MW00770508

FROM SALOONS TO STEAK HOUSES

UNIVERSITY PRESS OF FLORIDA

Florida A&M University, Tallahassee
Florida Atlantic University, Boca Raton
Florida Gulf Coast University, Ft. Myers
Florida International University, Miami
Florida State University, Tallahassee
New College of Florida, Sarasota
University of Central Florida, Orlando
University of Florida, Gainesville
University of North Florida, Jacksonville
University of South Florida, Tampa
University of West Florida, Pensacola

FROM SALOONS TO STEAK HOUSES

A HISTORY OF TAMPA

ANDREW T. HUSE

University Press of Florida

Gainesville · Tallahassee · Tampa · Boca Raton

Pensacola · Orlando · Miami · Jacksonville · Ft. Myers · Sarasota

Library of Congress Control Number: 2019954513
ISBN 978-0-8130-6640-0

The University Press of Florida is the scholarly publishing agency for the State University
System of Florida, comprising Florida A&M University, Florida Atlantic University, Florida
Gulf Coast University, Florida International University, Florida State University, New
College of Florida, University of Central Florida, University of Florida, University of North
Florida, University of South Florida, and University of West Florida.

University Press of Florida
2046 NE Waldo Road
Suite 2100
Gainesville, FL 32609
http://upress.ufl.edu

To Carol, Howard, and Tim

CONTENTS

PREFACE

When I first came to Tampa and learned of its history, two main themes impressed me. First, sleepy Tampa's influx of cigar factories and their immigrant workforce, beginning in 1886–1887, made the city a far more colorful and conflicted place than most other Florida cities at the time.

The establishment of Ybor City in 1885 made Tampa town a new global center for premium cigar production. A large influx of immigrants from Cuba, Spain, and Italy labored hard and had their own ideas about recreation, specifically on Sundays. A port town on the isolated Florida frontier, Tampa was both sought out and condemned as a center of gambling, prostitution, and violence. Tampa's diverse population aroused the resentment of nativists and some progressive activists, but it also created the City of Tampa, founded in 1887, rich with commerce, cuisine, and working-class culture.

There are many ways to examine the life of a person or city. Traditional history tends to focus on people in positions of power, wealth, and influence. More recently, however, historians have employed other approaches to the past, focusing on work, leisure activities, and popular culture to bring communities to life. Tampa's unique identity and often tumultuous past have drawn the attention of some excellent scholars. Most previous research has focused on ethnic studies, labor, and the cigar industry, but less work exists illuminating places of recreation and leisure. Such places—cafés, social clubs, cantinas, restaurants, and bars—have defined Tampa's culture outside the workplace.

Restaurants and bars serve as sensitive barometers of culture, commerce, and demographics, providing revealing contexts in which to examine a variety of social issues. "Going out" challenges normal rules of behavior and blurs distinctions between public life and private life. It is also through entertainment, cooking, drinking, and dining that communities vividly express themselves and form a collective identity. Bars and restaurants have frequently served as battlegrounds for conflicting values. As social laboratories of sorts, places of public consumption often expose countervailing cultural currents and become fixtures of conflict themselves.

In addition to the city's popular culture, I was also impressed by its illicit past, strewn with tales of organized crime and corruption, resulting in nicknames such as "Little Chicago" and "Sin City of the South." While many authors mention Tampa as a permissive "open city," none have attempted to explain how and why the city developed in such a way. As I researched these issues, I concluded that Tampa's popular culture and early corruption were entangled. As this book progresses, the city's corrupt trajectory recedes as a focus but still connects its history to popular places of consumption.

This book offers ten forays into Tampa's storied past, all focusing on conflict over various bars, clubs, and eateries and highlighting the city's shifting values and social contours. I begin with public debates over saloons, recreation, and Florida's sweeping Sunday law from roughly 1895 to 1902. I then explore lesser-discussed aspects of the Spanish-American War in 1898, eschewing legends of the "Splendid Little War" for a critical view of camp life in Tampa that includes price gouging, disease, and racial tension. The story then moves on to reveal the roots of civic corruption in saloons and Tampa's love-hate affair with risqué dancers between 1901 and 1916. The cigar industry, central to Tampa's history, affords a focus on collective institutions created by the immigrant workforce and suppressed by local authorities, including soup houses and cooperative stores. World War I unleashed fierce nationalism and wartime hysteria, sparking a number of controversies that stymied commercial bakeries and the local German American Club. Exploring the Prohibition era reveals the failure of the law through strong but flawed characters, including a police chief, a speakeasy operator, and a zealous judge. The rise of jook joints and the crackdown on sexual diseases occupy the chapter devoted to World War II, revealing a Tampa still mired in corruption and racism. I then trace the impact of the Bartke family, as they imported their "ultra-modern" steak house from upstate New York to

Tampa International Airport in the 1950s. The narrative next examines how young black activists dared to challenge racial segregation at the city's lunch counters in 1960. In the final chapter, I trace the stories of Las Novedades restaurant, Steak 'n Brew, and the El Goya Lounge, which all occupied the same Ybor City building in the dark days of urban renewal.

Understandably, it is difficult to find reliable sources about discreet places. Saloons, gambling halls, speakeasies, and jook joints are not known for keeping scrupulous records of their activities. The soup kitchens and cooperatives that provided sustenance to workers were ephemeral, rarely lasting longer than the crises they were meant to alleviate. Local newspapers, despite their biases and flaws, are often the best tools for exploring day-to-day life. I have augmented this research with other local sources, including City Council meeting minutes, ordinances, police records, government reports, and so on. The Hillsborough County Aviation Authority records helped to flesh out the later days of Bartke's Steakhouse. I have also drawn from oral history interviews when able, including several I conducted myself. Working as a librarian in the Special Collections of the University of South Florida's Tampa Library has been a great boon to my research, providing me with a variety of resources, including political papers, organizational records (such as the NAACP), personal papers (such as the Leo Stalnaker papers and *Tampa Life*), Bartke's scrapbook, the Cody Fowler Papers, and much more. While none of these sources are perfect on their own, together they provide reliable information on the subjects I explore. I have also relied on a wealth of secondary sources to reinforce and guide my own research.

As a firm believer in the power of stories, I feel that one of the historian's most vital functions is to salvage and/or synthesize compelling stories that tell a larger historic truth. I hope my humble contribution illuminates as it entertains.

ACKNOWLEDGMENTS

First, I would like thank Dr. Gary Mormino for the inspiration and encouragement over the years. For their reviews and comments, I thank Dr. Robert Kerstein, the Honorable E. J. Salcines, Dr. Brad Massey, and Rodney Kite-Powell. A special thanks to Dr. Charles McGraw-Groh for his valuable critiques. Also thanks to Karen Mayo, Carol Elwood, and Tim Huse for their proofreading and informal reviews. Many thanks to those who sat for interviews or oral histories, including Manuel Garcia III, Barbara and June Bartke, Clarence Fort, Dr. Jack Fernandez, Mary Henry, and Crichton and Alice McKay. Jennifer Dietz and the City of Tampa Archives provided many digitized records that proved useful, especially the minutes of the City Council.

Aside from Tampa's natural harbor, railroads became the city's most important link to the outside world after 1884. Here, a construction crew clears the way for a railroad. (Tony Pizzo collection, University of South Florida Tampa Special Collections)

INTRODUCTION

Boom Town on the Florida Frontier

Spain ceded Florida to the United States in 1821, and two years later, the U.S. Army concluded the First Seminole War with the Treaty of Moultrie Creek. The army then established a small outpost at the top of Hillsborough Bay called Fort Brooke, largely to isolate the restive Seminole Indians from trading opportunities with the British. A small town formed adjacent to Fort Brooke, but the settlement struggled to find its footing. Incorporated as a village in 1849, Tampa was reincorporated as a town in 1855 with about six hundred residents, most of them personnel stationed at Fort Brooke. Ravaged by the Civil War and yellow fever outbreaks, the population dipped and the government of Tampa dissolved in 1869. Completely isolated and intermittently ravaged by disease, the town struggled and its future seemed bleak.

A visitor's impressions in 1853 painted a stark picture: "Tampa is a small town, inhabited by the most worthless population in the world. They seem to be, well, the refuse of creation. Three or four lawyers, as many preachers, three stores—half a dozen grog shops, and these live on each other. I do not believe there is a dollar per head among them. They hate the sight of an honest man." Through small-scale farming and cattle herds, the fiercely independent Florida Crackers eked out a humble living, often relying on moonshine to barter for goods or cash. As a small town on the Florida frontier, Tampa became a place for the frontiersmen to trade, socialize, and misbehave.[1]

Tampa was a fairly typical small Florida town before the 1880s. For its part, Tampa's white population was decidedly Southern in temperament and political sensibility. The old families that dominated Tampa's elite tended to be unreformed Confederates. After Reconstruction, they were eager to replace the federal troops with Southern policies of white supremacy. Tampa's African Americans, about one-fifth of the city's population, suffered from substandard living conditions, lack of basic rights, and constant threats of violence to enforce perceived color lines. Bound together by strong churches and social clubs, Tampa's black residents also fostered a strong business community that eventually coalesced around Central Avenue.[2]

Tampa's population fell to a new low of 720 in 1880. When the military decommissioned Fort Brooke in 1882, it seemed that Tampa might die with it. Hillsborough County had no promising industry to speak of until phosphate was discovered nearby in 1883. Three developments in the next four years dramatically changed the course of Tampa's history. First, in 1884, Florida railroad baron Henry Plant extended his tracks to Tampa, later adding steamship routes and improving the port's facilities. Second, Vicente Martinez Ybor and other cigar producers founded Ybor City in 1886, a cigar town dependent upon skilled immigrant labor. Third, Tampa incorporated as a city in 1887, grabbing up Ybor City in the process.

On December 1, 1883, Henry Plant visited Tampa, a town of less than seven hundred, for the first time. His railroad soon followed after seven months of rushed construction through difficult terrain. At the time, no less than three new hotels were being built to accommodate more travelers and visitors. Plant's railroad connection to Tampa's harbor ended the city's days of isolation on the Florida frontier. Plant's fast steamships *Mascotte* and *Olivette*, named after popular operettas, became synonymous with Tampa, linking it with Havana, Key West, and New Orleans like never before. The railroad and port opened Tampa and the hinterland to international trade for the first time. Thanks to Plant's railroad, Tampa began a business boom that extended to the Great Depression.[3]

Plant and his rival, Henry Flagler, had a habit of leaving fantastic hotels in the wake of their Florida railroads. Construction of Plant's Gilded

Age palace, the Tampa Bay Hotel, began in 1888 and was completed in 1891 at astronomical cost. Plant's Tampa Bay Hotel attracted some ultra-wealthy curiosity-seekers for its first few seasons, but they soon sought out other novelties.[4]

Gavino Gutierrez, a Spanish importer and civil engineer, first visited Tampa with friend Bernardino Gargol in search of guavas. In November 1884, Gargol, a guava paste manufacturer, was disappointed to find rumors of wild groves to be false. Although bereft of guavas, Tampa seemed like an ideal location for cigar production, and Gutierrez thought of his friend Vicente Martinez Ybor. Born in Valencia, Spain, in 1818, Ybor became a Havana cigar magnate sympathetic to the cause of Cuban liberty. When Cuban rebels took arms against the Spanish Empire in 1868, Mr. Ybor's political leanings forced him to flee for his life. He relocated his cigar factories to Key West, but the small, isolated island was not an ideal permanent site for his empire. By 1884, Ybor was actively searching for new locations. Gutierrez proceeded to Key West, where he told Ybor of the promising site near Tampa.

Ybor's factories specialized in producing hand-rolled cigars using clear Havana tobacco, considered the best in the world. Along with the Cuban insurrection, a high U.S. tariff on finished cigars persuaded many cigar producers to relocate their operations to the United States. Tampa joined Galveston, Mobile, and Pensacola in trying to draw Ybor to their locales. Tampa's Board of Trade (later the Chamber of Commerce) sweetened the deal sufficiently for Ybor to buy property, and his friend and colleague, cigar producer Ignacio Haya, followed suit. The biggest challenge Tampa presented to the industry was the lack of skilled workers. Years of warfare in Cuba had forged a remarkably mobile multinational workforce built around Cubans.[5]

Ybor enlisted Gutierrez, who was a surveyor and an engineer, to plan a town built around cigar factories. He also attracted a workforce with offers of well-paying positions in factories with plenty of work. With a very low cost of living, Tampa offered workers a chance to get ahead. Most of the workers probably had no intention of staying for long. The first trees came down on October 8, 1885, to make room for the settlement known as Ybor City.[6]

For his namesake city to flourish, Ybor needed other large companies to build factories there. Some agreed to relocate to Ybor City as well, and none was more important than Sanchez y Haya, run by Ignacio Haya. When construction dragged, Haya reconsidered what must have seemed like a rash adventure in the Florida scrub. He quietly put up all of his holdings in the project for sale. When Ybor caught wind of Haya's reluctance to invest in the new cigar city, he thought it might be the end. A shrewd gambler by nature, Ybor decided to bluff. He offered to buy all of Haya's property near Tampa. After seeing Ybor's determination, Haya decided to stay. In turn, Ybor's own doubts melted away. They resolved to make a new start together. That night, they sealed the deal over a champagne supper.[7]

Ybor should have been the first to open with his Principe de Gales (Prince of Wales) factory, but a sudden strike delayed the opening of the facility. Ybor's all-Cuban workforce refused to labor under the supervision of a Spanish foreman, so Sanchez y Haya's all-Spanish factory opened in February, producing its first cigar by April. That same month, a fire in Key West destroyed Ybor's factory there, prompting many of the workers to relocate to his new facilities in Tampa. Ybor's Land and Improvement Company constructed hundreds of homes to sell to his employees on an installment plan. Many of the unpainted wooden houses did not last ten years in the termite-ridden elements of Florida. With local partners, Ybor and his close associate Eduardo Manrara also built a streetcar line connecting their settlement with Tampa. With an eight-minute streetcar ride, one could oscillate between the South and the booming immigrant world of Ybor City.[8]

In 1887, Ybor's colony still looked precarious. Ybor was afraid that low morale and fears of yellow fever would drive away his workforce for the holidays and that they would not return. Ybor and his wife acted fast by inviting every worker and their families for a Nochebuena (Christmas Eve) feast at "La Quinta," Ybor's newly constructed mansion. Carriages picked up each family and whisked them away to his estate. Enchanting scenes greeted the families, with Ybor's yard adorned with Japanese lanterns, candles in the trees, and large tables set for a banquet. Servers brought out wine and roast pork, turkey, red snapper, chicken, beans and rice, yucca, roasted potatoes, and vegetables. Dessert followed, with pastries, fruit, candies, nuts, and melons. Coffee and cigars rounded out the lavish celebration.

After dinner, Ybor presented a surprise. As a personal sign of gratitude, Ybor divided the profits the workers had generated for him in several months of operations, $6,000 in all, or about a month's wages per worker. Ybor's gesture won the workers' confidence. The small town blossomed into a bustling metropolis that sustained a vibrant immigrant culture.[9]

To the workers, Ybor was more than a factory owner or employer. He was their patron, a paternalistic figure who took a personal interest in their welfare. After some initial tensions, Ybor simplified matters by employing only Cubans. It was said that along with his Cuban partner, Eduardo Manrara, Ybor refused to hire Spaniards at all to avoid irritating his workforce. Haya's firm exclusively hired Spanish workers, keeping the warring people separate in different factories. When Ybor's first brick factory opened, he gave the old wooden factory to his Cuban workers to use as a gathering place. Renamed the Liceo Cubano, or Cuban Lyceum, the building housed one of the area's first Cuban patriotic societies formed in opposition to Spanish rule.[10]

Observers noted that the Cubans brimmed over with passions—namely, politics and recreation. In addition to the inherent instability of the tobacco industry of the age, Cubans remained mobile to avoid the violently fluctuating fortunes of their homeland. They roamed a vast international labor market linked by the steamship, moving between cigar factories in New York City, New Orleans, Cuba, and Florida. The Cubans became known as free spenders who lived with gusto. The labor troubles that Ybor hoped to avoid in his new location sprang up almost immediately. In 1887, tensions between Cuban and Spanish workers were high and they often refused to work side by side. Several workers were shot in a fracas during a strike.[11]

By 1888, Cuban patriots had formed the Liga Patriotica Cubana (the Cuban Patriotic League) to support independence of their land from Spain. Lectors read and reread accounts of the heroics of the Ten Years' War (1868–78), and Cubans constantly schemed for the coming struggle. Other patriotic societies sprang up, and Tampa became an important center of fundraising and political support for the revolutionary cause. The upstart Cigar City also made a profound impact on the tobacco industry in a short time. Two thousand immigrants had settled in Ybor by June 1887, with stores and restaurants quickly opening to serve them. By 1888, Tampa's cigar workers outproduced those of Key West, rolling more than 100 million cigars annually.[12]

Each of Tampa's largest immigrant groups formed remarkable social clubs and mutual aid societies. Since health insurance did not exist and health care was so scarce in Tampa, which was two miles away, the immigrants quickly created clinics of their own. Ybor encouraged Cuban doctors to relocate to the area, and Cuban and Spanish clinics formed in 1888. Health care was a big concern in Ybor City, where substandard sanitation and fears of yellow fever meant sickness was never far away. Enough of the footloose men had caught social diseases from local prostitutes to make health care a most pressing concern. Over time, the clinics expanded and provided some of the finest health care in the community.[13]

These immigrant social clubs and their clinics quickly became hubs of social life that exemplified the virtues of collective enterprise. The largest clubs eventually became Centro Español, L'Unione Italiana, Circulo Cubano, and Centro Asturiano. Whether one enjoyed rounds of coffee and games of dominos or chess in their cantinas, dances in their ballrooms, or entertainment in their theaters, members had it all, even cemeteries. The immigrant colony rose during the height of white supremacy and segregation in the United States. In 1896, the U.S. Supreme Court ruled in *Plessy v. Ferguson* to justify racial segregation. The decision helped to split the Cuban Club in 1899, spawning the Afro-Cuban La Union Marti-Maceo the following year. A sign at Sulphur Springs warned at the time, "No Dogs, Niggers or Latins Allowed."[14]

If Vicente Martinez Ybor financed Ybor City, Gavino Gutierrez was its mastermind. He led Ybor to the site, surveyed the land, and plotted out the streets. He designed the buildings and workers' casitas. Mass excursions to nearby parks for picnics became a popular Sunday ritual for clubs and families, favoring Ballast Point's beach resort or DeSoto Park, which was especially attractive because it had fewer mosquitoes than other areas. Owned by Gutierrez, the Spanish Park featured a popular racetrack and zoo.

DeSoto Park became the favorite of Tampa's immigrants. A private streetcar brought visitors to a pavilion tucked deep into beautifully manicured gardens. Immigrant families engaged in recreation, especially on Sundays, when it hosted baseball games, concerts, dances, and various performances. A respectable saloon discreetly sold drinks to the men. The park ran ads in the newspapers exhorting unsavory characters to stay out. Management reserved the right to throw out any disorderly patrons, and DeSoto Park was usually peaceful and relatively wholesome. The immigrants played soccer, delighted in cockfighting and gambling, and readily adopted baseball as their new favorite sport. From multiple-language newspapers to baseball teams, mutual aid societies to patriotic clubs, Tampa's immigrants created a society, a "radical world," that seemed familiar but was entirely new.[15]

By the late 1880s, Italian immigrants, chiefly from the Sicilian village of Santo Stefano Quisquina, began arriving in large numbers. First drawn by work on Florida's railroad, the Italians were eager to give up their jobs on the sugar plantations of St. Cloud. The industrious newcomers settled in the area, establishing macaroni factories, bakeries, small farms, dairies, and fishing fleets. In 1892, Scottish immigrant and attorney Hugh C. Macfarlane founded the new cigar colony of West Tampa (1895–1925), drawing more cigar firms. It did not officially become part of Tampa until 1925, but it was always in the city's cultural orbit.[16]

Led by growth in Tampa, West Tampa, and the city of Port Tampa, Hillsborough County leapt in population from 5,814 in 1880 to 36,013 in 1900. Tampa's population swelled from 720 in 1880 to 5,532 in 1890, then tripled to 15,839 in 1900. In 1892, two new homes were built per day in the city, but they could scarcely keep up with demand. The price of lots often doubled in one month. With a population that increased twentyfold in only fifteen years, the city's expansion was disorderly and often unpleasant. Tampa's boom attracted a wave of drifters and gamblers who had abandoned working life in search of the next score. Writer Kelly Reynolds set the scene in boom-town-era Tampa:

And from every point of the compass an army of cardsharps, whores and pickpockets converged on the suddenly overcrowded little city. At night, gypsy peddlers camped on the streets, unprecedented mountains of garbage accumulated, dog packs roamed, scavenging animals multiplied, and raw sewage clogged the gutters. . . . Rows of gimcrack saloons, restaurants, lodging houses, shanties and stables appeared, hastily assembled by roving journeymen. And everywhere, everywhere, were large and small tents of gray canvas—temporary homes that remained for years.[17]

Tampa had succeeded in attracting infrastructure improvements and a signature industry that employed skilled foreign-born laborers. The city's future peace and prosperity would depend on some degree of harmony between Tampa's United States–born "pioneers" and foreign-born immigrants. That harmony proved to be elusive, as Tampa's white Protestant establishment chafed both at the immigrants' recreation and the leniency of city officials toward vice.

THE SUNDAY WARS

Saloons and Recreation

In June 1887, the Woman's Christian Temperance Union (WCTU) held a picnic in the upstart Latin colony of Ybor City with a brass band and a swing-set, where organizers promised "all stiffness and formality will be left out entirely." On Independence Day, local temperance activists from Tampa played a major public role in the city's formal celebrations, singing "Hail Columbia" and "Dixie" back to back. At the time, the picnic and parade carried a deeper significance, a message to the small town and the newcomers in its midst. Ybor City, the cigar-producing immigrant enclave, had just been incorporated into the new City of Tampa a month before.[1]

It is telling that Tampa's chapter of the WCTU formed in 1886, the same year Ybor City produced its first cigars. Tampa had only six hundred voters in the city, all male and nearly all white. The *Tampa Morning Tribune* wrote, "The immigrants who are forced here are the paupers and criminals of the Old World. Europe has no right to send us her abject and forlorn." But the newcomers did not fit the description of poor, illiterate refugees. Instead, the arriving cigar workers were often the best-dressed, the most skilled, and the most educated people in town. Tampa's merchants reacted by tripling the price of their goods and gouging the newcomers. The immigrants were horrified to discover that the Tampa area had little culture that they could recognize. Games of dominos could only divert them for so long before they demanded a community to accompany their workplace. When a new arrival brought his wife to Ybor City from New Orleans in the late 1800s, she fell to her knees and wept at the ramshackle, sandy village she saw.[2]

Although Tampa's "natives" of the time looked on the immigrants with disapproval, the city itself gave little reason for such condescending pride. Aside from the burgeoning cigar industry, whose labor was dominated by foreigners, Tampa's fastest-growing business community was composed chiefly of its gambling houses, brothels, and saloons. Just a year into its existence, Ybor City began to serve as a place for Tampa's most mischievous to cavort. Wide-open saloons frequently resulted in "broken heads."[3]

The Ybor Improvement Company provided the infrastructure and basic services for the new cigar colony. When Ybor first came to town in 1885, he had a certain understanding with Tampa's elite Board of Trade that went well beyond real estate. First, they agreed to supply strike-busting police or vigilantes whenever his factories required them; second, Ybor made it clear that his workers would not tolerate a dry city. All the while, Ybor assumed he would preside over an independent municipality, with Tampa, its sister city, then two miles away.

Perhaps Ybor underestimated the Board of Trade, which waited until Ybor and Haya had both opened their factories to spring their trap. Under a special act of the state legislature, Tampa incorporated as a city, which comprised the former Town of Tampa, North Tampa, also known as Tampa Heights, and the new suburb of Hyde Park. Coveting the tax base of Ybor City, Tampa's leadership claimed that lacking police, Ybor City required Tampa's supervision. Being annexed into the City of Tampa was never Ybor's plan or desire, and he publicly objected.[4]

Tallahassee's territorial government imposed Florida's first Sunday law in 1832. The statute read in part, "whoever keeps open store or disposes of any wares, merchandise, goods or chattels on Sunday, or sells or barters the same, shall be punished." In the late 1800s, the maximum sentence for violating the law, whether one sold ice cream, fresh fish, or whiskey, stood at a whopping fifty dollars or six months in jail. The law did allow transactions for emergencies but otherwise saddled the entire state with an impossible ideal. Every county and city enforced the Sunday law according to the moods of local voters and the officials they elected.[5]

When his colony was taken under Tampa's wing, Ybor knew that disputes over the unpopular Sunday "blue laws"[6] were inevitable. The immigrants interpreted the "day of rest" much differently than Tampa's elite, favoring sports, games, dancing, entertainment, and activities of all kinds. These newcomers, along with what probably amounted to a majority of white and black natives, had no sympathy for the temperance movement and generally saw little wrong with alcohol, saloons, or gambling. None of the new workers could actually vote to change the Sunday law. Because most wage earners worked six-day work weeks, often with half-days on Saturdays, the Sunday laws prevented working people from conducting business or pleasure on their only free day of the week. The mismatch between the Sunday laws and Tampa's liberal immigrant workforce wrenched the community for decades. As Tampa expanded between 1886 and 1918, the city's voters succeeded in passing increasingly restrictive ordinances against saloons.

Even zealous temperance workers understood that Tampa's continuing prosperity was dependent upon the skilled labor of the immigrants. The *Tampa Tribune* urged tolerance, writing, "The people of Ybor City and Tampa will understand each other if let alone." Tampa's moneyed interests could stifle the complaints against the immigrants and their Sunday circuses, nonchalant gambling, and Sunday drinking for only so long.[7]

SALOONS AND RECREATION

Monday mornings were not a pretty sight in Tampa during the 1890s. Workers nationwide called the first day of the work week "Blue Mondays" because so many of them suffered from hangovers after bouts of drinking that often lasted all weekend. In Tampa, the city's courts returned to life on Monday mornings after being closed on weekends and a grizzled assortment of suspects appeared before the judge. In 1895–96, the police ledger reveals that between half and two-thirds of arrests were related to vice, primarily drunkenness, intoxicated violence, gambling, and prostitution. Another very common charge included passing out on private property.[8]

In relatively remote places like Tampa, common people played as roughly as they lived and worked. Drinking alcohol was not just a working-class activity but an almost universally accepted masculine pastime. For many working men in America's cities, the saloon served as a social outlet and networking hub away from home and work. Saloons often served as the only public places for working men to gather outside of church. Drinking places became centers of social life for most of Tampa's men, important as sources of business and social networks. Particularly on the isolated frontier, saloons became multipurpose social centers. Historian Thomas J. Noel notes that saloons "provided the cultural and social life of the French *salon*, the civic and political benefits of the Teutonic *saal* or public hall, the elegance of the Spanish *gala*, or parlor, and the sedate, private man's world of the British pub. Until government, churches, schools, banks, libraries, hospitals, theaters, museums, and other institutions became well established, the saloon served as a multifunctional institution."[9]

Men came to drink, to socialize, to find work, and to relax, but they also came in search of prostitutes and games of chance. For many, the saloon and the church represented polar opposites: the ways of the devil and the ways of Christianity. But few people are so absolute in their behavior. Some worshipped at both temples, on Saturday night and Sunday morning, respectively. In the southern United States, this love-hate relationship with alcohol was most pronounced, and it was said that men would vote their counties dry, even if they had to stumble to the voting booth to do so.

The unchecked expansion of unlicensed saloons across the country in the late 1800s, with their rotgut liquor, gambling, violence, and prostitutes, prompted a strong backlash against all saloons. Soon activists such as the Woman's Christian Temperance Union, which opposed alcohol in general, were joined by the Anti-Saloon League, a group bent on ridding society of saloons. Protestant and evangelical activists maligned saloons not just for the spirits they served but for who they served, namely, the lower classes, including undesirable immigrants and black people. Built on a mixture of religious conviction, racism, and xenophobia, the temperance movement grew steadily in Florida after Reconstruction. In 1887, the Florida legislature added article nineteen, known as the "local option," to the constitution, allowing individual counties to prohibit the sale of alcohol. Although church leaders rallied to make the county dry, Hillsborough's voters soundly defeated the measure in 1889.[10]

Tampa remained steadfastly wet, especially on Sundays. In 1891, the *Tribune* complained, "The saloons in Tampa Sunday, with few exceptions, did business in violation of law and order. Streams of people were passing in and out of the back doors of the saloons all day long. . . . Throngs of young men stagger about the street Sunday in all stages of intoxication." It became clear to all that neither the city nor the county enforced the blue laws or much else. Few businesses or professionals bothered to obtain state or local licenses for their enterprises.[11]

Ybor City's "saloons" modeled themselves on the cafés of Havana, which functioned as café, saloon, snack bar, and social club. A *New York Times* journalist noted of Havana's cafés at the time, "One grows very used to eating next to a bar. There is one in almost every café, and it is usually next to the tables with no screen or partition. I have heard that strangers sometimes try for hours to find a café that has no bar attachment. Here no one thinks of it after the first shock has worn off. Wine is very commonly drunk. As a result there is rarely an intoxicated man among the natives."[12]

The enforcement of blue laws fluctuated with the political winds and the annual mayoral elections. Initially, Tampa's leadership did not take the blue law too seriously in Ybor City, afraid to jeopardize tax income by upsetting the immigrant labor force with strict enforcement. In any case, Tampa's police were so chronically underfunded that it could never enforce the law everywhere. At the most, they could harass and suppress the immigrants at work and play. The Sunday law may have been a genuine expression of religious devotion, but it was also meant as a tool of social control, a way to pander to less tolerant voters, and a weapon to be used against political enemies.[13] The saloon question defined boom-era Tampa's social life and politics.[14]

When police actively enforced the blue laws, it disrupted routines that had been allowed to exist for years. Most police harassment fell upon legitimate businesses trying to serve customers at the times they were available. Tampa's immigrant entrepreneurs suffered business losses as a result of forcible closure and frivolous arrests. At one point in the 1890s, the cigar factories shut down on Saturdays to allow workers a day of liberty from the Sunday law, losing untold thousands of dollars in the process. No one was more pinched by blue laws than the saloon owners themselves. Saloons already encountered fierce competition from the area's blind tigers, unlicensed saloons that served unregulated whiskey of questionable quality. Because the proprietors of the blind tigers were unburdened by taxes, fees, laws, or decency, their profits were high, much of them siphoned away from legitimate saloons. The blind tigers gave all saloons a bad name by openly flaunting the law and serving bad liquor.

Closing on Sundays forced saloons to neglect customers on one of the most lucrative days of the week, compelling them to break the law to earn a profit. A saloon owner at the time in New York City observed, "A saloon week begins on Saturday, when the laboring men are paid, and from morning until midnight Saturday my bar was continually wet. But Sunday receipts average much more than those of any other day except Saturday. . . . So I found very soon that it was necessary to keep open on Sunday in order to make both ends meet." He refused to pay the police protection money to open on Sundays. Because he would not pay bribes for the privilege of violating the blue law, his entire business failed.[15]

The Booze Barons

In the 1890s, Tampa's thirsty population and visitors gave rise to a thriving saloon culture. Wealthy patrons drank under the minarets of Tampa Bay Hotel or shot billiards on the fine tables at Balbontin's Saloon. The White Swan and later the Saloon Columbia epitomized the simple pleasures of working-class saloons. Those at the bottom of the social ladder had the most places to choose from, a plethora of bars, drinking shanties, and blind tigers with floors of sawdust in place of spittoons.[16]

As Tampa's saloon culture boomed with the arrival of a new workforce composed largely of immigrants, a new class of immigrant entrepreneur rose with it. In the years since the founding of Ybor City, Tampa's saloons and alcohol sales had been expanded and largely taken over by immigrant entrepreneurs. Besides the cigar factories and social clubs, the most prominent symbol of immigrant achievement was the Florida Brewery, founded by Don Vicente Martinez Ybor himself. In 1896, national brewers and local prohibitionists opposed Vicente Martinez Ybor's formation of the Florida Brewing Company, but local boosters cheered. The brewery opened on May 18, 1896, at Thirteenth Street and Fifth Avenue, relying on Tampa's then-abundant spring water. The brewery was the first in the state and its beers became leading brands in Florida and Cuba. The brewery became the single-most profitable part of Ybor's sprawling business empire. In 1900, no other American brewery sent more product to Cuba. Newspapers typically dismissed the objections of dry activists in the interest of commerce. "The *Tribune* takes no stock in the objections raised to the brewery by a class of men who are too good for their own good."[17]

Locally, the wholesale liquor dealers benefited the most from the rich liquor trade. B. M. Balbontin and Robert Mugge became wealthy and influential as brewery agents for Pabst and Busch, respectively. They both used the leverage of their powerful employers to acquire exclusive outlets for their products. Both routinely bought saloons for themselves and their employers.[18]

Bautista Balbontin was born in 1863 in Romorose near Santander, Spain. In 1883, he moved to Birmingham, Alabama, where he became a waiter at a saloon and later acquired one with a partner. Evidently a casualty of a local "beer war," Balbontin came to Tampa in 1889, where he quickly found his footing. His career as a cigar maker lasted one week, after which he worked as a manager for Loera and, later, Pendas & Co. In 1893, he bought his first saloon in Tampa (Seventh Avenue and Fourteenth Street) and was elected tax appraiser. About a year later, he sued his former partners for debts and acquired a piece of East Ybor land in the process. In 1897, he opened a new saloon nearby. He closed his old bar while quietly planning his next enterprise.[19]

The *Tribune* wrote of Balbontin, "He has built up a trade that he is likely to take with him wherever he may go. No man in Ybor City has a wider circle of friends than Mr. Balbontin, who has won an enviable reputation as a caterer to the public. [He] enjoys the distinction of being one of the most popular caterers that Tampa has ever known." The saloon was "handsomely and effectively fitted in oak, and is brilliantly lighted by electricity."[20]

Balbontin had as much nerve as he had business acumen, and soon he seemed to take some satisfaction in challenging the Sunday laws and skewering its adherents. By 1901, he had entered the more profitable wholesale liquor business. When the brewery fell on hard times, Balbontin bought in as a partner in 1905. He retired from the brewery in 1909 and dedicated his time to the wholesale business.[21]

Born in Lauterberg, North Germany, in 1852, Robert Mugge became Tampa's other influential liquor dealer at the time. He came to the U.S. Midwest as a young jeweler-milliner in 1869, then briefly relocated to Cuba owing to his chronic asthma. He finally settled in Tampa in 1878 and became a citizen in 1879. Mugge's rise in Tampa began when he became the local agent of the powerful Anheuser-Busch breweries. His employers subsidized his investments and helped vault him into business as a liquor distributor in the 1890s. In the late 1890s, Mugge was able to buy new real estate with regularity. The *Tribune* observed, "R. Mugge is determined to control the saloon business in Tampa, or at least a majority of it." Mugge could lease his saloons to franchisees and sell them his beer and liquor without much regard for the proprietor's take. In the words of the *Tribune*, "Many saloons in this city have been practically run by the Anheuser-Busch Brewing Co. Mr. R. Mugge is their agent and through him the Company paid the license, and the operators paid their backers so much each week for these considerations."[22]

Mugge's intellect manifested itself in many ways. He spent years dabbling with technology as a source of income with varying success. Mugge's most successful enterprises included an ice plant, a distillery (Central and Cass), and a bottling plant on Marion Street adjoining his home. In Tampa's often unrelenting subtropical heat, Mugge made his own refreshing soda, specializing in lemon, strawberry, and sarsaparilla (comparable to root beer) flavors. Mugge pioneered the use of slot machines and other mechanical gambling devices. Trying something new always came with risks. He became the test defendant for a nickel slot machine that the city had already licensed for use.[23]

His son remembered how Mugge would relax on Sundays. Never

one to waste time, he leisurely paid his bills and maintained his account books in the presence of friends and "wisecrackers." In 1912, he bought the black-only Central Hotel and built the Bay View Hotel in 1915, the year of his death. Mugge's intellect set him apart from many of his contemporaries, and he became one of the most outspoken opponents of the Sunday laws, often penning persuasive editorials in his letters to the newspapers. The ambitious German had built a small empire of saloons and real estate by the time of his death in 1915.[24]

The heavy liquor traffic in Tampa soon attracted national attention. As competition reached fever pitch, many owners turned to America's largest breweries for support, such as expensive fixtures, license fees, and other business expenses. Of the national brewery giants, Anheuser-Busch came to dominate Tampa's saloons by 1896. According to a saloon owner, only three of Tampa's approximately thirty-five saloons were actually owned locally in 1897.[25]

THE LAW AND ORDER LEAGUE

In 1895, blue law opponents mocked dry activists by presenting to City Hall a petition that measured seventeen feet long. The unwieldy petition was, according to the *Tribune*, an "awe-inspiring document [that] had evidently been signed by a large number of respectable citizens in ignorance of its contents." The petition objected to the ringing of church bells or the collection of church donations on Sundays "upon the ground that they involved manual labor." The effort was probably a response to the police arresting people, such as fishmongers, for a variety of Sunday infractions that did not involve alcohol. The city ignored the petition, but City Attorney Pat Whitaker wrote (and council passed) a new blue ordinance allowing the operation of streetcars, railroads, ice works, lumber kilns, livery stables, barbershops, bathhouses, restaurants, coffee shops, delivery of groceries, and certain necessary work in cigar factories. This more liberal interpretation of the Sunday law did not last beyond the next election in 1896.[26]

In August 1895, days after city hall received the irreverent wet petition, dry-minded citizens formed the Law and Order League as a lobby group through local Presbyterian churches. Bartow had formed a similar

E. MANRARA, President.   HUGO SCHWAB, Secretary and Treasurer.
J.W. CODINGTON, Vice-President.   A. C. MOORE, General Manager.

The Florida Brewing Co.

BREWERS OF ABSOLUTELY

PURE BEER

Only the Purest and Best Materials Used.

PATRONIZE HOME PRODUCTION.

The Tampa Bay Hotel and the Best Saloons, Patronized by the Best Citizens of Tampa, use it, some of them, exclusively.

It has also taken front rank in Cuba as the LEADING BEER of Havana.

EXTRA PALE,
STANDARD,
CULMBACHER,

On Draught or in Bottles.

When you Drink Beer ask only for that of

THE FLORIDA BREWING CO.

There was no greater symbol of the conflict between immigrants and Tampa's dry elites than the Florida Brewery, the first in the state. (Tony Pizzo collection, University of South Florida Tampa Special Collections)

Prohibition group several weeks before. Tampa's league organized with two hundred members, dominated by Hugh Macfarlane, the founder of West Tampa, and criminal judge G. A. Hanson.[27]

The City Council complained of "laxly enforced ordinances bearing on gambling, Sunday opening [and] vagabondage." Minor blue law offenders filled the courts: Butchers, grocers, and stable keepers constituted most of the list, and Mugge was arrested for delivering ice. Judge Simonton presided over their cases with little enthusiasm for the law. The judge asked each of ten defendants one day if their goods or services comforted the public. When each man replied affirmatively, he discharged them all. He even discharged an honest saloon owner (W. T. Boyd) who openly admitted to hosting gambling.[28]

In 1896, the famous Prohibition activist Frances Willard rallied Tampa's dry activists with a visit. As founding president of the Woman's Christian Temperance Union, she identified herself as the "standard of purity" and represented half a million zealous members. Willard's Christian worldview could be described as severe. Her most ambitious project: an international petition to ban alcohol worldwide.[29]

Perhaps as a reaction to Willard's visit that year and the efforts of the league, voters elected Myron E. Gillett as mayor in 1896. Gillett promised a campaign against gambling, particularly the irrepressible games of the immigrants and professional criminals. The *Tribune*'s comments on the subject are worth noting at length.

The high-handed manner in which the gamblers, monte-banks, harlots, and flim-flammers, have played their games in this city for several years, has been more like their conduct in the wild and wooly west in the 70's, than in a civilized community in the 90's. The town has been run wide open, and the violation of all law sacred to civilized history has been of the most flagrant type.

Tampa's population is cosmopolitan in the highest sense of the word; in fact nearly one half of her population are foreigners, whose social and national customs are quite different to ours. These people love pleasure, they know little else, and to bring them at once under restraint to observe our customs would have proven disastrous to our interests. While their ideas of life are so much unlike our own, they are not a criminal class, but on the other hand, peaceable, industrious and prosperous. Against such there is no law. Through a misconception of the principles and customs of these people, the law has been so lax that a crowd of greedy vultures have swarmed, and pitched their tents here to prey upon the city, sucking the very life-blood of our prosperity like vampires.

The gamblers have found a fat "take" in Tampa, they have made good use of their opportunity. Many hard working people have been robbed of their earnings and some rich ones have fallen into their dens and lost heavily. In several instances during the past winter, men who have come here for either business or pleasure, lost thousands of dollars. The last Sunday in May, little more than a week ago, one visitor dropped five thousand dollars in a dive in Ybor City. Such things have been a common occurrence.[30]

In June 1896, Mayor Gillett took office determined to clean up vice. For him, law and order began with clearly written laws. At the time, Tampa had accumulated a mess of more than two hundred ordinances. In his first meeting with City Council, Mayor Gillett said,

I had no hand in framing the present laws against gambling, prostitution, and Sunday closures of saloons, but, when I took the oath of office, I agreed to enforce them. The election demonstrates that the people want it done, the law breakers expect it to be done, and it is my desire not to disappoint either side. The only way to stop these open violations of the law is to *STOP* them.[31]

Gillett's campaign aggressively rounded up gambling and blue law offenders in the most dedicated effort against saloons to date, but it also routinely filled the court docket with minor cases. Weekly Sunday sweeps rounded up a handful of immigrant barbers, butchers, and ice men, with their charges flippantly thrown out in court the following day. Such application of the law made no one happy. Reformers saw it as being soft on criminals. Immigrant entrepreneurs saw it as frivolous harassment. Even Balbontin and Mugge were arrested for selling on Sundays.[32]

Tampa's saloon owners adapted to the hostile police. They claimed that when they left their establishments alone on Sundays, thieves stole stocks of liquor stored in and behind the saloons. This justified them building fences behind their back doors as high as eleven feet. They used screens and partitions to block the visibility of their windows so police could not peer inside. They also opened more flagrantly on Sundays to sell innocent ice cream drinks while still quietly peddling liquor. The *Tribune* observed, "Now it appears these saloon keepers propose to fight the city government and have thrown down the gauntlet."[33]

By October 1896, Gillett's campaign of increased enforcement and licensing fees had thinned out the saloon market. Tampa lost ten of its thirty-one saloons, DeSoto Park closed one of two, and West Tampa closed three of five. Out of a total of thirty-eight saloons, well over one-third had closed, leaving twenty-four and an estimated $2,500 loss in city license revenue. The dry campaign had made a real difference.[34]

Police took a special interest in Balbontin's namesake saloon. During a raid in 1896, police forced their way past Balbontin's lookout, a young black boy, and into his business. There, they found the liquor baron sitting in his empty saloon reading the newspaper. Officers arrested him and his bartender for being open on a Sunday. Balbontin challenged authorities in the courtroom, and his court case in 1896 aroused passions on both sides of the liquor question. The same could be said for City Solicitor Peter O. Knight, who became a champion of personal liberty and won powerful friends when he defended blue law offenders pro bono. As the city's solicitor, he should have been *prosecuting* cases against suspects, not defending them.[35]

Knight enraged the Law and Order League when he appeared in court to defend Balbontin, asking for a delay in the trial to research the case. Knight admitted he was the prosecuting attorney for the state "and if he believed his client was guilty he would advise him to so plead, as he could not afford to defend in one court and prosecute in the other, on the same charge." Although Knight referred to him as his "client," he also claimed that he was merely there to be sure justice was done, not as an official attorney. The bizarre case proceeded with Knight as Balbontin's unofficial, unpaid attorney.[36]

The mayor personally prosecuted the case but had no evidence. Police accused Balbontin of slyly tapping kegs from the rear of his fridge while making them appear disconnected. Knight poked holes in the mayor's case. Balbontin's saloon shared a back door and common hallway with a neighboring barber who may have left it open. He accused a police officer of being a dedicated cockfighter and gambler who held matches every Sunday in West Tampa with impunity.[37]

Mayor Gillett had no case. The barkeep wasn't even in the saloon, but next door getting a shave at the barber. No one was found buying alcohol from the saloon. The *Tribune* joked that Balbontin was on trial for leaving the back door of his saloon open. The mayor must have been chagrined when he had to admit defeat. He had merely embarrassed himself, the league, and their cause. Peter O. Knight, the would-be prosecutor, argued that since there was no evidence, there was no real trial and no wrongdoing on the part of himself or his would-be client. Knight accused Mayor Gillett of pandering to voters, promising saloon owners lax enforcement and dry activists strict enforcement.[38]

When Knight represented the Spanish Club on a similar charge, members raised $200 to pay him, but he simply donated it back so he could not be accused of being a paid attorney. Knight became such an effective defender of Tampa's wet merchants that Louis Athanasaw of the notorious Imperial Theater paid him the dubious honor of naming his son Peter O. Knight Athanasaw.[39] For more than a year, the Law and Order League relentlessly pursued charges against Knight for dereliction of duty and tampering with paperwork, in particular some delayed indictments against Mugge and Balbontin. The league also peppered City Attorney Pat Whittaker with accusations for the next year, including being part of a conspiracy with Knight to clear Balbontin of charges. City Council moved to sustain charges made against Knight, but could not muster the votes. When the league submitted evidence of Knight's alleged wrongdoings to Governor Bloxam, he did not find cause to intervene.[40]

Balbontin accused the league of "unwittingly laboring to jeopardize the commercial prospects of the town under the hypocritical cloak of morality." He suggested that all other places of amusement be closed on Sunday and that the cigar factories be stopped from employing operatives to work.

If a few fanatics and hypocrites that have made dismal failures out of all their undertakings are now to ruin Tampa's prosperity and sacrifice the vast fortunes that our people have invested here and drive from our doors the very people that have made this city the Queen of the Gulf, then we say turn the reins of control over to these people and show no favoritism.[41]

"Indiscriminately arrest every [violator of the blue laws] for a few weeks," Balbontin suggested, and support for the law would evaporate. The *Tribune* emphatically agreed. Several weeks later, just over a year after the anti-vice campaign launched by Mayor Gillett, the *Tribune* expressed its exhaustion with the protracted struggle over saloons. Just ten years after Ybor City had been annexed, the *Tribune* blamed the Sunday laws for the city's mounting social and financial problems.[42]

> The moment a few fanatical busybodies succeed in imposing upon the general public legal restrictions that are not sanctioned by public opinion, that moment the law becomes inoperative and its enforcement difficult. Nothing is more dangerous than the presence upon the statute books of laws that are not or cannot be enforced; and there can be no more dangerous class in any community than extremists who force upon the public legislation that is neither desirable nor necessary.
>
> That Tampa is afflicted with the pernicious activity of such a class is obvious. That the great mass of our people are tired of their officious ministration is equally obvious; and it is only a matter of time when the city will turn upon its heel and burst the fetters these self-appointed censors have sought to impose upon it.[43]

Just a year before, the *Tribune* had cheered Mayor Gillett's announced crackdown on gambling. But in practice, the enforcement push seemed to be a veiled political campaign against immigrants and political opponents. Attorney Hugh Macfarlane, who had founded West Tampa in 1895, led the Law and Order Society with other attorneys. The newspapers duly took sides in the political contest being played out every Sunday, with the *Tampa Daily Times* siding with the Law and Order League and Macfarlane and the *Tribune* lining up behind Peter O. Knight, Balbontin, and Mugge.[44]

A larger conflict farther from home interrupted the Sunday wars,

Christian activists railed against alcohol and saloons in Tampa for thirty years before Florida finally went dry. The tax cuts that would supposedly follow Prohibition never materialized. (Tony Pizzo collection, University of South Florida Tampa Special Collections)

throwing Tampa into the center of international events and a war with Spain. Tampa's merchants were unanimous in their desire to exploit the War Department's selection of their city as a port of embarkation for the invasion of Cuba. To stamp out blind tigers and their often-dangerous rotgut, authorities allowed anyone to open a legitimate saloon on any unoccupied property, and Tampa's drinking places quickly expanded.

THE DAY OF REST AT DESOTO PARK

DeSoto Park, Ybor City's most popular private resort, became the booze barons' signature enterprise and a symbol of immigrant defiance of dry laws. Mugge built the pavilion at DeSoto Park in 1895 with an accompanying saloon. Over the years, the park was leased by Mugge and Balbontin. "Great crowds came," Mugge's son wrote in his memoir, "mostly of the Cuban population—and it was quite a treat for them on a Sunday afternoon."[45] Mugge installed more fixtures such as bowling alleys and bathhouses. Balbontin leased the park in 1896 and made improvements of his own, including a new temporary refreshment stand, newly spruced-up grounds, a bandstand, a carriage driveway, a restaurant, a bar, a water-side promenade, and a huge dance pavilion large enough for a hundred couples, all lit by two hundred electric lights around the park.

In the first years of the twentieth century, Desoto Park was still one of the most popular local destinations for recreation. On a typical Sunday, the park planned a cakewalk dance, followed by the performance of a military band, and finally a "Spanish American ball" with more music and dancing. The park also featured vaudeville acts, hot-air balloon daredevils, trapeze artists, and high-wire jugglers. The baseball diamond there hosted countless hotly contested innings between local teams, also held on Sundays in defiance of the Sunday laws.

DeSoto Park and its saloon was an intolerable nuisance to Tampa's moral guardians, and it became the ultimate prize in the Sunday wars. In 1899, when Greek immigrant Louis Athanasaw of the notorious Imperial Theater leased the park and supplied vaudeville entertainers for shows there, opponents must have been seething. Located in Fort Brooke, a lawless hamlet outside Tampa city limits, Athanasaw's racy theater challenged the community's standards of decency. It did not help matters that the park's saloon was run by none other than Balbontin and Mugge. This trio of immigrants became the sworn enemies of local dry activists.[46]

The concerns of reformers did not end with public drinking. Entertainment of any kind could not be tolerated. In 1897, police arrested the entire Forepaugh family when the trapeze act performed at DeSoto Park. Police also shut down popular baseball games. The *Tribune* opposed the strict enforcement of the Sunday law.[47]

The manner in which DeSoto Park has recently been handled by the authorities on Sundays is a case in point. The resort is one of the most beautiful and picturesque in the vicinity of Tampa, and Sunday is the only day in the week upon which it can be conveniently utilized by the cigar-makers who have been prominent among its patrons. To close such a place on Sunday means one of two things. The people must either be deprived of their rational enjoyment, or lose a working day in order to secure a little recreation. This means closing the cigar factories for a day, and a consequent loss of four or five thousand

dollars. This is what is actually taking place in Tampa today, in consequence of the uneasy exertions of a set of people who are so deeply
impressed with a sense of their own superiority that nothing will satisfy them but the imposition of their own ideas upon the majority of
their fellow citizens.[48]

In 1902, four prominent ministers mounted a new campaign against local saloons that did not observe the Sabbath. Their loud protestations
spurred police to enforce blue laws for the first time in two years, and
every saloon in town was closed—all but one nestled in the pavilion at
DeSoto Park. The holy men then visited the park one Sunday afternoon
while hundreds of thirsty patrons collected around the pavilion's bar. As
the ministers made their way through what they called "The Devil's Play-
gound," watching the various amusements with disapproval, "a crowd of
at least five hundred men and boys, Americans, Spaniards, Cubans, Italians, and negroes, followed in their train," mocking the holy men.

They finally came upon the saloon and pressed on inside with the
crowd, until they stood atop the bar's footrail watching drinks continue
to be sold as they cried out for arrests. Some drinkers brazenly invited the
ministers to join them for a taste. Police arrested the bartenders and park
managers, B. M. Balbontin and G. Ferlita. The *Tribune* observed, "Having
accomplished the arrest of the drink dispensers, the preachers went to
the baseball grounds, where the Tampa team was in the act of pound-
ing the West Tampa nine all over the diamond." The ministers demanded
that police arrest everyone involved, but they only arrested the ticket
seller. To avoid a possible riot by spectators, nervous police summoned
Sheriff John T. Lesley to the scene, who flatly refused to arrest anyone
else and accused the ministers of mounting a political campaign against
him.

The ministers withdrew and swore out warrants for Balbontin, four
bartenders, and the man who sold tickets for the baseball game. When
solicitor Simonton neglected to file the charge against the baseball ticket
man, the preachers learned they had no remedy. The subsequent trial of
Balbontin and Ferlita that summer divided Tampa's citizens between wet
and dry. The prosecution never presented evidence that beer was indeed
being sold and consumed in the saloon that day. Two of the ministers

testified they could not be sure that beer was sold as they had never even tasted the beverage. Reverend Anderson testified that he so hated the liquor trade that he went to the park that day to stop it or die trying. The trial dragged on into the fall. When the ministers could not positively identify the beverages they saw as intoxicants, the case fell apart, ending twice in mistrial. The police apparently did nothing to secure evidence. Finally, G. Ferlita was convicted, but Balbontin escaped punishment.[49]

A merchant, "one of the few teetotalers in this city," wrote an anonymous editorial to the *Tribune*. "Had the preachers begun their work at home, yea under the very shade of the edifices of worship, and accomplished anything, then it would be with becoming grace to attack the vice of Sunday beer dispensing at the park." In other words: If the preachers' flocks were truly faithful, the community would obey the Sunday laws, and no dry campaign would be necessary. A reform-minded political faction called the Citizens League took up the reform mantle of the Law and Order League, then five years gone. This time, reformers put up a slate of candidates and managed to elect the politically independent Mayor Frank Wing, all the while opposing "open city" advocates such as Peter O. Knight.[50]

Mayor Wing ordered "the bluest Sunday in Tampa's history," according to the *Tribune*, allowing only pharmacies to function. It may have been the city police's most earnest effort to enforce the state law to the letter. The mayor listed examples of the kinds of places the police would be scrutinizing, calling out "saloons, coffee shops, fruit stands, ice cream parlors, cigar stands, soda water stands, barber shops, news stands, bootblack stands, ice cream carts, ice wagons, drays, and wagons" and clarifying that "all [are] included in the order, and must not be operated today. Delivery teams for dry goods, grocery and other stores were ordered in the stables by midnight last night." Mayor Wing announced, "No one will work in Tampa tomorrow but the policemen. . . . The people made a demand for this sort of Sunday observance, and [we] will give it to them." He even publicized a surprising statement of compliance issued by the Liquor Dealers' Association:

We, the licensed liquor dealers of the city of Tampa, having complied with your order of closing our places of business on Sunday, the first day of the week, and endorsing your policy in this matter, do hereby request of you that you will cause the Sunday law, as it appears in the Revised Statutes of the State of Florida, and in the ordinances of the City of Tampa, be enforced strictly to the letter. We now realize that our clerks need the rest given them on Sundays and believe that all other employees and animals should enjoy the same. Respectfully, The Liquor Dealers' Ass'n. of Tampa. By B.M. Balbontin, President. Attest: Max Caras, Secretary.[51]

And in a reversal of the earlier loosening of the blue laws, City Council ordered that all streetcars be shut down the following Sunday.[52] Officers made the rounds giving notice to close "in some cases supplemented by the comment: 'It's the Goo Goos who are doing this,'" blaming the crack-down on uncompliant immigrants. "The barrooms were closed in the city limits," the *Tribune* observed, "but were wide-open just across the line in Fort Brooke and West Tampa. The thirsty throngs took car rides and got all they wanted; and, because it was harder to get, most of them took more than usual. The result was there was more visible drunkenness in the city than has been seen on any previous Sunday."[53]

While the city maintained pressure on saloons, it loosened other Sunday restrictions, announcing, "Business necessary to the existence and comfort of the people will be allowed to operate today. Saloons will be closed, but barbershops, meat markets, soda fountains, etc., will not be restricted." The *Tribune* noted with some satisfaction, "The 'blue law' regime lasted only one Sunday." DeSoto Park's saloon turned away many disappointed regulars and tried to mollify them with soft drinks. When five milkmen were brought before Judge Peeples, he dismissed them all, fretting for the children.[54]

In June 1902, newly elected Mayor James McKay wrote to the local ministerial association announcing that the wrenching Sunday crusade was over. He spoke to a mass meeting about "bettering the moral condition of Tampa" but had resolved to run an open city. He would close only unruly saloons on Sundays. McKay had been elected on the "Good Government ticket," and he made no secret about appointing Balbontin and Mugge to the Board of Public Works. He said that "prominent businessmen" had suggested that he "give a liberal interpretation of the law in such matters. I think a majority of people in Tampa were in favor of such a liberal interpretation." A *Tribune* editorial read, "The ministers appear to be wasting their time in their crusade to give Tampa a blue-law Sunday."[55]

Concerned citizens periodically organized reform efforts against Sunday drinking, gambling, prostitution, and corruption, but their efforts were always muted by several factors. The city's rationale for allowing vice to flourish was economic. First, the "foreign population . . . demanded a lax enforcement of laws," the *Tribune* wrote. The city's leadership believed that a permissive "wide-open" city would become the most prosperous. Second, a strong laissez-faire attitude prevailed, in which the city did not tax citizens enough to fund basic services. Through the fluctuating administrations starting in 1887, the police had been perennially underfunded. While reformers demanded crackdowns and some politicians promised change, no one was willing to raise taxes for the purpose. Voters consistently elected lenient constables and judges. Finally, there was no shortage of illicit financial incentives for city officials to be friendly to saloons, gambling, and prostitution. No wonder most of Tampa's leadership publicly scoffed at "goody goody laws."[56]

Tampa had succeeded in attracting infrastructure and investment, but its prized cigar industry relied on skilled immigrant labor. The city's future peace and prosperity would depend on a certain degree of harmony among Tampa's pioneers and immigrants. This harmony proved to be difficult in practice owing to the white Protestant establishment chafing at the activities of the immigrants and the leniency of city officials.

"SOME OF THE SOLDIERS DID ALL THEIR FIGHTING IN TAMPA"

The Spanish-American War

Cuba's quest for independence from the Spanish Empire was long and painful. Known as the Pearl of the Antilles, Cuba was Spain's most vital New World possession and one of the few colonies still ruled directly from Madrid. The long-ignored Cuban desire for autonomy fermented into a movement for complete independence. In 1868, Cuban rebels launched an insurrection with little chance of success, and the Ten Years' War (1868–1878) drove much of the island to ruin. Cuba's racial and class tensions divided the rebellion, which the Spanish contained to the eastern part of the island.

In the 1890s, a new rebellion was at hand, led by a pantheon of patriots. At the end of the last war, General Calixto García shot himself in the head rather than give up the cause of Cuba Libre. Scarred but unbowed, García returned to the revolutionary fold for a new insurrection in 1895. The old Dominican warhorse Maximo Gomez would mastermind the guerilla war. Always on horseback, the "Bronze Titan" Antonio Maceo tenaciously took the fight to the Spanish.

A squabbling junta based in New York City provided inconsistent political leadership for the movement. One revolutionary outshone them all. José Martí became the spiritual leader and intellectual voice of the revolution, raising vast sums of money from Cuban exile communities in the Americas and drafting the program of the United Cuban Revolutionary Party. His poetry caressed the heart. His newspaper writing informed a scattered exile population. His speeches, some of his finest given in Tampa, galvanized Cuban patriots to sacrifice. It is no wonder that Martí was a legend in his own time.

Most importantly, Martí's philosophy shaped the revolution in profound ways. First, he appealed to Cuban nationalism above all. Disturbed by racism during and after slavery in Cuba, he called for racial unity, since half of the island's population was considered black. As a journalist and speaker, Martí was intimate with the Cuban diaspora, colonies of Cuban patriots scattered among Mexico, Florida, and New York. Between 1890 and 1894, Martí toured the Cuban exile communities to rouse the people, raise funds, and arrange filibusters, expeditions of arms, recruits, and supplies. Martí's principles remedied the mistakes of past struggles and reinvigorated the revolution.

Tensions between the Cubans and the Spanish in Tampa became unbearable during the 1890s, leading to their division in their respective clubs. Even boardinghouses had to "stack" guests by political affiliation. In 1891, Cubans stoned gentleman cigar magnate Ignacio Haya—one of Ybor City's founders—and his wife in the street for employing Spaniards in his factories.[1]

During a minor strike in August 1892, crowds congregated in front of the cafés and saloons, heatedly discussing the situation. Throngs of workers took to the streets armed with clubs. For their own protection, "scabs," or strikebreakers, were allowed to carry pistols and displayed their weapons on the street and in the restaurants.[2]

The workers enjoyed their promenade on Sunday morning as usual. Then, a hotheaded Spaniard named Salvadore Valdez quarreled with a passing Cuban. When bystanders parted the men, Valdez picked up a stick to use as a weapon. Unable to find his intended victim on the crowded street, Valdez became infuriated. Wielding his club, he insulted the first person he saw and, "like a ruffian," said one onlooker, challenged everyone around him to combat.[3]

As the Cuban crowd on the street boiled into a mob around Valdez, his brother-in-law Modesto emerged from his nearby restaurant, El Piral.

Modesto brandished a baseball bat, followed closely behind by a friend with a pistol. They, too, challenged the crowd "in a manner denoting unquestioned bravery." The pistolero fired two shots and dashed into the restaurant with his friends. The crowd, now raging, attempted to subdue the men, but the gunman fired from the restaurant.[4]

By three o'clock that afternoon, several hours into the ordeal, a mob of three hundred enraged Cubans besieged El Piral restaurant. Modesto Valdez holed up inside with four other Spaniards. The pistolero fired through the windows at the gathering crowd, which was "frantic and unruly as a wild beast." Although the mob worked over the building with bricks, bats, and bottles, the five Spaniards survived, and the two groups traded accusations through letters to the *Tribune's* editor. Police hauled several of the Spaniards to jail that evening. After being laughed at when ordering the crowds to disperse, Mayor Herman Glogowski enlisted forty temporary policemen to maintain order.[5]

The bad reputation of an owner could ruin any Ybor City restaurant. In 1892, workers at Lozano, Pendas & Co.'s cigar factory, walked out when management hired Modesto Valdez, the Spanish owner of El Piral restaurant. The strike fizzled, but workers boycotted his restaurant, and Valdez learned that few businesses could survive Cuban disapproval.[6]

An incident late in 1892 brought tensions to a new height. Secret agents of the Spanish Crown tried to kill José Martí, the soul of the Cuban revolution, while he visited Ybor City. He had stopped in Tampa several times over the years, where he said he was "happy amongst warriors" in the exile community. On December 16, spies acting as his orderlies poisoned his Vin Mariani, a popular wine at the time infused with cocaine (much like Coca-Cola). Martí was just settling down in his private apartment after a long day of meetings and speeches. He sent an assistant for a glass of the elixir, which Martí used privately when engaged in his nightly writing and correspondence. Upon taking a sip, Martí immediately knew it tasted wrong and spit it out. It had been spiked with something that sickened him, probably some sort of toxic acid.[7]

Paulina and Ruperto Pedrosa nursed him back to health in their private home, where Ruperto slept in front of the door to Martí's room. Martí swore the doctor to secrecy and protected the would-be assassins from retribution. One of them came to ask forgiveness, and much to the shock of his advisors, Martí granted a private audience. The would-be assassin left with newfound revolutionary fervor and went on to become Commander Valentin Castro Cordoba, another hero of the Cuban struggle. Martí soon recovered and was back on the fundraising circuit.[8]

A new Cuban insurrection seemed to be inevitable. By 1894, Ybor City and West Tampa could count forty-six Cuban clubs and patriotic societies. Every week on *El Dia de La Patria* (The Day of the Fatherland), participating workers gave the day's wages to the cause of Cuban liberty. On October 12, Martí gave his final speech in Ybor City at the Emilio Pons factory. Together with the generals and junta, Martí made the final arrangements for the revolution to proceed. On January 12, 1895, disaster struck. American authorities seized three ships docked at Fernandina (north of Jacksonville) loaded with weapons and equipment that Martí had purchased for the revolution. It was a massive loss, but the revolution was poised to begin despite the setback.[9]

The secret order to launch the revolution against Spanish rule was rolled into a Cuban cigar made in Tampa. The city became a vital offshore base in the Cuban war for Independence. The Cuban Revolutionary Party set up a war headquarters in Ybor City, and Emilio Núñez raised a regiment for Cuba Libre. The war began on February 24, 1895, with a successful uprising in the east of the island. In April, new contingents of troops led by Gomez and Maceo reinforced the rebels. Martí died in a skirmish on May 19 at Dos Rios, a martyr for Cuban liberty.[10]

The sensational Yellow Press found the perfect villain in Cuban governor Valeriano "The Butcher" Weyler, an unsentimental Spanish general who instituted a cruel and cunning strategy of "reconcentration" in 1896. By driving three hundred thousand peasants off their land and forcing them to reside in the cities, Weyler deprived the Cuban guerillas of support in the countryside. His inhumane policies were denounced by the Cuban junta and the press, and Weyler became known as a ravenous beast. While thousands of *reconcentrados* faced starvation and disease, the general himself couldn't understand what all the fuss was about. "One does not make war with bon bons," he quipped.[11]

The weapons and supplies provided by the Cuban exile community infuriated Weyler. The general responded with a ban on tobacco exports from the island. He wanted to cripple the cigar industry in the United

States, depriving the rebellion of a vital revenue source. Henry Plant's steamer *Olivette* began a marathon run to bring as much tobacco to Tampa as possible before the export ban took effect. Every inch of the vessel brimmed with the product during its last runs in 1896. The Spanish reopened trade some months later, throwing a lifeline to Tampa's cigar industry. Due to political turbulence in Spain, Weyler lost support and resigned in 1897. His brutal policies were effective militarily, but they created a furor in the United States, which suddenly seemed concerned about human rights in Cuba. By 1898, Cuba had been at war for over almost three years, with both sides putting a torch to most of the country, causing extreme hardship and economic dislocation.[12]

In a display of power, the United States dispatched the battleship *Maine* to Havana Harbor, where it mysteriously exploded on February 15, 1898. The cataclysm was caused by an accumulation of coal dust belowdecks, but most of the nation assumed the devious Spanish were at fault.[13]

The Plant Line's *Olivette* evacuated some of the survivors of the *Maine* to Tampa on March 28 to a rousing welcome. Less than one month later, Spain and the United States had declared war on one another. The Stars and Stripes eclipsed the Cuban revolution, and Tampa played a key role in the brief struggle that became known as the Spanish-American War. Mayor Gillett called for fair treatment of Tampa's Spaniards: "These citizens and businesses of Tampa are not to blame for the existing state of affairs.... There has thus far been no clash between our Cuban and Spanish Citizens and I firmly believe the leaders on each side will give wise counsel to their people."[14]

The interruption of Cuban exports caused a chill in the U.S. tobacco industry. The insurgency had hobbled Cuba's tobacco productivity beginning in 1895, but the real crisis struck when war commenced in April 1898. The first obvious problem was the cutting of Cuba's tobacco shipments, especially the Havana leaf, which was so important for wrapping cigars. "If you want to smoke Havanas next Christmas," the *Tobacco Journal* warned in June, "you better buy them now and save them." Even if trade with Cuba flowed uninterrupted during the war, the scorched island had little to offer.[15]

If the cigar industry found itself in a tough spot, its workers suffered the most. By April, three thousand Cuban refugees had settled in and around Tampa, straining resources further. Eduardo Manrara of the Ybor Company opened a soup kitchen to feed up to eight hundred struggling workers and destitute Cuban refugees twice daily, but he could never fulfill demand. For breakfast, the restaurant served hash, rice, ham, and cornbread; for dinner, it served soup, beef, rice, beans, potatoes, and bread. While some residents opened more soup houses for the hungry, the Cuban junta continued to raise more funds for the war. Cuban volunteer guerillas could now drill out in the open.[16]

As the United States and Spain teetered on the verge of war, Henry Plant's keen business sense led him to dispatch Franklin Q. Brown to Cuba in April to identify possible business opportunities. Upon his return, he visited President William McKinley to persuade him of Tampa's value as a springboard for the invasion of Cuba. His advocacy must have made an impression. The War Department designated Tampa as one of the assembly camps for the invasion of Cuba. The Plant System operated the line going in to Tampa and had made improvements to the port. Although the small town offered minimal amenities to soldiers, officers could enjoy the incongruous luxuries of Plant's Tampa Bay Hotel, a fanciful palace across the river from the hardscrabble town.[17]

Cocksure Henry Plant promised the War Department that his single railroad could handle the deluge of railcars coming from the north, but the deployment in Tampa was a mess from the beginning. Only one other line ran into Tampa but was owned by Plant's bitter competitors, the Florida Central Railroad. The two companies relentlessly undermined one another, compounding confusion and stoppages.[18]

It seems natural that Plant's railroad would be massively overburdened, but the chaos in the military proved to be much worse. The day after the declaration of war against Spain, the War Department shipped 150,000 rations to Tampa, including canned goods, bread, meat, medicine, clothes, rifles, and camp equipment. But no one had seen fit to catalog the contents or label the train cars, making it impossible to unload the cargo directly onto the appropriate ships. The result: Plant's line was backed up for miles with trains waiting to be unloaded, sorted, and inventoried. Some trains dumped their cargo anywhere and everywhere. With no warehouses available in Tampa itself, supplies languished in the open or were stored on ships.[19]

For many years, historians and local enthusiasts have focused on the exploits of U.S. military forces and turned out stories of heroism, but these do little to help us understand what happened in Tampa. A focus on the consumption of the soldiers while in Tampa reveals that many of the challenges faced by soldiers of the day revolved around consumption, including the profiteering disguised as hospitality, drunkenness, racial tension over access to saloons, and food-borne disease.

TAMPA HOSPITALITY

Private Charles Post documented his insatiable hunger during his unit's long train ride to Florida. "Guards were posted at each car door, and no one was allowed off the train. Our breakfast came: a can of corned beef to each man as his day's rations, six hardtack, and swell up [with] water." Soldiers like Post used every opportunity to obtain food and drink from the public while on the move. In Waycross, Georgia, a scene quickly unfolded when a train station began charging individual soldiers for coffee that the army had already paid for. The clerks began demanding a nickel per cup, then a dime, and finally a quarter, until the troops were on the verge of a riot. By the time the soldiers reached Florida, they had been subsisting on poor rations, gone without bathing, and had been gouged at every opportunity.[20]

Getting to Tampa could be a challenge. "In 1898 the soldier trains were blockaded in Plant City for miles," Minnie Waver remembered. "For three days they lived on water and hard tack. It was on Sunday, the merchants opened up their stores and supplied all the food necessary to feed those hungry men. The Fifth Ohio Regiment came to our kitchen—had the band on the lawn while we cooked the juicy steaks for them all day long. . . . It seems understandable that many of the men were short on patience when they arrived in Tampa."[21]

A correspondent from the *New York Times* seemed crestfallen when he first eyed Tampa. "It is poor in architecture, poor in population, and worse as regards streets and highways than any city I have yet seen. It is impossible to drive half a mile out of town in a carriage. The wheels will simply mire in the soft white sea sand."[22]

Tampa did not impress most of the new arrivals. One New York recruit had an especially bad first day in camp, where he was "bitten by mosquitoes, stung by a tarantula, [had] a touch of malaria . . . [sat] down on a giant ants' nest, [stepped] on an alligator, and [had] a snake in his boots." With questionable food and no sanitation, the camps soon brimmed over with filth, and the foul smell surrounded the city. The *New York Tribune* observed, "Tampa combines in a curious way a certain Southern shiftlessness with the bustle and enterprise of a Western boom town." Some soldiers hated the sound of Spanish being spoken, even if it was uttered by Cuban patriots who had fought the Spanish for decades.[23]

Journalist George Kennan's description of Tampa is really a tale of two cities: the extravagant grandeur of the Tampa Bay Hotel and the sandy, ramshackle town itself. "It was a warm, clear Southern night when we arrived," Kennan wrote,

> The scene presented by the hotel and its environment, as we stepped out of the train, was one of unexpected brilliancy and beauty. The impression made upon a newcomer, as he alighted from the train, was that of a brilliant military ball at a fashionable seaside summer resort. . . . The showy architecture, beautiful grounds, semi-tropical foliage, and brilliant flowers of the Tampa Bay Hotel raise expectations which the town across the river does not fulfill. It is a huddled collection of generally insignificant buildings standing in an arid desert of sand, and to me it suggested the city of Semipalatinsk—a wretched, verdureless town in southern Siberia, colloquially known to Russian army officers as "the Devil's Sand-box." Thriving and prosperous Tampa may be, but attractive or pleasing it certainly is not.[24]
>
> Long trains of four-mule wagons loaded with provisions, camp equipage, and lumber moved slowly through the soft-deep sand of the unpaved streets in the direction of the encampment; the sidewalks were thronged with picturesquely dressed Cuban volunteers from the town, sailors from the troop-ships, soldiers from the camp, and

war correspondents from everywhere; mounted orderlies went tearing back and forth with dispatches to or from the army headquarters in the Tampa Bay Hotel; Cuban and American flags were displayed in front of every restaurant, hotel, and Cuban cigar shop, and floated from the roofs and windows of many private houses. . . . Thousands of soldiers, both inside and outside the sentry-lines, were standing in groups discussing the naval fight off Manila, lounging and smoking on the ground in the shade of army wagons, playing hand-ball to pass away the time, or swarming around a big board shanty, just outside the lines, which called itself "NOAH'S ARK" and announced in big letters its readiness to dispense cooling drinks to all comers at a reasonable price.[25]

Augustus Mugge, the son of "Booze Baron" Robert Mugge, recalled that his father "had a huge saloon built in an orange grove near the camp in the northern part of the city, near Michigan Avenue. The contractor had to build the entire structure, including fixtures and ice-box, in one day. The counter had a length of eight feet, and the soldiers were served by eight bartenders. It was open day and night and was known as the 'Noah's Ark.' A train of beer was shipped from St. Louis to Tampa."[26]

Tampa's residents rode the great wave of patriotism of the day, but they also calculated the profits to be reaped from visitors. The small town of 15,000 was suddenly home to twice as many free-spending soldiers. The army paid out $175,000 on a routine payday, most of which went directly into Tampa's economy. A *Washington Post* correspondent wrote, "The Tampa shopkeepers are making so much money that the city banks will hardly hold it. Even a lemonade man, equipped with a bucket and two tin cups, can make $25 a day."[27]

Tampa had been overwhelmed not just with soldiers and materiel but also with opportunity. A *New York Times* journalist observed:

Tampa has the largest share of this glory and prosperity. It has at one stride taken its place as the first city of the state, and is somewhat abashed and overcome by its sudden rise to such great importance. It has not yet been able to adjust itself to its new conditions. It knew what was coming, but was appalled by the very magnitude of its good fortune.[28]

By May 1898, every hotel and boardinghouse was "running over with guests." Restaurants and bars sprang up overnight. Cockfights and dog fights drew huge crowds at Sportsman's Park. "Some good birds will be pitted," the *Tribune* noted. "The dogs to fight are 'Bull,' belonging to the [local] firemen [against] a crack fighter, the property of one of the soldiers now in camp here. Much money will change hands on the result." The ladies of Hyde Park held a "hop" so Tampa's upper crust could mingle with the officers. The *Tribune* couldn't print enough papers to satisfy demand. "It looks like the whole world belongs to Tampa."[29]

CAMP LIFE

Soldiers cursed their wool uniforms in Tampa's heavy heat and humidity. The arriving troops set up camps with an eye toward getting relief from Florida's sun. Gathering what material they could, the men fashioned elaborate "bowers and arbors" and "porticos of pine poles, thatched with palmetto leaves, and under the grateful shade of these shelters loll[ed] about and enjoy[ed] what little rest they manage to get between drills and tours of camp duty."[30]

The troops passed the time in Tampa training for combat and pursuing leisure wherever they could find it. John P. Jones of the General Joe Wheeler Camp remembered:

> There was good fishing and a splendid bathing beach, while many of the men made a little extra money by gathering seashells and shipping them north. There was a baseball diamond (which we made ourselves), also a lawn-tennis court[,] a small library, and last (but by no means least) the canteen. This was an old building[,] about 100 feet long and 20 feet wide, furnished with a bar, at which was served beer, sandwiches, soft drinks, cigars, cigarets [*sic*], and a number of small tables and chairs for card and domino-playing. This was our club and it was an interesting place, as we put on amateur theatricals, and some of the boys were good singers and musicians.[31]

Besides the heavy uniforms and unbearable heat, the lack of tasty food compounded the misery of the soldiers. Military food was an acquired taste at best, with hard tack, cheap coffee, and semi-rancid beef being the primary foodstuffs of the campaigning army of the day. When asked if his unit had received rations, a New York Volunteer replied, "Oh we had some crackers that ought to have been used for paving stones. Coffee that you could hardly call by that name, and some fearful beef." For one unit, meals consisted of a breakfast of coffee, beef, bacon, and light bread. Beef stew with tomatoes and beans served as lunch with hardtack or bread. Dinner was simply bacon and bread with coffee.[32]

A journalist embedded with the soldiers in Tampa spoke for many when he wrote in *Harper's Weekly*, "In this hot climate we yearn for fresh fruits and vegetables, for anything that will quench thirst and at the same time cool the blood. Meat and all heating things we try to avoid by a wise instinct. The troops, however, are supplied only that which is most unseasonable—greasy pork, and beans of that brown quality that makes one ready to spend the rest of the day in the watermelon patch."[33] The men found food where they could get it. A large group of men left camp to be fed by the nuns of the Catholic convent, who thought the army had not been feeding them.

> The good Sisters placed tables under trees and waited on the men. The soldiers literally came in squads. We were somewhat surprised to see the continuance of this the second day. More men applied at the convent for food than on the day before. Three good meals were served to any soldiers who took the trouble to apply. The next two days were the same. The Sisters ordered large quantities of food, got up at 4 o'clock in the morning to prepare it, and worked hard all day long. During this time the men were receiving their regular camp rations, and none of them paid the Sisters a cent for what was so freely given. Some of the men who had been most regular in their attendance at the convent meals were afterwards seen buying ice cream and other luxuries on the main street of Tampa. Finally the colonel called upon the Mother Superior and offered to reimburse her for what she had paid out, and the sisters found out they had been feeding men who were not starving—as they had represented—but were merely dissatisfied with camp fare.[34]

Missionaries and temperance workers exhorted the men to match their courage with godly virtues. Cuban women full of revolutionary fervor baked for the camps and distributed cigars, often raising money for the Cuban junta in the process. Future Tampa mayor D. B. McKay remembered of the visiting soldiers, "The brawling, drinking, gambling groups were not typical of the mass of fine young patriots who assembled here for the invasion of Cuba. The vast majority were temperate in their habits and devoted themselves earnestly to the task of becoming trained for the job ahead of them. It was very noticeable that many of them carefully observed their religious duties while in camp here."[35]

Catering to this sect of soldier, the Woman's Christian Temperance Union passed out literature and cold water at camp. In a pamphlet titled "Christian Work in Our Camps," trailblazing female journalist Anna Northend Benjamin wrote an optimistic characterization of the American soldier, including the claim that "while there is a good deal of drinking in the army, there is very little drunkenness." Mrs. Benjamin must have traveled to the camps only during the day, as one night at Fort Brooke would have changed her mind about the tendencies of soldiers. To tamp down the rowdy men, the military dispatched the "Christian General" Oliver Otis to inspire them to improve their behavior. It did not work.[36]

Soldiers commandeered streetcars and fired pistols as they careened around the city. Alcohol fueled their wildest antics. The war brought an estimated $3 million to Tampa. The soldiers bought a whole variety of products and services, but it is no surprise that their greatest idle pleasure besides good food was liquid refreshment. Tampa's heat and humidity made cold drinks of any kind a sought-after relief. A single soda fountain cleared $1,100 in a week. Some of Tampa's merchants were notoriously greedy. One peddler charged soldiers two cents for a gallon of smelly drinking water. Captain M. B. Stewart wrote, "Their [Tampa's] patriotic endeavors were limited to a partially successful effort to relieve us of as much pay as was consistent within the pale of the law. . . . Pie factories and beer saloons multiplied and increased." Saloons such as the White Swan, the Yellow Dog, the Green Goose, and Sid Tipple's joined Noah's Ark in slaking the thirst of the soldiers. Officers gravitated toward the ornate delights of the Tampa Bay Hotel.[37]

Demand for strong drink was so high that the city allowed entrepreneurs to operate makeshift saloons in any vacant storefronts or lots.

With saloons came the homes of other vices, like dance halls and bawdy-houses. Fort Brooke, independent of Tampa (and even more lawless), and Ybor City became the favorite destinations of the soldiers. After being paid, Charles Post recorded that his unit cleared out of the camp and went into town.

> That night out of approximately a thousand men, there were only eighty-five privates left in the camp. We eighty-five were all there were . . . to round up the others, who were in Tampa drinking it dry. So, commanded by officers, we marched out of camp in column of twos, down into Tampa. Every saloon brought forth its amazed prisoners. With fixed bayonets, we formed them in a column of twos. The column grew and, as we turned back to camp, it stretched away down into the darkness of the scantily lighted street. . . . The Regulars, far wiser, sent out no Provost Guard. They shut their eyes on paydays, and until the night after. I think that without a doubt we made ourselves ridiculous.[38]

On the march back to camp, Post saw a welcome sight at the end of the streetcar line. A newly built barn "boards still a fresh sawmill yellow" beside an orange grove: "Known as Noah's Ark, it was a gambling house and offered chuck-luck, keno, roulette, and faro. The barn was packed to the doors; not an officer could get in. But here, at the trolley terminal, under flaring gasoline torches, was an ice-cream and soda fountain forty feet long. Here were soap, coconuts, oranges, lemons, writing paper, and sandwiches. On the counter, soldiers were playing chuck-luck and craps."[39] The soldiers were so footloose that some escaped their captors long enough to buy goods at the improvised store. Clearly, it was almost impossible to reign in young volunteer soldiers on pay day.

THE HAZARDS OF FOOD AND DRINK: TYPHOID AND EMBALMED BEEF

Concerns about the sustenance of the men mounted before a shot had been fired. As the troops began assembling in Tampa, the *New York Times* revealed an early scare over the water supply: "Threats have been made to murder the army wholesale by means of poisoned water. The tanks

Because their officers sometimes chose poor ground for campsites, soldiers fashioned hammocks to avoid floods and pests. (Ensminger Brothers photo collection, University of South Florida Tampa Special Collections)

which supply the city with its water, and from which the soldiers also get their quota, are accessible, and only a few days ago an attempt at poisoning these tanks was reported to the police and to the military authorities. Happily, it was proved to be a false alarm, but the mere suggestion that it carried was sufficient to show the soldiers how easily their lives might have been sacrificed."[40]

The worries about food and drink were not unfounded. The war against the Spanish proved to be a quick affair, but widespread sickness among the troops became the biggest killer. Within days of the *New York Times* article on Tampa's water supply, soldiers in Tampa became sick. While the populace had been whipped into hysteria over what evil the sinister Spanish might do, the soldier's very worst enemy was himself. The U.S. troops would later mock the Cubans for their unsanitary villages, but the camps of the American soldiers were deadly. Typhoid fever infected its first victims within days of setting up camp in Tampa. Although army physicians fretted about tropical diseases, typhoid became the more lethal danger, with many men being infected before shipping out to Cuba. About 20 percent of personnel were infected overall, one in five of them fatally. More U.S. troops died of typhoid fever (2,622) than those killed and wounded in the entire war (1,973).[41]

Roughly 30,000 troops camped around Tampa, some for more than six weeks. Campsites went up near Port Tampa, old Fort Brooke, DeSoto Park/Palmetto Beach, west of the Tampa Bay Hotel, and just north of town. It proved to be an unpleasant stay for most of the soldiers, especially after torrential rains in June that flooded several camps, forcing their relocation. The army did not supply enough clean water to the camps, prompting the men to drink out of nearby civilian wells. The troops dug fresh "sinks," some for latrines and others for wells, but the ground was so soft and the water table so high that the task was rendered impossible. Instead of staying in a deep hole, the human waste simply sat at the top of the brimming latrines. Torrential rains spread filth, and the water table underground linked latrines with wells.

Much of the ground around Tampa was simply not suitable for mass camping sites. Even Sun Tzu, who wrote *The Art of War* in ancient China, exhorted, "If the health of the troops be considered, and they are encamped on high and sunny ground, diseases will be avoided, and victory made certain." The authorities who chose Tampa as a site for troop concentration would have done better to heed Sun Tzu's advice. There was no winning against typhoid on such ground, especially the sites closer to the water along Palmetto Beach and DeSoto Park. The very act of concentrating so many men together in a small area "supercharged" the spread of the disease in a short time. Cuban volunteer Antonio Norona was the first to die in Tampa's camps.[42]

Besides camp sanitation, officers were preoccupied with soldiers obtaining infected food and drink from locals in Tampa, or as one surgeon called it, "indiscretions in eating." A Major Barnett of 157th Indiana Volunteer Infantry recalled, "[I] asked the colonel to issue an order forbidding the use of alcoholic drinks, liquors, uncooked fruits of any kind, pies and cakes [instead of] buying and eating so much at shacks and canteens." Major Davis of the Second Georgia Volunteer Infantry said, "on my recommendation [my Major] closed all the stands selling the abominable 'soft drinks.' These stands used the water from the shallow wells to prepare their drinks." Captain John Fuchsius saw men buying lemonade from a "local huckster" who drew his water from a well within feet of latrines. Major Frank Henley said, "My only regret is that the men who were thus reckless and careless were not severely punished." Despite the strong urging of medical personnel, most officers made no effort to enforce the order to boil all water before drinking. Other medical authorities suggested empowering more unit canteens to keep soldiers on base and prevent them from buying products outside of camp. The profits could be used to comfort their sick comrades. Alas, the idea never caught on.[43]

After its victory in Santiago on July 3, the U.S. Fifth Corps became so wracked by disease in Cuba that it gave rise to the notorious "round robin" letter likely written by Teddy Roosevelt and signed by nine officers asking to be withdrawn from Cuba immediately. The letter was leaked to the press on August 2. The secretary of war withdrew the units while some of the men could still march. A federal investigation of the epidemic began on August 18, less than a week after hostilities ceased. Research proved that several units had brought typhoid with them when they arrived in Tampa. With such haphazard organization there, the infections inevitably spread. Despite the adverse conditions, the camps in Tampa suffered fewer cases of and deaths from typhoid fever than any of the army camps, including Jacksonville; Chickamauga, Georgia; Falls Church, Virginia; and Middletown, Pennsylvania. The typhoid fever plague worsened over the coming months whether one was shipped overseas or remained in camp stateside. Soldiers suffered even more from dysentery, but it wasn't nearly as fatal.[44]

Food poisoning was less pervasive and less fatal than typhoid fever, but it was still a problem. Two dozen soldiers were sickened with ptomaine when they ate some spoiled canned corned beef, and reports recall their vomiting and "great depression." The treatment presented another ordeal: apomorphine, calomel, and soda; and for the depression, injections of strychnine and nitroglycerin. The incident blew over quickly enough, but the canned beef scandal had not yet begun.[45]

Suspicions about poor military food seemed to be confirmed by Alexander B. Powell. A New York City–based meat broker, he came to Tampa with five sides of beef and a marvelous secret method for preserving raw beef for rations. The ambitious meat dealer had fumigated the beef with sulfur and claimed that it would not spoil for seven or ten days, even in the Caribbean heat. He had written to President William McKinley touting his preservation technique and pleading for a government contract. He boasted of his many clients among Florida's restaurants and hotels, including the Tampa Bay Hotel. When he received no response, he decided to pitch his product more directly. Powell received six sides of beef from Armour Company to fumigate. After performing the procedure, Armour retained one side of beef for observation while Powell shipped the other five to Tampa in hopes of demonstrating his technique to the supply officers.[46]

Powell was just one of many men who had converged on Tampa hoping to make a quick buck, and he was apparently right at home among the hucksters. He offered his beeves to military officers and ship skippers and succeeded in getting four sides into larger shipments bound for the front, including the *Yucatan*, which carried the Rough Riders to Cuba, and the *Panama*, bound for Puerto Rico. Powell hoped that once on the island, the soldiers would eat his treated beef in a smashing publicity stunt, and their praise would win his company a massive contract with the War Department. He retained one side of beef to observe under Florida's harsh sun, but he seemed more interested in attracting attention to himself. He finally convinced the captain of the transport ship *Comal* to hang the side of beef above the deck of his docked vessel, where it glistened in the sun for all to see. A Major Daly thought the beef still looked fresh after several days, and dared cut off a small slice to cook at camp. He became sick after eating Powell's beef, but admitted he was unsure if his meal sickened him or the three falls from his horse he took in the field that day. The beef was the likely culprit, as it spoiled soon after embarkation. Powell's beef was thrown into the sea by the soldiers it was supposed to feed. The story of Powell's failed experiment should have ended there, but it soon stoked as much outrage and fear as any Spanish attack.[47]

Powell had attracted a lot of attention with his eager display. No one was more concerned about the quality of the rations than the soldiers themselves. General Nelson Miles saw Powell's beef perched aboard the *Comal* and apparently assumed he was demonstrating the preservation method used in the canned beef the army supplied its soldiers. With a shudder, he assumed the canned beef had been "embalmed" using Powell's secret technique. The quality of the canned beef, which the army apparently thought was superior to reliable bacon, left much to be desired. The canners had boiled low-quality cuts of meat and canned them with no seasoning. The military then issued the canned meat as rations even though the beef had been purchased specifically to be prepared in stews, with sauce, or cooked with vegetables in field kitchens. Instead, the men had to rely on uncooked beef as protein for days or weeks at a time, such as when they were on the move. Many of the soldiers could not force down the smelly morsels at all. When rumors ran through the ranks of troops that they had in fact been issued "embalmed beef," they were inclined to believe it.

Private Charles Post wrote about his first encounter with crates of the meat product. "We came across some cases of canned beef and read the name of the consignee; it was us, all right, our U.S. Army. But on the other side of the case the name of a previous consignee could still be seen, burned into the wood: 'Yokohama, Japan.' It had been intended for the Japanese soldiers in the China-Japan War of four years before—1894. Its contents were indicated as 'Roast Beef' [but were] ground up cow, bone, gristle, cartilage, and gullet, with stringy fibers scattered through a semiliquid mess."[48]

Before Carl Sandburg became a famous poet, he was a common soldier who wouldn't touch the stuff. Sandburg wrote of the canned beef ritual among his mess companions,

A tin of "Red Horse" would be handed to one man who opened it. He put it to his nose, smelled of it, wrinkled up his face, and took a spit. The next man did the same and the next till the eight men of the mess had smelled, grimaced, and spit. Then that tin of "Red Horse" was thrown overboard for any fishes of the Atlantic ocean who might like it. Somehow we got along on cold canned beans, occasional salmon, and the reliable hardtack. What we called "Red Horse" soon had all our country scandalized with its new name of "embalmed beef."[49]

No soldiers had died from consuming embalmed beef, but the scandal transfixed an outraged public wary of the meat trusts. Much of the public had only recently become accustomed to eating refrigerated beef that had been slaughtered hundreds of miles away. Most were strongly skeptical of the giant meat companies such as Armour and Swift, and for good reason. Upton Sinclair wouldn't write *The Jungle* for another ten years, but he only revealed what most already thought to be true: meatpacking was (and is) a very dirty business.[50]

The government formed a commission to investigate the canned beef and typhoid infections. After much confusing testimony and finger-pointing, the investigations proved that the War Department had not served embalmed beef, but what it did serve was not quite edible. The commission scolded the Commissary General for buying seven million pounds of an untested product, sight unseen. If Mr. Powell had left his experiment at home instead of displaying it in Tampa, all the confusion might have been avoided. The study of the typhoid epidemic led to a massive groundbreaking study written largely by military physician Walter Reed.[51]

DISORDER AND RIOTS

The Imperial Theater earned a notorious reputation during the war. Owner Louis Athanasaw was a "burly Greek" whose brick building stood just outside Tampa and inside Fort Brooke. Featuring vaudeville performances, girly shows, and lowbrow theater, D. B. McKay remembered,

> The place never closed day or night, nor even on Sunday. There was a liquor saloon in front and a vaudeville theater in the rear. This was a favorite rendezvous of the troops, and seldom a day or night passed without some serious disorder at the place. Jack Stephens was Fort Brooke's only peace officer, and he was not able to cope with the disorderly mobs—even with the help of military police. As much ammunition as would have been used in one ordinary battle—the place was

"shot up" times without number, but Athanasaw was not discouraged. He was making too much money.[52]

When a drunken group of soldiers claiming to be Rough Riders were turned away by a bordello's madam, they attempted to storm the place and take the women by force. To the soldiers' surprise, the women returned fire and repulsed the attack. One prostitute and one soldier were injured.[53]

The lawless atmosphere of Fort Brooke brought out the worst in many. John P. Jones remembered Fort Brooke as "a festering sore on the body of the community." Soldiers seeking vice found it in Fort Brooke and parts of Ybor City, and the worst places flourished where those two municipalities met.

Jones recalled, "It was a horrible example of how low human beings can fall when all moral and legal restraints are removed and anyone who ever visited that place could exclaim with the poet, 'I have seen far down the Infernal Stair / And seen the spirits congregated there.' . . . Everything was wide open and the police force [of three] seldom interfered unless things got very bad, such as physical violence or a display of weapons."[54] Soldiers meted out their own brand of justice when they demolished the many gambling shacks along Michigan Avenue, piled up all the implements, and burned them. History did not record whether the troops disapproved of gambling or the specific methods employed at the houses. After an article appeared in one of the newspapers criticizing the behavior of the troops, only the intervention of the Provost Guard (an early version of military police) saved the building from arson. The Green Goose, a "tough" saloon at Port Tampa, was not so lucky and was burned down by some troops.[55]

African Americans served with honor during the war, even if they were rarely treated with honor by the white community or the press. Violence against black people in the United States was reaching a peak at the time, driving Chaplain Prioleau to write, "Talk about fighting and freeing poor Cuba, and of Spain's brutality, of Cuba's murdered thousands, and starving reconcentrados. IS AMERICA ANY BETTER THAN SPAIN? Has she not subjects in her very midst, who are murdered daily without a trial of judge or jury?" Regiments comprising veteran Buffalo soldiers from the West (Ninth and Tenth Cavalry and the Twenty-Fourth and Twenty-Fifth Infantry) became some of the most decorated in the army. When the first black troops arrived in early May, Tampa's black ministers and their congregations greeted them with celebrations. Black unit bands regaled the citizens with song.[56]

The relations between Tampa's white community and visiting black soldiers became an immediate source of friction. The white citizenry resented the presence of black soldiers in uniform, and most businesses refused to serve them. White racists routinely jeered at black soldiers and insulted them in public, while many black soldiers were determined not to be discriminated against while passing through the South. The *Tampa Tribune* reacted strongly against the black soldiers: "The colored infantrymen stationed in Tampa and vicinity have made themselves very offensive to the people of the city. The men insist upon being treated as white men are treated and the citizens will not make any distinction between the colored troops and the colored civilians." When insulted by white citizens, black troops stationed in Lakeland shot into a crowd, killing a white resident.[57]

In a letter from Tampa, a concerned observer described the rising tensions in May. It was bad enough that Tampa residents were so rude, but the treatment of black soldiers by saloons made matters worse. "Even the grogshops shut their doors against them—that is, the white grogshops do. Here and there in Tampa one sees the sign, 'Colored Bar'—and it is only there that the negro defender of his country can buy a drink. After he has become somewhat inflamed with such liquor as he obtains here, it is little wonder that, when joined by several of his fellows, he attempts to force an entrance to a 'white bar': and then an affray is likely to follow, and the whole black soldiery, which really contains few bad men, gains a bad reputation. Perhaps sometimes the colored soldier is unduly afraid that he will be humiliated, and is as a result unduly self-assertive."[58]

On May 2, the soldiers had been paid and about two hundred black soldiers went to Fort Brooke to celebrate. When Marshal J. J. Stephens arrested a black man who argued with a white saloon operator, fifty black soldiers beat the lawman, stripping him of his gun and prisoner. The battered marshal barely escaped the mob with his life and later arrested one of the men responsible. Days later, the Missing Link saloon (Franklin and Cass) refused to serve four black soldiers. The *Tribune* wrote,

> Upon this refusal the negroes became very boisterous and swore that they would have whiskey or blood. Seeing that the clerk was not to be bluffed, they left the place after using some very rough language toward the whole of the white race. They swore to return last night and demolish the place, but evidently forgot to do so. It is indeed very humiliating to the [white] American citizens and especially to the [white] people of Tampa who pay such enormous taxes to be compelled to submit to the insults and mendacity perpetrated by the colored troops that are not camped in this city on account of the inadequacy of the police force. On several occasions during the past few days Mr. Joe T. Symons has been compelled to close his barroom in Ybor City to prevent bloodshed. The colored soldiers have sworn vengeance against his place because he would not serve them in the white apartments of his resort.[59]

Symons appealed to the mayor and police for protection, and the *Tribune* called for more security against black soldiers. If Mayor Gillett lacked the police, concerned citizens said, he should have appealed to the governor or one of the generals on-site. A similar incident took place at the Greater New York concert hall (Seventh Avenue and Fourteenth Street), a "whites only" establishment that refused service to black soldiers, who threatened to "clean out" the place. The soldiers and officers, the *Tribune* reasoned, "must know that there is no law to compel a man to sell goods to a person whom he desires not to" and if white-owned saloons began serving black people, "they would soon lose all of their best customers."[60]

On the night of June 6, knowing they were about to ship out, many soldiers visited the town they had learned to despise one last time. It took only one incident for Tampa to descend into a drunken orgy of sex and violence. The *Tribune* reported,

> While the mob of soldiers were having sport breaking up the furniture, and stealing the property belonging to the saloon keepers, in Fort Brook[e] and Ybor City one party of men caught a little colored child about two years old and decided to have some fun. One

of the men held the child by the legs with one hand and spanked it with a shingle. This caused great laughter among onlookers. The child was then held at arm's length, by the feet with head down, and the man holding it called to another to shoot at it. The man with the pistol might have been a good shot and had no intention of hitting the child, but the escape was a close one. The bullet from the pistol passed through the sleeve of the child's light dress, and grazed its arm. This satisfied the brutes and they returned the child to its mother.[61]

Having heard news of the horrific shooting game, the black Twenty-Fourth and Twenty-Fifth Infantry regiments "stormed into the streets firing their pistols indiscriminately, wrecking saloons and cafes which had refused to serve them, and forcing their way into white brothels." It is difficult to tell how much of the ensuing disorder was caused by racial tensions and how much was the result of a drunken outburst by men about to ship into the unknown. Perhaps it began with the indignant reaction of the black soldiers to the shooting incident, but white soldiers soon joined in, and the chaos became absolute. Men began ransacking saloons and cafés in search of more liquor. Tampa's five policemen could do nothing in the face of such a numerous and well-armed insurrection.

John P. Jones was drinking at the Imperial Theater Saloon when the riots began.

> Fort Brooke had been reaping a golden harvest from the free-spending soldiers, and on this particular night the "Imperial Theater" was [a] sea of campaign hats, a long bar at the end of the building was crowded with patrons, while a troupe of girls rendered a program of songs and dances on the stage. During brief lulls in the general hurly-burly there could be heard the whirr of roulette wheels and rattle of dice, indicating that the gambling room next to the theater was also doing a rushing business. The streets outside were crowded with soldiers, both white and colored[,] but there was nothing to indicate that anything unusual was brewing. The first intimation of trouble was a fusillade of shots outside, followed by the screaming of women in a resort across the street. The show-girls paused in their act then fled into the wings for as if at a signal, the whole audience rose to its feet and then the shooting started. After wrecking the theater and gam-

bling joint next door the crowd proceeded to shoot up the whole place and by the time a reinforced provost guard reached the scene[,] every saloon, sporting house, and gambling hall in Fort Brooke was completely wrecked.[62]

An interracial mob of soldiers swept down on Tampa's saloons like a pillaging army. Starting at Francisco Ysern's saloon, they stole all of the liquor and destroyed the furniture, firing their pistols to keep the provost guard at bay. At Café Cantante, the soldiers shot up the saloon, pillaged all of the liquor, and "citizens fled for their lives." The mob then split up, with half of it blazing a trail of destruction to Ybor City and the other half ransacking the saloons of the Scrub, a poor black neighborhood north of downtown. The debauchery continued as the sun rose the next morning.[63]

Only after deploying the Second Georgia Volunteer Infantry Regiment, a white unit of zealous segregationists, did the drunken rampage end. Twenty-seven black troops and several Georgia volunteers, all wounded, were transferred to Camp MacPherson near Atlanta for treatment. A military-mandated press blackout in Tampa conveniently coincided with the ugly incident. Locals armed themselves in response to the news, and sleepy chapters of temperance activists were roused to action.[64]

After the riots cleared, the *Tribune* wrote of Fort Brooke: "Not a whole window light was left in the place, and all the saloons were wrecked. The white troops said it was the work of the negro soldiers, and the negroes laid it to the whites. Whoever did it seemed to have done a good job of it. No other casualties reported except a complete destruction of obnoxious places."[65]

Immediately after the disaster of June 6, the army began embarking soldiers for Cuba. For concerned Tampa residents and the soldiers alike, the invasion of Cuba couldn't come soon enough. The only exception proved to be the merchants who catered to soldiers, who assembled on a dusty track on the approaches to the wharves. The bustling little village became known as "Last Chance Street." Sheltered by umbrellas stuck in the sand, black women fried chicken on Cuban clay stoves and bartenders peddled drinks and women from makeshift counters in tents.

Chaos permeated the preparations to invade Cuba from Tampa, resulting in bottle-necks of men and supplies along the railroads and at the port. (Ensminger Brothers photo collection, University of South Florida Tampa Special Collections)

A just-built two-story house advertised itself as a restaurant but offered only women.[66]

Once the soldiers were aboard their transports, the men might wait days to depart. Private Post recalled a mess cook on his transport who "dumped the required number of cans of corned beef into a wash boiler, broke some hardtack into it, and then, on deck, turned a steam pipe from the engine room into it. It was not bad; the steam seemed to soften the hardtack, and perhaps it was the boiler scale from the fire room down be-low that gave a tang to the corned beef. Coffee was made the same way."[67]

Less than half of the soldiers actually sailed for Cuba and Puerto Rico, and the rest stayed behind. In another drunken incident later in June, sol-diers raided the newly built Noah's Ark saloon, demolishing the building, fixtures, and billiards tables while stealing all of the liquor. No black sol-diers took part in the disturbance, and accordingly the episode received little attention in the press. By the time the soldiers began embarking early in June, the army reconsidered the use of Tampa as an assembly point, ordering all troops out by summer's end.

On July 4, flush with news of recent victories in Manila Bay and Santiago de Cuba, the Tampa Bay Hotel featured a special menu laced with the names of war heroes and place names. The victors of Manila Bay were honored with "Consomme Dewey," while a daredevil from the naval battle of Santiago was enshrined in "Cream Hobson," another soup offering. Rear Admiral William Sampson was named in a red snapper dish, while Allyn Capron, the man who formed the Rough Riders and who died fighting in Cuba, was recognized in a "Boiled Weakfish" preparation. Worth Bagley, the only American naval officer to have been killed in action against the Spanish, made do with potatoes, while Admiral Winfield Scott Schley could claim a roasted shoulder of lamb as his own. Commanding General of the U.S. Army Nelson Miles had stuffed tomatoes served in his honor, while Consul-General to Cuba Fitzhugh Lee lent his name to rice pancakes. The pudding was named after the *Merrimac*, a coaling ship that was sunk to block Santiago harbor. No officer or politician was named in the ribs of prime beef, but the sauce served with the turkey was named after corpulent General William Shafter.[68]

The glut of men and money had passed through town like a storm, leaving Tampa soggy with booze. The carousing soldiers, the overwhelmed police, and the drunken riots had all made saloons "obnoxious places" to the community, and the choice between temperance and order or saloons and disorder seemed to be clear. A writer for the Works Progress Administration, looking back thirty-five years later, wrote, "The foundation of these sinks of iniquity had been laid long before the Spanish-American War. Gambling dens and houses of prostitution had flourished in the old Government reservation of Fort Brooke since the date of its founding, and it needed but the influx of the volunteer regiments to make things hum. . . . Many soldiers did all their fighting in Tampa."[69] The crush of saloons persisted after the war. Between 1898 and 1904, the number of legal saloons quadrupled to 134.[70]

THEATER OF SHADOWS

Vice, Corruption, and Indecency

In the 1890s, local judges and journalists joked that no white man had ever been charged with gambling in Tampa. Such crimes were distasteful only when committed by black people or immigrants. When white showman R. R. Glenn was arrested for running a lottery a few years later in 1901, Judge Peeples thought him innocent of any intention of violating the law and suspended his sentence.[1]

A reform-minded political faction called the Citizens' League formed to purge the community of vice and corruption. At first, it acted as a pressure group like the Law and Order League had several years before, but soon it would emerge with its own slate of candidates. In August 1900, the Citizens' League appealed to the city to close down the gambling halls once and for all. A judge sympathetic to the league's goals announced his intention of cleaning the gambling out of Tampa. The following February, City Council passed a new ordinance specifically "to prohibit lotteried games of policy, and all games of chance," while preserving "similar innocent diversions" such as horse-racing and church raffles. New state laws expressly banned lotteries. In July 1901, the *Tribune* noted, "Policy was exterminated in this city about six months ago by the vigorous measures adopted against it by the police. It sought refuge in Fort Brooke, but its reign there was brief."[2]

Of all the immigrants' cultural fixtures, perhaps none had more of a political impact than bolita, a numbers game similar to "policy" gambling in other parts of the United States. The lottery was popular in Spain and especially Cuba, and those who moved to Tampa brought their fervor for the game with them. Once imported to the United States, the numbers racket went underground. Gambling had already become popular and accepted in most of Tampa before the immigrants arrived. While the Latin immigrants enthusiastically embraced baseball, Tampa's white and black residents took up bolita with gusto.[3]

In 1903, the *Tribune* described the game: "Bolita is a favorite gambling device in Ybor City and consists of 100 wooden balls. With 99 chances to lose and only one chance to win it seems strange that sensible men place their money against such odds." One could bet as little as one cent on a number (though standard bets of ten cents or one dollar were encouraged), allowing the poorest residents to play often. The house kept ten dollars per round, and the winning bettor received ninety dollars. The details for payouts and revenue sharing might have changed over the years, but the game remained the same.[4]

Tony Pizzo remembered a man in a suit, tie, and tails standing on a stage with one hundred numbered ivory balls.

> Slowly he'd drop each of the balls into a velvet bag, mixing them as it filled. Then when the last ball would be inside it, he'd tie the drawstring and hand the bag to a member of the audience who'd mix it again, pass it on to another bettor who'd mix it once more and pass it on. A man in tails would walk up with a big silk red ribbon. He'd give the bag a final shake and usually choose a woman to select a single ball by feeling through the bag without opening it. Then he'd tie the ribbons around the spherical bulge and walk to the center of the stage where he'd pick up a pair of shiny scissors. Then with great flourish, he'd cut the bag, just above the ribbon. Then slowly, he'd untie the knot and drop the sacred ball into his palm. Holding the ball aloft he'd call the winning number.[5]

People like J. L. Montajo inspired struggling workers; he bought the Victoria Hotel (Ninth Avenue and Sixteenth Street) with money won in a

"Little Havana" lottery, a sly reference to Tampa's own racket. The lotteries of Cuba and Honduras, whose results were telegraphed to Tampa, were gradually replaced by games held in Ybor City. The rise of locally run bolita games soon required a syndicate to control operations, a "bank" to ensure prompt payment, sellers to distribute tickets for a commission, and runners or "bag men" to distribute tickets and deliver funds. Sellers assumed the legal risks, while the bank assumed the financial risks and reaped the greatest profits. Over time, the operation fell into the hands of the most notorious organized criminals in the city. Bolita became so ingrained in Tampa's culture that the city police reportedly laundered the proceeds, money that helped influence the outcome of any election between 1900 and 1960.[6]

Bolita probably arrived shortly after the first workers disembarked from Key West in the late 1880s. Some say that the numbers game arrived when Manuel "El Gallego" Suarez closed his saloon in Key West and relocated his bolita balls to Tampa. In the early 1890s, he opened a new saloon in the Sevilla building (on Fourteenth Street and Eighth Avenue). He threw the bolita bag at 9 p.m. everyday and twice on Sundays, taking advantage of the increased traffic in saloons. It did not take long for Suarez to find the heartbeat of Ybor City at the upscale Cherokee Club, where he was arrested for running games in 1902. "Bolita writers were everywhere," Tony Pizzo wrote. "No one looked down on them. They visited the workshop and the office and haunted the streets." Street vendors who sold various snacks and sweets were also bolita salesmen. The *Tribune* reported that black men were stealing soap from their women, who often washed clothes for a living, to sell for bolita money.[7]

It became a common myth that the Latin immigrants were instinctive gamblers, but Tampa's white and black communities had spent their time and money playing games of chance long before the immigrants arrived. It was true, however, that gambling in the immigrant enclaves was engaged in more openly, with no opposition from within. Bolita began as a quaint immigrant novelty, but over the years, it became Tampa's greatest amusement and most wicked curse.

Ambitious politicians did not just covet the tax revenues the immigrants produced. Criminal wealth could be exploited even more ruthlessly. Saloon owners dependent on the lenience of friends were left in a vulnerable position. Involvement in illegal enterprises made protection by local police and politicians a necessity. Networks established by numbers games and saloons were easily adapted to political networks geared toward getting out the vote to protect their interests. Since so many profited from or participated in gambling, legitimate businessmen and citizens often supported gambling interests over efforts at reform. As another way of paying for influence, underworld leaders often provided charity and dispensed favors, further consolidating their influence among constituents whether they gambled or not, just as long as they voted.[8]

Tampa's political organization meant that each local ward elected its own constable. It had become an unspoken American tradition that "local politicians, through control of local police, could coordinate the marginal businesses of the community." Tampa designated Ybor City as a ward, and initially its constable became a position of vital importance for those engaged in vice. Corrupt officials protected their friends in a variety of ways. When saloon owners had to be arrested for the sake of public appearance, authorities used the power of their positions to dismiss charges, tamper with records, or levy inconsequential fines. Unchecked saloons with special privileges led to pervasive gambling and prostitution, activities that usually thrived in blind tigers. In the process, Ybor City became an unofficial district for gambling and vice. In short order, the saloons had become as bad as the blind tigers. But worse, they were organized.[9]

A good example of a nuisance saloon can be found in the old Saloon Columbia before it became the opulent restaurant we know today. In December 1903, Spanish businessman P. A. Vazquez developed the property he owned on the edge of Ybor City along Seventh Avenue and Twenty-Second Street. His first new business, the Columbia Café, joined Tampa's crowded saloon market on December 23, 1903. In 1904, he opened the Columbia Kitchen above the café and constructed two more buildings, to feature a bowling alley and an "elegant pool-room, refreshment and fruit store."[10] Priding itself on Spanish and American food, the Columbia Kitchen opened above the café on June 12, 1904, with a private feast for Tampa's elite. The guest list included such local luminaries as Mr. and Mrs. Peter O. Knight, John Perry Wall, D. B. McKay, and members of the Ybor family, among others.[11]

In 1905, Vazquez sold the saloon to the Florida Brewing Company, and it did not take long before it joined Tampa's lawless fraternity. Sheriff's deputies arrested operator (and future owner) Casimiro Hernandez Sr. for selling bolita tickets in 1906.[12]

Vicious fights erupted with such regularity at the Columbia that the neighborhood boys would gather at the intersection to watch the nightly beatings. Besides the Columbia, the Seminole barroom across the street provided reliable entertainment. Virgilio Valdez said, "I used to go down there with the other kids. There wasn't much to do at night for the kids you see, so we used to go down and stand outside the bar to look through the windows at the cowboys who kill each other."[13]

In 1909, a barroom dispute between two men at the Columbia spilled out into the street. Police tried to break up the fight, and when one of the men was being restrained, the other brawler slashed him twice, "disemboweling him and cutting a huge piece of flesh almost free from his side." The police reported it was the worst stabbing they had seen in years.[14]

Local temperance activists pointed to the murder at the Columbia Café as the latest example of the wickedness of saloons and those who haunted them: "At different times there has been much complaint among residents and business men regarding the character of the saloon at Twenty-Second Street by C.M. Balbontin[.] It is alleged that the character of those who make a habit of loafing about the place is not the best. Although little has been done previously, it is possible that action will now be taken to have the place closed."[15] Closing the secretive Spanish-run saloons was easier said than done. Sherriff Hobbs had repeatedly tried to raid a club next to Centro Espanol, but a series of locked doors with electric push-button releases always kept the police at bay, and by the time they gained entry, all evidence was gone. Hobbs said,

> The foreign saloon element of Hillsborough County is composed largely of Spaniards. They want to sell liquor on Sunday and gamble all the time. They have approached me for protection and I can call their names. I am reliably informed that every Spanish saloon in Hillsborough County operated bolita, a pernicious form of policy gambling. It is almost impossible to catch the scoundrels, as they place their numbers on the wall and sell tickets to men, women, and children. . . .

The gambling dives in and around these saloons are protected by stool pigeons, electric bells, etc. They know my office deputies by sight several blocks away and sound the alarm or give warning. It is a sight to see the gamblers run. . . . I want to say right here that the Spanish saloon element is more persistent in resisting the enforcement of the law than any other nationality in Hillsborough County.[16]

The owner of the Columbia, C. M. Balbontin (brother of Bautista), who bought the saloon in 1905, passed away in 1911. Manager Casimiro Hernandez obtained the deed and licenses for the Columbia Café, and it joined the thin ranks of independent saloons that had not been bought out by the breweries and their brokers. In 1917, Hernandez was arrested for selling liquor without a license, which begs the question of whether the Columbia was *ever* licensed to sell liquor.[17]

PROFILES IN CORRUPTION AND CRIME

As early as 1894, the corruption in Tampa's police department was already well established. City and county police jealously guarded profitable criminal rackets and the kickbacks they provided. If Tampa seemed racy and raucous, Hillsborough County could be downright lawless. Fort Brooke, a separate municipality composed mostly of squatters, gamblers, sports, and prostitutes, had a paltry police force that seemed to exist solely to supervise and skim off the gambling there. To the east, dry, rural Polk County became a hotbed of blind tigers, many with small camps of prostitutes, especially around the phosphate mines.[18]

It is possible to document the rot of corruption setting in at the Tampa Police Department, particularly with Ybor City's elected constable. In the fall of 1905, City Deputy Nobelo Madruga made the rounds among Ybor City's saloons to spread the word. Louis Callenberg had been elected constable. To serve drinks and throw bolita all week long with no hassles from city police, Madruga notified each owner of their obligation to discreetly pay him five dollars per week. For any saloon owner in search of high profits, such a proposition was all but impossible to resist. Most minor bolita peddlers made $110 per week; $60 from Monday to Saturday and $50 on Sundays, when two numbers were thrown. Sundays

While typical saloons in the United States were obvious in their intent, Tampa's Latin "cafés" proved to be amorphous, oscillating between snack counters and shady refuges for bootleggers and gamblers. (Tony Pizzo collection, University of South Florida Tampa Special Collections)

were also the most profitable at the bar, when most men were completely free from work.[19]

In August 1905, Celestino Rio and his fellow saloon owners felt quite safe with their numbered balls when Deputy Sheriff J. J. Stephens burst in unannounced. Stephens hauled in Serafin Montiel, E. Villamil, Joaquin Sierra, Rio, and Manuel Suarez, also known as "El Gallego." After his arrest, Rio complained that he had been blackmailed by the constable. Rio claimed to have collected the constable's weekly tribute from his fellow saloon owners. Deputy Stephens worked for the county and was clearly not in on the arrangement. Montiel told the same story, being informed of his "duties" after the elections of the previous fall. Constable Callenberg and Deputy Madruga were both arrested.[20]

Tampa's leadership showed no interest in the scandal. Judge Raney offered to dismiss the case, but the men demanded a full investigation and public exonerations. The city refused to present a case against its officers at all. The defense brought out a battery of witnesses. Upon Madruga's easily won acquittal, his father threw him a celebratory banquet at Las Nuevitas, one of Ybor City's finest restaurants.

Some citizens wondered how bolita was allowed to stay in operation after the discovery of the payoffs. Impotent to intervene, Sheriff's Deputy Stephens responded by sending the depositions of the suspects he arrested to be published in the *Tampa Tribune*. But no crackdown, no state investigation, and no meaningful change ensued. More than anything, the sheriff's ploy seemed to be an effort to embarrass his counterparts in the city.[21]

While responding to a fire later that year, Constable Callenberg died by contact with a live electric cable. Madruga became notorious for extorting saloon operators and arresting them when he was not satisfied. Several of those he arrested initially complained in court of Madruga's demands only to withdraw their disputes later. Judge Young said that it was common knowledge that thirty-two bolita shops operated in Tampa, and he urged police to immediately raid them all. Sheriff Jackson put twenty-five county bolita operators out of business in short order, but city police apparently did not participate.[22]

Allegations of corruption dogged Madruga, but he briefly became constable two years later when the office was left vacant. Accusations and reproach didn't dissuade Madruga from running for reelection in 1908, although he lost at the polls. He stepped down and considered opening a coffee shop, he told the press. He must have been winking when he gave the location as the corner of Ninth Avenue and Fourteenth Street, home of a notorious drinking and gambling den that he had raided months before. The owner of that bar may have financed his own hostile takeover through bribes, five dollars at a time.[23]

For every corrupt cop, there were several dozen saloon men, gambling house operators, and professional "sports," men who usually supported themselves through gambling and crime. Luke Palmer provides a good example of a Tampa sport. A chronic gambler as a player and operator, Palmer seemed to be a born grifter and schemer. Known for brawling in public, gambling in private, and riding horses recklessly, Palmer was hotheaded and impulsive. When a rival insulted him in public, Palmer punched him in full view of police, costing him a night in jail and a $120 fine.[24]

In December 1900, itinerant worker H. G. Morton (who went by the unimaginative alias Moore) drifted to Tampa and found Luke Palmer's unnamed gambling house in debauched Fort Brooke. The visitor proceeded to lose every penny he owned, so he offered to pawn his pistol and pocket watch for more money. Palmer refused to buy them, instead suggesting that if Morton "had the nerve" there was "good money in the city." Palmer promised Morton "plenty to eat" if he would steal for them. By sharing the proceeds, the luckless gambler could enrich his new friends and earn some money of his own.

First, Palmer sent one-legged Frank Logan begging door-to-door in Hyde Park and Tampa Heights, where he scouted out houses for burglary. After a string of break-ins over two weeks, Palmer compensated Morton only in poker chips, which he always proceeded to lose gambling. Police arrested Morton for his crimes, at which time he gave up the entire plot to police, implicating Palmer and his other accomplices. Louis Athanasaw, owner of the Imperial Theater, and beer baron B. M. Balbontin bailed out the suspects. Here was open proof of collusion between Tampa's saloons and career criminals such as Luke Palmer, who had never run a legitimate business.[25]

Morton admitted to his crimes in the courtroom, and testified against his accomplices. The court acquitted Luke Palmer and his gang and sentenced Morton to five years in the state penitentiary. Their victory was remarkably short-lived, as police arrested all three immediately after their release for running a gambling house, which they had freely admitted to on the stand.[26]

Just days later, before the fresh gambling controversy died down, Luke Palmer and fellow sport (and former hunting guide for the Tampa Bay Hotel) Arthur Schleman captivated the city with a bet. Palmer and Schleman each put up $200 deposits for a race between their respective horses, Adelia and Silver Duck. Tampa's gambling laws did not extend to the presumably gentleman's pastime of horse racing. The race became a cause for excitement and festivity, and each rider put up another $300 on the day of the race for a total of $1,000 at stake. Others bet a total of about $4,000 or $5,000 on one of the horses before the big event. Instead of racing himself, Palmer asked Fort Brooke constable (and former sheriff's deputy) J. J. Stephens to ride in his stead. (As a gambler and a policeman in wide-open Fort Brooke, respectively, the two men had already worked closely together.)[27]

On September 4, 1903, the hotly anticipated race proved to be a blow-out, with Schleman winning resoundingly. Palmer heatedly protested that Schleman had kicked Stephens, although the judges said no kicking occurred. Tension between bettors of both horses threatened to break out into a gunfight at the New American Theater, but Schleman cooled tempers when he offered to let the purse stay for a rematch and insinuated that the old bets should be reimbursed, as well. At this, the heavily armed bettors dispersed to stew in their favored saloons. No rematch ever took place.[28]

Palmer spent the next six years running gambling games in Fort Brooke. A recent cleanup campaign in Tampa had pushed more sports into Fort Brooke, further raising the stakes for whoever could control gambling there. He was arrested at least four times and fined $500 each time he appeared in court.[29] In 1906, Palmer was arrested for running a gambling house, this time with a young Charlie Wall at La Brisa Saloon on Water Street. Judge Gordon gave each a $500 fine and a reprimand. Over the next thirty years, Wall climbed to the top, or perhaps the bottom, of Tampa's underworld.[30]

Palmer was laid low in 1909 in a hail of bullets aimed not by a criminal rival or an honest police officer but by his wife of one year, Pauline. Mrs. Luke Palmer shot her husband several times after she allegedly caught him trying to press his affection onto a thirteen-year-old girl they had taken in. Her son offered conflicting testimony, but she was acquitted after a riveting court case. The *Tribune* described Luke Palmer as "generous but vindictive, straight in his business dealings but a gambler by vocation, a lover of horses but often brutal in his treatment of human beings under him for hire, he was at once the antithesis of himself and his own worst enemy. He was courageous to a marked degree and was a man few cared to cross in anger. His one failing, his friends agree, was his love for women of the underworld."[31]

Tampa's most notorious sport was also its most unlikely. Born into one of Tampa's most influential families in 1880, Charlie M. Wall never quite fit in. The son of Dr. Perry Wall, former mayor of Tampa and the first doctor to attribute yellow fever to the mosquito, Charlie was born into

Tampa's establishment. His middle name was even McKay, another surname synonymous with Tampa's most powerful, as the two families had intermarried. For whatever reason, Charlie always seemed to be a bad seed, showing signs of violent and scandalous behavior at a young age. At the age of twelve, he tried to kill his stepmother, but the .22 caliber rifle did not do the job. Dispatched to a military academy, the school returned the troubled boy after he escaped to visit a brothel. Upon Charlie's return to Tampa, his father, it seems, gave up trying to domesticate him and allowed him to roam around town. The only places young Charlie seemed comfortable in were the saloons and gambling halls, where he eventually learned the trade of a professional sport, to which he applied his impressive mathematical acumen.

Over the years, Charlie Wall was arrested regularly for fighting and gambling. His activities can be traced fairly closely through his arrests. By 1904, he was running his own joint above the New York Exchange on Lafayette. In 1905, he worked with Luke Palmer at La Brisa. Two years later, he ran games out of a room above the Metropolitan Theater in Fort Brooke.[32]

By 1911, Wall had clearly climbed higher in the underworld when he was arrested with police officer J. A. Killebrew, who was later disgraced and removed from office for drinking in saloons while on his beat. Wall and Killebrew were charged for beating Ed Cantreras, who accused Killebrew of taking bribes. Leading dry advocate Don McMullen complained that new mayor D. B. McKay looked out for his cousin Charlie Wall. In 1913, the young sport was building a home designed by prominent architects Bonfoey and Elliott for the princely sum of $4,000.[33]

By 1914, Wall had become influential enough to have others run his operations for him. When police raided Wall's Bronx Club on Fortune Street, Wall claimed to have subleased the property to Henry Webster, who just so happened to be dead. Wall said he assumed the Bronx was a legal business but did not have a hand in running it. The police had seized the account book of the club, complete with the names and numbers of many well-known residents. For their part, Wall's disgruntled partners claimed that "Wall was the 'high mucky-muck' and 'silent partner' who 'seldom came about the place' because he 'was too busy on the outside,' but that he 'collected hush money and his share of the profits.'" City

Solicitor Jackson was mystified by the jury's ruling to acquit, as the city had gathered a very strong case based on evidence of the lease and the testimony of witnesses. He grumbled, "The verdict was not found on the evidence, but in spite of it."

The case had also revealed Wall to be Tampa's gambling kingpin. When gambler James Uncles lost big while out of town, he returned to Tampa, probably in 1913, hoping to replenish his coffers by running a gambling house of his own. He soon discovered that Tampa was no longer as "wide open" as it appeared. In his testimony, Uncles said he quickly learned that Wall "claimed to own all the gambling in Tampa. . . . Any man would be crazy to open a gambling house in this city without having first seen Wall about it." He eventually opened the Bronx Club with Wall's blessing, but Uncles resented the new gambling order in the city. He sought a hit man to kill Wall but could never raise enough money. Uncles soon faded from the scene, but it would not be the last time someone would plot Wall's murder.[34]

Just as the temperance activists traded their call for moderation for one to prohibit alcohol altogether, the local forces of corruption and organized crime were consolidating. Charlie Wall achieved two important things sometime between 1905 and 1915. First, he supplanted the Cuban bolita operation with one run completely in Tampa. Historian Frank Alduino writes, "It is highly probable that Wall was encouraged and even financed in his takeover attempt by Tampa's elite business community, which did not like the idea that gambling revenues were leaving the city." Localizing gambling operations was only the first step. Second, Tampa's bolita racket became much more centralized. In the early days of the 1890s, it appears that multiple bolita games occurred in various gambling houses. By the time Florida outlawed alcohol in 1918, Charlie Wall had organized a large operation around his own lottery. Competitors and smaller bolita operations jockeyed for position, but Wall and others at the top kept them at bay for the next twenty years or so.

Wall sustained his power not only by running rackets but also, likely, by exploiting his family connections. It is probably not just a coincidence that the rise of Charlie Wall as a criminal mastermind coincided with the political career of his cousin. In 1910, Donald Brenham (D. B.) McKay was elected mayor (1910–1920, 1928–1931) and was never far from the levers of power. During the same period, Charlie's brother, Perry G. Wall, was also mayor (1924–1928), stepping aside to let McKay hold the office again in 1928.

With his family and associates, Wall could decide any election in Tampa by stuffing the ballot boxes in the "hot" precincts of Ybor City and, after it was annexed in 1925, West Tampa. That is how the regime maintained candidates tainted with criminality. He constantly bought the loyalty of the Latin districts through charity and unexpected gifts. In 1910, Wall fed nine hundred cigar workers and their families in the midst of a strike. Those acts of kindness were not soon forgotten. At least six rivals for Tampa's numbers racket died trying to unseat Charlie Wall. Enterprising Wall was always finding new angles. By 1916, Wall wasn't only fixing the elections but running betting pools on them, too.[35]

The Rise and Fall of the Imperial Theater

One night in 1902, the semi-lawless hamlet outside of Tampa called Fort Brooke roared with cheers and jeers. Billy Hill, manager of the Imperial Theater, wrestled with "an excited individual" in front of the venue while a boisterous crowd gathered around. Police arrived at 10:00 p.m. and the man, rumored to be an escaped convict, gave Hill and three officers a great struggle before they secured him with three pairs of handcuffs on his wrists and shackles and chains on his legs. By this time, a large crowd had collected on the street in front of the theater, and police dragged the suspect inside until a wagon could arrive. The Imperial's boozy patrons shuffled back into the theater thinking the excitement was all over, but the show had just begun.

Somehow, the suspect broke free and rushed onto the stage, where he was left unmolested while he maneuvered out of every impediment. One by one, the cuffs and chains fell to the stage floor. The man was never arrested because there never was any escaped convict. Manager Hill revealed with delight that the now-unchained man was none other than The Great Gay, an escape artist who would be engaged at the Imperial all week. The fracas on the street was just a prelude to his stage act. As The Great Gay bowed before the riveted crowd, the police, who apparently were not in on Hill's publicity stunt, "sought sudden seclusion." It is impossible to know today if the police were duped or in on the act.[36]

Burly Greek immigrant Louis Athanasaw presided over countless nights of surprise, spectacle, disturbance, and hilarity at his Imperial Theater. The Imperial remained unconstrained by the respectability of the Tampa Bay Casino or the rising artistic intentions of the immigrant theaters. Instead, the theater aimed its entertainment at working-class men, and it became permissive Fort Brooke's most popular attraction. Management prominently featured titillating girlie shows, "leg shows," and "coochee-coochee" dancers to satisfy the male clientele. The theater also deployed a bevy of young beauties to shake down patrons for drinks. Men who bought drinks for the servers and performing soubrettes could retire to semi-private booths or "boxes" with one side open to the stage to drink and flirt. The Imperial was among the most notorious and popular venues around Tampa. The *Tribune* helped spread the word of every new entertainer at the Imperial, drawing nightly crowds. One woman known as La Culebra (The Snake) was a special dancing attraction.[37]

Most lower-class theaters sold beer, mixed drinks, and "champagne" that was actually carbonated pear cider. Show business magazine *Variety* saw the Imperial as a reminder of theater's less refined days: "[The] 'acts' are supposed to serve drinks in the many boxes, besides entertaining on the stage. It was a revival of the old 'variety days' so often heard of as relics of the past, when 'wine rooms' were the principal source of income to the house." Since the show continued constantly throughout the night and selling booze took priority over any pretense of art, female performers who were popular with the men would simply skip their onstage cues when engaged with patrons, leaving the other performers to ad lib in compensation. No one would confuse wine-room performers with the Royal Shakespeare Theatre Company.[38]

Typical entertainment at the turn of the century included dazzling diva Helene Mignon, who sang in four languages, the Bollis singers, who catered to lovers of lowbrow opera, the Lehmanns, who specialized in skit comedy, Englishman Henry Steele, who provided standup, and the entire company of twenty-four entertainers who engaged in a nightly burlesque. "Crowded houses are assured every night," the *Tribune* wrote.

Producer Harry Sefton's "comic opera burlesque" offered "a new departure entirely from the old style of vaudeville. There will be a change in burlesque each week, and he guarantees to give new faces in rapid succession." Such ads suggested a clientele of regular customers.[39]

On July 4, 1902, the Imperial hosted an extravaganza spilling over with color, music, drink, and flesh. Athanasaw decked out the Imperial with "flags, banners, bunting and sweet-scented roses galore." A brass band played popular tunes, but the real attraction, as usual, was the women.

> Such a galaxy of pretty girls with shapely forms, both brunettes and blondes, charming singers and sprightly dancers for the eye to feast upon, have never before been seen at any one time at a vaudeville entertainment in this city; and still not half has been told, for Manager Frank Binney, who has a faculty for doing things as they aught to be done, has a rare treat in store for lovers of breezy vaudeville in the shape of a ticklish burlesque, with a musical frolic bubbling over with bright bits of button bursting comedy, introducing the entire company of unexcelled artists. Now the Imperial is the place to see a show that is worth seeing and bear in mind a good clean show with no objectionable features.[40]

A Syrian dancer named Freda Mad came to Tampa as part of a midway show at the Plant Railroad depot. After the engagement, Mad took a job at the Imperial Theater as a "coochee-coochee" dancer. Her act drew great crowds, but some in the community thought her act "indecent" and called her a prostitute. When ministers protested against the popular Sunday concerts at the Imperial, Athanasaw began to promote "sacred" recitals with much the same music.[41]

One night in 1903, the unthinkable happened when a woman walked into the Imperial Theater. It was not that unusual for a woman to search saloons for their wayward husbands, but her intended disguise attracted attention. She arrived disguised as a man. She did not find her husband but was instead arrested for attempting to drink in a saloon. After she cried and "pleaded piteously to be freed," she posted bond and went back home. "The incident," winked the *Tribune*, "created a sensation," and the laughter roared at the Imperial Theater. The county had passed an ordinance against women drinking in saloons precisely to crack down on places like the Imperial.[42]

The Imperial's occasional wrestling and boxing matches may have been of questionable authenticity, but the passions they aroused in the spectators were nonetheless real. In March 1900, actors Jim Bailey and Frank Walsh were scheduled for a twenty-round boxing match, drawing a capacity crowd an hour before the fight. Police had already warned Athanasaw and the pugilists that they would not allow the unsanctioned fight to occur. By the scheduled time of ten, the crowd chanted,

> "Fight! Fight! Fight!" with a vehemence that frightened the scantily-clad soubrettes who were trying to keep them amused with rag-time melodies. Jim Bailey, who was figured in the previous pretended fights which have occurred at the Imperial, declared that he would go into the ring anyhow. Frank Walsh, his prospective opponent, who is one of the song and dance artists of the theater, was also willing. By 10:30 the place was a regular bedlam. Spaniards, Cubans, Greeks, Italians and Americans were shouting at the tops of their voices.

The fighters stripped to their waists and as comedian/MC Billy Hill was trying to select a referee, the police intervened, threatening the fighters with arrest. When the crowd grew unruly and rushed the stage, police somehow cleared the entire theater and averted a drunken riot.[43]

After years of promoting the Imperial through ads and endorsements, the *Tampa Tribune* apparently had seen enough by 1903, perhaps because the Imperial no longer bought ads in the paper. "The Imperial Theatre continues to thrive. Hell has been filled years ago with better people than the shysters who conduct this den of iniquity and it behooves the authorities to either shut the thing up or put it under special police protection." For the next decade, Tampa's moral guardians campaigned to have the popular theater closed, singling out the establishment as a fount of depravity.[44]

In 1907, when the City of Tampa annexed Fort Brooke, it had long been known as "Athanasaw's Hell's half-acre." The Greek impresario closed the Imperial Theater and leased the space to a tenant. After evading Tampa's authority in Fort Brooke for years, the impresario opened a new theater, the Criterion, in Ybor City. Hopes of a cleaner theater scene faded when Athanasaw put the Verdier Sisters on the Criterion's stage. The trio were already infamous in Tampa for performing an unmentionable song called "The Iceman." Apparently, their act was even racier in 1905 when police arrested them and manager Billy Hill for staging a vulgar act.[45]

Whether it was a case of deceit or honest rebranding, several months after opening the Criterion Theater in Ybor, the crafty Greek renamed it the Imperial, and the den of indecency was officially reborn, this time in Tampa's city limits. The city commission tried to hobble the Imperial with a barrage of ordinances and Sunday raids.[46]

In 1907, a city ordinance banning vaudeville shows connected to saloons effectively closed the Metropolitan Theater, the site of the old Imperial in Fort Brooke. Athanasaw closed the Imperial for an extended period "until a way was found to evade the state and city laws forbidding a theater and a saloon to run in connection." The anti-vaudeville ordinance banned a theater from operating with a saloon, so Athanasaw accordingly jettisoned any pretense of culture by not booking any entertainment. The soubrettes and their secluded booths remained open for business. The *Tribune* complained that the Imperial was just a glorified saloon and, in the process, outlined the business model of the "Wine Room Theater." "They cannot rely entirely upon vaudeville features of their houses for profitable patronage, then being merely an excuse for introducing the drink-selling soubrette and her style of 'boosting' business for the whiskey and beer interests of the establishment."[47]

Reformers targeting liquor and corruption pointed to the Imperial Saloon as an example of Tampa's wickedness. The theater's latest show in 1909 had outraged the usual group of citizens. After years of lethargic response from the city, Mayor Wing vowed to react. He singled out the Imperial saloon as a menace, pointing to its steady business on Sundays and urging police to pay a visit. When Athanasaw landed in court for selling alcohol on Sundays, he absurdly claimed he had never been in court before, despite a long list of arrests.

Athanasaw finished 1909 with one last defiant act when he "imported a Cuban hoochee coochee dancer" for a special Christmas Eve show. The unamused *Tribune* complained, "The Oriental dance is bad enough in itself . . . done by women whose costumes can't be described because they didn't have any to describe." While the act appeared to shed all artistic pretense and clothing, the dancers wore full-body stockings that revealed their feminine form all too well without exposing flesh. Police arrested Athanasaw for exhibiting a "fallen woman" with "an unmentionable costume" in "an indecent manner."[48]

When surveying the "disgusting exhibition by the Cuban woman," the court found that her dance, as demonstrated by witnesses, was far more vulgar than other previous dances such as "the 'hooch,' the 'Salome,' and the 'Vampire.'" In his defense, Athanasaw claimed no responsibility for the offending act. He claimed to have taken in a Cuban troupe that had a hard-luck story and was stranded in Tampa. After hearing their story, he resolved to help them earn the money for steamer tickets back to Cuba. After his show concluded for the night, Athanasaw had allowed them to employ their own stagehands and ticket sellers and accepted no money for the use of his theater. When asked if he knew the act would be "immoral," Athanasaw said he found nothing offensive about the dance, saying, "You gentelmens knows it was ze Spaneesh dance." The prosecutor questioned his eyesight.[49]

With Athanasaw's daring exhibition becoming the talk of the town, copycat acts sprang up to exploit the buzz. City Council complained of Nelly Nell, a soubrette engaged at the Alhambra Theater in Ybor City, and her provocative dancing. The council "requested in the name of decency" that the police forcibly close the theater, revoke the license, and expedite any connected criminal cases. In a special session of City Council, Police Chief Woodward said that theaters "kept a watch out for the officers and would cut out the immoral part of the performances when an officer was present." It was also very difficult to get any witnesses to testify against the theaters. Council passed a new ordinance allowing the city to close "objectionable" theaters.[50]

Considering his success in avoiding incarceration thus far, Athanasaw either led a charmed life or made friends in all the right places. Instead of the proverbial book being thrown at the repeat offender, Athanasaw's sharp and influential attorney John P. Wall found Police Judge Peeples to be rather understanding. When a deputy noted the Imperial's lively clientele, Athanasaw insisted with a straight face, "Only soft drinks and near beer, your Honor." Mayor Wing told Athanasaw publicly in court that he had to close on Sundays, and for once, he sheepishly agreed.[51]

The *Tribune* complained, "The man was brought before this [corrupt] police judge and you never saw such craw-fishing." (Incidentally, catching crawfish sometimes calls for reaching deeply into dark spaces.) Judge Peeples found several pretexts to delay Athanasaw's trial, but reformers accused him of avoiding his duty to mete out justice. In the meantime, "some poor unfortunates who were not organized for crime were fined twice and three times" more than connected men like Athanasaw, the *Tribune* observed.[52]

Athanasaw's hijinks only made the Imperial harder to defend. A new city ordinance passed in 1911 barred women from entering saloons, loitering, or working in them. This ordinance was meant to dismantle the Imperial's business model and reinforce a long-standing effort of the city to minimize the public spaces where the potentially volatile mixture of alcohol and the pursuit of sex took place.[53]

As Tampa fitfully matured into a modern city, the Imperial seemed to belong to another time, when the city was a mere outpost on the wild Florida frontier. Perhaps the rumors were true—namely, that Tampa was too wicked a city to oust the Imperial—because it took federal agents, federal charges, and an innocent teenage girl to finally jail Athanasaw and shutter his business.[54]

Young Agnes Couch stepped off the train in Tampa as the sun rose early one morning. The seventeen-year-old from Atlanta was recruited by an agent to take a job as a "chorus girl" in Tampa for the Imperial Musical Comedy Company. She leapt at the opportunity to make it in show business. According to her contract, she would be paid a salary, stay at the theater, and receive a commission of 20 percent on all drinks sold. The final clause of the contract should have given Couch pause, but she signed anyway, probably impressed with the free train ticket she was given.[55]

Couch assumed she was on her way to the big time and rode the rails to Tampa with two other female recruits for the stage. Upon laying their eyes on the seedy Imperial, Couch's fellow would-be showgirls immediately recognized it as a low-class dive and left. But Agnes, young, naive, and probably broke, went inside. The young recruit was led to her private bedroom to catch up on her rest. While eating lunch with her fellow performers during the first day, "she realized she was in depraved surroundings." The coarse women seated with her cursed and smoked, and Couch could scarcely eat a thing out of fear and disgust.

The young lady would rehearse a group stage act by day and work the booths selling drinks by night. Following an afternoon of rehearsal, Athanasaw visited Couch in her room, telling her she would soon like the place and the money she made from the men there. He predicted the attractive young lady would be a hit among the patrons and told her that he wanted her to be "his girl." Athanasaw inferred that she should not get too intimate with patrons and revealed that his bedroom adjoined hers. He kissed her and left her to prepare for work, saying he would return that night.

After this unsettling visit, Couch was thrown into the maelstrom of the Imperial's rough audience. She was appointed a booth at nine that evening to begin her shift in "the boxes." Couch was rather meek and had never drunk alcohol before, making her especially unqualified to hold her own in a booth with drinking men. No doubt billed as the "new girl," Couch began the night with four men crowded into her booth. They all bought drinks and insisted that she join them. After refusing for some time, Couch gave in and choked down a bottle of beer, the first taste of alcohol in her life, she later testified.

Couch desperately thought of a way to escape but was too scared to try. One of the men in her booth, none other than hunting guide, game warden, and dogcatcher Arthur Schleman, sensed her anxiety and thought she was practically being forced to drink. The concerned customer sensed she did not want to be there, and he took her to another box to speak privately, where she revealed her predicament. After talking it through, Couch confessed she would probably get used to being a server. Schleman protested that she "better not" get used to working in such a place and resolved to remove her from the premises immediately. When he tried to rush her out the back door, bouncers said he couldn't leave with an employee. Schleman left and summoned the police.

When officers arrived to investigate, Athanasaw came forward to say he would not detain Couch if she wanted to leave. He offered to cancel her contract on the spot and send her to Atlanta the next morning. She herself had never actually asked or tried to leave. She elected to go with the police with her story, and dry activists denounced Athanasaw, saloons, and the officials who had let them run wild for so long.[56]

Couch's story was just the kind of sensation the newspapers loved, and all of Athanasaw's bad press finally caught up with him. The federal government had fashioned a new law for just such cases. Congress passed the White Slave Traffic Act (aka the Mann Act, after Congressman James Robert Mann of Illinois) in June 1910 in response to growing concerns about the nation's white women falling into prostitution. The act was another brainchild of reformers who pushed for Prohibition and other new government powers and was aimed at minorities and immigrants like Athanasaw. According to the logic of the time, black people and immigrants were increasingly exploiting white women as prostitutes, taking them across state lines for nefarious purposes. Although Tampa's leadership never seemed interested in closing the brothels, they did have a resilient public nuisance in the form of Mr. Athanasaw and his theater. Prosecuting the Greek entrepreneur for violating the White Slaver Traffic Act seemed like a tidy solution to a long-standing problem. Best of all, federal courts would dispatch the suspect much more assuredly than the city courts presided over by corrupt laggards like Judge Peeples.[57]

The *Tribune* warned that if local authorities did not act to suppress the Imperial now, the theater would be run the same way, with or without Athanasaw. According to the *Tribune*, the morality of the entire community was at risk, as places like the Imperial turned women into prostitutes and men into full-time "sports."[58]

> The women in these wine room resorts are, for the most part, experienced artistes[.] These girls do not hesitate to tell smutty jokes and submit to as well as give caresses to gain their ends, and the more drinks they sell the more money they will make in commissions. . . . There has arisen a set of men, young some of them, who are having an easy living drinking and carousing without working or having any visible means of support. . . . Something ought to be done with these parasites.[59]

In response, City Council unanimously passed yet another theater ordinance, this one aimed squarely at the embattled Imperial, "an ordinance to regulate theatres, picture or vaudeville shows, dance halls and similar acts of amusement, in the city of Tampa, Florida, and to prevent women and girls employed in or connected therewith from entering, loitering or drinking in any box, booth, stall, room or apartment connected therewith." The Imperial closed for several weeks while Athanasaw appealed the ordinance. He was soon up and running with female servers again. Critics used the scandal as proof of Mayor D. B. McKay's corrupt rule. The fire chief had testified at Athanasaw's trial of his good moral character.[60]

Athanasaw's experience in federal court would seem a world away from "crawfishing" with Judge Peeples. Spectators crowded the federal courtroom at Athanasaw's trial, the *Tribune* reported, paying special attention to the young witness.

> She said she thought it was her chance to get a start in show business, but upon her arrival here she learned that the theater expected her to "sell drinks and entertain a low class of men in a wine room show surrounded by houses of ill fame." She is a well-appearing girl, plump and rosy. She parts her hair on the right side, binding a slanting braid across her forehead. Her timid, woe-begone expression, her blue eyes staring fixedly at the floor, and her chaste language, indicated nothing of the usual type found in dismal dives.[61]

Couch testified:

> After lunch I went to my room, and about 6 o'clock Louis Athanasaw, one of the defendants, came and said to me I would like it all right; that I was good looking and would make a hit, and not to let any of the boys fool me, and not be any of the boy's girl; to be his. He wanted me to be his girl; to talk to the boys and make a hit, and get all of the money I could out of them. His room was next to mine, and he told me he was coming in my room that night and sleep with me; and he kissed and caressed me. He told me to dress for the show that night and come down into the boxes.[62]

Athanasaw's able attorney, John P. Wall, offered a solid legal defense against the charges. Athanasaw denied wrongdoing and pointed out that the city and state allowed the theater to remain open. According to a court summary, "Athanasaw denied that he made improper proposals to the girl, and it was testified that at the preliminary hearing she did not charge him with such. In all else, however, her testimony was not contradicted, and it was supported as to the character of the house and as to what took place." Since the court and Athanasaw agreed he made no improper advances, legal logic assumed he was an innocent man. But the white slavery law was a new kind of measure that was cunningly adaptable in its vagueness. In essence, no actual crime had taken place, but Athanasaw was being tried for what he allegedly *intended* to do and whether that might have led Couch toward certain disapproved of lifestyles.

The judge asked the jury, "Did they intend to induce or entice or influence her to give herself up to debauchery?"

> The language of the statute is directed against the transportation "of any woman or girl for the purpose of prostitution or debauchery, or for any other immoral purpose, or with the intent and purpose to induce, entice, or compel such woman or girl to become a prostitute or to give herself up to debauchery, or to engage in any other immoral practice."
>
> The question here is of intent; what was the intent with which they brought her; that she should live an honest, moral, and proper life? or that she came and they engaged and contracted with her for the purpose of her entering upon a condition which might be termed debauchery, or lead to or would necessarily and naturally lead her to, a condition of debauchery just referred to?
>
> You have heard the testimony in the case in regard to the circumstances in which she was placed. You have viewed the scene where she was employed. You have examined by the testimony and your observation what was the character and what was the condition or influence in which the girl was placed by the defendant. Was or was not it a condition that would necessarily and naturally lead to a life of debauchery of a carnal nature relating to sexual intercourse between man and woman?
>
> The plan might have succeeded if the coarse precipitancy of one of the defendants and the ribaldry of the habitues of the place had not shocked the modesty of the girl. And granting the testimony to be true, of which the jury was the judge, the employment to which

she was enticed was an efficient school of debauchery of the special immorality which defendants contend the statute was designed to cover.[63]

Despite fighting the White Slavery Law all the way to the U.S. Supreme Court, Athanasaw received a sentence of two and a half years of hard labor beginning in 1913, while his partner (and brother-in-law) Mitchell Sampson was sentenced to eighteen months in federal prison. While waiting to serve his sentence, Athanasaw was arrested once again when he held an unsanctioned prize fight at the Imperial.[64] Even without Athanasaw and Sampson, who both began serving their sentences in 1913, the Imperial continued to outrage. After a shooting at the Imperial, the *Tribune* reminded readers, "Not the slightest change was made in the method of operating the Imperial. [It is] the same low dive, where women induce men to drink, where there is the most shameful intermingling of the sexes, and where there are absolutely no pretensions to even the semblance of decency."[65]

Much to the relief of local dry activists, the Imperial Theater closed in mid-1913. In 1915, a newly released Athanasaw opened a theater in Ybor City, but his glory days had passed. Police raided the new Imperial to enforce new alcohol regulations in 1917, and Athanasaw insisted there was no booze on the property. After a search that lasted an hour, the officers finally found the stash: eight iced bottles of beer, at which time Athanasaw quickly drank three bottles of "extra pale" to demonstrate they were for personal use, not for sale. The police soon located a much larger hidden cache and arrested the veteran offender. The wily Greek kept a low profile during Prohibition and died in 1931 at the age of seventy-three when he was mangled by a train he apparently could not hear at Sixth Avenue and Fifteenth Street. Like so many other things in Tampa, there is probably more to that story, too.[66]

THE SAWDUST TRAIL

In 1915, no one could deny that change was in the air. The White Rose saloon's old location (213–215 Lafayette, now Kennedy Boulevard), dating back to 1888, was torn down in 1915 to make room for a new brick building. "As only a vacant lot will remain," the *Tribune* commented, "the White Rose will be marked by no monument of modern architecture for it will join the shadowy army of memories, unmourned."[67]

The White Rose was a casualty of the Davis Package Law, a statewide measure aimed specifically at saloons and passed in 1915. The new law prohibited customers from drinking alcohol in the same place it was purchased, limited the sale of liquor to the hours between 7:00 a.m. and 6:00 p.m., prohibited the sale of alcohol in amounts less than half a pint, and banned women from places that sold alcohol. The financial blow to the city was considerable, and at least a hundred workers were unemployed. Other saloons became private clubs or built partitions to more easily serve their clientele away from prying eyes. Only two hundred saloons remained in Florida, with only seventy-five retail or wholesale shops.[68]

The Davis Act had the desired effect. Out of Tampa's seventy-five saloons, more than fifty closed on October 1, 1915, the day Bill 222 became law. While the drinking public may have been aghast to find only one-third of Tampa's saloons still in business, St. Petersburg retained only two. Despite the new law, drinking in Hillsborough County and six other Florida counties was still legal. Hardworking, hard-drinking Tampa would not loosen its grip on the bottle so easily.[69]

Florida's prohibitionists neared their goal, but Tampa's government seemed as corrupt as ever. Recent civic reforms had instituted the White Primary that excluded black people from voting in Democratic primaries, ostensibly to remove "purchasable votes" from the electoral process. Through ballot-stuffing, especially in Ybor City and West Tampa, the Democratic Party was able to fix elections. Mayor D. B. McKay and his political allies formed a durable regime that would last into the 1930s with little interruption.[70]

Sharply aware of Tampa's moral shortcomings, dry Presbyterians, stern Methodists, and zealous Baptists from twenty-five local churches raised $8,000 to bring Henry W. Stough's Evangelistic Crusade to town. Stough was well known as a touring revival preacher who took a special delight in pointing out the sins of his host cities. By inviting him to town at such cost, many of Tampa's Christians announced their disapproval of Tampa's culture and government. A vocal muckraker who backed down from no one, Stough was notorious for his "fiery temper and lack of political finesse." The year before, he was sued for slander after insulting an alderman and several saloon owners in Harrisburg, Pennsylvania.[71]

Stough may have had sacred intentions, but his large campaign staff required heavy funding. The twenty-five participating churches each paid Stough $225 weekly during his stay, built a massive wooden tabernacle, provided entertainment, and paid for the party's train tickets. In February 1916, volunteer workers began assembling the great lumber chapel on Franklin Street in the Garrison neighborhood. Although the temporary cathedral could hold eight thousand, the crowds were expected to exceed its capacity. It was the biggest auditorium in the state until the crusade moved on.[72]

The crusade's train rolled into town on March 5, and a chorus of five hundred heralded their arrival at the tabernacle, singing "His Love Is Far Better Than Gold." Stough arrived with Dora Cain, who ministered especially to the women and took charge of the choir. A nursery allowed mothers to worship without constraints, drawing three thousand women to exclusive daytime sermons. Stough set up his headquarters at the upscale DeSoto Hotel. He and his staff made day trips to various surrounding towns such as Tarpon Springs, but the focus of his crusade was the stage of the massive wooden tabernacle in Tampa.

A thousand worshipers welcomed him to the stage on an unseasonably cold night. Stough did not kick off his campaign with any of the fiery bombast he was known for. He spoke about James 5:16, "Therefore confess your sins to each other and pray for each other so that you may be healed. The prayer of a righteous person is powerful and effective." To conclude his opening speech, Stough said, "This city needs a revival. Lots of folks blame the gang for the condition of things here. Wherever you don't till a field or a garden patch, weeds will grow. Let us till this city for God."[73]

A group of locals took Stough on a tour of the undesirable parts of town one night, scribbling the license plate numbers of cars parked in front of the bawdy houses in hopes of unmasking their owners to the public. After touring Tampa's bars and brothels, Stough did not disappoint his fans when he called the city "the most damnable wide-open and rottenest town this side of hell." With his sense of outrage duly aroused, the preacher performed his sermons—with titles such as "Red Lights and Search Lights" and "Home Makers and Home Breakers"—with such poise and fervor that the *Tribune* declared them "masterpieces." Although Stough believed in the power of the spirit, he also espoused eugenics as a way to reduce crime. "There is but one way to get rid of criminals," he insisted. "Stop raising them." For wayward children who were otherwise well bred, he recommended prayer and hickory.[74]

Stough did not originally plan to stay for Tampa's municipal elections on April 17, but his ardent followers pleaded that he help unseat corrupt mayor D. B. McKay. Always spoiling for a war of words, Stough agreed to stay for a discreet fee. His civic-minded followers gave him anonymous letters with explosive allegations, which he read quite publicly in his sermons for worshippers and journalists to hear. The writers of the *Tampa Daily Times*, owned by Mayor McKay, were openly hostile to his presence in town. Due to Stough's allegations and testimony, a grand jury found irregularities with poll tax records regarding voters registering in multiple wards and being registered and paid to vote by criminals. He alleged that the police department had used kickbacks from prostitutes to finance their new automobiles.[75]

When Stough took the stage at a night service on April 5, he said, "We have been skirmishing up 'til today. The city has never been stirred as it is stirred right now. This city must be won for Jesus Christ to accomplish permanent good. A mere reform election will not bring the results." Stough warmed up to mayoral candidate (and former mayor) Frank Bowyer, who was at least willing to pay lip service to cleaning up the city's vice.[76]

McKay lashed back in his own way. His friendliness to the Latin population and use of racism as a political issue meant he was probably responsible for starting the rumor that Stough had dismissed Tampa's Latin population as no better than "Negroes." Tampa's police accused Stough of mounting a campaign of political propaganda. An officer fined one of Stough's drivers fifty dollars for speeding, but a café owner who sold liquor to a minor on Sunday was discharged with no punishment the same day. The *Times* even insinuated that Stough's attractive female assistant helped him in matters more carnal than spiritual. The preacher dismissed the story, McKay, and the *Times*. "I wouldn't use that dirty little sheet to wipe my dog with."[77]

In a sermon to a packed audience, Stough accused Tampa's police of allowing vice to flourish due to commands from "higher up the ladder." He led the audience in prayer for Mayor McKay. "I can exactly see how a city like Tampa got into the hands of pirates. People came here and bothered only about themselves and did not take the city to heart, and you know what the consequences have been."[78]

Stough was not joking during a sermon he made on April 2 in which he preached to an all-male audience that "immoral" women held too much power. "Why is it some men wouldn't run for mayor?" he asked the audience. He then answered, "It's because Hilda Raymond and Genie Gilbert won't let them." Raymond and Gilbert, Stough claimed, were "sporting women," and they held enough secrets about Tampa's power structure to cause "murder and riot, and divorces and bankruptcies on Franklin Street." Tampa's two "madams" of prostitution were certainly well-connected, and their facilities popular.[79]

Throughout all of the revelations and allegations about Tampa's growing criminal-political machine, the name Charlie Wall seemed to hang in the air like the name of the devil, often alluded to but never spoken aloud except in hushed tones. Wall was no doubt the "young man from one of the wealthiest families in town" who witnesses saw taking groups of drinkers and gamblers to pay their poll taxes in time for the elections. Stough knew the answer before he asked, "Is any man or any company of men who might be called an invisible government controlling you?" Several voices in the congregation shouted, "Charlie Wall . . . Charlie Wall."

Although Stough lost his attempt to help defeat Tampa mayor D. B. McKay, his followers had reason to take heart. Stough had galvanized voter registration and turnout while revealing the workings of Tampa's invisible government. If a clean opposing candidate had run, Stough said, McKay would have been beat. "I haven't heard the gang crowing very loud. They are trembling in their boots. When the heart of a city is stirred and a majority are for the right, I see a brighter day dawning for Tampa.

She will never be the same." After six weeks, 3,882 souls "walked the saw-dust trail" and were born again.[80]

One weeping woman told Stough just before his departure, "Tampa will never be the same because you were here." But evidence of his campaign faded quickly. On April 28, the massive tabernacle, once the largest in Florida, was razed to the ground. Tampa's machine roared on into the 1920s.[81]

COLLECTIVE ACTION

Soup Houses, Boycotts, and Cooperatives

In the late 1800s, Havana had become a political pressure cooker known to produce a radicalized, assertive—even combative—workforce. Most workers arrived in Ybor City deeply politicized by harsh experiences in their previous homes and workplaces. In the Gilded Age of robber barons and monopolies when workers enjoyed few rights and little respect, the value of labor unions seemed self-evident. Aware of the demand for their skills, cigar makers were accustomed to being treated as artisans with a certain degree of deference in the workplace. The immigrants built upon their principle of strength through collective action and applied it to the workplace, the marketplace, and the political sphere.[1]

Workers routinely engaged in collective action through their social clubs, patriotic societies, and labor unions. The Cuban workers who had followed the factories to Key West found no organized labor on that island, so they organized their own unions and expressed little interest in the politically moderate American organizations. American unions blamed Latin workers for being difficult to organize, often based on their disinterest in the less radical unions of the United States. Besides these issues, racism and the lack of compassion for Cuban nationalism hurt any attempts to organize Latin workers in American unions.[2]

Cigar workers were remarkably aware of literature and politics. The bustling but relatively quiet industrial worksite gave rise to a novel educational institution: the *lector*. The readers had roots in Cuban jails, the center of political and labor discontent on the island. Educated prisoners with strong voices read to their fellow inmates, their words echoing through the cell blocks. *Lectores* became the mouthpieces for worker-produced newspapers in Havana during the 1860s, which made them a popular fixture in cigar factories. In Havana and Tampa, the workers in every major factory hired *lectores* to read to them during the workday. They began the morning with news and politics, foreign and domestic, translating on the fly. In the afternoon, *lectores* read dramatically from various international novels in daily installments that anticipated the radio serials of mid-century.[3]

When Vicente Martinez Ybor and other cigar firms left war-torn Cuba for Key West in 1869–70, the cigar workers followed. Over the following decade, the small island resembled the political hotbed of Havana. By the time Ybor and his peers planned to leave Key West, they were seeking ways to avoid repeating the cycle of strikes and negotiations. To encourage Ybor's relocation to Tampa, the Board of Trade promised to defend the cigar industry against strikes and other forms of labor activism by "any means."[4]

Ybor built his namesake city assuming it would be his to run in traditional Latin "patron-peon" fashion.[5] The unionists had other ideas. When Ybor's factory was less than a year old, his workers established a local chapter of the Knights of Labor and demanded an increase in wages. On January 17, 1887, just three weeks after Ybor's Nochebuena feast for his workers, the Knights of Labor staged a strike. Two days later, the loyal workers and the strikers clashed at the factory, leaving five wounded and one killed. The opening salvo in Tampa's labor wars had begun, and the stakes would only rise with time.[6]

When the strike commenced, Ybor and other factory owners pleaded with Tampa officials to help police their unruly labor force. Tampa's Board of Trade vowed to "guarantee full support and protection for their lives and property by every legitimate means." On February 12, a group of "municipal authorities" banished the foreman and about seventy-five workers from the area, prompting protests by workers across a variety of occupations. Rumors of Spanish involvement in the crackdown aroused the indignation of the Cubans. Most of the expelled workers were eventually allowed to return to their jobs and homes. The Board of Trade succeeded in stifling the strike, and the demands of the workers had not been addressed. As the colony's workforce grew, crushing unions by force would not be so easy. Between 1887 and 1894, workers staged twenty-three walkouts, an average of three per year, and the big strikes hadn't even begun.[7]

If the immigrant clubs and clinics represented "peacetime" applications of the cooperative approach, the soup kitchen was the variant devoted to the class struggles foretold by Karl Marx. Like the barricades of the Paris Commune, union commissaries and soup kitchens were often the only bulwark against the strength of the ruling class. Striking workers depended on these food dispensaries for months at a time. The soup kitchen grew in importance because the antagonists relied on attrition over negotiation to resolve strikes. When the market failed the workers and prices went haywire, workers responded with cooperative retail enterprises. By using their collective buying power, they established an alternative and bypassed the markups of retail stores. The immigrants' class consciousness, labor temples, and cooperative medical care flew in the face of the way most Americans understood capitalism. When the immigrants formed cooperative retail stores and restaurants as a response to the steep rise in prices, many saw them as a threat to the city's livelihood.

Despite Ybor City's great success, the economic life of most of its citizens remained precarious. Strikes in the factories meant a loss for everyone who depended on the wages of the cigar workers. Because the cigar workers earned the majority of the city's payroll, the economic life of the city depended completely on functioning cigar factories. Ybor's merchants usually offered to mediate conflicts between labor and capital, especially because they stood to lose many thousands of dollars in trade every week. The *Tribune* observed during a strike, "It seems as if everybody are at the mercy of the strikers. Will the strikers have mercy on the business interests of Tampa?"[8]

Merchants may have disliked business slumps, but zealous strikers proved perfectly willing to go hungry for their cause. Hunger took on the status of a political sacrament for some; having gone hungry before, they did not fear it. Instead, deprivation became an act of devotion and rebellion. In 1893, an impetuous labor leader shouted to a crowd of supporters, "We will never give in. We are making a stand now for our rights and we'll starve before our surrender." Union leadership repeated the bitter promise countless times, and cigar manufacturers tested it time and again.[9]

Labor stoppages dragged on for many months, making strikers dependent upon union-funded soup kitchens to feed their families. During the strike of 1893, the *Tampa Daily Times* reported that many faced starvation. Desperate Spaniards camped on the shores of Palmetto Beach to live off the seafood they caught in the bay. Some fled to Cuba, hoping to find jobs there, and the Spanish government in Havana paid for their passage. More than two hundred Spaniards embarked for Cuba one night, leaving an irate saloon owner behind. A whopping $1,200 in bar tabs sailed with the Spaniards.[10]

Soup kitchens may have nurtured the workers and their families, but they quickly drained the union's coffers. Hardship and hunger became the orders of the day. Butchers and grocers, often encouraged by factory management, cut off the union's credit. A defiant gesture by a striker added to the misery when he set fire to O'Halloran & Company's factory in newly founded West Tampa, burning down two city blocks.[11]

THE WEIGHT STRIKE

At the end of 1898, with Cuba theoretically independent under the tutelage of the United States, some workers felt that the broad labor struggle had been deferred for the sake of Cuban liberty. Workers had refrained from strikes for several years to maximize the funds pledged to the revolution. The Cuban War for Independence, which concluded with the Spanish-American War in 1898, had laid waste to the island, and its political situation was in disarray. Staying in Tampa seemed like a better idea to most Cubans than going hungry in Havana. As a result, the end of the war did not lead to a Cuban exodus from the factories, nor to the factories moving back to the island.[12]

Coincidentally, just as the workers turned their political attention to the workplace, large U.S. corporate firms bought up many of Tampa's largest cigar factories. Whatever workers thought of old man Ybor, he was their patron, a visible father figure to praise, ridicule, or scorn. That worker-patron relationship may have been strained in the first place, but it was also a familiar tradition. The very idea of the gentleman cigar tycoon seemed to have died with V. M. Ybor himself in 1896. Perhaps it is best that Ybor did not live to see the massive, faceless tobacco trusts in New York dominate the industry in the following years. The Havana-American Company snatched up ten factories in Ybor City before being bought out by bigger trusts along with most of the industry. Predictably, the new corporate masters of the cigar industry wanted to make their new acquisitions more efficient and profitable.[13]

In 1899, a Chinese restaurant owner went to Tampa's courthouse with a grievance. A cigar factory worker had not paid his large tab of ten dollars. When confronted with the bill by police, the man refused to pay the owner directly but instead settled the bill through the court. He was so incensed by the ordeal that he insulted the city's prosecutor, drawing an additional fine. The man returned to work at the Ybor and Manrara factory, where he gave an impassioned, impromptu speech on the virtues of organized labor and the evils of capital. The man's rant resonated with his coworker's widespread resentment of the new corporate rules, leading the factory's workforce to stage a walkout and a strike by four thousand workers. Threats of assassination by unionists persuaded many manufacturers to shutter their factories for the duration of the ordeal.[14]

The cigar workers had already been chafing under the strict regulations of their new corporate masters. Most egregious of all was the presence of the tobacco scales in the workplace. The old regime allowed workers to take product home to smoke or practice their technique. The trusts required workers to weigh the tobacco they brought to their benches. The new weighing procedure not only deprived cigar makers of an accustomed perk, but it was also seen as calling the consistency of their skills into question. From the distance of New York City, this seemed like a simple, innocuous new procedure to ensure uniformity and profitability. From the factory floor, the scales represented everything wrong with the direction of the cigar industry.[15]

The "Weight Strike" commenced at the beginning of 1899 and the workers demanded the removal of the scales from all of the factories. The

Tribune singled out the Cubans and labor agitators, two common scape-goats, as the instigators of the strike.

> The American cigar makers [and] Spaniards are reasonable and con-scientious people and are not individually concerned in such unrea-sonable demands. They are willing to listen to reason, but the Cuban to a great extent, are led entirely by incendiary speeches from their leaders, who are generally men of little to no education.[16]
>
> If blame must rest on one particular element, it should fall upon the anarchistic leaders who have urged the strikers into this defi-ance and its results. There can be little doubt that the . . . strike was directly inspired by professional agitators, probably sent here for that purpose.[17]

In the early weeks of any strike, workers typically fell back on their own resources, consuming any reserved food and money before relying upon the soup kitchens. A sister union in Havana reportedly sent eight thou-sand dollars to sustain the strikers. The *Tribune* noted with dread, "Ru-mors of the institution of a soup-house and free-lunch stand were not verified." Two weeks later, the union opened several soup kitchens to signal it was ready for a long fight. "In front of the free soup houses," the *Tobacco Journal* observed, "can always be seen a crowd discussing the sit-uation with the wildest gesticulations, and usually denouncing the manu-facturers in the severest manner possible."[18]

Although most soup kitchens undoubtedly served limited fare, a sneering *Tribune* article in 1899 questioned the public's image of such places.

> The people who believe the idle cigarmakers are anywhere near starvation are victims of a ludicrous delusion. Go out to the "soup houses," as they are called, and take a note of the character of the "charity" on which the cigarmakers are now subsisting. Instead of the supposed crust of bread and small bowl of thin soup which rumor as-cribes to their commissary stores, they have plentiful repast of various meats, vegetables, good bread and cakes in abundance, and strange to relate—good wine. It is of little wonder that the labor troubles con-

tinue. A perusal of the bill of fare of the Cuban "soup houses" will make the average lunch stand patron green with envy.[19]

The strike ended three days later in victory for the union. Workers celebrated their triumph with a gloating Labor Day Parade in Ybor City, with a thousand revelers joining the festivities. The parade began at noon, punctuated with banners that read, "Labor produces all, capital nothing," and "Down with the scab!" A dark-skinned Queen of Labor lorded over the festivities from a float drawn by four horses. Another horse, hungry to the point of emaciation, represented those fed by wages before the victorious strike.[20]

The Resistance

Capital and labor had both drawn lessons from the Weight Strike. Heartened by their swift victory, workers created a new union called La Sociedad de Torcedores, or La Resistencia. As a homegrown union, La Resistencia reflected the radical ideas of the workers, not the moderate union bosses of New York. In addition to cigar makers, the radical union served as an umbrella organization for immigrant bakers, waiters, clerks, bartenders, and laundry workers. To give the upstart union more credibility, its leadership negotiated a shaky agreement with a small local of the moderate International Cigar Makers Union.[21]

La Resistencia became the militant voice of workers in the workplace and the community. For workers who could not vote in local elections, the union provided influence. La Resistencia was willing to acknowledge that the cigar manufacturers and the City of Tampa were intimately connected. Strikes, or just the threat of them, became leverage to demand change: infrastructure improvement, new streetcars, more courteous streetcar conductors, and so on. In the spring of 1901, the Fortune Street bridge linking Ybor City to West Tampa collapsed, a major inconvenience for workers. When no repairs were forthcoming, the union threatened to strike if the city did not repair it. The city complied, but the new union probably did not endear itself to the Board of Trade and its vigilante Citizens' Committee. In fact, La Resistencia was a threat to all of the local power brokers, including cigar manufacturers, local elites, elected officials, and other labor unions.[22]

During the next strike in 1901, Tampa's Board of Trade reacted much more forcefully. The *Tobacco Journal* wrote of the union, "It is foreign in its origin, foreign in race, foreign in tongue, and antagonistic to our laws, customs and government. They want to boss the bosses and abuse the hospitality Tampa has granted them." The tobacco companies grew weary of the frequent strikes and had been unimpressed by the city's intervention against the last walkout. If the city could not protect their interests as promised, they implied their willingness to leave. Just as they had fled Havana and Key West before, some manufacturers plotted their escape from Tampa. They eyed Pensacola and Jacksonville as possible locations for branch factories and even for wholesale relocation.[23]

Prepared to preempt such a move, La Resistencia demanded that all proposed branch factories be snuffed out. It also insisted that all manufacturers recognize the union's exclusive right to represent all of the cigar workers in Ybor City. La Resistencia wanted nothing less than to claim every unionized worker in Ybor City regardless of profession. The general strike began on July 26, 1901, and five thousand cigar makers left work. In a city of about twenty thousand residents (if one includes West Tampa, Fort Brooke, and Port Tampa, which would all be incorporated into the city), the effects of such a strike cannot be overstated.[24]

The cigar manufacturers met with Tampa's Board of Trade at the upscale Cherokee Club to discuss how to react to the strike and the union's sweeping demands. The board mustered a new posse of vigilantes. The *New York Times* described Tampa's so-called Citizens' Committee as a quaint tradition for a small town in distress, as if from a natural disaster. "There is nothing turbulent about these summary proceedings," wrote the *Times*. "They are conducted with a certain formality, and the body of citizens directing them possesses in some degree the character of a vigilance committee, called into existence to meet a public emergency."[25] The Citizens' Committee would use force as necessary, but hunger remained its most effective weapon.[26]

The union announced it would use reserve funds not to pay workers stipends but to fund collective soup houses. La Resistencia opened nine of the cantinas on August 2: four in Ybor City, one at Port Tampa, one at

Palmetto Beach, and three others on Tampa's outskirts. Although union leaders flaunted savings of $32,000, they spent $7,000 to stock and open the cantinas. Thereafter, the union claimed to spend $2,000 a day to run the soup houses.[27] With a large store of groceries and meat at their central commissary at Fourteenth Street between Eighth and Ninth Avenues, La Resistencia prepared for a long strike.[28]

On the opening day of the commissaries, cooks butchered a dozen cattle and ordered seven thousand chickens from New Orleans. The *Tribune* noted, "The strikers propose to live as well as possible under the circumstances." The good life, as it was, would not last for long. The first signs of trouble came from within the union, when a revolt broke out in La Resistencia's ranks. Union leader José Padilla saw a great number of angry visitors the day the soup houses opened. Some complained of the soup itself, claiming it was "too thin," "that the beef soup was unacquainted with beef, the chicken soup a total stranger to chicken." Workers claimed that a strike could not survive for long "on such weak and watery stuff." It was not an encouraging sign on the soup houses' first day of operations.[29]

Other workers preferred cash to thin soup from the unions, hoping to pay rent and stretch their food dollars. Landlords did not readily tolerate tenants with no money, especially those on strike. Large-scale evictions quickly followed on August 13. The *Tribune* suspected that a mere one-third of strikers actually ate at the soup houses. But as the strike wore on, more workers depended upon the food served there.[30]

On August 5, after three days of food service, "a committee of the leading businessmen notified the soup houses that they must close and feed no more people." Days later, police raided the soup houses for being "instrumental in prolonging the strike" and arrested some of the workers there on "various charges." Contrary to its own reporting, the *Tribune* falsely claimed the cantinas had operated "unmolested" by outsiders. With their kitchens wrecked, cantina workers distributed uncooked food for strikers to prepare at home.[31] La Resistencia announced that its members would starve before they surrendered.[32]

Next, the Citizens' Committee singled out the leadership of the union for rough handling. Their plan began with a flag of truce. According to the *New York Times*,

A great open-air meeting had been arranged, to which all the Resistencia leaders had been invited, the purpose being to catch them all together. They were all present. Music had been provided, and the streets were lined with thousands of persons. . . . When the leaders were warned of the approach of a posse, they dispersed, but the men were snatched from the crowd. They were kept in carriages with guards on either side.

The Citizens' Committee publicly announced to the confused crowd,

> To the Anarchists and professional labor agitators: We say that your days in Tampa are at an end. We cannot and will not permit you to destroy this prosperous city. If you regard your safety, you will shake its dust from your feet. In conclusion, we notify the manufacturers that this movement of citizens is not in your interests, but in the interest of the entire community.[33]

The vigilantes had shipped the kidnapped union leaders to Honduras aboard the freighter *Marie Cooper*, where they were abandoned on a remote beach.[34] After being threatened, La Resistencia leader José Padilla hid with some Italian friends for three days. Then one evening, hiding behind an American newspaper, he took a train to the port and sailed for Havana. Alejandro Rodriguez took his place, who promptly announced, "There is no danger of our being starved into surrender."[35]

After just over a week of service, several soup houses closed down. Putting a brave face on things, the union claimed they had "no use for so many." If La Resistencia had no use for so many cantinas, it was because their food supplies had been effectively cut off. Tampa's wholesale butchers refused to extend more credit to the union. Produce dealers doubled and quadrupled prices to register their dissatisfaction. Merchants turned down the union's urgent requests for loans. To make matters even worse, the cooks at the soup houses prepared to strike against the union![36]

As supplies waned, the scenes at the cantinas became more desperate. The *Tobacco Journal* noted on August 17, "There has been a great dissension among the strikers regarding the soup houses, two were closed today in West Tampa and one in Tampa ran short on provisions long before the number of people dependent on their house were served. As a consequence many went hungry, and this will be an inducement for them to search for work."[37] On August 20, a "large number" of members left the union. Seventeen labor leaders were warned to leave the city within twelve hours, and they complied. The *Tribune* claimed (probably falsely) that strikers had begged for their own "filthy" soup houses to be condemned. "They say the sanitary department should have them either closed or cleaned out. They are vile and filthy to the extreme, and, as one of the men expressed it, they are bad enough to produce typhoid or yellow fever."[38]

The police chief swore in a new squad of policemen, and the Citizens' Committee issued letters to La Resistencia Secretary Alejandro Rodriguez and other labor leaders warning them to leave town. But the new secretary did not intend to be driven from his post so easily. Rodriguez took the letter out into the street, spat on it, and ground it into the dirt with his heel, all the while raving, "Damn the Americans; they can't make me go." Forty-eight hours later, vigilantes kidnapped and deported Rodriguez and six of his comrades. Tampa's union-busters became so enthusiastic in forcibly deporting immigrants that they sometimes did so in error. Overly zealous vigilantes accidentally deported Crescencio Gonzalez to Key West, but authorities recognized they had erred and allowed the shaken man to return.[39]

At the end of August, the *Tribune* reported with satisfaction that the union was "on its last legs, torn by dissentions within and opposition without, without cohesive power to direct its own affairs. If it ever succeeds in gathering itself together again, it will be surprising." Cantinas lacked food, the union ran out of money, and landlords drove destitute strikers from their homes. A thousand workers broke ranks to return to their positions. Key West unions sent another $1,200 for the strikers, but workers continued to trickle back into the factories. Employers compelled returning workers to promise not to recognize any union in the workplace. Expecting trouble, the mayor asked the police to swear in more deputies to preserve order.[40]

La Resistencia asked members employed in restaurants not to serve workers who returned to the factories before the strike ended. Restaurant owners replaced all cooks and waiters who complied, adding to the long list of unemployed and needy union members. In despair, a female worker suggested they burn down all the factories. La Resistencia's leadership resorted to starting a rumor that all those returning to work would be deported.[41]

By the end of August, the cantinas served one ration a day, consisting of weak coffee and cooked corn meal. There was no meat or even soup to be found in the soup houses. Like a triumphant general, the *Tribune* announced the futility of further resistance. "They must see that persistence in their present course is suicidal. They can never win this fight. Its only result will and must be the annihilation of their organization, and their unconditional surrender. The extermination of *Resistencia* is as certain as the rising sun."[42]

On the other side of the conflict, a newspaper writer for the leftist *L'Alba Sociale* wrote in Italian,

> Tampa, before the workers came here, used to be a small town, a town that not even dogs would have wanted to come to. Six thousand workers came here in this desert of quicksand, marsh, and nothing else just because the capitalists, for economic reasons, were offering them a deal. We are asking ourselves, what is this committee of horrible citizens, which claims to be so patriotic, proposing to accomplish by carrying out such monstrous acts as they have committed at the expense of the workers? Let Tampa become what it once was, a desert of sand populated by animals—a very biased kind of animal which the bourgeoisie can get along with better than they can with us.[43]

Public opinion turned against the strikers on September 14 when President William McKinley died by an anarchist's bullet in Buffalo, New York. As the cigar manufacturers shipped in hundreds of German replacement workers from across the nation, union soup kitchens closed for lack of food and funds. The *Tribune* complained of the zealous strikers, "It looks as though a large proportion of them do not care to work for lucrative salaries as long as soup houses and hand-outs and sympathy is extended them. The soup houses have been ordered closed."[44]

The Citizens' Committee smashed up the cantinas that remained, "poured the soup on the ground, and put out the fires. Some of the cigar makers assisted in the work." The *Tribune* said the hungry strikers "are now simply whistling to keep up courage." The union bought tickets for strikers to leave the city, alleviating the pressure to feed them. On September 16, owners reopened their factories, inviting the strikers to drop their demands and return to work.[45]

Vigilantes had cleared the last of the soup kitchens by September 24, when a sallow, weak, and nervous striker visited the *Tribune* office with the daily ration for himself and his family of seven. Declaring he could not live on such fare, he turned over his "measly and putrid" ration to the editors. When they weighed the meal meant to feed eight, they found a quarter pound each of corn meal, rice, and beans and an ounce each of salt, bacon, and lard. "The provisions that this poor fellow brought to the *Tribune* office would have turned the stomach of a hungry dog," the editor revealed. "Had they been fresh and wholesome, they would not have appeased the appetite of a child, much less seven grown people." The weary striker said his wife and six children were weakened by hunger. "Ravenously hungry" himself, the man vowed to abandon the strike and return to the factory for work the next morning.[46]

By October 17, 1,100 others had returned to work as well, more than one-fifth of the strikers. Police and deputized citizens escorted strikebreakers back to work and charged the uncompliant with vagrancy. The charge carried a sentence of a month on road gangs. After Tampa passed a harsher vagrancy ordinance, Ybor City's working-class women responded by marching on city hall while fronted with a brass band. A posse of citizens turned away the activists, but courts quietly curtailed the use of the newly stiffened vagrancy ordinances. The Citizens' Committee continued to round up union leaders. A new agreement with immigrant grocers kept the soup houses supplied, and able Italian strikers refused rations for the common good.[47]

The strike finally fizzled in November as manufacturers imported more labor, especially from Havana. By November 23, nearly two thousand workers filled the factories. Five days later, the union sued for peace. The bitter strike of 1901 had concluded, and La Resistencia folded the next year. The only beneficiary was La Resistencia's rival, the Cigar Makers' International Union (CMIU), whose workers never participated in the strike or missed any meals. The Citizens' Committee had carried out its strikebreaking work with gusto, but no politician in the city would openly take responsibility for its excesses. Mayor Francis Wing said he was not in town when the abuses against strikers were carried out but doting at the bedside of his ailing mother.[48]

"The dove of peace once more brooded over a fretted populace," the *Tribune* noted, but a general business malaise followed the strike. "Business in Tampa was never so poor as at that period." According to historian Durward Long, unionism declined sharply in Tampa for years, along with pay and working conditions.[49]

In 1904, the major manufacturers tried to abolish unions from the factories and introduce machines for producing cigars. The workers quickly joined unions again, and it seemed a new showdown was brewing. The Joint Advisory Board, the decision-making organ for the local unions, issued a manifesto that pled, "Tampa has but the cigar industry as its only source of revenue and it is to the interest of us all to maintain that life to insure the future of our city, our industry, and ourselves."[50] While labor tensions smoldered, manufacturers recruited "apprentices" younger than ten in so-called school factories. According to previous agreements, manufacturers could employ children as 6 percent of their workforce, but soon one of every four employees was a child.[51]

A perceptive "Anonymous Businessman" shared his observations with the *Tribune* on how the trusts and not the unions would bring the death of Tampa's cigar industry. "You can't kill unionism," he wrote. "You or I or all the manufacturers in the world can't do it." He contrasted "True unionism—conservative, righteous, fair-minded and broad," with "lawless violence, anarchy and brute force. Union men are going to learn to make this distinction, to separate one from the other, to use brain instead of brawn."

> True unionism is right and it is necessary with the advancement of the trusts. There is no other way to meet combines except with combinations. Unionism is stronger in Tampa than it ever was. You can't kill the union by oppressing the workmen, for by so doing you only show them more clearly the need of it, and when they are oppressed or driven into the streets that their union becomes of greatest benefit.

It is when a man is working peacefully along, still having to pay his dues, that he is liable to forget the benefit of his union.

The writer keenly pointed out that the large tobacco trusts could much more easily survive strikes and fights with unions while putting smaller, local competition out of business. He argued that the old local manufacturers such as Ybor, Haya, and Fuente had built Tampa's reputation. The tobacco trusts had since started purchasing smaller competitors to cash in on Tampa's reputation for quality and association with clear Havana tobacco. "Their policy has always been to cheapen labor and to reduce the number of workmen by using different patent machines. This not only kills the trade of high-quality cigars, but it reduces the volume of workmen earning living wages that has permitted Tampa to prosper."[52]

Mob Violence

Both sides in labor disputes increasingly relied on violence to achieve their aims. As it expanded, Tampa's cigar industry only deepened the city's dependence on foreign-born workers. In 1910, Tampa and West Tampa claimed more than 46,000 residents and the cigar industry employed 10,500, with 6,000 of them members of the Cigar Makers' International Union. Cigars accounted for 65 percent of the city's revenues and 75 percent of its payroll.[53]

When factories began replacing unionized employees without cause, the CMIU demanded a stop to the practice and recognition for the union. Factories responded with a lockout, and workers retaliated with a walkout on July 25, 1910. The union asked the Board of Trade to mediate, but the manufacturers were not in the mood to negotiate. The CMIU called for a strike, sending eight thousand men and two thousand women into the street, where they quickly made their presence known. The CMIU demanded recognition, a closed shop, and fair wages. The manufacturers wanted to rid themselves of the union. Rampant violence on both sides of the struggle eclipsed the prominent role of the union soup kitchens and commissaries.[54]

Antonio Albedo, a nonunion cigar maker, gave an impromptu speech

If the immigrant social clubs and their clinics represented the "peacetime" application of communal enterprises, then union soup houses were the type used in times of struggle. These remarkable images from the Weight Strike of 1899 show a diverse and resolute workforce. (Tony Pizzo/Ramon San Feliz collection, University of South Florida Tampa Special Collections)

in the street urging his fellow workers to return to the factories, but he was soon mobbed by union loyalists who rushed him. Albedo ran into a nearby saloon in hopes of finding safety, but he was "roughly seized and dragged in a shameful manner to the Union hall, where he was almost terrified to death," according to the *Tobacco Journal*. After being interrogated for some time, the workers took him to Palmetto Beach, where he was warned to leave town. It was much too early in the strike for most workers to consider giving up.[55]

By September, tensions had risen further. Police had to use fire hoses to disperse a large confrontation outside the Antonio Santaella factory, the largest in West Tampa. A saloon owner was murdered in the street with no witnesses. A massive Labor Day parade stoked passions while the union raised money. The unionized carpenters pledged their support for the cigar workers, and the other trades joined in. Gunplay on the streets was common and the situation was getting out of control.[56]

On the afternoon of September 14, a striker shot and killed Bustillo Brothers bookkeeper J. F. Easterling as he tried to enter the factory. He was the "first American" to be attacked during the strike. Two assassination attempts of factory foremen failed. Brawls and stabbings became common. Cigar firms secured new locations in Miami, Palatka, Key West, New York, New Orleans, and so on. The manufacturers issued a statement to the "Public of the City of Tampa," announcing they would close their factories indefinitely until conditions made it possible for them to resume business.[57]

While campaigning for election earlier that year, newly elected Mayor D. B. McKay had proudly bragged about his role in the "Citizens' Committee" that helped neutralize the strike of 1901 through extralegal means. As the son of a leading local Scottish family and the husband of Aurora Gutierrez, daughter of Gavino, one of Ybor City's founders, McKay felt doubly duty bound to repeat his triumph.[58]

The arrival of replacement workers brought tensions to a fever pitch. Eight hundred "prominent citizens" joined a new extralegal Citizens' Committee, which declared itself "the only law." The committee recruited toughs from the surrounding countryside to patrol the streets, attack strikers, and protect the replacement workers. After a large Labor Day celebration by workers, McKay ordered three hundred more toughs to be sworn in. Drawn from the hinterland, these fresh police were generally of low character, enlisted not to enforce the law but to supersede it.[59]

A week after the death of Easterling, police claimed to have caught his assassins when they arrested two unemployed Italians. There was no evidence that Castenge[60] Ficarotta, forty-five, or Angelo Albano, twenty-five, had committed the murder, but it hardly mattered. There would be no trial. While being taken to the county jail on September 20, the prisoners were abducted by a mob who robbed the carriage at gunpoint. The two men were lynched from a stately oak at Grand Central[61] and Howard Avenue. The mob, probably enlisted or encouraged by the city, left the following note: "Others take notice or go the same way. We know seven more. We are watching. If any more citizens are molested, look out." Italians were often singled out as the worst ethnic troublemakers for generously supporting the strikers. Albano and Ficarotta paid the heaviest price.[62]

Authorities left the lynched bodies hanging aloft until well after morning for all to see. To amuse themselves, the perpetrators had stuck a tobacco pipe in the mouth of one of the corpses. Neither victim belonged to the union or even worked as a cigar maker. Constable James Keagin said there was nothing to be done. None of the painted faces of the assailants or their cars could be identified. A *Tribune* editorial claimed the lynching was "a lesson" and that some courageous men had circumvented the "the weaknesses and inadequacies" of the courtroom. "Every person in that group deserved hanging," the editor wrote. Union leaders received threats of lynching, and Mayor D. B. McKay's "stress squads" roamed the streets, attacking isolated workers. McKay wrote in the *Times*, "It is impossible to understand the attitude of the American Union working men of the city who have been misled into sympathizing and supporting the cigar workers."[63]

When two thousand workers protested the lynching, Mayor McKay responded by banning all public assemblies. On October 1, arson destroyed the Balbin Brothers factory, and firefighters narrowly saved the *Tribune* building. The union's Joint Advisory Board began to ship workers from the city to protect them from vigilante violence. Thousands more shipped out of Tampa to try their luck elsewhere or wait out the strike in safety.

On October 4, Tampa's business elite, including McKay and the *Tribune*'s Wallace Stovall, met to form a new Citizens' Committee. They placed attorney and West Tampa founder and cigar producer Hugh Macfarlane in charge of the squad. The committee announced that any violence on the part of workers would be blamed on the union. On October 17, Macfarlane led the armed throng into the labor temple, drove workers onto the street, seized the union's records, and smashed all else. On its way out, the committee left a sign on the door reading, "This place closed for all time." Although the posse never identified itself as officers of the law, they later claimed to be gathering evidence for Easterling's murder, including the arrest of three union leaders. Police dropped the charges of murder against the men, but they were convicted of lesser charges and sentenced to a year each on a chain gang. A grand jury later concluded there was no connection between the union and Easterling's murder.[64]

In the meantime, the union's soup houses had gradually run out of provisions. A West Tampa woman visited the *Tribune* office looking worried and haggard,

> bearing in her hand wrapped in a bit of greasy paper, a half pound of the fattest fat bacon. She is the wife of a cigarmaker who has been out of work, on account of the strike, for fifteen weeks. The piece of bacon was the piece de resistance of the dole of sustenance given her by the order of the Joint Advisory Board. A dog would not have eaten it. This was meat for man, woman, and six hungry children. In addition, she got ten cents worth of stale beans, ten cents worth of wormy grits, and a few ounces of cooking necessaries.[65]

The streets had become too hazardous to brave without protection. "Hundreds of armed citizens" patrolled the factories. Special police roved around town, riding four to a car, looking for vulnerable unionists. Only the most zealous strikers still remained in Tampa. Some wandered the street armed with clubs, resolved to beat any scab who dared try to work.[66]

The manufacturer's association met with the Citizens' Committee and announced plans to reopen thirty-six factories. The strike had clearly waned by November, and Governor Albert W. Gilchrist visited Tampa, taking pains to legally clear the locals of any wrongdoing toward strikers.

By the end of January 1911, the desperate workers voted to end the strike. Most of the branch factories established elsewhere closed their doors, and workers converged on Tampa seeking jobs. Tampa's businesses lost an estimated $350,000 every week of the strike, and the cigar industry lost $15 million. The union was not recognized, but workers returned to the factories free of reprisals, with the wage scale intact and the promised exclusion of child labor, which factory owners had used extensively in the years leading up to the strike.[67]

Labor newspaper *El Internacional* spoke for the anguish of many workers when it wrote, "Why do they who own Tampa expect me to care what becomes of it? I have no lands, no factories, no bank full of glistening ore. The very streets we paved and paid for do not belong to us. We, the sovereign American citizens, after elections are called a mob and ordered like stray dogs from off the streets we built and yet this same mob elected sheriffs and mayors to its undoing."[68]

COOPERATIVES AND BOYCOTTS

"Socialism to be practiced here," the *Tribune* announced in 1908, "co-operative store established in Ybor. Plan originated in France." Ybor City's immigrants found strength in numbers and solidarity. Their mutual aid societies supplied health care and social activities. Most blue-collar workers could only dream of affordable health care for their families. The ethnic social clubs and clinics seemed harmless enough to business leaders because there were no private health-care providers for them to compete against. Local retailers expressed alarm when co-ops threatened traditional retail groceries that sought profits from food and other essentials.[69]

Two hundred stockholders invested in the French-inspired co-op named Crecherie that summer. According to the practice of Ybor City's typical co-ops, investors paid a nominal entrance fee, worked there a set number of hours per month, and bought goods at cost. Nonmembers shopped for 10 percent above cost, which was still cheaper than the average markup on groceries today (13 percent). The principle was not much different from a retail store, except that investors could buy cheap goods and reap profits through a small investment and a little work. The "stockholder plan" was the most successful model, in which each investor received a 4–5 percent annual return on investment and a second payment derived from profits.[70]

Designed by and for working people, most co-ops opened at the end of the workday and closed at eight or ten each night. Each cooperative's board of directors appointed clerks to the stores for given periods. The positions were rotated regularly, and workers were not compensated. Wholesale purchasing agents also rotated in and out of positions, but because they had to work during the day and lost time from their regular jobs, they made a salary. Tampa's traditional businessmen were not pleased, especially because the co-op practice expanded as the economy floundered in the decade after 1910.[71]

World War I posed economic difficulty to working people across the United States. Between 1912 and 1919, the cost of living increased by 135 percent, with raises increasing pay by only 12.5 percent. Union rolls in Ybor City also more than doubled, from three thousand to seven thousand.[72] Tampa's elite and the immigrants responded quite differently to the severe inflation during World War I. Tampa's wealthiest housewives exercised their influence through progressive groups such as the National Housewives' League, pressuring City Council to pass a flurry of ordinances to protect their interests. The wealthiest citizens led the most prominent attempts at reform but also ensured their failure. For example, the Housewives' League gave up on the idea of a community farmers market because there would be no practical way to exclude immigrant shoppers and Italian peddlers.[73]

During one of the worst spikes in prices during March 1918, the workers of each major cigar factory sent two delegates to a meeting at the Central Trades and Labor Assembly temple to decide how to proceed. The five hundred in attendance voted to begin a boycott of potatoes and onions. Anyone familiar with Spanish and Cuban cuisine knows how kitchens must have suffered as a result.[74] Even when a shipment of Irish potatoes from Maine brought Tampa's housewives running, the immigrants suspected the cheap prices were only "bait" to disrupt the boycott. Storekeepers claimed to be selling them at a loss and some stores threatened to stop carrying them.[75]

Claiming that the warring nations in Europe enjoyed cheaper produce than the United States (when they could obtain it at all), a cigar worker wondered, "The governments of those countries saw that it was convenient to put into practice some of the socialist theories, and they have regulated the process and distribution of all commodities. They have done away with the middlemen. Why can't Uncle Sam do something like that here? Do we support our government for the benefit of the people or for the welfare of capital exclusively? Who rules in this great land of 'freedom and democracy,' our government or our capitalists?"[76]

In February 1919, a meeting was held to promote a cooperative store at the Labor Temple (1612 Eighth Avenue). A wintering Harvard professor of political economy and psychology, Professor Greenwood, said, "The co-operative stores are making a success of their mission wherever they are tried and placed in the hands of experienced merchandisers." A co-op store in Manatee had already enjoyed success. Tampa's number of co-ops grew from two in 1915 to twelve in 1919.[77]

At their peak in 1918–19, the cooperatives complained to the Board of Trade that retailers and wholesalers had unlawfully colluded against them. Some local wholesalers claimed they were pressured by the retailers not to do business with the co-ops. In time, only three remaining wholesalers dealt with the co-ops: Jose Franquiz, Jose Guerra, and A. Massari. Co-op membership stood at 1,298 with almost $70,000 in monthly business, or $750,000 per year. Apparently acting as their private counsel, Municipal Judge Tom Watson presented the grievances of the co-ops, which he described as "safe, sane, and businesslike." Watson described the behavior of Tampa's business establishment as forming "an illegal combine formed for the purpose of putting the co-operative stores out of business."[78]

Chairman James Bryan, a dry goods wholesaler himself, was intensely involved in the case. Board member J. Edgar Wall was a rare retailer who supported the co-ops, claiming that they would not put any retailers out of business. Wall said that he could not tell businessmen who to associate with but that the co-ops had the right to operate. Cigar manufacturers H. S. Foley and Enrique Pendas testified that the co-ops were good for the cigar workers and the industry as a whole. The Board of Trade appointed an ineffectual committee to look into the dispute.[79]

Tampa's concerned retailers then went much farther up the food chain to choke off the co-ops. A wholesaler who supplied the co-ops claimed he was "boycotted by the broker." According to wholesaler Jose Guerra, the saboteur was former food administrator and present member of the Merchants Association Hafford Jones. Guerra claimed, "Jones is now saying that the banks and brokers are not going to recognize wholesalers who sell to the co-operatives." After taking Guerra's large order of Quaker Oats products for the co-ops, the Bonacker Brothers brokerage refused to fill it. When Guerra contacted Quaker directly, they said they would not do any more business with him until "the matter is adjusted." Guerra showed a series of telegrams between the three parties, which the *Tribune* confirmed corroborated Guerra's story. Guerra planned to sue the brokers if needed, hoping Franquiz and Massari would join him.[80]

The remainder of 1919 was not kind to Guerra's business, which slid from more than $50,000 per month to less than $3,000 after being shunned by the larger business community. That fall, the County Food Board temporarily revoked Guerra's wholesale license for allegedly profiteering in sugar.[81]

Various boycotts persisted for several years, reaching their peak in the fall of 1919. Late in October, a committee of cigar workers declared a boycott against local stores, including dry goods, clothing, and shoes. The initial boycott would last ninety days in an effort to bring down prices, or at least to allow the market to correct itself. Workers passed out handbills with details of the plan and *lectores* read them in the factories. The shopkeepers responded that a ninety-day boycott would drive them out of business without changing prices. Merchants worried that the workers would rely on mail-order catalogs, draining money from the city. But leaders of the movement denied this, saying that they had enough clothes, shoes, and other products for ninety days. The *Tribune* was so opposed to the idea that it would not even print the word "boycott" after the initial report.[82]

Ybor's merchants formed their own committee to cope with the crisis. The merchants wanted to provide proof that they were not profiteering but merely charging prices dictated by the market. They invited the worker's committee to select any two businessmen or accountants in the country and offered to bring them to Tampa to report on the honesty of their businesses. A member of the worker's committee said, "We are not attempting to bring harm to Tampa. The retailers tell us that conditions are horrible, that they cannot get goods to sell us, that the demand is far ahead of the supply—and this is just the condition we are attempting to relieve." He considered such actions to be a "patriotic duty" to go without. When asked what would happen if prices did not dip, he replied, "Then we'll extend it another ninety days, maybe two years, until they do come down. We do not intend to make it a laboring man's movement. It should be taken up by the entire public."[83]

Early in November, the retail boycott commenced. The participating shipyard workers numbered two thousand alone with a payroll of $50,000 per week. The cigar workers earned $300,000. The *Tribune*'s editors were clearly upset by the boycott, writing about the perils of class warfare: "Since there has been no class consciousness in this country among the employers[,] that latter have not yet formed any great organization for the purpose of carrying on class warfare. Whether or not they will do so in the future undoubtedly will depend on the future attitude of organized labor." The editorial concluded with a plea to the state and federal government to ban strikes and lockouts. An accompanying editorial titled "Shame on the Boycotters" reminded workers that retailers had extended them credit, donated to their churches and associations, and provided employment outside the factories. The editor acknowledged the "condition of inter-dependence" between workers and merchants: "Neither can get along without the other. Suppose the merchants of Tampa should announce that they will not sell goods to a certain class of people except under conditions which that class declares impossible for them to meet. Those who have started this unholy thing at a time when mutual forbearance is needed have no right to expect the backing of the best element of Tampa, have no right to call themselves American citizens, and should be ashamed to meet the average patriotic man or woman even on the streets."[84] One could have pointed out that Tampa's segregated business community did indeed refuse to sell to a class of people.

The *Tribune* accused boycotters of being dishonorable and unpatriotic. The editor vented again the next day,

The only thing that can be accomplished by a "boycott" is to demoralize business as a whole, financially embarrass individuals, and add to the troubles of those who precipitate this "boycott." It is the most unfair method of attempting to correct a supposed wrong that can be devised. It gives absolutely no chance for defense. It is a dagger stuck in the back, a slugged "blackjack" hitting the back of the head from behind a tree in the dark. No considerable body of men ever yet joined in a "boycott" that did not repent it soon. Over that nation it is looked on with as much favor as we did the casting of "mustard gas" into the sleeping ranks of our boys in the trenches. No true-hearted American patriot will use the "boycott" as a weapon against defenselessness in the dark any sooner than he will sacrifice his honor to keep flying the red flag of disruption and ruin.[85]

Several days later, on November 8, the *Tribune* reported a "nationwide roundup of 'Reds,'" a thousand in all, after a series of raids across the nation, though no such action occurred in Tampa.[86]

THE STRIKE OF 1920

After the inflation of the war years with no increase in wages, Tampa's cigar workers found it difficult to survive. Their co-ops functioned well but had been sabotaged by jealous retailers. A recent federal commission estimated the average worker would need $100 per month to live. The wages for cigar workers averaged only $60 monthly. A strike seemed imminent in 1920, so after the end of the winter rush on cigar orders, the manufacturers staged a preemptive lockout. This triggered a strike by the Cigar Makers' International Union, which demanded a "closed" union-only shop in April. More than 7,600 union workers left their jobs. Another 3,500 jobs servicing the cigar workers disappeared for the duration of the strike. At the beginning of July, union coffers stood at $60,000 swelled by outside contributions. Union members in Chicago, Hartford, Denver, San Francisco, Boston, New York, St. Louis, Cincinnati, and Philadelphia all participated in a "Tampa Day" to donate their wages to striking workers.[87]

The strike dragged on for months with no result except violence and anger. As usual, the soup houses served as the backbone of the union's efforts. The *Tribune* complained, "over-paid and corn-fed agitators are gloating over the fact that they intend to absolutely annihilate the cigar industry in this city."[88] Labor-based newspaper *El International* wrote, "The gentlemen who compose this union-busting association have never suffered the pangs of hunger—champagne and caviar have always been at their service when thirst or hunger threatened—and they don't know the anarchist-breeding effect of hunger on the victim. Even with the twin methods of starvation and falsehood the manufacturers seem to be playing a losing game."[89] The manufacturers didn't think it was a losing game. Union member Domingo Cuesta discussed the opening of a makeshift union-funded "restaurant" and the predictable reaction by police: "All the cigar workers on strike were fed here. However, the manufacturers made some combination with the authorities. One day policemen came to this place, destroying everything they could lay their hands on. The food, already cooked, and all the groceries were thrown out onto the street."[90]

The destruction of the commissary dealt the union a deadly blow. The notorious Citizens' Committee personally visited the homes of strikers, warning them to leave town. They vowed that union men "would be found decorating trees and telephone poles," strung up by nooses. The committee clearly wanted strikers to remember its two lynching victims from the strike ten years before.[91]

Before long, even the most motivated strikers began to cave in. One confessed to the newspapers, "I have never had a part in breaking a strike until now and I am forced to work because my seven children need food and clothing." Hysterical union leaders refused to back down. In a manifesto issued by the Strike Advisory Board, the young men of Ybor City were ordered to work in the phosphate mines, where several had already died in accidents, and the old men to "shoot their brains out if they could not get food." After enduring a month without union benefits, workers had practically formed a fishing colony to feed their families.[92]

Only four thousand of Tampa's ten thousand cigar workers remained in the city, most flocking to Cuba or New York in search of work. The workers panicked as Christmas approached. One such desperate man was Jake Menendez, who became a scab so he could eat. Angry striker El Pescador ("The Fisherman") Flores shot Menendez in a café on Twelfth Avenue and Eighteenth Street and then fled to Jacksonville.[93]

After ten grueling months, the strike ended in February 1921 with $12 million in wages lost. The strike of 1920 exhausted the cigar workers, their

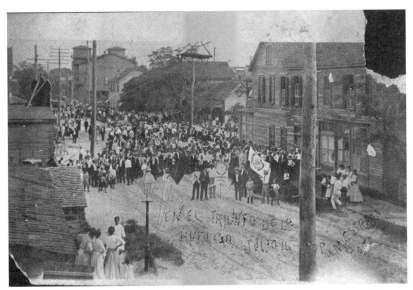

After six months of striking in 1920, workers meet at the Centro Asturiano theater. (Tony Pizzo collection, University of South Florida Tampa Special Collections)

unions, and several factories before they admitted defeat. The union paid out $1 million to members without attaining its goal of recognition and a workplace closed to other unions. The only thing they won was the opportunity for workers to earn the same paltry wages as a decade before, and those had been severely undermined by inflation.[94]

That year, when hungry workers heard of a factory nicknamed Arroz con Pollo (Chicken and Yellow Rice), it must have been music to their ears. Laureano Torres at the E. Regensberg & Sons factory enjoyed supposed worldwide fame "as a master of the art of blending tobacco as well as arroz con pollo." Such a meal must have seemed like the good life to hungry strikers.[95]

The Russian Revolution and civil war sent shockwaves through American culture. The Red Scare made many Americans fearful of any communal enterprise, political or economic. During the 1920s, cooperative marketing by livestock and produce growers flourished, but the idea of cooperative consumerism was seen as a threat to capitalism. For the invisible hand of the market to function, consumers apparently had to remain powerless and divided.

In 1929, the workforce of Tampa's cigar industry peaked, with factories employing thirteen thousand workers and producing 500 million cigars annually. But the cigar industry's painful decline had already begun, made worse by the Great Depression, mechanized production, and increasing preference for cheap cigarettes. Workers went on strike that year for more wages.

During the strike, a "scab" named Manuel Cabrera brought sandwiches back home from a nearby restaurant. A block from his destination, a familiar man approached, drew a pistol, and shot Cabrera dead. Uneaten sandwiches lay scattered in the street.

Joe Lopez was a zealous striker. With his gun still warm, Lopez walked into Cabrera's home, where he rented a room with his girlfriend Clara Thomas. Lopez confessed to Ms. Thomas that he had gunned down their landlord for breaking the strike. The lovers argued, and an emotional Lopez left the house in a hurry. Upset by the incident, Ms. Thomas fled to a neighbor's house.

Lopez burst into Pedro Arez's café looking crazed and worried. In a state of extreme excitement and despair, Lopez stammered to his friend behind the counter, unable to find words fast enough. In an attempt to calm him, Arez asked Lopez if he had been drinking, which he denied. Trying to think of some worthwhile advice, Arez suggested that his haunted friend lie down and relax.

Instead, he rushed to see Clara. He was afraid she might call the police about Cabrera's murder. When he knocked on the neighbor's door, she refused to see him. So Lopez quietly snuck into the house through the back door.

A series of gunshots broke the silence in the dwelling. Police found a gruesome scene. Lopez blew off Clara's head with four .45 caliber bullets while she lay in bed. In a fashion, Lopez followed his friend's advice to lie down. Police found him on the floor beside the bed with a self-inflicted gunshot to his tormented heart.[96]

Like Cabrera, Lopez, and Thomas, the relationship between labor and capital ended badly in Ybor City. In the decades after the unions broke, the factories themselves followed suit. In the early 1930s, young residents moved away to find work. Machines soon dominated cigar production and debased Tampa's reputation for fine hand-rolled cigars. Riddled with termites, the old Ybor company housing faced mass demolition. The emptying cigar factories loomed over the remnants of Ybor City like disapproving sentinels. Over the following decades, city fathers watched the factories close with regret—and saw the unions dissolve with relief. The cigar industry in Tampa was destined to be a tenuous, contested, and ephemeral creation. Tampa would never fully recover from the loss.[97]

WAR, FEAR, AND BREAD
DURING WORLD WAR I

In early February 1917, two months before the United States entered World War I, local authorities in Tampa, Florida, required German aliens over age thirteen to register with the federal government. That month, the city's German American Club entered an extravagant float in the city's annual Gasparilla Fiesta parade. The float, one of only six that year, depicted a mighty waterfall. The Great War cast a long and dark shadow, unleashing a flood of fierce nationalism and suspicion across the U.S. home front. The conflict gave a new focus and urgency to anti-immigration fears across the nation, and the presence of so many influential German Americans in society took on sinister implications. The presence of the previously popular German American Club became an irritant to many of Tampa's most ardent patriots. Even German music allegedly became a tool of sabotage and sedition.[1]

On April 6, 1917, the United States declared war on Germany and the Central Powers. War offered potential benefits to the upstart city, namely, an influx of federal money. Ernest Kreher, president of the newly formed Tampa Shipbuilding and Engineering Company, traveled to Washington to gauge the availability of government contracts. He returned promising welcome news for "Tampa's newest industry." Instead of being lauded as a captain of industry, Kreher and his family found themselves embattled with the public because of his Germanic roots.[2]

For about a century, the United States had accepted wave after wave of new immigrants. But between the 1890s and 1917, new anxieties surfaced, provoking a trend of nativism, Prohibition, and immigration restrictions. Suddenly, Germans and Germany became touchstones on issues from bread to beer to books. The *Tampa Tribune* opined in the days leading up to the U.S. declaration of war, "They are either Americans or Germans. There is no middle-ground. . . . In Tampa, we believe that anti-American ones and even the lukewarm-American ones, can be counted on the fingers of two hands. . . . We have no fear of the great majority of German-born in the event we get into war with Germany." This sentiment waned quickly, however, and the people and newspapers of Tampa had convinced themselves that there was plenty to fear and question about their neighbors of German extraction. Cloak-and-dagger rumors of German spies abounded in Tampa but led nowhere.[3]

Paranoia about Germans came and went in acute spasms of fear, but special resentment was reserved for suspected profiteers. Most of Tampa's anxiety was focused on more mundane matters, namely, the price and quality of staple foods. Perhaps no other food was scrutinized more than bread: its price, purity, and provenance. Throughout 1917 and 1918, City Council issued a flood of ordinances tightly regulating bread in an effort to placate Tampa's angry housewives. Frank Allen was Tampa's most successful baker, but wildly fluctuating prices and the wrath of the public made the war especially difficult for him. For the next two years, Tampa's chief vexations focused upon bread, Germans, or both.

This essay seeks to examine wartime anxiety in Tampa during World War I, a chapter of the city's history that has been only cursorily studied by historians. Moreover, the material covered here is not of the kind kept alive by patriotic societies and military enthusiasts. The historiography of the war has changed radically in the last century, and the home front of the United States has been broadly reinterpreted in the recent years. Writers immediately after the war characterized the home front as fraught with German sympathizers and spies, justifying the violent actions taken by vigilantes. A few courageous writers at the time opposed this view, but it would take several decades before historians reached a new consensus that vigilantism posed a bigger threat to America's freedoms than the Germans ever did. Scholars specializing in ethnic studies have supplied new works about German Americans and their place in American society before, during, and after World War I. There are some invaluable lessons buried in this chapter of U.S. history about the tensions and paranoia often prevalent in the homeland of the United States, where the line between vigilance and oppression is a thin one.[4]

BECOMING A WARTIME BAKERY

Pioneer baker Frank H. Allen was born in Georgia in 1870 and settled in Tampa at the age of twenty-one. He oscillated between owning a bakery and a grocery for the next two decades.[5] He fought a court battle in 1915 to trademark "Allen's Butter Crust Bread." By 1917, Allen's bakery had climbed to the top, overtaking its greatest rival, Tampa Steam Bakery.[6]

Allen's business emerged during a transformative era. In the second decade of the twentieth century, commercial bread became a national obsession as production shifted from a special comfort of home to a manufactured necessity for most Americans. As the population shifted from agriculture production to wage-earning jobs and as families moved to crowded urban areas in the early twentieth century, fewer working-class women had the time or resources to bake fresh bread on a regular basis. For centuries, small bakeries supplied limited amounts of fresh bread to the market. By 1920, much of the bread consumed by Americans was made on an industrial scale for a mass market, and commercially produced bread was more widely available than ever before. Fluctuations in food prices jeopardized the availability and affordability of bread, provoking an emotional response from the public. Between 1910 and 1920, the prices for flour, bacon, butter, and eggs more than doubled, and white sugar and steak tripled in price. The cost of potatoes rose fourfold. As war broke out in Europe, Americans read about starving Belgians even as their own food costs escalated.[7]

The food industry and consumers were at odds over prices, with retailers such as Allen's bakery stuck in the middle trying to eke out a living.[8] Frustrated consumers responded to climbing prices with boycotts, cooperatives, and activism. By 1917, many of Tampa's most influential women had formed a local chapter of the National Housewives' League, a group of consumer activists first organized in New York City by Jennie Dewey

Heath. The tough economic times and Heath's aggressive campaigning drew a half million members by 1913. The league focused on several issues: unsanitary stores and markets, impure food, false weights and measures, and price gouging. The Tampa Housewives' League immediately became a strong political force and put fear into the hearts of the city's grocers and bakers.[9]

Tampa's bakers had been panicked since the war began overseas in August 1914, when flour prices shot up. At the time, Allen admitted, "I don't know what we will do. At the rate we are now paying for flour, bakers will be bankrupt very shortly." Allen's Bakery may have felt the pinch, but so did its competitors. Smaller bakeries were forced to reduce the size of their loaves. For most bakers, the size of their loaves fluctuated with the wholesale price of flour. Manipulating the weight attracted less attention than changing prices did.[10]

At public meetings of the league, consumers aired their grievances and Allen served as spokesman for the bakers. Outraged housewives brought in rolls infested with cockroach nests that they had obtained at a local bakery and were served by public schools. Jennie Sauls, president of the Housewives' League, claimed that Allen's bread was frequently inconsistent in weight. The housewives demanded that every loaf have a wrapper stamped with the date of production. Allen explained this would likely drive up the price by as much as a penny per loaf. He emphasized wartime labor scarcity, noting that he had been forced to hire black labor for wages that would have been unthinkable before the war.[11]

Consumers became so sensitive to rising and falling prices that the newspapers regularly printed lists of food prices (wholesale and retail) offered by the Hillsborough County Food Board, one of four thousand such groups formed by states to regulate the production, sale, and conservation of food during the war.[12] Late in 1916, the *Tribune* reported that most loaves were under standard weight, prompting another tense meeting with the bakers. As the newspaper reported, "The irate housewives did not stop at questions of dollars and cents but went so far as to demand an explanation for such tactics as have led up to the present small loaf, which has been approached gradually and without announcement, in fact leading the consumers to believe they were still getting their twenty-four ounces of bread." Although bread received the most attention in the press and from the public, other food industries regularly manipulated prices and the size/weight of products to adjust to fluctuating commodity costs.[13]

In Tampa, 1917 was the year of the bread ordinance. Concerned that local oversight of bakeries would cease, allowing merchants to gouge customers, consumers worried that they could face food shortages as easily as Europeans did. For most of the year, the City Council, the bakers, and the Housewives' League wrangled over labels and weight, none of which made bread any more affordable. The city seemed eager to appease the Housewives' League and minimized the concerns of the bakers. A month after the United States joined hostilities, City Council voted to suspend all recent ordinances, which had not yet been enforced, involving bread weight and composition so they could be renegotiated with bakers and the Housewives' League. For Allen, the torturous process of defending Tampa's bakers began yet again.[14] Sauls of the league confessed to the *Tribune*, "The bread situation has reached a crisis. We find only one baker in town able to talk for the rest of them. At our recent meeting Mr. Allen said plainly they would not give in one inch."[15]

In May 1917, city food regulators arrested five Tampa bakers (beginning with Allen) when they refused to stamp the weight on their bread as ordered in a new ordinance recently passed by City Council. "The arrest of the five bakers is the latest step in the fight on the part of the public and housewives of Tampa to regulate the weight of the loaf sold, and to secure some measure of relief from what is considered a very unsatisfactory local bread situation," the *Tribune* explained. Allen charged that the bread-labeling ordinance might put Tampa's bakeries out of business, as their profit margins were so thin and the Housewives' League howled every time bakers passed on their expenses to consumers. He warned that bakers would be forced to raise prices to supply the loaves of accustomed size.[16]

TAMPA'S GERMAN CLUB

The German American Club's status immediately came into question when the United States joined the war. The club had been popular with non-Germans, but those cordial relations cooled quickly.

Tampa's Deutsch-Americkanscher Verein, or German American Club, was formed in 1901 to celebrate German culture and provide opportunities for socializing and mutual aid. Its forty influential founders elected former four-time Tampa mayor Herman Glogowski (1886–1887, 1888–1889, 1890–1891) president. It should be noted that Glogowski was born in Germany but also identified as Jewish, as did other fellow founders.

In 1909, the club opened a beautiful three-story clubhouse. The city's political and commercial elite attended a lavish New Year's Day dinner honoring the German ambassador, who came as a special guest. An "expert mixologist" from the North German Lloyd Steamship Line manned the bar. The club seemed especially welcoming to non-Germans, and by 1912, the members' roster included more than one thousand men in a city of about thirty-nine thousand residents. Indeed, Tampa's German immigrants were considered a model group at the time: industrious, literate, patriotic, and white.

When the United States joined the war on April 6, 1917, the German club reacted by offering its building to the Red Cross as a hospital. A similar club in Jacksonville had done the same thing in an attempt to avoid wartime tensions by demonstrating loyalty to the U.S. war effort. Within days, classes on nursing techniques had already begun in the building. Card parties held at the club turned all jackpots over to the Red Cross instead of issuing prizes to winners, but otherwise activities seemed to proceed normally.[17]

Despite these good-faith efforts, all things "German" quickly fell into disfavor in Tampa as elsewhere. *The Plant City Courier* wrote, "Tampa has helped in the war by the complete capture and subjugation of the German Club over which old Glory waves triumphantly and continually." But the subjugation was by no means complete. One of the final bastions of German culture to come under attack was music. German bands and conductors fell out of favor during the war years. The *Nation* warned, "German music, as a whole, is dangerous . . . a combination of the howl of the cave man and the roaring of the north winds."[18]

The club's affiliation with the Red Cross did not disrupt its more routine functions such as weekly dances and the annual May Ball, which continued as normal in 1917 with a radically altered musical menu. Gone were any trace of Bach, Beethoven, Wagner, and Liszt. The dance opened with the one-step "All America," proceeded with other songs such as "It's Time for Every Boy to Be a Soldier," and concluded with "Let's All Be Americans" and "Home Sweet Home." No strains of German music would be played.[19]

No one was safe from anti-American accusations. A maestro about town, German-born bandleader Charles A. Heidt had lived in Tampa for thirty years and at the time was Tampa's best-known musician. In 1917, he led the German Club's house band and Tampa's municipal band. "Die Wacht am Rhein" (The Watch on the Rhine) was a popular old German martial air. During a routine party at the German Club, in the midst of a charming medley, Heidt's band played the strains of the patriotic German song.[20]

Police Captain James McCants heard the offending song from the street, beautifully rendered by Heidt's distinguished orchestra. To officer McCants, it seemed unthinkable that an American of any origin should play such a song. McCants believed it was against the law to issue any speech aiding the enemy cause, and he apparently viewed German music as enemy propaganda. The officer threatened to arrest Heidt for the offense. Just playing the notes represented "a violation of the law during wartime," the officer insisted.[21]

Heidt reportedly replied that he would play what he pleased. The leadership of the club reacted in a similar fashion, initially dismissing the charges. McCants was surprised to find that "the attitude . . . of several Germans in the room was rather truculent," and he admitted "that for a few moments he thought there was going to be trouble." Heidt later explained that he had forgotten the song was a part of the medley played that night, but McCants and others concluded it was a deliberate act of sabotage.[22]

When asked by city officials if he was aware that playing the national anthem of a warring nation was against the law, club president George Stecher said, "There is no law against playing music." (In any case, the song in question was not the German national anthem.) But under pressure from public officials, the club's trustees fired the orchestra and agreed not to play or sing any German songs for the duration of the war. Judge W. Alonzo Carter, who had once been a member, suggested the club officers change its name altogether or resign to allow others to do so.[23]

Some citizens thought there were more deserving objects for public investigation. Harry Howard asked in a letter to the *Tribune*, "Why Charles Heidt's band has been expelled from the German Club because he thoughtlessly played a part of a Germanic air? I will admit it was in poor taste, but no great harm was done. But what about that councilman who is said to have offered his services to a baker for $900? Is there any expulsion for a grafter? Consistency, thou art a jewel."[24] For one citizen, bread prices seemed more alarming than old German songs.

Vigilance against Germans and their songs only increased. That fall, the Florida Federation of Women's Clubs met at the Tampa Bay Casino, combining a suffrage convention with social and political events. The overture planned for the opening ceremonies was protested by the membership when it appeared in the program. Von Weber's "Der Freischütz" was slated to be performed by the Friday Morning Musicale Orchestra, conducted by Hulda Kreher. Women offended by the planned performance of the song wired their protests from Miami, reading in part, "German music has no place on a program where food conservation, Y.M.C.A. war work, Red Cross work and war relief work of all sorts for the American soldiers in the trenches are discussed."[25]

Not everyone agreed with Captain McCant's interpretation of the law. After several members protested the appearance of German music and language in the program, the performance was cancelled. President W. S. Jennings of the Federation said, "I thought the president made it very plain that we were at war with the German autocracy and not with the German people. Therefore, why we should discard music that has been standard and accepted as such merely because it was written by a composer with whose country we later went to war?" The musical selection was probably that of conductor Hulda Kreher, a classically trained violinist and sister to Paul and Ernest Kreher of Tampa Shipbuilding and Engineering Company. This incident blew over, but the hostile home front was not finished with the Kreher family.[26]

After the United States joined World War I in 1917, the local German American Club allowed the Red Cross to conduct wound-dressing classes in the facility. (U.S. Archives)

Liberty Bonds

In January, Tampa Shipbuilding and Engineering Company (hereafter referred to as Tampa Shipbuilding) President Ernest Kreher caught the imagination of Tampa when he made inquiries to officials in Washington about government contracts. Weeks before, Kreher had become president of the newly organized company and absorbed the Tampa Foundry and Machine Company in the process. Kreher's forty-acre site on the estuary served as home for the company, which would add shipbuilding to its existing services. The company's other site was located on the Hillsborough River. The other officers in the company included prominent attorney Peter O. Knight as vice president, cigar manufacturer Angel Cuesta, Tampa Gas Company President Frank Bruen, and other well-known Tampa businessmen.[27]

Born in Kimmitz, Germany, in 1874, Ernest Kreher crossed the Atlantic after completing his engineering apprenticeship, arriving in New York at the age of sixteen. By 1893, Ernest had relocated to Tampa and found work as a ship repairman at the port. During the Spanish-American War, he and his crew reportedly worked five days straight with minimal time for naps. At the end of the marathon shift, Ernest's boots had to be cut off his swollen feet. He later moved to the Krause and Wagner machine shop, located on the Hillsborough River between Platt and Lafayette (now Kennedy Boulevard), eventually buying the business and renaming it the Tampa Foundry and Machine Works. Kreher's latest company, Tampa Shipbuilding, combined the river facilities with those on the estuary.[28]

The first order came quickly: two 8,500-ton freighters. The company embarked on a crash course to upgrade its capabilities in time to fully exploit the demands of war. Kreher fretted about the labor shortage, wondering how he would be able to recruit the one thousand men needed to complete the work. In the meantime, crews rushed the construction of the steamship *Poughkeepsie* to make way for wartime vessels.[29]

In June 1916, several distinguished members of the original downtown Rotary Club's Liberty Loan committee made the rounds among Tampa's well-heeled businessmen to raise money for the war. When the men visited Tampa Shipbuilding and solicited subscriptions for the Liberty Loan, Ernest Kreher erupted.

Kreher reportedly said:

> I left my country [Germany] to evade military service, being opposed to militarism. I did this legally, as I left the country before I was of age. I swore allegiance to this country. I will not subscribe to the liberty loan to assist in starving those who are dear to me. It is not a question of my ability to subscribe; but the point that offends me is, to ask me to subscribe to a loan to assist in starving my own people. It is not necessary to further discuss this matter, as I state positively that I will not. You can cut my head off, but that is all you can do, as I will not subscribe.[30]

Kreher must have been agitated and distracted as he responded to the request for bond subscription, because he seemed oblivious to the fact that one of his visitors was Wallace F. Stovall, the influential publisher of the *Tampa Morning Tribune*, who took note of his every utterance. The *Tribune* noted, "He was emphatic in his refusal, and the story of his attitude and his expressions, spreading over the downtown section, was the subject of discussion by animated groups on the streets last night."[31] The committee members duly reported the incident to U.S. District Attorney Herbert Phillips, but it was not a crime to refrain from buying war bonds, a patriotic act that was intended to be voluntary.[32]

The publisher of the *Tampa Daily Times*, D. B. McKay, who also happened to be mayor, could not help but weigh in: "This paper has always respected Mr. Kreher as a man and developer, and it appreciated the fact that he naturally has a feeling of sympathy for the people of his native land, but as he has long claimed the rights of American citizenship, and has prospered under those rights, he should be an American in fact as well as name. When one claims to be an American one must be an American, heart and soul."[33] In the wake of the episode, Kreher asked to retract his comments to the Rotary Club. When he offered to buy a Liberty Bond from the Rotary committee, they declined to sell him one. Instead, Tampa Shipbuilding bought $5,000 worth of bonds as a company. Claiming the rigors of being the president and general manager of Tampa Shipbuilding were too great for one man, Kreher resigned as president but kept his role as manager. The Kreher brothers—Ernest and the elder Paul—were the largest stockholders in the company.[34]

Immediately after the comments were reported, all three hundred of the company's workers went on strike, both to protest Kreher's sentiments and to demand a (nickel) raise and fewer working hours (nine-hour shifts). Workers had used the lull in work to better organize their union. After meeting with striking workers in conferences, the new president of Tampa Shipbuilding, L. H. McIntire, agreed to grant them a five-cent raise.[35]

In September, Kreher revealed that the company had eight berths with plans to complete a new dry dock. Other locals formed Tampa Dock Company in search of more government largesse to build wooden ships. A representative from the United States Shipping Board visited the facilities in July, noting with approval that ten ships could be produced simultaneously in Tampa. In September, the shipping board took charge of the

Tampa Shipbuilding and Engineering Company's facilities as it did with shipyards across the country, favoring the construction of smaller 3,500-ton vessels. The site also produced prefabricated housing to be used behind the front. That fall, the company's facilities were leased to the Oscar Daniels Company, who had a large contract to build ten vessels. Tampa's new shipbuilding industry prospered, thanks in large part to Ernest Kreher, the German pacifist.[36]

Tragedy in the Bay

Tampa Shipbuilding used its steel launch to shuttle men to and from work, but government regulators found that the launch was being overloaded. The workers, who were eager to return home, rushed to catch the first trip away from the facility rather than waiting for the launch to return. Federal inspectors suggested the company use smaller boats that were not subject to regulation. The company constructed two "flimsy flatbottomed skiffs" to shuttle its workers. The vessels were powered with a single, large rear-mounted oar.[37]

About one hundred and fifty workers depended upon these small boats to get to work every day. Because it was often the quickest way back into the city, workers tended to crowd the boats at quitting time, ignoring the more stable steel launch. The foreman of the estuary plant had a thankless job at the end of each shift. Every day, he chided the men not to overwhelm the boats, but it was always a struggle to get some to wait for the next ride. The discipline of the workers disappeared after their shift ended.[38]

Chief Deputy Sheriff A. C. Logan watched Tampa Shipbuilding employees leaving work in January 1918. Day after day, the workers piled into the small boats until they had room only to stand. Logan predicted the workers would go too far one day and capsize. A week later, the workers piled in as normal. Twenty workers crammed into one of the boats, forcing the occupants to stand. The foreman warned those in the boat that it was overloaded, but all were in a hurry to get back to town before the darkening sky opened up. An occupant on the boat yanked the boat's chain out of the foreman's hand and the vessel was free from the dock.

Just as it shoved off, another man jumped in, and some witnesses later said that the boat was taking on water before it even launched. At least sixteen men piled into the other boat, and the skiffs started their slow crawl across the Ybor Channel. None of the passengers thought it unusual that the boats were loaded within an inch of the waterline, because it was typical practice at the time.

The wake caused by the company's passing steel launch was enough to overwhelm the two boats. Many of the workers, over half of them black, did not know how to swim. In their panic, workers grappled with one another in an effort to stay afloat. Some men swam ashore, while others calmly held on to the submerged skiffs and awaited rescue. The shipyard closed while crews dragged the channel for corpses. Since the tide was going out at the time, some of the bodies flowed out of the channel into the bay. Of the approximately thirty-eight men on the boats that day, seventeen died.

The public furiously sought a scapegoat for the tragedy. Blaming the workers for their haste was unthinkable. The steel launch pilot was never pursued as a culprit. Instead, Tampa Shipbuilding and Engineering was blamed for not regulating its rowboats more carefully. Once again, the name Kreher dominated public discussions and press coverage. As additional bodies were found, Ernest and a young worker went out in a boat to collect them. Rather than eliciting support for the beleaguered industrialist, his act of compassion or contrition only goaded Tampa's patriot warriors.

The press and some members of the public called for the Kreher brothers to be expelled from their own shipyards. The year before, President Wilson issued an order barring all foreign citizens from war labor. After the drownings, U.S. District Attorney Herbert Phillips and a federal marshal scrutinized the company's employees and barred seven noncitizens from work at the shipyards, including Paul Kreher, Ernest's elder brother.[39]

Two weeks later, tempers flared when Paul Kreher was reinstated in his position. Some whispered that he regained his employment largely due to his reported $16,000 stake in the company. This seemed to be an exception to President Wilson's order excluding enemy aliens from war work. When the people of Tampa heard of this decision, an unsettling wave of grumbling began. Some people wanted an example made of Kreher, not an exception.[40]

As public anger swelled, so did paranoia. Some directly questioned the loyalty of the U.S. district attorney and the marshal. District Attorney Phillips responded to critics that Kreher could be banned only from the foundry plant, not the estuary plant, because of the differing nature of the work done at those locations. He also added that the newspapers, especially Mayor McKay's *Tampa Daily Times*, had misinterpreted President Wilson's order. The explanation did nothing to satisfy Tampa's patriot warriors. In fact, it seemed to stir Mayor McKay into action.[41]

McKay seemed to jump at the opportunity for the public spectacle the situation afforded. The mayor held a town meeting in the courthouse, where an angry crowd aired a list of grievances. The assembly bristled with anger and denunciations at the outset. The public event was not a legal trial but a local response to a perceived federal injustice. Sore feelings against the federal government lingered in many of Tampa's oldest families going back to the Civil War and Reconstruction. Since then, Tampa's most influential families had also discovered the riches to be extracted from Washington. Fort Brooke had provided Tampa's original inhabitants with free security, and a flood of riches came in 1898 during the Spanish-American War. But in times of trouble or unrest, Tampa's citizens had always formed citizen committees to enforce the will of local elites. As early as the days of Reconstruction, vigilante riders defied federal mandates to protect the recently freed slaves and enforced a brand of frontier justice tinged with racism. Since the immigrants' arrival in 1886, squads of armed vigilantes were routinely brought to bear against striking immigrant workers. These brutal "committees" formed to enforce justice when more legitimate means might fail.[42]

Mayor McKay declared the meeting open and called upon the crowded courtroom to nominate a chairman. Hearing his own name, he quickly accepted and proceeded to the matter at hand. Attendees demanded answers, but no federal representative had been invited to explain the government's position. Instead, frustration built as the public repeatedly shouted accusations to the sole target of all their angst, Ernest Kreher. They asked why Paul Kreher was allowed to remain employed in the company, especially because he was not a naturalized citizen. Others accused Ernest of defying the wishes of government inspectors and wondered why the nation's flag did not fly over the shipyard. The indignant throng blamed Kreher for the drownings of the workers in the accident the previous month.

Mayor McKay conceded that the federal officials had the legal right to make their decision, but they had no "moral right" to reinstate Kreher. This pleased the crowd and seemed to sum up their unfocused sentiments. Having found fault with the response of federal officials in enforcing the president's wishes, McKay and his fellow citizens essentially appointed themselves to the job and took satisfaction in their duty. "There has been a devious trail between this city and Washington," one man said, "and Wilson and the men behind him don't know the facts."[43]

An incensed attendee took the stand to speak of Paul Kreher: "I know Paul Kreher personally. His is my very nearest neighbor but he hasn't done me the honor of greeting me or speaking to me in more than a year. I know the individual and the government from which he came, his intuitions and his inclinations, and I say, to have him engaged in our commerce is dangerous for our people." Another man said, "If Mr. Kreher has a right to return he is unfortunate in accepting that right." Others shouted that the Rotary Club should come forward to once again discuss Kreher's reaction to the solicitation of Liberty Bonds the previous June as long as Ernest was present. Some called for Peter O. Knight, the company's attorney, to be run out of town.

Mayor McKay cautioned against wild accusations and unsubstantiated rumors but then admitted that he had a rumor of his own to share. The mayor repeated the question he'd supposedly overheard among shipyard employees: Why didn't the U.S. flag fly above the worksite? When Ernest Kreher asked for permission to explain his reasoning, McKay ignored his pleas and continued with his story, which concluded with the news that workers had pitched in for a flag but that Kreher simply kept it folded in his desk instead of flying it. McKay then allowed Kreher to have the floor. The embattled engineer pled that although he had a large flag, there was not yet a pole to fly it from, but the crowd was in no mood to listen and booed him off the floor.

Another man connected German Americans with rumors of food sabotage. He repeated a rumor he had heard that a German cook had been sent to Camp Wheeler (in Macon, Georgia) along with Tampa's first recruits last fall. This cook had been discharged from the military after his unit accused him of putting ground glass in their food. When the cook returned to Tampa, he allegedly headed straight to Ernest Kreher's home. "It may not have anything to do with this but it shows you that they will stick together," the man said. "There are only two roads, one to Washington and one to Berlin, and we can tell by the way they walk which road they are on. From now on when I hear them on Berlin road, they've got me to answer to." Another man pointed to larger conspiracies, saying he had heard a man denounce the president and wish every American doughboy death in France. The man supposedly reported what he heard, but then the would-be spy left for Newport News. Days later, there was a great "calamity" there, he said, without specifying what it was. Many impressionable Americans were convinced that German agents were burning factories and sabotaging the war effort with impunity.[44]

Supervised by Mayor McKay, the attendees of the meeting passed a resolution to ban all un-naturalized citizens from defense work. They tried to pass a resolution in which the local government would call for the removal of the U.S. attorney and the marshal who allowed Paul Kreher to be reinstated, although not all supported this step, and it was shelved. James A. Griffin, an officer of the Exchange National Bank, was appalled by the proceedings, and over the shouts and stomping of his fellow citizens, he expressed disappointed surprise that Mayor McKay would preside over such a disorderly meeting and that the people of Tampa would so quickly question the loyalty of federal officials. "It seems amazing that the mayor of your city here [is] trying to pull down others in authority." The hoots and boos rose as Griffin said that he for one would trust the president and the federal government. Some in the crowd began throwing things at Griffin.[45]

Then McKay circled back to Ernest Kreher, grilling him as to why Paul was not a naturalized American citizen. Kreher explained that Paul had filled out the papers twenty years ago but lost them. He had applied six years before, but the war stopped the paperwork just about the time it should have gone through. This explanation satisfied no one. At this, the meeting broke up after all vowed that they would return to any similar meetings the mayor called.

Public pressure mounted for Kreher and all German workers to be banned from the facility, but federal officials did not budge. Kreher finally agreed to withdraw his services to Tampa Shipbuilding and to stay off the company's property "to satisfy public opinion." His brother Paul was similarly run out of the company. Ernest, his brother Paul, and his sister Hulda remained the dominant stockholders.[46]

Some citizens were relieved that McKay's moment of demagoguery had passed, sensing how closely the town hall meeting resembled a lawless citizens committee. The *Tribune* wrote, "This city came perilously near making a sorry spectacle of itself in the eyes of even itself[.] Tampa, with all her patriotic fire and enthusiasm, will preserve her poise, keep her balance, and never allow her 'Hotspurs' to lead her into disgraceful action, or regrettable deed." This episode proves that Tampa had still not abandoned its impulse toward vigilantism, but there were also modest signs of progress. No one had been beaten or killed in the same city that saw two Italians lynched by a "Citizens Committee" during a strike in 1910. The incidents in Tampa were not isolated to Florida or the Deep South but were similar to the convulsions of paranoia in communities all over the nation. A common thread running through most of the recent scholarship is the destructive tendencies of patriotism and vigilance on the home front, and the episodes in Tampa described above confirm these conclusions.[47]

THE GLASS SCARE

While much of Europe went hungry, Americans bickered about wheat substitutes. By 1918, Tampa's supply of flour ran so low that only a few weeks of bakery operations could be projected. Tampa's bakers began to use wheat substitutes, with corn meal or rye flour comprising 10 to 12 percent of the "wheat" bread. Hillsborough County Food Administrator Hafford Jones announced, "I do not wish to unduly alarm anyone, but the situation is that there is only enough flour in Tampa to last about forty-five days, and the outlook is that unless extreme economy is practiced there will be a period of about twenty days when Tampa will have no flour. . . . Substitutes of all kinds must be used."[48]

The situation became so dire that Allen called for a meeting of Tampa's bakers at the Bay View Hotel to review the impasse. The "American" bakers collectively decided to focus upon three loaves, "American-French bread, rye bread and mother's bread."[49] They also agreed to suspend the production of rolls and buns, which tended to be more wasteful. Tampa's "Latin" bakers restricted themselves to one type of "Italian" loaf and one kind of "Spanish" loaf, which was probably Cuban-style bread, as it was already universally popular in Tampa. Several bakers refused to phase out pastry and cookie production, arguing that such a drastic measure would put them out of business.[50]

Despite the difficulties of the day, Allen's aggressive business instincts told him to expand. In January 1918, the ambitious baker bought a full-page ad on the front page of the *Tampa Tribune* inviting the public to tour his new bakery at the corner of Pierce and Polk Streets. Offering refreshments, an orchestra, and a singer, the grand reopening of Allen's Bakery was a major event in Tampa. Unlike other bakeries in the city, Allen had built a state-of-the-art automated facility the likes of which had never been seen locally.[51]

"Baking today," Allen's ad read, "in a few of the most modern plants such as Allen's, is one food industry that is free from human contact and bread is perhaps the most absolutely sanitary product. Allen's Butter Crust Bread is not touched by human hands from the time the flour is dumped into the first bin until the finished product is opened in the home." Allen's ad also described the entire production process, down to his final flourish, when the loaves were "run through an automatic wrapping machine which covers and seals 1,800 loaves an hour." For a public increasingly concerned with cleanliness and purity, the presence of a bakery that was entirely automated and free of human contact seemed thoroughly modern. Allen trademarked the name "Big Butter Crust Bread," and the people of Tampa loved his soft machine-made loaves. By 1918, Allen was selling half the bread purchased in Tampa. His delivery squadron expanded from one wagon to four "team" wagons and five autos. According to Allen, he delivered as far north as St. Cloud and DeLand, as far south as Punta Gorda, and all points in Pinellas.[52]

Allen pleased the Housewives' League and offended some of his peers when he unilaterally added wrappers that other bakers could ill afford. Allen had reportedly fought with Fred Reynolds of the Tampa Steam Bakery over the issue. Another baker, F. W. Mohr, publicly vowed to put Allen out of business.[53]

It did not take long for trouble to find Allen's bakery. In April 1918, Tampa police arrested street food salesman J. N. King after receiving a Citizens' complaint.[54] When the detainee was brought before city officials, they sternly told the vendor to step forward and present his bread. They closely inspected the loaf until they said they had found a foreign substance. They found several coarse shards of glass that appeared to have been pushed into the bread's crust. Police arrested the deviled crab man, and city officials hoped the contaminated bread represented an isolated incident. The paper wrapper for the contaminated loaf read "Allen's Butter Crust Bread." More complaints of glass in bread emerged, and the label on every tainted loaf led investigators to Frank Allen.[55]

Rumors of ground glass in food were quite common in the United States during the hysteria of World War I. The federal food board advised citizens on March 31 "to be most careful in the future when eating bread, rolls, cake and pastry" as jagged bits of glass had been found in flour and wrappers. The board issued the warning with the caveat that it was not suspected to be a widespread problem but the product of angry employees. Sacramento Union, no. 32, April 1, 1918. This brief warning appeared in multiple newspapers across the country. In a matter of days, the articles had touched off a national scare.[56]

An overzealous (and possibly mentally ill) member of the military police became convinced that German saboteurs adulterated food with ground glass. Major Noel Gaines, who supervised the military police of the Nineteenth Division in Texas, announced that fifty enlisted men were ill as a result of ingesting ground glass introduced into their food. When government chemists found no glass in an initial investigation, Gaines claimed the lab assistants were composed of an Austrian, two Germans, and a Turk, all of whom had migrated from homelands that were at war with the United States. He falsely claimed that further tests confirmed the presence of glass and the negligent lab assistants were "dealt with." The reaction of the people to the baseless rumors was immediate at a time when concern over bread was already high. The *Literary Digest* complained, "Rumor undoubtedly has done much to incite the people. There have been numerous reports of ground glass in food, for example [and] fires in factories."[57]

On April 8, 1918, the Tampa *Tribune* republished the Gaines story from Texas, thereby spreading and validating the rumors of Germans sabotaging the food supply. The first local consumer complaints of adulterated bread surfaced in the following days. A far more accurate article appeared in the *New York Times* in April 8 that the *Tribune* never reprinted. The *Times* tried to reassure readers, writing the headlines, "Federal agents find only one authentic case in more than 200 investigated. More Hysteria than glass: US Marshal finds no German plot to make food dangerous to life." The only injuries reported occurred in Fort Smith, Arkansas, where an angry employee adulterated a loaf of bread with glass and the bread was served at an orphanage. Such investigations seemed to be willfully ignored in Tampa, where the ground-glass hysteria took on a life of its own.[58]

On April 10, County Food Administrator Hafford Jones called a town meeting at City Hall to provide a public forum for people to report suspicious food. City investigators began by interrogating and arresting a deviled crab peddler, who claimed to know nothing about the shards of glass that had been found in his loaf. For every person who brought evidence, there were dozens who provided nothing more than wild rumors and hearsay. Nevertheless, a hasty conclusion developed among the public: these sabotaged loaves must have been the work of German spies who conspired to undermine the U.S. war effort.[59]

Because the wrappers on the adulterated bread bore the name of Allen's Bakery, authorities launched their investigation at the massive gleaming new facility that had opened three months earlier. All fingers initially pointed to an eighteen-year-old registered alien from Germany by the name of Bremer. Allen admitted that he previously had fired every person with German extraction on his staff, but young Bremer remained to run the wrapping machine. Under public pressure, Allen fired the young immigrant, but he was never found guilty of anything besides being Teutonic.[60]

When federal officials became involved and began planning arrests,

"Mr. Allen was frantic in the turn affairs had taken. He said he put everything he had in the new bakery . . . which is one of the most modern shops in the country." The embattled baker said, "I am as anxious as anyone to know the truth of the matter." Allen sifted his flour three times before processing it, and the theory of "glass going through into the flour was out of the question." Allen also supplied military personnel in the area, including the "aviation camp" at Arcadia. All the glass found by investigators was far too large to go undetected.[61]

"Officials here believe the glass found in Allen's bread was placed there to do him injury," the *Tribune* read, "and evidently the purpose was accomplished, temporarily at least, as his bread sales have fallen off thousands of loaves in the past few days and his out-of-town orders have with a few exceptions been stopped completely. Working on this theory, the officials dove deep into the history of the local bakers and brought to light a fight between Allen and Fred Reynolds, of the Tampa Steam Bakery. The situation between Allen and baker F.W. Mohr was also aired[.]" After inspecting Allen's bakery, city officials released a statement saying the facility was safe and Allen innocent, but the paranoia only grew.[62]

It appeared that fellow baker Fred Mohr enjoyed Allen's dilemma enough to become a suspicious person himself. Mohr was a longtime Tampa baker who built up his business much as Allen had. Going back to the turn of the century, he was especially well-known for his excellent cinnamon buns. After splitting with a partner at Stein and Mohr bakery in 1896, he announced the opening of his own grocery-bakery (at Central and Constant) but was soon arrested for baking without a license (which was not unusual at the time). Mohr thrived in Tampa, moving to a brick building at Tampa and Washington Streets and opening a new $14,000 facility there in 1908. Allen's bakery made Mohr's look dated by comparison.[63]

Mohr became the center of the glass investigation. He allegedly said he knew of an incident involving ground glass two weeks before popular reports but did not go public with it because it was "none of his business." Before the glass incidents, Mohr had gathered a large supply of bread bags from Allen's bakery and suggested to many around town that Allen's bread had been doctored with glass. Mohr crowed to his acquaintances, "you can't find glass in my bread," spreading word of Allen's adulterated product. The *Tribune* pointed out that Mohr himself was born in the United States but was of pure German ancestry. In fact, Mohr was unabashedly pro-German until the United States entered the war, at which time he changed his allegiance.[64]

The problem spread. Allegedly, glass also was found in the flour of a smaller bakery. Glass was discovered in sausages and cakes made by other local companies. A slice of chocolate cake at King's drug store was similarly doctored. Days later, glass was found in Tampa Steam Bakery's bread as well as a sought-after cinnamon bun produced by Mohr. When the problem persisted, police rounded up the employees and proprietors of Allen's bakery and Tampa Steam Bakery for questioning.

Allen testified that he thought his bread had been swapped out on the delivery trucks and replaced with tainted product clad in his wrappers. Allen quickly equipped his delivery trucks with locks and hired two guards to prevent tampering. A couple weeks later, Allen sought an injunction in court prohibiting Mohr from using his wrappers. Mohr had been ordering the wrappers from a printer and admitted to using them but offered no explanation for his actions. The court upheld the injunction and made it permanent. Mohr could no longer use or possess Allen's wrappers. During the crisis, Allen ran an ad promising "EVERY PRECAUTION!" was being made to ensure safety and cleanliness.[65]

News of the events in Tampa quickly spread, and new reports of glass-tainted food proliferated across the state. A. J. Frank Smith of Pensacola sent more than thirty parcels of food allegedly containing glass to the Florida Department of Agriculture, including flour, sugar, bread, and candy. Of the total of thirty-eight specimens analyzed by the department in 1918, none contained ground glass, but four of the items contained large pieces of broken glass that could have done damage to a consumer's mouth but would not have been ingested. The most common adulterant was sand. A writer recorded after the hysteria had subsided, "When the people in the U.S.[,] through receiving the daily German atrocity lies, became really war-crazy, they began in numerous places to taste ground glass in their food. Of course [they thought] it was the German in the U.S. grinding up old bottles and putting glass in their food. Not one case was proved, but many a butcher, cook and baker kept the dustpan away from the eats, and lying served at least this one good purpose—cleanliness."[66]

Many state food regulators received hundreds of reports of glass, and in most cases, no glass was found at all. In a few rare cases, it appeared glass had been hastily added to a food article. A food regulator in Pennsylvania later wrote, "With one or two exceptions these stories proved to be without foundation, the fears of the people being aroused by glistening fragments of crystallized sugar which were mistaken for glass." The glass scare had pressured many civilians to practice "Voluntary breadless days."[67] Americans saw glass everywhere. A government lab in Washington, D.C., tested a wide variety of consumables for glass, including cakes, cheese, corn flakes, hominy, ice cream, canned tomatoes, olive oil, and jelly.[68]

Paranoia over food sabotage coincided with changes in the flour supply. The reports of glass in bread and flour circulated as the government mandated the use of wheat substitutes in the nation's flour. The Indiana State Council of Defense finally issued a report that put all questions to rest. When baked quickly, bits of germ (or endosperm) in corn flour could take on a glassy appearance. "In bran flours, a nervous person might easily fancy that particles of the hard outer crust were glass. And dextrin sometimes solidifies into a hard, transparent mass which might be mistaken for glass." The council advised, "Bakers would do well to preserve this information carefully and in event the 'glass scare' raised its head again, the local authorities should be acquainted with the real facts."[69]

The *Lakeland Ledger* put it best when the editor wrote, "The alleged discovery of ground glass in the bread of a Tampa baker, seems to have been merely a mare's nest [an illusory discovery], pointed out by some malicious or hysterical person. Charges of this nature may not only ruin a man's business, but they are very disturbing to the people generally. The person who makes such a charge should be made to produce mighty good reasons for doing so." The cases quickly disappeared from Tampa's newspapers. Although newspapers such as the *Tribune* never missed the opportunity to pass along unfounded rumors, the press was much slower to investigate, dispel rumors, or defend suspects.[70]

The true conspiracy was not a German plan to poison America, but an American illusion to galvanize its populace. United States Attorney

General Thomas Watt Gregory announced in the *Army and Navy Register* that the glass and poison rumors were false, but no such announcement was made to the general public. Gregory briefly mentioned the ground-glass hysteria in his annual report and noted that the government had opportunistically used the unfounded rumors to scare the public. The Justice Department had the power to dispel the craze but instead allowed the paranoia to flourish, which in turn created local controversies such as Allen's. Certainly no baker of German extraction was safe from allegations. The attorney general's report read:

> The Department has also been hampered by the circulation of un-founded reports, running into the hundreds, of supposed unpunished alien enemy activities in the way of fires alleged to have been caused by enemy agents [and] alleged uses of ground glass. In view of the necessity for constant vigilance on the part of the public, it has not always seemed advisable to this department to enter into controversies as to the truth of these irresponsible reports[.] The best answer to rumors of this type is the present general state of good order. When it shall become possible to make known the true facts in regard to these vague rumors it is believed there will be no cause for lack of approval on the part of the general public.[71]

In the national ground glass episode, no one in the chain of rumors and lies had been held accountable. A warning to local consumers in New York was amplified by patriot warriors, the press passed it along without scrutiny, and the government quietly acquiesced to dreadful witch hunts across the country. Certainly German merchants suffered the most, but even those without Teutonic roots like Allen were not immune to rumors wielded as weapons. Through newspaper ads, Allen assured the public of the safety and cleanliness of his products, but the bakery business did not get any easier. Later in 1918, Allen was cited for allegedly failing to use enough substitute in his bread, an offense routinely committed by other local bakers. Allen contested the charges and the case went to court. He was exonerated for lack of evidence.[72]

While the Independence Day celebrations of 1917 had been restrained, patriotic fervor appeared to be on full display during July 4, 1918. The *Tribune* extolled: "Tampa, cosmopolitan Tampa, the melting pot of loyalists from Spain, from Cuba, from Greece, from far off Syria, joined in the festivities of the celebration . . . with American and foreign-born joining hands, cheering for democracy and rekindling the fires of hate in their hearts against the principles of Prussianism, barbarism and kaiserism." Brass bands, cannon salutes, and maneuvers by the "county guards" filled the day, culminating in a parade. A committee of foreign-born citizens planned the festivities.

> Among the features of yesterday's program was the appearance of a giant flag in the parade, carried by German and Austrian-born men who came to this country to escape the oppression of autocracy, to cast their lot in a land of equality where right is might. Yesterday they flaunted themselves in the face of the Kaiser, true to the land of their adoption: men broad enough to denounce the principles of the land of their nativity, unashamed of their birth; proud of their allegiance.[73]

Among the two dozen flag bearers: George Stecher, former president of the German American Club; Julius and Abe Maas, the German Jews who founded one of Tampa's most important retail stores; and Paul Kreher of Tampa Shipbuilding. The *Tribune* headline read: "Nations melt in accord in Tampa's great celebration."[74]

Recent events had left Tampa's German Club in limbo. The National German-American Alliance acted as a national umbrella group for local German clubs around the nation. The alliance had largely been funded by brewery and distillery owners, and by 1918, it had become vilified by nativists in the United States for the group's vocal opposition to Prohibition, desire for neutrality during the war, and active support of the German war effort through fundraising and service groups. In 1917, when government officials wrote to German clubs across the country urging them to publicly announce their support of the United States, the president of the German-American League of Minnesota replied acidly that the league "does not need and resents the arrogation of your society to advise them in regard to conduct by German-Americans in this war."[75]

The very existence of a national German-American Alliance became a sensitive issue in the heat of war. Of the alliance, Teddy Roosevelt said, "If congress does its duty, it will revoke the charter of that organization and make a provision that membership in it constitutes treason against this country." Pressure against the alliance was so strong that the group disbanded in April 1918. By August, President Wilson felt justified in revoking the charter of the moribund alliance.[76]

On a day that has been withheld from history, probably sometime between April and August 1918, Tampa residents gutted the German American Club's building of its fixtures in a violent outburst that seems to have been allowed by police. Newspaper writers at the time did not feel the need to cover the event, but many years after the fact, Tampa journalist and historian Leland Hawes recorded an account with an eyewitness. Hasdrubal "Drubie" Arango spent his childhood in a house adjacent to the German American Club. The families of cigar workers lived around the large clubhouse, and many were members despite their different nationalities. Arango's father had no Teutonic ancestry, but the German Club welcomed him anyway. Drubie and his brothers played around the club, helped set up the pins in its bowling alleys, and watched club members slaughter fowl for feasts behind the building. He especially remembers the music and singing that drifted from the three-story clubhouse's windows.[77]

On a date that has been lost to history, Drubie watched a mob of "rednecks" wreck the club, drag busts of Goethe and Beethoven down the sidewalk, ransack the club's records, and vent wartime tensions with steel bars, hammers, and paint. Vandals wrote across the front door, "To hell with the Kaiser," and "Take the Kaiser to Hell." The ornate cornerstone was smothered in fresh cement, and the large window that bore the name of the club in German painted over with white.[78] For all practical purposes, Tampa's vigilantes had "lynched" the German American Club house.[79]

Although an end to the war appeared to be in sight late in 1918, Tampa was in a rush to dispose of the old German American Club as quickly as possible. It is indeed an irony that city fathers brokered a deal to transfer the building from the most hated group in the city—the German immigrants—to a more traditional object of scorn, the labor unions. Tampa's labor unions in 1918 were many and powerful, and the German American Club's beautiful building would make a fine new labor temple, the reasoning behind the deal went. Unions could house offices there with plenty of room left for worker recreation. The original deal was for a quarter of the asking price to be paid as a down payment, with the rest of the $20,000 paid in installments. Eventually, the Labor Temple paid just $500 up front and likely could never have afforded the purchase, especially after what would be a long, costly strike by cigar workers in 1920.[80]

The U.S.S. *Tampa*, a merchant vessel in which city residents took much pride, had been sunk by U-boats in the Atlantic on September 26, 1918. Mayor D. B. McKay, who always seemed to have an outsize idea of his own importance, called for the unconditional surrender of Germany in the press, in part to avenge the loss of the *Tampa* and the 147 men aboard.[81]

In the meantime, Tampa's upstart shipyards continued to churn out new vessels to carry Uncle Sam's war effort overseas. In mid-October, formerly embattled German Club conductor Charles Heidt led the Tampa Dock Company's band in launching the *Coulter*. About a week later, he took ill with Spanish influenza, which had wracked Tampa beginning in October. He died on November 1 after an illness of only one week. Heidt had lived in Tampa for thirty years and had led Tampa's Municipal Band. Just over a week after his death, the armistice ended the war.[82]

To celebrate victory over the German foe, the local Red Cross's canteen committee organized a novel party for Tampa's most influential citizens. After the guests congregated at the YMCA building, they drove in a procession, led by a Red Cross ambulance carrying Tony Guida, a doughboy who had just returned from Europe. The next car was a military one, which carried the new, fictitious "Governor of Berlin," played by a gloating Mayor D. B. McKay. Howell Lykes (founder of the Lykes Brothers Company) and his wife played the King and Queen of Belgium, with other locals taking honorific European titles and playing at being royalty.

The first stop was the Elks Club, which in this case stood in for France. The Masonic Temple stood in for Egypt, where heavily veiled "geisha girls" danced barefoot. The Catholic Club assumed the identity of Japan, with its interior being redecorated as a Japanese garden. There, geishas played hostess and danced. The Italian Club capably emulated a visit to Italy. A young amateur dressed as an Italian peasant girl made an act out of feigned stage fright. Centro Español became Andalusia and Centro Asturiano became Madrid. The long progressive spectacle ended with the occupation of Berlin in the form of the old German Club. Mayor McKay was sworn in as the new overlord of the German capital. At the party's conclusion, the guests were sent off with doughnuts and coffee provided by the ladies of the Salvation Army.[83]

Several days later, at the opening celebration of the labor temple in the German American Club building, labor leaders remarked how far unions had come in Florida since the early 1890s. At the event, State Senator Doyle E. Carlton said with no apparent irony that the building would be at "the center of a brotherhood of man." Perhaps it seemed unpatriotic to point out that the club had been forcibly seized and sold in direct contradiction to the ideal Carlton extolled.[84]

Apparently in reference to the anticipated new use for the club, another speaker thought the building was like an old "spinster" who was at last getting married. The rhetorical marital union did not last long. It appears that the unions never had the money to buy the building in the first place, and the deal quickly fell through. Dances began to be held under the auspices of the congregations of local synagogues. The Young Men's Hebrew Association occupied the building until 1944, but the German American Club would not return for many years.[85]

CONCLUSION

This essay only begins to explore Tampa's history during World War I. The heated atmosphere of war has always provoked passions on the home front, but this new industrial kind of war called for efforts across all strata of society. Since workers and consumers felt intimately connected to the war, it was not a leap for individuals to think that suspicion of their "fellow man" would serve the war effort, as well. Citizens took advantage of wartime pressures to attack rivals old and new. While residents bellowed about liberty and brotherhood, their actions reveal that the more intolerant and irrational dark side of patriotism usually won the day. While Lady Liberty held aloft the torch to guide the huddled masses to safer shores, America's warrior patriots wielded it as a weapon against their neighbors. The loudest patriots won.

One might think that by surviving beyond war's end, Allen's path would have become easier. It did not. The public could not get enough of his bread, but by the end of 1920, he had had enough of the volatile baking industry. Allen sold his business, Tampa's first truly modern bakery, to manager E. B. Lewis and head baker E. D. Williams.

Under the control of Oscar Daniels, Tampa Shipbuilding facilities produced ten ships during and after the war. In 1923, Daniels returned shipyard operations to Ernest Kreher, who had been restored as president. It must have been a thrill to open his long-deferred dry dock in 1933. The facilities masterminded by Kreher became the backbone of Tampa's waterfront industry and its maritime war effort during World War II.

The German American Club remained dormant during Prohibition, perhaps because no meeting fit for Germans could convene without beer. Although the German American Club was later reorganized, it would never reclaim its building. It is difficult to imagine a more fitting monument to the dark side of patriotism and the days when Tampa surrendered to those impulses.[86]

THE NOBLE DISASTER

Prohibition and Speakeasies

In 1916, the "Cracker Messiah" Sidney Catts won the Florida gubernatorial race with a mixture of hard campaigning, fiery Baptist-style speeches, support of Prohibition, and anti-Catholic bigotry. Although Catts sometimes drank in private, in public he was an intolerant prohibitionist. After falling out with the Democratic Party, he joined the Prohibition Party's ticket and won in a remarkable landslide. He accused the "murderous monks" at the nearby St. Leo Monastery in Pasco County of routinely practicing human sacrifice. Catts further warned that the Catholic immigrants in Ybor City were stockpiling weapons at their churches for the coming religious war in the United States. Like today's demagogues, it mattered little to Catts if his stories were true, as long as they mobilized his unquestioning followers. Only Ybor City's precincts went on record as opposing Catts in Tampa.[1]

In the off-year of 1918, many did not bother to vote in yet another statewide referendum on alcohol. With the seeming suddenness of a thunderbolt, Florida voted itself dry. Still not satiated by his signal victory, Catts reconvened the legislature to rush through other measures against liquor. He was largely motivated by a rush on the part of Tampa's saloons and distributors to sell off their stocks. Catts wanted to prevent Tampa's dealers from cashing in one last time.

And just like that, after over thirty years of struggle, Florida went dry. Between 1918 and 1919, various states voted to amend the constitution by banning alcohol, culminating with a national ban on alcohol. In January 1919, enough states approved of the Eighteenth Amendment for Congress to ratify, and it went into effect a year later. In October 1919, Congress passed the Volstead Act, which provided criminal penalties for violating the Prohibition Amendment.

On January 1, 1919, Prohibition became Florida law, and the nation followed about a year later. The Reverend Billy Sunday exulted when Prohibition passed: "The reign of tears is over. The slums will soon be only a memory. We will turn our prisons into factories and our jails into storehouses and corncribs. Men will walk upright now, women will smile, and the children will laugh. Hell will be forever for rent." For generations, dry activists had promised that heaven on earth would follow the passage of Prohibition.[2]

Florida Brewing Company found itself with vats of beer it could not sell when the Internal Revenue collector visited. The brewery emptied the vats, disposing of the beer through a drain in the floor. As the sudsy torrent ran from the mouth of the sewer several blocks away, crowds of children scooped up the beer with buckets, bottles, and dippers. The flood would have been worth $36,000 before Prohibition.[3]

The day Prohibition went into effect, a sailor named John Branch stood before a judge for public drunkenness. "You will be turned over to the state next time you get drunk," the judge told the sailor. If caught drunk again, Branch would be charged with a misdemeanor, fined up to $500, and sentenced to up to six months in jail. The third offense would be treated as a felony, with a maximum fine of $3,000 or three years in prison.[4]

Some say the true targets of Prohibition laws were not drinkers but immigrants who ran the liquor, wine, and brewing industries. B. M. Balbontin, Tampa's influential alcohol distributor and saloon owner, understood the implications.

My opinion is that [Prohibition] was an evolution of terrible reach. For example: 98% of the beer plants in the United States belonged to Germans. 95% of the [liquor] refineries belonged to Jews. 90% of the importers were Spaniards, Italians, French, and Germans. More than 90% of the retailers in liquor belonged to the nationalities expressed above, all foreigners. With that evolution called Prohibition, they confiscated more than 95% of the investments of these foreigners. They annulled their political force[.][5]

More recently, scholar Edward Behr has written, "Prohibition was the rearguard action of a still dominant, overwhelmingly rural, white Anglo-Saxon Protestant establishment, aware that its privileges and natural right to rule were being increasingly threatened by the massive arrival of largely despised (and feared) beer-swilling, wine-drinking new American immigrants."[6]

Whatever the motives of Prohibition, it was never enforced with much conviction. Politicians, many of them responsible for passing dry legislation in the first place, refused to fund enforcement effectively. Just as Tampa had traditionally neglected to fund a decent police force, members of Congress and their constituents (many already weary of the recent income tax, imposed in 1913) gave up on funding Prohibition before it began. Local law enforcement received precious little additional funding. As interest increased in Florida real estate, many businessmen and politicians thought dry laws would discourage visitors and investment.[7]

Some Florida hotels set their tables with black cloths to mark the occasion of going dry. Though the dark color indicated mourning, many restaurants and hotels never intended to abide by the law. T. H. Weigall, a keen observer of boom-time Florida, writes,[8]

Florida, from my own experience of it, was the wettest country I have ever known. The state legislature had definitely abandoned any attempt to enforce the provisions of the eighteenth amendment; and the united factors of a tropical climate, the proximity of areas where liquor of all sorts was obtainable at all hours and at the lowest prices, and the presence of a vast amount of ready cash in the hands of people eager to spend it, combined to render quite abortive the intermittent efforts of the federal agents. Practically all of the hotels served these drinks quite openly, and indeed there was no particular need to conceal them. . . . The amount of drinking that went on all over Florida, especially in the larger towns, was simply astounding.[9]

After the onset of Prohibition, Tampa's activists solicited donations to fund the nascent Florida Educational and Temperance Association. The new organization focused upon persuading local authorities to enforce the measure. The Tampa chapter's efforts to raise funds fell on deaf ears. Even a speech by legendary orator and presidential candidate William Jennings Bryan failed to raise the needed funds. Just as the dreams of the temperance movement were being fulfilled, popular support, which had peaked during the stresses of the war, was already slipping away.[10]

SMUGGLING AND SPEAKEASIES

The word speakeasy, referring to a blind tiger or unlicensed saloon, had been around for decades. But during Prohibition, the speakeasy became a contradiction of sorts: an iconic cultural institution on the shadowy margins of society. African American jazz burst onto the national music scene out of radios, on phonographs, and across speakeasy dance floors everywhere, reflecting the heady excitement of the times. Prohibitionists and suffragettes had unwittingly ushered in a new wave of women's liberation, just not the kind they envisioned. Precocious young ladies enjoyed their new freedoms by doing the Charleston, smoking cigarettes, and drinking bathtub gin. Their prohibitionist elders were not pleased.

Prohibition warped the marketplace in a variety of ways. In his revealing study of gay life in New York City, George Chauncey touches upon many of the biggest changes wrought by dry laws, including the criminalization of nightlife, corrupt police, the rise of crime syndicates, and the erosion of respect for the law. Perhaps most importantly, Prohibition ushered the middle class into working-class bars and restaurants that were previously considered too low-class for more respectable patrons. The desire to drink and socialize had done what had been considered impossible before, or at least highly improbable: The working and middle classes recreating in the same spaces. These illegal bars became a zone outside other socially proscribed places where people of wildly different backgrounds might meet. Speakeasies became cultural laboratories, where the rich were more likely to mix with the poor, men with women, white with black, criminal with lawful.[11]

Tampa's saloon owners had to find new businesses overnight. Prohibition set off a collective mad dash on the part of tavern owners to reopen their establishments as restaurants. At the time Prohibition went into effect, saloons occupied many of the best business locations in the city. The *Tampa Tribune* noted, "Already one place has been turned into a pool room. John Nelson said he expected to turn his place into a restaurant with the dawn of the new period." But the new era didn't look immediately different from the old one. Another business awkwardly renamed itself The Tavern Coffee Shop (101 Zack Street) and registered as a restaurant in 1925. One key feature disappeared overnight, the *Tribune* mused: "The prohibition law has brought something else to Tampa: a second-hand market flooded with mahogany fixtures."[12]

Tampa had been run (and known) as a wide-open town for many years, and the Prohibition era gave rise to a new breed of daredevil saloons. The speakeasy varied widely, from tiny drink stands and converted homes to restaurants and full nightclubs. Entrepreneurs of all kinds—some legitimate, others from the criminal underworld—cashed in on the insatiable demand for booze. As with today's illegal narcotic trade, the potential for profit was too great to resist. In 1930, about 130 retail businesses in the city sold liquor in addition to their usual articles of trade.[13]

Immigrants became the foot soldiers of the wet underworld. One of the unintended consequences of Prohibition, of which there were many, was that the dry years actually afforded many immigrants more economic mobility (and attendant risks) than the legitimate liquor industry did. As Prohibition wore on, upstart Italian bootleggers aggressively joined the trade, augmenting their incomes by distilling liquor for sale. Spanish and Cuban criminal networks already controlled vice in the city, including bolita. As many as half of Ybor City's families were involved in the liquor trade. It seems every café and fine restaurant in Ybor City and West Tampa doubled as a speakeasy. Even the most innocuous street vendors, including pirulli candy salesmen and deviled crab vendors, sold bolita tickets. After years of conditioning, Tampa had become hard-wired for crime.[14]

It did not take long before the raids began. In 1919, government agents raided Garcia's coffee shop (1601–1603 Michigan Avenue) while they supervised a "gang of Negroes" who destroyed $10,000 worth of booze, "rotten whiskey, good whiskey, domestic and imported wines and even cold beer." The haul of evidence included two hundred gallons of whiskey, at $10 a quart. Manuel Garcia was arrested for trying to rescue parts of the stash. Garcia also ran a bottling operation in which whiskey from barrels would be conveyed to bottles, then labeled with "Old Cutter" or "Mumm's Extra Rye." The operation had all the necessary labels, paste, brushes, bottles of various design, coloring agents, corks, wax, and so on.[15]

Over time, Ybor City boasted an elaborate system of lookouts on every street corner whereby businesses could be warned well in advance of any trouble by police or Prohibition agents. Since whiskey was usually poured from pitchers, not bottles, it was easy to quickly pour down the drain. Since people took liquor in demitasse cups, servers only had to pour a little coffee in the cups to appear legitimate. At Manuel V. Lopez's downtown restaurant, police found whiskey stowed in special compartments built under his tables.[16]

Bootleggers, who were often legitimate liquor distributors before being put out of business, needed new outlets to sell their product. Aside from restaurants, soft drink stands and soda bars often replaced saloons, serving a sweet substitute for something harder. The name "soft drink" was meant to stand in sharp contrast to "hard liquor" by marketers. It is one of history's ironies that "soft drink" fountains and ice cream parlors often acted as fronts for bootlegging and retail liquor sales.

In 1919, on the eve of nationwide Prohibition, Tampa supported only nine soda fountains. A year later, with the United States a dry nation, there were forty-nine, a sufficient number to replace most of Tampa's saloons. In 1924, 115 soft drink retailers populated the business community, peaking with 131 in 1930. It should come as little surprise that the number of soda fountains fell sharply immediately after Prohibition was repealed. Within three years of repeal, half of the fountains closed, and the numbers continued to fall steadily.[17]

Billiards halls followed a similar pattern. Billiards began as a gentlemen's game, but the Prohibition years would give pool halls a seedy reputation as a haven for illegal liquor and gambling. On the first dry day in Florida, a Tampa saloon reopened as a pool hall, and others were

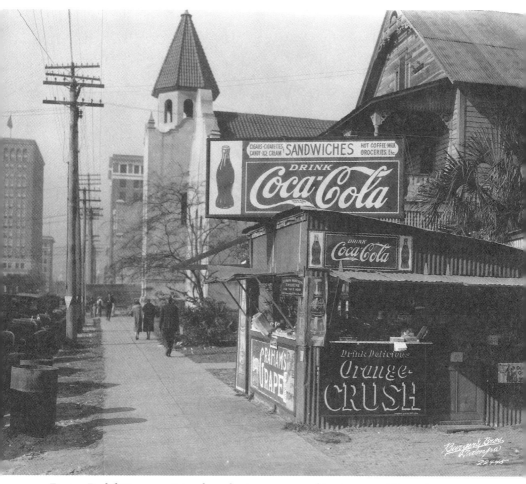

During Prohibition, a variety of new businesses opened to circumvent liquor laws, including soft drink and/or sandwich "stands" so small and numerous there were difficult to regulate. (Burgert Brothers photograph collection, Tampa-Hillsborough County Library System)

expected to follow. Pre-Prohibition numbers averaged about eight establishments in Tampa. Prohibition saw that number balloon to twenty-two in 1925 and twenty-seven in 1932, only to drop to eleven just three years after repeal.[18]

Some of the city's most respected Spanish restaurants never stopped selling liquor and wine. Even with the nuisance of raids and an occasional arrest, the funds supplied by illegal alcohol sales were indispensable to most in the hospitality business. El Pasaje, Rubin's, and the Columbia were notorious. Most speakeasies stood in sharp contrast to the fine restaurants. The majority served the working class with much less pomp and fine food. Prohibitionists claimed that national alcohol consumption had dropped since the ban began, a trend hardly in evidence in the smoky rooms of Tampa's restaurants and bars.[19]

One thing that unified these disparate speakeasies was the products they sold. During the early dry years, a large amount of premium liquor still sloshed around the state, but as supplies dwindled, Tampa's drinkers relied chiefly upon doctored beverages. Home brewers sold their own beer and wine in large quantities, but moonshine became a staple of dedicated drinkers whether they knew it or not.

Two rivers ran through Hillsborough County and into Tampa at the time: the Hillsborough River, fed by the springs of the Green Swamp to the northeast, and the torrent of moonshine collected from countless stills in the surrounding counties. The city itself percolated with café con leche and brazen moonshine.[20] Much of the city's supply came from rural stills, but bootleggers distilled in Ybor City and black Central Avenue, as well. Tampa's gangsters eventually controlled the moonshine racket, with outlying sheriffs as accomplices in the trade.[21] Northern Hillsborough County became a hotbed of distilling. Resident Walter Burrell recalled,

> This area used to be full of whiskey stills. That was a big business back then. I would go around to some of the stills and buy mash from the owners to feed my hogs with. One man would have control over all the stills in the area. He would let you run a still if you gave him some of your whiskey to sell. There were so many stills out here that moonshiners had a standing joke. They said the reason Gunn Highway was so crooked because it ran from still to still. One moonshiner heard he was going to be raided and he loaded his entire still on the back of a flatbed truck.[22]

An international network of smugglers and rum-runners augmented local moonshine operations. Tampa was among the busiest of illegal destinations on the Gulf coast, along with Mobile, New Orleans, and Galveston. To import their cargoes, the "Black Ships" anchored in international waters more than twelve miles off the coast to avoid the police and coast guard. A "Key Man" supervised the loading of the liquor into small boats and then ashore. From there, high-performance cars or covered trucks smuggled the liquor to central points for distribution and sale.[23]

Most rumrunners came to Florida from Bimini, Nassau, or Cuba. Respectable men, even preachers, became involved as rumrunners. In 1921, Captain Bill McCoy founded Rum Row in the Bahamas aboard the *Henry L. Marshall.* He himself did not drink, but he was an honest smuggler who dealt only in premium liquor, or the "real McCoy." He brought his first shipment to Savannah in 1921, made a small fortune, and rum running was born. In 1917, Nassau imported 50,000 quarts of liquor for consumption on the islands. Five years later, the Bahamas took in ten million quarts annually, with most being earmarked for profitable export to the United States. The most effective vessels were built by the same contractors who constructed the Coast Guard's boats, but with higher specifications for speed.[24]

Smugglers devised the "ham" as the most efficient way to stuff as much hooch into limited spaces by stacking six bottles in burlap sacks (like a pyramid, with three on the bottom), using straw as a cushion between the bottles, and weighing them down with salt. If a sack had to be thrown overboard, it would initially sink, but as the salt dissolved the bottles would gradually float again. Rumrunners sometimes used submersion tanks, chained below the keel and barely buoyant. These cigar-shaped tanks could be towed ashore by smaller boats and were easily sunk if police intervened.[25]

Despite the great efforts of smugglers, the amount of premium liquor imported would never be able to meet demand. With premium liquor available only at extravagant prices, most workers settled on moonshine and home brew. One might purchase what appeared to be a premium bottle of liquor, even with a label, but in fact contained doctored moonshine. In 1929, a raid in Hyde Park revealed a typical counterfeit liquor operation. A journalist noted, "The kitchen and dining room was equipped as a bottling works, where the booze was flavored, [colored,] labeled and rubbed over with wet sawdust to give it the appearance of being smuggled in from the boats."[26]

Other regular drinkers didn't delude themselves with labeled bottles of rotgut but were content to drink moonshine, also known as "white mule," "third rail," or "pale poison." It became common knowledge that Florida grapefruit "satisfactorily disguises the taste and odor of all degrees and varieties of the prevalent 'corn' as grapefruit juice when used as the weaker part of the bootleg highball or cocktail. This has created a big demand for the Florida product and all . . . speakeasies carry sufficient stocks of this alleviating accompaniment."[27]

While some people at the time could laugh in their sleeves about liquor smugglers, the same operators brought a deadly serious wave of narcotics along, as well. Although opium dens had operated in Tampa for decades, the 1920s brought the twin scourges of cocaine and heroin. According to historian Frank Alduino, Tampa was "notorious for drug peddlers, large and small, both as a winter resort and a base of operations, and as an especially lucrative field in itself on account of the great number of vacationing addicts, addicted hotel employees, and addicts who poured into the state to work their rackets on the tourists." The *Tampa Tribune* claimed that five hundred addicts lived in the city, and crime spiked any time they became desperate. The city stockade reserved small detached, sunbaked huts called "dog houses" for severe addicts or unruly prisoners.[28]

In 1920, Tampa harbored more drug traffic than Chicago, New Orleans, or Philadelphia. Only New York City moved more dope than Tampa. The market was so flooded that a federal narcotics inspector said the street value of morphine, cocaine, and heroin was lower in Tampa than in any other city in the nation. A raid in 1925 yielded more than $1 million worth of cocaine and morphine. The ringleader was an eighteen-year-old Italian named Joseph Cacciatore who called himself "king" of Tampa's drug trade. He had conducted his business in Ybor City's restaurants and cafés using children as salesmen. Cacciatore was sentenced to nine years in federal prison and a $3,000 fine. The real kings of narcotics proved to be Charlie Wall and George "Saturday" Zarate. In 1928, their arrest for selling morphine to an undercover informant rocked Tampa's underworld. Both proved to be remarkably resilient in and out of the courtroom, but both were murdered in Tampa, Zarate in 1936 and Wall in 1955.[29]

It should come as little surprise that in the waning days of Prohibition, enterprising forty-two-year-old resident Lee Cox was working on a

Ybor City goes underground. Investigators excavate a large cache of liquor as on-lookers gather at the fence. Note the "hams" on the left, typically five bottles of liquor stacked in a burlap sack for shipping. (Tampa Bay History collection, University of South Florida Tampa Special Collections)

mutant hybrid beverage: liquor spiked with narcotics. Police sent an informant to get a drink at a speakeasy at 1014 N. Florida Avenue. After a couple small sips, the informant felt a numbing sensation. Cox had been doctoring his liquor with pills, likely opioids, at a hideout two doors away. Judge Tom Watkins gave Cox one of his stiffest sentences in memory, a mere four months in jail and a thousand dollar fine.[30]

LAW AND DISORDER, 1921–1924

The early years of Prohibition in Tampa are best exemplified by the careers of two men: Police Chief Frank Williams and speakeasy operator Leo Isaac. Federal Prohibition Agent Frank M. Williams made a splash with a big bust in Pasco County in 1920 that caught the attention of Tampa's City Commission. The commission appointed Williams as police chief in February 1921 after his predecessor resigned. A veteran of World

War I and a performer in Buffalo Bill's Wild West show, the flamboyant Williams sported a large handlebar mustache and top credentials as a federal Prohibition agent. After decades of indifferent enforcement of blue laws and Prohibition, Tampa's teetotalers eagerly awaited a crackdown on booze and vice. Soon after, the new police chief's home was ransacked by burglars as a sort of welcoming party. As if to demonstrate how brazen criminals had become, thieves stole all of the liquor Tampa police had secured as evidence. A truck pulled up to City Hall one night and the thief used air vents to gain entry into the evidence locker.[31]

Williams began his tenure with a flurry of raids and arrests. In the first six months of 1921, besides traffic violations, charges of disorderly conduct (411 arrests), gambling (199), and drunkenness (100) were the city's most common offenses. Prohibition violations totaled ninety-nine, moonshine stills netted nine, and narcotics twenty. Tampa's crime wave seemed unfazed by Williams's activity.[32]

In 1922, Williams promised to turn things around. He fired twenty officers, hired new ones, and imbued the department with military-style discipline. Under Williams, Tampa police made plenty of arrests, but the routine offenders were barely fined by lenient judges and rarely served any jail time. In this context, it made sense that those apprehended smiled when arrested, politely paid their fines, and went back to work. Many establishments were warned of raids in advance so they could hide their inventories of fine liquor, leaving a little cheap moonshine to be confiscated. After a quick trip through court and a minor fine, the owners could open back up again.[33]

Chief Williams noted that the landscape had changed since Prohibition, and the alcohol trade had melted into the city. "Many of these places [speakeasies] operate under the guise of cold drink stands, but that is only their alibi."[34]

*　*　*

Running a speakeasy could be profitable if one didn't mind the notoriety that often came with the job. Leo L. Isaac, a man of about forty, was one such person. He arrived in Tampa ostensibly to take a job as a clerk in 1919 but soon opened a cold drink and cigar stand (Zack and Nebraska) that caught the attention of police. In November 1921, federal Prohibition officers raided Isaac's stand but found nothing except a mysterious safe. Isaac demanded a warrant and refused to open it. A government-sponsored safe expert could not open it, so they left a wax seal on it prohibiting anyone from opening it. The case disappeared quickly and Isaac was left to climb the underworld.[35]

In 1922, Isaac opened the Nebraska Café at the corner of Nebraska and Sixth Avenue. He sold alcohol in his club and ran a lucrative delivery business, as well. The flush entrepreneur renamed his speakeasy Isaac's Nest and bought a posh house in Hyde Park at 245 Bay Street. Armed with cunning attorney Pat Whittaker, Isaac always seemed to escape serious punishment. He hired bodyguards, mocked the police, and with his wife, Rose, built a life selling liquor at Isaac's Nest.

Isaac became infamous overnight when Reedy Rinfore, a nineteen-year-old "woman of the underground," stopped at his joint in March 1922. She had been at a party with several undisclosed men and appeared to be distraught. When they sent her home in a taxi, she asked to stop at Isaac's Nest for a bite to eat. When she arrived, she sat in a private room with the cabbie. The young lady only ordered a Coke, which she used to wash down a deadly dose of bichloride of mercury. The cabbie Leo Day grabbed her by the throat in an attempt to avert her suicide, but she had already ingested a fatal dose.

Laid low with pain, authorities brought Rinfore to Gordon Keller hospital. Doctors announced they could do nothing to save her life, predicting she would die within a day or two. Rinfore pled in the press, "I wanted to die then, but I want to live now!" While the community craved answers, the young lady said nothing about the events that drove her to suicide. She had been living in a downtown hotel and only recently moved into the house of an unnamed individual. Rinfore was not intoxicated when she poisoned herself, so alcohol was ruled out as a factor. Still, dry advocates decried the episode and Isaac's Nest as monstrosities produced by liquor. Rinfore's heartsick mother took her back home to Dade City to die.[36]

Less than one month after the Rinfore incident, federal agents raided Isaac's Nest. They arrested Isaac and his bartender with ten half-pints of moonshine, some colored to be sold as whiskey, buried just outside the back door. Because agents had written an incorrect address on the warrant, the evidence was inadmissible and the case thrown out. Federal agents had more luck in June, when they arrested Isaac for selling liquor again. The suspect posted a whopping one thousand dollars bond and walked.[37]

Isaac managed to avoid attention until January 1923, when forty police officers participated in a large wave of raids of known speakeasies. Chief Williams had recruited Atlanta police officer J. I. Perryman as a secret agent in December. His investigation set up the sweep, but in fourteen raids, police seized only ten quarts of liquor. Lookouts or leaks prevented larger hauls of evidence. Raids took place at Ideal Café (1233 Franklin), Isaac's Nest (1629 Nebraska), El Boulevard (Nebraska and Palm), Grand Orient (Seventh Avenue and Sixteenth Street), Las Novedades (1416 Seventh Avenue), Alhambra Café (Ninth Avenue and Fourteenth Street), Garcia's Restaurant (1324 Franklin), El Pasaje Café (Ninth Avenue and Fourteenth Street) and more, some of the most established restaurants in the city.[38]

In March 1923, U.S. District Attorney W. M. Gober tried to bring injunctions against twenty-five known liquor dealers in the state, forcing them to close for one year under the "nuisance" or "padlock" clause of the Volstead Act. The list included Isaac's Nest, Victor Licata (who would open the Seabreeze Restaurant outside of city limits in 1925), and other places in Jacksonville and Miami.[39]

Chief Williams began to stake out common offenders with "sentries," hoping to hamper their trade with constant scrutiny, but traffic just flourished elsewhere. The *Tribune* noted, "One 'restaurant' which is known as a gambling and liquor 'joint' didn't sell more than a dozen cups of coffee Thursday night because of the presence of the policeman outside." This "sentry" method was impractical, and Williams lacked the manpower to seriously consider such an approach. The limited police force could not be everywhere at once.[40]

Chief Williams complained that the courts were not cooperative in prosecuting liquor cases, or issuing warrants, rendering evidence inadmissible in court. The courts dismissed between one-third and one-half of liquor cases between 1920 and 1923.[41] By late 1923, Williams had clearly failed to tame Tampa's liquor problem and found himself assailed by city officials. Gone was the swashbuckling war hero. "Enforcement of the prohibition law is the most thankless and most discouraging job in the world," Chief Williams told the *Tribune*.[42]

Williams must have been frustrated with his job when he drove past a beer parlor (Cuba and Spring Streets) operated by the Daniels brothers. When one of the brothers ducked in to warn the other, Williams decided to pay them a visit. He forced his way into the business and began smashing all he saw, glasses, bottles, and furniture. He battered his way through locked doors and destroyed their stocks of beverages. When he found five-gallon kegs of guava wine fermenting, he threw one at Frank Daniels, covering him in guava juice. "Don't you like it? If you don't I'll just as soon wreck you, too," he said. The Daniels brothers backed off, and Williams finished his destruction before calmly driving away as a crowd that collected outside looked on.[43]

Dry activists did not just carry banners and placards. Some carried axe handles. Some carried blackjacks, guns, or knives. In Florida, the Ku Klux Klan was the muscle behind the reform movement. In 1922, the Klan expanded and modernized its mission by adding new targets for its hatred. In addition to black people, the Klan added all foreigners, Catholics, Jews, labor unionists, Communists, and the liquor trade to the list of those its members loved to hate. In the eyes of the Klan, Tampa was decadent, leftist, Catholic, corrupt, and un-American.

Perhaps 1922–23 was the peak of the Klan's influence in state politics, when it became a "self governing realm in the Invisible Empire." In northeast Florida, the Klan promoted its own slate of candidates for election. In 1922, Florida residents killed eight African Americans in Rosewood (in Levy County roughly fifty miles west of Ocala), and the small black town was abandoned. Many of Tampa's churches invited Klansmen to speak about the Klan's efforts and recruit new members from parishioners. In the early years of Prohibition, when it became apparent that few people took the law very seriously, the Klan asserted itself as a pressure group for enforcement. When that failed, the Klan intervened to make examples of prolific offenders.[44]

In August 1923, the Klan paraded in public after the death of President Warren Harding, winding through Tampa and Ybor City on slow-moving Ford Model Ts. Most wore white robes but saw no need to hide behind hoods. Police Chief Williams offered the Klan an honorary police escort for its impromptu parade. Later, Williams received a letter of thanks that read in part, "The Knights of the Ku Klux Klan are standing back of you to a man, ready and willing at any time to assist you in the proper performance of your legal duties as an officer. Should the occasion arise we can place at your disposal several thousand Klansmen on very short notice." These were not the officers that Police Chief Williams needed.

The Klan held a grand ceremony in Lakeland by the light of an electrically illuminated cross. There, three hundred members inducted a hundred and fifty new recruits. A Methodist pastor gave a sermon afterward. In a Bradenton demonstration, the Klan marched with banners reading, "bootleggers beware," "America for Americans," and "100 percent Protestant teachers" for all schools.[45]

On Halloween night 1922, Leo Isaac sat in front of his bar. When he saw the two Fords pull up and call him over, he probably wondered if the police had come to shake him down again. Hooded thugs wrangled Isaac inside one of the cars and drove him to the Six Mile Creek area east of town. Isaac was not alone as an abductee. The Klan had also kidnapped Enrique Rose, headwaiter at the upscale El Pasaje Restaurant, and Andrew Williams, a black entrepreneur and suspected bootlegger. Then, in the remote darkness outside of town, the Knights of the Ku Klux Klan applied the lash to the evening's three victims. The assailants then presented each victim with a letter warning them to cease their illegal activities, signed "Que, Que, Que," and released them. "Mend your ways and live as a decent law-abiding citizen or we will make an example of you. YOU ARE BEING WATCHED," the letters read. Similarly signed letters appeared in the wake of Klan violence in other attacks, and the Klan would go on to mail warning letters to another hundred and fifty suspected bootleggers.

Leo Isaac needed a doctor's attention after the severe beating. The El Pasaje waiter received a much lighter treatment but still spent several days in the hospital. Andrew Williams simply disappeared from public sight. After being told to close his business within ten days in the letter, Isaac told journalists in a panic: "I am at a loss what to do. I have recently spent a lot of money in remodeling my place of business and stand to lose heavily no matter what course I may pursue. I have never been guilty of the things with which they accused me. I have been the victim of many

In Ku Klux Klan meetings outside Tampa and Lakeland in the 1920s, an electrically illuminated cross stood in for the flaming variety. (Tampa Bay History collection, University of South Florida Tampa Special Collections)

malicious charges, and will not contest those which I may have merited, but I do deny that I have ever taken any part in the perversion of true women."[46]

Several days after the beatings, Isaac reportedly received a new message from the Klan indicating that he could continue to operate. The sheriff's investigation went nowhere and Isaac continued to run his business. When Harry Church, owner of the Owl Café, received a threatening letter from the Klan, he welcomed the opportunity to mete out some punishment of his own. He told the *Tribune*, "If this thing comes to the worst . . . I can safely say there will some 'soft singing and slow driving' or some of their relatives will have undertakers measuring pine boxes for them."[47]

The local Imperial Wizard of the Klan, Dr. Hiram W. Evans, denied the beatings, saying the perpetrators must have come from outside the vicinity. Doctor A. M. Bennett, pastor of the Palm Avenue Baptist Church, celebrated the violence and suggested that a fifty-man committee supervise

Tampa's morality. When the *Tampa Tribune* offered a reward for information leading to arrests in the beatings, the Klan threatened to dynamite the *Tribune* building and kill the sheriff. The *Tribune* subsequently denied the Klan was involved, saying the floggings were due to "private grievances." No arrests were made. Klansmen burned down the Green Lantern bar and beat its operators. E. P. Martin, former Hillsborough County solicitor, was also flogged, ostensibly for taking bribes from the underworld. Vigilantes abducted cigar maker Ramon Castello to the Hillsborough River, stripped him of clothing, and painted the letter K across his chest. The Klan's violence and disrespect for the law did not endear it to the community. Instead, they resembled the very criminal element they had vowed to oppose. Tampa found itself caught between two of the most intemperate groups of the day: the Klan and the criminal underworld.[48]

Bruised but unbowed, Leo Isaac must have been a little suspicious of the quick reversal: one week the Klan beat him senseless to close his business, the next, they politely sent him a letter inviting him to continue as normal. Isaac did just that, and a month later, at midnight on December 11, 1923, city detectives found one hundred quarts of "red liquor" in a shoe repair shop that adjoined Isaac's "restaurant." Isaac told the detectives they were trespassing. While detectives left two policemen to guard the premises, they went to the home of a judge to obtain a warrant. Police had been watching the business for some time and arrested Isaac again.[49]

With this latest reversal looming, on January 15, 1924, Leo Isaac, the self-made speakeasy maverick, died of a heart attack. Leo's sudden death left his wife, Rose, alone with one of the most notorious speakeasies in Tampa. She elected to continue to run the "café" and made a few changes, renaming it the Cameo Tea Room. Three months after Leo's death, Rose held a banquet specializing in chop suey and chow mein. Apparently, Rose had learned to cook Chinese American cuisine. Assuming that Leo and Rose Isaac were Jewish, she probably would have learned in New York, where Jewish Americans had fallen in love with Chinese American food. Rose went on to run Miss Isaac's Tea Room out of the old speakeasy, which specialized in chop suey and Chinese American food. On October 29, 1924, almost exactly a year after her husband was abducted by the Klan, Rose faced alcohol charges of her own, but the judge dismissed them. In the 1930s, she moved the business to 4715 Florida Avenue and in the 1950s to Frances Street. About twenty years after Leo's death, Rose's nephew Bern and his wife, Gert, came to visit Rose from New York City. They ended up staying and founded Bern's steak house in the 1950s.[50]

Before the elections of 1923, the *Tampa Tribune* had denounced Chief Williams for allowing crime to flourish in Tampa. Williams responded that the *Tribune* was of no help to Tampa's police. He also defended his record, but no one could deny that crime in Tampa was out of control. The *Tribune* cited the pervasive liquor trade, the undisturbed gambling establishments, and the rise of "cowardly assaults upon the citizens" and threatening letters by vigilantes such as the Ku Klux Klan.

Whether Williams made a genuine effort or not, he had very little to work with. The courts were all soft on alcohol, and he never had enough quality police officers. In 1918, the year before Florida went dry, Tampa had only twenty-seven patrolmen (with a maximum of nine men on duty) who earned a mere seventy-five dollars per month, while most city workers earned fifty dollars per week, all in a rowdy city of fifty thousand. When police petitioned for raises in the midst of terrible postwar inflation, they received a mere five dollars raise per month. Federal efforts were of little help, hampered by lack of funding, lack of trustworthy personnel, and a lack of conviction on the part of many federal judges. The city doubled in size to one hundred thousand between 1920 and 1925 in part because of the annexation of West Tampa, stretching resources further. During those same five years, Tampa's murder rate rose by 420 percent, averaging 44.26 per hundred thousand. Between 1923 and 1925, criminals stole six vehicles from federal Prohibition agents in Tampa. In 1923, one resident counted 142 speakeasies or booze sellers within city limits alone.[51]

When Williams dismissed two officers to reconcile the department's limited budget, the city demanded he reinstate them. The standoff led to the chief's dismissal in May 1924. Immediately after his firing, the *Tribune* praised his honesty and integrity, saying he seemed incapable of a dishonest act.[52]

In April 1924, several police officers were implicated in the robbery of Alonzo Clewis, which netted the robbers a handsome $24,000. Tampa police did not seem interested in investigating and soon dropped the case. When Peter O. Knight of the Exchange Bank hired private investigators from the Burns agency to look into the crime, they found that several Tampa police officers had masterminded the heist.[53]

It did not help appearances when Williams was arrested for the heist and implicated as an accomplice to Edith Conway, his former secretary with whom he was having an extramarital affair. When her would-be accomplices threatened her and offered hush money, she agreed not to alert authorities.[54]

The press all but confirmed the romantic relationship between Williams and Conway. Their financial relationship proved to be just as scandalous. Conway had reportedly loaned Williams $1,500 before the heist. After the robbery, she gave him a payment of $3,300, allegedly to keep him silent. Williams refused the money but then accepted it as "an investment." When investigators uncovered the plot, Williams immediately paid back his ill-gotten funds. At Conway's sensational trial in a packed August courtroom, her attorney accused Knight of trying to protect more powerful friends. When the jury acquitted Conway, Williams pushed his way through the crowded courtroom to passionately kiss his lover. The exasperated judge dismissed Williams's case, he said, to avoid another courtroom circus. So through a stroke of luck or an act of corruption, Williams escaped prosecution altogether. The *Tampa Times* denounced the "courthouse fiasco," editorializing, "Justice is only a name in this county—a discredited impotent thing, which, with the aid of influential friends, smoothtongued lawyers, and a jury deaf to law and evidence, any criminal may laugh and scorn!"[55]

When Perry G. Wall was elected mayor in 1923, voters could rightfully ask themselves "Which Wall?" they elected: Perry Wall or his brother, Charlie Wall, lord of Tampa's criminal underworld.[56]

THE ARSENIC JUDGE

In 1927, thirty-year-old Leo Stalnaker already had a reputation as an uncompromising crusader. The young attorney had fought Rex Farrior for his Florida legislature seat in 1926. Driven by his strong beliefs against drinking, gambling, and graft, the young judge had powerful dry allies, from Tampa's most righteous churchgoers to the Ku Klux Klan. As a state representative, he sponsored a controversial bill that banned teaching the theory of evolution in the state. The bill failed to pass, and Stalnaker accepted an appointment as municipal judge in Tampa in 1927. City Council appointed him after hearing incessant complaints that criminal penalties were far too low, especially for alcohol- and gambling-related charges. Stalnaker promised to bring his headstrong Methodist sensibility to the bench, this time against vice instead of evolution.[57]

By the time Leo Stalnaker took the bench on June 16, 1927, Tampa was buzzing with speculation. Voters had seen a procession of federal Prohibition agents and local elected officials promise to crack down on crime, but the situation only seemed to get worse. Stalnaker had a full docket on his first day and was not surprised to find that most of the suspects were repeat offenders who had enjoyed lenient sentences under previous judges. They were shocked when the young, cocky judge multiplied fines by two, three, or four times and threw the book at gambling and alcohol violators. When Jack Davis went to court for possession of alcohol two months before, he drew a fine of $200. Stalnaker gave Davis a sentence of forty days in jail and a $450 fine. If the fine was not paid, an additional sentence of sixty days would result.[58]

During his first day in court, Stalnaker handled an impressive fifty-three cases, issuing heavy fines and stiff jail sentences that reportedly "shook the underworld of Tampa to its foundations." The calculus of corruption had been overturned in a matter of hours. Satisfied with his day's work, Stalnaker said to reporters, "I am afraid I will have to be harder on my patrons after I learn to know them better. No doubt the new policy will frighten prisoners caught by the police. So I am raising bonds for bootleggers from $100 to $500 and sureties for bolita operators from $50 to $300. Only cash or certified checks will be taken as security."[59]

One local newspaper noted with apparent glee, "The continual stream of [raised jail] sentences sent scores [of courtroom onlookers] scurrying back to bolita parlors and bootleg dives with bad tidings. Even the police officers were startled by the extraordinary punishments." When the *Tribune* condemned Stalnaker's heightened fines for "victims of vice," the judge seemed pleased. "It is the hit dog that howls," he quipped. "The so-called prominent citizens, or 'higher-ups,' who are connected to the liquor interests are certainly not pleased with the manner in which I am handling the office of Municipal Judge."[60]

Just five days into Stalnaker's tenure as judge, the steady tempo of raids and sentences resulted in much more subdued weekends than normal. After one month, the campaign against liquor and gambling in the city prompted a strong reaction. The usual booze stands stopped selling individual drinks to customers and would only sell bottles. Bootleggers began operating out of private homes to make legal searches more problematic. In a sure sign of trouble, the city's two largest bolita rings would sell tickets only over the telephone.[61]

Several weeks of Stalnaker's tough sentences overwhelmed the city stockade with prisoners. Crowded conditions forced the city to create a "pardoning board" to send groups of prisoners home. On its first day, the board dismissed twenty-one prisoners and asked that female inmates sleep at home and return to the stockade daily for work. This practice made the stockade a temporarily male-only facility, with a capacity of 150, plus a little more room in punitive "dog-house" huts reserved for drug addicts and problem prisoners.[62]

Over the summer of 1927, Stalnaker heard cases with pleasure as he sipped cold bottles of Coca-Cola. The vice squad began gathering evidence through the plumbing and carried pipe wrenches to raids. When police burst into the café of F. Strickland on Fortune Street, they found him pouring corn liquor into the sink. Officers salvaged enough of the liquid from the pipe to present as evidence in court. Stalnaker ordered that the evidence be poured on the floor and lit with a match. When it caught fire, he passed his sentence, thirty days in jail and a stiff $300 fine. Local newspaper readers wondered how Stalnaker could dispense justice in under a minute. The judge had recently completed 142 cases in just three hours.[63]

Champions of the dry cause rallied to Stalnaker's side. City Councilman Sumter Lowry vocally supported the judge. Local ministers and the Ku Klux Klan had long considered Stalnaker an ally. City attorney (solicitor) E. E. Graves wrote a flurry of anti-alcohol ordinances for the City Council to consider: banning blinds in the windows of all places selling food and drink, banning heavy doors at all stores and restaurants selling food and drink, cracking down on lookouts for speakeasies, and boosting fines of speakeasy operators to $1500 and 180 days in jail. Few of the dry ordinances passed.[64]

Graves also wrote a "drastic" Prohibition ordinance that would have made it illegal to be in a speakeasy whether one knew it or not. Aimed at restaurant patrons who drank on the sly, it would make all those who frequented "known bootleg establishments" subject to arrest. Such a wide-ranging law may have nabbed wet patrons, but it would have criminalized dry ones, too.[65]

With the radical speakeasy ordinance under consideration, the *Tribune* expressed alarm for "the Spanish Restaurants of Tampa. They may or may not violate the law by serving or permitting liquor. But we do know that these restaurants of the better class are and have for years been distinctive features of Tampa entertainment and hospitality—and this ordinance would by driving customers away from them, put them out of business without any corresponding benefit to public safety or community morals." The ordinance never passed.[66]

A newspaper reader was so pleased with the judge's performance that he/she suggested that Tampa declare "a Stalnaker Day and celebrate the fact that we have one man who will do his duty. Resign? Never! Give us more like him instead of asking his resignation. He is just doing what our law calls for—enforcement. One battle Moses fought was so hotly contested he would have lost the day had not his followers supported him by holding up his hands. He was enabled to put the enemy to flight. Hats off to Stalnaker. Let's hold up his hands." The Baptist Ministers Conference of Tampa publicly supported and praised Stalnaker.[67]

One newspaper wrote: "We shall judge not, hoping that we shall be not judged by him." No wonder Stalnaker had come to be known as "The Arsenic Judge."[68] Beyond the enthusiasm of some local churches, Stalnaker could not draw on much public or institutional support for his fight. Just days after taking the bench, Stalnaker received threatening notes from Ybor City. The young judge said to the press, "Poorly written, the contents cussed me up on one side and down the other and hinted at all sorts of terrible things that might happen if I didn't 'ease up' on gamblers and bootleggers." In response, Stalnaker plainly restated his unwavering agenda, "My four major crimes are driving while drunk, possession or sale of liquor, sale or possession of narcotics and operating games of chance."[69]

In an editorial, Wallace F. Stovall of the influential *Tampa Tribune* said that he agreed with the heavy fines but felt that Stalnaker "has been almost completely illogical and unreasonable in imposing those sentences[,] dealing out severe sentences indiscriminately, making the victim of vice as great a criminal as the operator. We would suggest to the judge, however, that he ask the voters of Tampa for a vindication of his policy, if he adheres to it without change, when the time comes to elect a Municipal Judge."[70] When word of Tampa's tough new judge spread, roadside placards appeared in Lakeland and other small towns, reading: "Stalnaker will get you if you go to Tampa, Trade at Home." In response, *Tribune* editor Wallace Stovall lashed out against Stalnaker's crusade:[71] "What an advertisement for Tampa! What an inducement for tourists to visit 'Florida's Greatest City!' The zealous fanatic more often than not has in his mind's eye the picture of himself as a martyr, suffering and to suffer for the faith that is within him. If Judge Stalnaker thus envisions himself, a continuance of the course he has followed since he took his place on the Municipal Court bench seems likely to result in making that vision a grim and tragic reality."[72] City Commissioner James McCants denounced Stalnaker's stiff sentences and called for his resignation after several days. (In two years, McCants would become the chief of police.) Others criticized Stalnaker for cracking down on those in possession of small amounts of home brew, which was considered an "antidote" to bootlegging and hard liquor.[73]

The constant stream of suspects must have been gratifying for the "crusading magistrate," but they were also misleading. Tampa police had the unfortunate habit of accepting false identities when making arrests, or criminals paid surrogates to face their trials and serve jail time in their stead. When Stalnaker learned of these practices, he called for an ordinance requiring police to record the correct name and address of everyone arrested, especially for alcohol-related offenses. The discovery of such widespread corruption seemed to vindicate the young judge's dismal view of Tampa's government, which was shaken by the allegations. The judge perturbed organized criminals to the extent that they

Young Judge Leo Stalnaker, *center*, and his two honest policemen launched a crusade for a dry city in 1927. (Burgert Brothers Collection, University of South Florida Tampa Special Collections)

sent messages threatening his life. He reacted by keeping several loaded shotguns around his home at all times.[74] Soon, Judge Stalnaker became embroiled in the most sensational speakeasy case in Tampa's storied history and, in the process, discomfited residents in its highest and lowest places.

In 1917, Achilles "Archie" Cerf was a legitimate saloon owner who conducted his business within the bounds of the law. He had worked at the Saratoga Saloon (802 Franklin) back in 1898, ran the saloon at the Florida State Fair in 1905, and spent many years running the New York Exchange Saloon. His businesses provided enough income for Cerf to summer in Chicago. In the years leading up to Prohibition, dry laws forced Cerf to sell the South Florida Mail Order House (at 101 Lafayette), where customers could order liquor a quart at a time. Forty mail-order houses had recently proliferated to circumvent laws against saloons, but state laws prohibited all alcohol sales in 1919, about a year before Prohibition took effect nationwide.[75]

The *Tribune* wrote of Cerf,

> For twenty-six years Archie Cerf has conducted a liquor business in this city. Much of the time he had one or more bars and a wholesale business as well. During all that period Mr. Cerf conducted his business strictly within the law, and at no period of his career was he charged with an infringement or even requested to appear in court in connection with his business. His record is an unusual one and stamps him as not only an astute businessman but a law-abiding citizen. He has made good money out of his business and retires from it with a comfortable competence. Mr. Cerf has not yet decided what line of business he will engage in, but his friends feel certain that whatever he undertakes will be carried through successfully.[76]

Cerf stayed true to form over the following decade. Ten years after his profile in the *Tribune*, he opened an exclusive speakeasy in the heart of the city. In January 1927, he had formed the Eagle Club as the operating officer, with fellow founders attorney J. Craig Phillips, cigar factory owner Val Antuono, and J. M. Mitchell, a state senator from Pasco County. The bar was a "stone's throw" from the police department, and members of the invite-only club were issued unmarked keys for access to the front door. Members used a password when approaching the club's second door at the top of a stairwell.

Only the most discreet members of the city's elite were invited to join.

Key Club members vetted potential recruits for their fitness: "The ability to drink hard liquor and remain perpendicular was thoroughly tested by a committee, and his character, insofar as keeping secrets is concerned, was carefully scrutinized. The would-be member was escorted into the club, admitted into the 'holy of holies,' which consisted of a suite of lavishly furnished rooms. There the high priest of the shrine—a beetle-browed bootlegger [Cerf], squirming and perspiring in evening clothes—bestowed the badge of membership, or the key to the outer door."[77] Stalnaker was transfixed by the glittering prize of what became known as the Key Club. Police knew of the club but, lacking evidence, did nothing to stop it. One night that summer, club employees drove a member home who had over-imbibed, and the man arrived home drunk and cursing loudly. The man's wife, tired of her husband's many hours at the Eagle, stole his key and duly sent it to the police.

Stalnaker made the crushing of the club his obsession and personally supervised the police investigation. Working with a few honest officers and a personal cameraman, Stalnaker staked out the club's entrance. This time there would be no doubt as to the suspects' identities. With expensive motion picture cameras and a telephoto lens, detectives watched the entrance of the club from across the street. Stalnaker often arranged for a car to be parked in front with a pretty young woman inside. As the club-goers passed, they tipped their hats to the lady, giving Stalnaker's Kodak a clear shot of their faces.[78]

Two detectives raided the club on July 23, but not even the police could get their stories straight. Initial reports had the men dressed undercover in fancy suits. Subsequent reports claimed that when the uniformed detectives passed the club, they heard a woman scream inside. They entered the club without a search warrant and instead of finding a damsel in distress, investigators found a "real bar, with brass footrails, sawdust on the floor and an atmosphere reminiscent of pre-Volstead days." The detectives rounded up Cerf, the doorman, and three waiters.

Days later, Judge Stalnaker announced that the city's most exclusive speakeasy and its many prominent patrons would be exposed in a film shown in his courtroom. Stalnaker secured the investigation's film in a safe deposit box in a bank. Several prominent elected officials were expected to appear in the hotly anticipated feature, including two men who were running to replace Stalnaker as judge. Anticipating the screening of the film, which he titled "Wages of Sin," Stalnaker said, "The picture should be more popular than any feature movie ever exhibited in Tampa. To see ourselves as others see us is not always pleasant, but in a case like this, I believe Tampa will be taught a great moral lesson." Stalnaker even asked for a pipe organ to be brought into the courtroom to provide a suitably grim soundtrack to his feature presentation. One investigating officer said that multiple additional arrests could be expected stemming from the film.[79]

The case would be dogged by procedural irregularities that the defense lawyers seized upon as proof of bias. The suspects appealed for Stalnaker to be prohibited from presiding over the case for overstepping his bounds. Four city police officers backed up the defendants' testimony. If the appeal succeeded, and Stalnaker was taken off the case, Mayor Wall could appoint a special judge. At that point, the case would certainly disappear.[80]

When the defense attorney petitioned for Stalnaker to be disqualified from the case, the judge's temper flared. His voice trembled with emotion when he shouted down the appeal and ordered the defense attorney to shut up. Stalnaker dug deep into the law books to deny the disqualification, saying that in this case it was the judge's decision. When the *Tampa Daily Times* wrote an editorial critical of Stalnaker and his methods, police arrested two journalists from the newspaper for allegedly being in the club at the time of the raid. The journalist defendants accused Stalnaker and the police of retaliating for unflattering newspaper coverage.[81]

Stalnaker rushed the cases into the docket before he could be taken off the case. At the judge's request, detective Ponder recorded testimony in the official court transcript, describing the founding of the club, its members, and its officers. The defending lawyer objected to the introduction into the public record of unsubstantiated information, but Stalnaker allowed the testimony to continue to build an official record that would embarrass his enemies. On August 29, while a crowded courtroom of two hundred looked on, Stalnaker issued sentences of ten days each. The defendants immediately appealed and were released to their attorneys. Two weeks after the trial, Stalnaker discovered that the court record had been stolen from the court reporter's office, who said she had no knowledge of the theft.[82]

Mayor Wall called for Stalnaker to resign and openly admitted to being a member of the drinking club. His following argument harks back to the days of Nullification, saying, "I'm a member of the Key Club and don't care who knows it. There will never be any progress in government if the citizens bow to any law that certain interests have passed. I believe we have the same right as our forefathers had to oppose the British laws. [Prohibition] is destroying officials and breaking governments."[83]

The screening of Stalnaker's film soon became more complicated. The city's electrical inspector and fire chief ordered the screening to be postponed while they investigated the health and fire hazards arising from such an exhibition. A detective conferred with the inspector and assured everyone that the film was not flammable or explosive. The fire department was concerned with the projector and the capacity crowds expected to attend the screening. Stalnaker's courtroom was located directly above the police garage, where large amounts of fuel was stored, the fire inspector said. City officials worried that even a small fire could spread out of control.[84]

Burglars ransacked the homes of Detectives Lawrence Ponder and Harry Myers in search of the Key Club film. Concerned for the safety of this key piece of evidence, Stalnaker asked Ponder to keep quiet and deliver the film to the U.S. Attorney General in Washington. When Ponder departed, Detective Myers took a ten-day vacation and reportedly would not return to the vice squad. Days later, Department of Justice employees said they knew nothing of the Key Club case and had received no film. Federal Prohibition officials said they had never met with Ponder at all.[85]

Ponder resigned from the vice squad and left Tampa in the midst of the Key Club cases being brought to court. His resignation supposedly would not prevent him from testifying. Ponder's father said his son resigned at the request of his parents, who were worried for his safety.[86]

The entire family realized that the powerful forces of the Tampa underworld, which are mightier than most people imagine, would inevitably crush Lawrence because of his activities against members of the local bootleg ring. No one knows what my boy has had to contend with. Jealousy of fellow officers, open hatred of some and the constantly mounting weight of political influence bearing down harder and harder upon him were in themselves worry enough. But the threats, telephone calls and anonymous letters really broke his mother and his wife. After the Key Club affair, more powerful forces were brought to bear. The higher-ups were worried evidently by the threatened exposé of the films. The threats came faster and seemed to me to be more deadly.[87]

Cerf appealed his case all the way to the Florida Supreme Court, but it was not expected to be handled before mid-September, so Stalnaker would have no chance at trying the case unless he was reelected. When the official court docket reportedly went missing, Stalnaker declared he would run for a complete term as municipal judge. The misplaced docket covered the time of Stalnaker's term, forcing the judge to use an incomplete clerk's docket to try to re-create an accurate record of his time on the bench. Written notes on the Key Club cases also disappeared. Before Stalnaker could even run for election, his legacy was already crumbling.[88]

Election

Resistance to Stalnaker's strict interpretation of the law began immediately, but the Key Club case had given him nationwide publicity. While many churchgoers cheered their dry champion, Stalnaker appeared to be increasingly isolated as his tenure wore on into the fall. First, City Manager W. Lesley Brown ordered City Attorney E. E. Graves, the judge's only true partner in the struggle, to cease acting as a criminal prosecutor, instead spending his time trying tax cases. Dry City Commissioner Sumter Lowry's actions at the time did little to help: He publicly called Tampa police lazy while cutting their funding. With no effective allies left in the city government, Stalnaker was then challenged from without.[89]

Tom O. Watkins announced he would run for Stalnaker's post to restore "dignity" to the bench. It was probably no coincidence that Watkins's campaign was managed by Archie Cerf's attorney, C. J. Hardee. Five other candidates stepped forward.[90]

For his part, Stalnaker was in no mood to back down. The *St. Petersburg Independent* wrote, "Judge Stalnaker and his friends appear to have decided against Mayor Wall," who actively campaigned for Watkins, while Stalnaker intimated that Wall himself was a bootlegger. For many, Mayor Wall's criticism of Stalnaker was proof of the judge's honesty. A local wrote, "Passing history of our city proves that 'crime' is not confined to slums and evil resorts. It flourished in high places. 'Criminals' are not all behind the bars. They boldly walk our streets." Another reader implicated Tampa's elite. "Are laws which are enforceable when directed against out-of-state corporations not to be enforced when Tampa men are the violators? Are laws against bootlegging, bolita and contraband drugs only to be enforced when the poor and friendless are the defendants?"[91]

Other locals were not so trusting of Stalnaker's methods or motives: "Stalnaker in his campaign accused everybody who was not for him of being with the underworld, against law enforcement and for a wide open town."[92]

Through some means Stalnaker was elected a representative in the legislature—whether it was through the influence of the hooded wearer of sheets [the Ku Klux Klan], whose main stock in trade seems to be hatred of foreigners, or by other means, is unknown to this writer. If we can now learn from our citizens of foreign birth that art of self-control as it is practiced in their countries, we could avoid all the bitter wrangles and strife growing out of the liquor question. For with them there is no prohibition and no need for it. There is no liquor question. There is no drunkenness—except when some occasional American gets under the influence. And yet we are asked even by a few ministers (whose sincerity we don't question, but regret their being so badly misled) to vote to keep in office a judge who becomes rabid at the sight of a foreign-born citizen or even to hear his name called. This judge whose extreme sentences, we are constrained to believe, arise not from a desire to suppress crime or to do justice, but solely from a desire to add to his notoriety.[93]

It seemed the entire city had turned on Stalnaker by the time of the October elections. As the contest neared, both local newspapers refused to print his campaign ads. The *Tribune* printed a story saying that Stalnaker had conceded defeat and asked all of his supporters to support Watkins instead. The next day, Stalnaker wrote the *Tribune* denying he had ever made such a statement. Stalnaker took to giving speeches directly to his base at church congregations.[94]

With no other press to turn to, Stalnaker invented his own. His home-grown newspaper, the *Municipal Judge*, appeared before the election to attack his opponents and the newspapers. "I am standing alone in this race," he wrote, "fighting to the last ditch for civic righteousness. I am being ridiculed, criticized, abused, falsely accused, and persecuted by the press, and I am not given the privilege to defend myself through the columns of the press, in paid advertisements, and otherwise." Stalnaker's campaign printed 40,000 copies to distribute for free.[95]

It must have been humiliating when the proud judge visited the *Tampa Tribune* to ask for his disastrous election results. Voters had swept Stalnaker out of office, at least if the municipal election returns could be trusted. He carried only two of the twenty-six precincts. "Nobody in Tampa in the last two weeks had doubted the result," the *Tribune* crowed. Tom Watkins, Stalnaker's opponent, won 6,004 votes to Stalnaker's 2,680. Partisans threw a street celebration when it was clear Stalnaker had lost the bench, "not so much because Watkins had won but because Stalnaker had lost."[96]

In November, with his time on the bench dwindling away, Stalnaker defiantly began "personally conducting raids against disorderly houses." One Saturday in November, the maverick judge personally led a sweep that caught thirty-four offenders. He also indulged his love for embarrassing his victims with a "personal camera man . . . [who] went right along and photographed the militant judge and the officers as they put the pinch on alleged lawbreakers. Close-ups, fade-ins, cutbacks—all the tricks that seasoned movie men toy with—followed one after the other in succession Saturday night as Stalnaker, a judicial Cecil B. DeMille, directed the photographing of gambling dens, gambling paraphernalia, and the men and women who must face film on charges of general disregard for the law." Stalnaker must have known that their criminal cases might be compromised by his zealous participation, but he clearly enjoyed it too much to care.[97]

Stalnaker's crusade in politics came to an abrupt end little more than a year after winning a seat in the legislature. His two honest city detectives were gone; one resigned and one was fired. The council that appointed him was gone. The police chief retired. It does not appear that Cerf or any of the other Key Club suspects were ever tried for their crimes. When Stalnaker left the bench, he dismissed all the cases in his docket. The Key Club testimony, film, and suspects all disappeared from the justice system, and Tampa's dark criminal machine roared on as if Stalnaker had never existed. Former mayor D. B. McKay, one of the architects of Tampa's regime, had just been elected for the fourth time.

TAMPA LIFE

Even off the bench, Leo Stalnaker would not back down. Frustrated but not defeated, he tried to parlay his experience and public image into a career as a journalist. Instead of a judge's gavel, the crusader wielded the printing press as a weapon against Tampa's corrupt government, which welcomed back D. B. McKay as mayor in 1928. Early in 1929, a small publication called the *Spade* appeared in Tampa, devoted entirely to exposing the city's rampant crime and corruption. Stalnaker probably played a part in the *Spade*, which listed W. J. Griffin as publisher. After the short-lived *Spade* disappeared (its second and final issue appeared in April 1929), Stalnaker established a full newspaper called *Tampa Life* with partners two months later. *Tampa Life*'s coverage of corruption was far more relevant to Tampa's plight than anything else printed in the city at that time. Stalnaker had an axe to grind, but denied slinging mud at his enemies. Instead, he called his muckraking "strong, stalwart, fearless, Christian aggressiveness against cussedness."[98]

Stalnaker's paper had three chief obsessions: exposing corruption, espousing racism, and teaching the Holy Bible. One story pointed out that a black deputy was a confessed chicken thief. While other newspapers ridiculed the Klan, Stalnaker defended it. He also printed weekly Sunday school lessons for his readers.[99]

On the back cover of the *Spade*, the editors listed some Tampa restaurants engaged in the liquor/gambling rackets, most of them cafés in Ybor

City or downtown.[100] Liquor sales became so brazen that the Blue Bird Café offered curb service. Gambling houses were similarly out of control. Tampa was in the throes of bolita mania. Big bolita houses began paying out two numbers a throw, then three, in a power play to win players away from the smaller independent bolita bookies. Police raided cafés, filling stations, and cigar and drink stands, pulling out fifty slot machines in a single day.[101]

Hyde Park Deputy J. E. Pentecost caught Anderson Harley running the biggest moonshine-still operation in the county. When Judge Tom Watkins (Stalnaker's replacement) asked him if he had made the rotten moonshine that had been circulating around town, Harley denied it, saying, "That ain't no rotten liquor, that's the best shine in Tampa. Try some of it and see. If you all put me in the stockade for selling liquor, I want it to be for selling good liquor, 'cause I don't mess with any other kind."[102] Police Chief James McCants and Judge Tom Watkins fixed fines at very low levels for vice offenders.[103]

A new slate of elected city officials assumed duties in 1928 and 1929, including Mayor D. B. McKay. The *Spade* "wanted to be fair and give them a chance" to be honest before condemning them.

> We venture to state that there is more gambling, bootlegging, bolita, more open saloons and more lottery operating in Tampa right now than ever before since Prohibition, and are operating more openly than they have done in years . . .
>
> The Mussolini of Tampa [Mayor D. B. McKay] . . . is a man with no conscience, no feeling for little children (outside of his own kin), a man whose greatest love is for gold and silver of which his coffers are running over, a man who has accumulated fortunes by many political schemes. . . . He has plenty of time to confer with the higher-ups of the gambling world, but little time or sympathy for a desperate man with a starving family who has fallen before his corrupt political gun. . . . We feel that there are enough red-blooded, conscientious citizens in Tampa to help us trample this old political machine in the mud— this old political machine that was first built by the Mayor [in McKay's first three terms, 1910–1920] in the by-gone days of open saloons and gambling halls, long petticoats and bustles.[104]

Allegations ranged from negligence to unbridled debauchery. On the south end of the Twenty-Second Street Causeway (just outside city limits), the fine Embassy Club had an opening night party that two Tampa judges allegedly attended. The drinking lasted until daylight, with erotic dancers performing. Another recent affidavit named two judges as visiting Nellie's Roadhouse just north of Tampa, where one of them was said to have intercourse with a nude dancer. In 1928, Florida's sheriffs held a convention in Miami, so local police threw a party for many who visited on the drive down, serving $500 worth of liquor at the event.[105]

Stalnaker's position as manager of *Tampa Life* was almost as short-lived as his stint as judge. After one tumultuous year, *Tampa Life* went out of business, but the controversy it caused lived on. In May 1929, *Tampa Life* had printed an inflammatory sermon preached by Rev. Ira E. Williams, the young pastor of Eighth Avenue Methodist Church, where Stalnaker attended services. The sermon accused twenty-two local high school girls of "immorality," but the specifics have been lost to history.[106] Ed Blackburn, president of Hillsborough High School's Dad's Club, accused Stalnaker of libel, and Judge Cornelius gave warrants for the arrest of Stalnaker and of *Tampa Life* business manager George W. Coulie. Unapologetic, Stalnaker was finally acquitted, as his authorship could not be proven in court.[107]

Stalnaker continued to work as an attorney until late 1930, when allegations surfaced of "violating the confidence of a client and perpetrating fraud in handling the $16,000 estate of Florine Brandon, a minor." Stalnaker received a $9,000 loan from the girl's trust and failed to file the proper disclosure forms for several months. He invested the money in real estate that promptly flooded. Unable to pay back the loan, Stalnaker left his young client's trust bereft of more than half of its funds.[108]

The Florida Bar suspended Stalnaker's membership, ordering him to pay back the $9,000 he had received from his client's trust. He appealed to the Florida Supreme Court in 1931, which upheld his suspension. Desperate for income during the 1930s, he wrote detective stories to make a living. The embattled Stalnaker never repaid the loan, instead asking Florine Brandon to claim she was satisfied with his payment of just $1,000 and property valued at $500. He resumed his legal career only in 1941, after a split court decision restored his license (he was judged not on what he had actually paid but by his ability to pay). Stalnaker went on to practice law for the rest of his life, but he will forever be known for his stand against evolution, his stormy six-month tenure on the bench, his muckraking newspaper, and his fall from grace, all between 1926 and 1930.[109]

RAW DEALS

The outcome of Prohibition in Florida must have been a great disappointment to the activists who brought it about. Coupled with the buzz of the Florida land boom, the years of state and national dry laws had only served to further saturate the state. In the face of Prohibition laws, virtually everyone participated in or casually accepted crime as a matter of routine. If allowed to continue indefinitely, what kind of society would Prohibition produce? As the late 1920s wore into the 1930s, even some former supporters of Prohibition had to admit that the laws had given too much power to police and criminals alike while undermining the legitimacy of the church and state.[110]

By 1928, Prohibition was an obvious failure. In New York City, socialite-activist Pauline Sabin rallied the wealthy (including women!) to repeal the dry laws. The business community had soured on Prohibition, as it felt it had given the government too much power over regulation. Enforcement had led to an erosion of civil liberties and property rights. The Volstead Act led to the rise of federal police such as the FBI. Most importantly, the wealthy erroneously thought that the return of alcohol-related taxes would lead to the elimination of the hated federal income tax.

In retrospect, it seems easy to blame the failure of dry laws on powerful gangsters and corrupt police and politicians, but no law can be effective among an uncooperative public. At the time, Dr. C. W. Duke said of Tampa, "Laws must be enforced to be effective. . . . Responsibility for their enforcement or their lack of enforcement in the last analysis rests with the people."[111]

Congress repealed the Eighteenth Amendment in February 1933, but Florida was still technically dry. Despite a flurry of lobbying by die-hard Prohibitionists, the Florida Legislature voted to legalize 3.25 percent beer, and Governor David Sholtz signed it into law. Beer became legal again in Florida on May 8, 1933, while Tampa's drinkers sang "Happy Days Are Here Again." Dozens of trains, trucks, and ships converged on Florida's hardest-drinking city, bringing in 3.2-percent beer from New Orleans and Cuban beer prized for being stronger. The freighter *Pawnee* arrived just as the Beer Bill was signed, with enough suds to fill three railroad cars. In the first fifteen wet days, Hillsborough residents drank 250,000 bottles of beer and 17,000 gallons of draft, more than any other county in Florida: a daily average of two and a half bottles per person. By May 1933, well over five hundred businesses were selling beer in Tampa, but only sixty-nine had bothered to obtain licenses.[112]

JOOK JOINTS, WORLD WAR II, AND "VENEREAL DISEASE"

On New Year's Eve 1939, writer Stetson Kennedy visited Ybor City to document life there for the Works Progress Administration. He and his wife, Edith, visited her relatives, Pedro and Estrella. Their children stared at Kennedy and said in Spanish, "He's an *American*. He sure looks it, too. You can tell by looking at him." Kennedy wrote:

"Would you like to go somewhere tonight?" asks Estrella.

I suggest a cafe of some sort, anywhere we can dance and buy drinks.

"You don't mean a *jook joint*, do you?" Estrella asks. "Jooking is for unmarried men."

"That's what you think," replies Pedro, "plenty married men go jooking."

"I know they do, but that's not so good."

"You don't know what jooking means. Jooking means having a good time anywhere, drinking and dancing."

Seventh Avenue was the only Ybor City street illuminated by streetlights. Estrella worried that her guest would want to leave Ybor City for the well-lit "American" streets of Tampa.

I assure her that we would prefer to stay in Ybor City, so we drive along Seventh Avenue. Narrow, and with a street car track down the center, it is well lighted with neon signs. Most of the shops have Italian and Spanish names. The cafés, barrooms, and restaurants are thronged with people, many of them dressed in tuxedos and evening gowns. The restaurants are being heavily patronized by Americans from Tampa.[1]

After cruising down the strip, they parked the car and strolled and window-shopped before stepping into a jook joint, or small dance club. They spent many hours there, eating Cuban sandwiches and mixing Cuba Libres (rum and Cokes with lime) at their table. The jukebox was stocked with ten records—eight of Cuban music, two of American—and customers constantly fed it nickels to keep it playing. Children set off fireworks on the brick streets, joined at midnight by carousing policemen who fired their pistols and shotguns into the air. Buckshot spattered onto the sheet metal roofs. Revelers shouted and laughed into the night. Couples danced the rhumba until the sun rose.

Kennedy's party passed clues of the harsh changes that lay ahead as they romped down Seventh Avenue. Posters on storefronts read, "Aid the Spanish victims of Fascist Aggression," referring to the Spanish Civil War, which was then in its final throes. The signs of propaganda, with imagery of bombers, gutted cities, and suffering civilians, would be familiar to all of Tampa in a short time. World War II began in Europe that September, and the United States plunged into the conflict about two years later.

After the Japanese attack at Pearl Harbor and the U.S. entry into World War II in December 1941, Tampa's New Year's festivities became more subdued, overshadowed by talk of war, the draft, and invasion scares. No children set off fireworks in the streets, and the *Tampa Tribune* announced, "To prevent confusion over blackout warning signals, owners of sirens and loud whistles were asked not to blow them at midnight tonight, as in years past." German U-boats operated along the coast, and far away, the Japanese war machine roared through the Pacific.[2]

The war interrupted peacetime routines and overthrew inhibitions. Tampa had long maintained a reputation as a place with an active nightlife teeming with all manner of vice. When the United States joined World War II, typical jook joints became the frontlines of another war, a war against rampant sex and vice that sabotaged the war effort with

Jook joints served as recreation centers on rural worksites across the South, offering a place for music, gambling, drinking, and the pursuit of the opposite sex. (Florida Memory Collection, Florida Archives)

sexually transmitted infections (which will hereafter be referred to as venereal disease, or VD, in the parlance of the times). The city's jook joints became the focus of anti-VD enforcement efforts. The military soon questioned the willingness of city fathers to clean up vice at all.

FROM JOOK TO JUKE

In April 1941, journalist Theodore Pratt wrote an article in the *Saturday Evening Post* calling Florida "The Land of the Jook," which sparked the public's imagination, resulting in the movie *Jook Girl* the following year. The national attention prompted the *Miami Herald* to devote column space to Florida's history of jook joints. "We learned that the term 'jook' originated at a turpentine still and that the name is almost as old as the industry itself. It is a name given by the negroes to a building or dance hall set aside for their use. After their week's work, the negroes would congregate on Saturday night to dance and frolic at the 'jook.' The music supplied usually came from guitars and banjos manipulated by the negroes with the particular kind of music that they like and play."[3]

By the 1940s, a new generation of white Americans had discovered jazz music and dancing, some opting for more raucous and raw variations popularized by hot jazz, jump blues, and frantic jitterbug dancing. At the same time, white Americans became more aware of jook joints and the role they played as wellsprings of black song and dance. Curious white people were fascinated by the latest black entertainers, and some wanted a closer look.

But while distant observers saw carefree frolics and parties, jook joints dwelled in the squalid shadows of the Sunshine State. Jooks would not have existed at all if Florida's poorest workers had been treated fairly. Instead, after Emancipation, Florida functioned much like the rest of the South, as a feudal society that coerced its peasants to provide the labor necessary for property owners and businessmen to profit off the land. Self-sufficient black subsistence farming was actively suppressed. In 1941, journalist Theodore Pratt recognized jooks for what they were: a necessary cog in Florida's merciless agriculture machine. Pratt traced the origin of jook joints to Florida's turpentine industry.[4]

Instead of a lighthearted look at the song and dance of black workers, Pratt's article read more like an exposé of Florida's shameful labor conditions. Pratt described a hundred jooks, most of them black, less than a hundred miles from the luxuries of Palm Beach County's coastal towns, with hundreds more across north Florida, around the vast farms of Lake Okeechobee and the budding enterprises north of the Everglades. Each cluster of jooks claimed its own death toll, usually several stabbings and beatings each weekend. Guns, ice picks, razors, and fisticuffs were simply ways of life in jooks, with most conflicts arising over women or gambling. Pratt wrote, "The frontierlike violence of the region is a product of the most outrageous kind of farming practiced in America, which draws thousands of migrant workers, large numbers of whom live in the most abject poverty. The jooks are an escape from this life." Only the worst working conditions could make the squalor of jook joints attractive as an escape. Growers reserved the easier and more lucrative jobs in the packing plants for white workers, usually desperate sharecroppers from elsewhere in the South looking to augment their negative incomes.[5]

Pratt described a faceless, soulless farming industry where "the growers are not farmers but soil miners gambling with Nature in a speculation usually financed by northern commission houses, which furnish seed and capital, if need be, and take their profit in the handling of the crop." Only about one-third of attempted crops succeeded financially, leaving growers to rent land and operate at a loss while the financiers reaped certain profits. Local growers felt "little or no responsibility for their workers. [T]he result [is] that the condition of the muck-land casual workers was worse than anything in the Grapes of Wrath."[6]

"Many of the migrants," Pratt wrote, "white and black, continue to live in indescribable squalor in ramshackle camps, boardinghouses, tin and burlap shacks, broken-down trailers, trucks, old automobiles—and the screaming jooks. Occasionally Negro migrants still sleep in the open in the tall grass around a fire built in an empty oil drum." Survivors still spoke in hushed tones about the fatal hurricanes of the 1920s that killed thousands of unsheltered workers. Many rural black people had little choice but to comply when the barkers called over loudspeakers from flatbed trucks to press workers into service for this camp or that harvest.[7]

Much like saloons, jook joints would always carry a stigma in the white press as dangerous places. Although this was true, there also seemed to be a great variety in the quality of jook joints, and some were known more for good times than for bad. Women rarely ventured into the saloons of old, but jook joints were places for men and women to interact and dance. The only thing that set jooks apart from typical bars was the addition of music, either a live band, a piano, or a jukebox.

Besides the meager pay, most work sites provided one source of comfort and recreation: Saturday nights. Plantations and large-scale enterprises typically paid their workers on Saturday afternoon and gave them Sunday off. Since agricultural labor took place in rural areas, often hours away from any major town, the owners of plantations and work camps provided a company store to sell goods (often at inflated prices) and a small space to serve as a bar, cantina, and recreation center. Sometimes they were little more than clapboard shacks, primitive lean-tos or repurposed railcars. The facilities provided just enough shelter and comfort to prevent workers from trying to leave after payday.[8]

For most African American workers on these sites, recreation meant drinking, gambling, dancing, and pursuit of the opposite sex. Music held these recreation centers together, with workers often playing music for free drinks. Sometimes the worksite owners provided a piano. It is said the first jukeboxes were the crate the pianos had shipped in. At the end of a night of music, the player boxed up the piano once again, which probably afforded more protection than the flimsy shack in which it resided.

All over the state, migrant farm workers, road gangs, and other rural workers relied on jook joints for entertainment, socialization, and easing stress. Many workers lived for Saturday nights, when their bosses left them alone to live out loud. Workers had the most time and money on those Saturday nights, and they determined to make the most of them. Don Gavin of Wakulla County recalled, "These jooks were just the only place to be. Actually we couldn't afford to do anything else even if we would have liked to." What mattered most is that workers could express themselves and entertain one another.[9]

Without music, there would be no "jookin'." Not the low, steady work songs moaned in the harsh sunlight, but music of the night, songs of full of exuberance and desire, humor and heartache. Jook joints became cultural incubators, where workers in every region of the South developed their own songs and dances according to local taste. The music was not the only thing jumping and swinging in jooks—bodies in motion characterized the jitterbug dancing of the 1930s and 1940s. It was a style of dancing typically restricted to young black people, but like the jooks themselves, it caught on with others.

Of course, music and booze set the scene for the jooks' other delights, namely, pursuit of the opposite sex. Since male workers predominated at the hardest-working camps, the bosses often imported truckloads of women, prostitutes or otherwise, into the camps for Saturday night. Putnam Lumber Company used a train to ship women to its jook joint in Clara sixty at a time. It was often the only way to keep the men on-site week after week. With few amenities and no privacy, it was not unusual for lovers to stumble off into the woods and couple in the darkness. Other jooks provided small curtained cubicles in the back for "strictly dishonorable" purposes. By 1940, many jook operators hired young women to act as servers, but they were more akin to "B-girls" who sold drinks to customers and ostensibly drank with them, though the girls only drank fruit juice to improve the profits of the joint and preserve their sobriety for the next customer.[10]

Workers also enjoyed gambling. Company agents issued tokens to serve as credit. Workers typically gambled for tokens and spent cash on drinks and necessities. Poker was eschewed as too slow-paced, with the men usually preferring to play craps or a card game called "Skin," or "Georgia Skin," while women's card games were often devoted to "patting." Bolita was so pervasive that when it had been stamped out in Palm Beach County, black workers refused employment at the enterprises there until the lottery returned. Ministers complained that some congregants went to church only to get the Bible verses from the gospel to play as bolita numbers. Even the games had their own songs. Zora Neale Hurston can be heard singing such a song, "Let the Deal Go Down," in her field recordings for the Works Progress Administration.[11] Hurston put it best in her novel *Their Eyes Were Watching God*: "The jooks clanged and clamored. Pianos living three lifetimes in one. Blues made and used right on the spot. Dancing, fighting, singing, crying, laughing, winning and losing love every hour. Work all day for money, fight all night for love."[12] The jook proved to be a durable concept in the 1930s and 1940s, when couples dancing had reached new heights in popular culture. Many were run by people not associated with larger work sites. Some had full kitchens, while others served only pickled snacks out of jars. When people started importing the idea of rural jooks into cities like Tampa, they tended to become more well-appointed nightclubs and differed little from the urban bars and saloons already found there.[13]

Coin-operated machines became a new craze. Beginning in the 1930s, the coin-operated mechanical phonograph, juke-organ, or jukebox began to replace pianos and live entertainment in urban jooks. In 1935, the U.S. mint tripled the production of nickels and dimes in part because of these contraptions. By 1940, fifteen million nickels were being spent in jukeboxes daily.[14]

As jook joints went from rural dives to more urban locales, they became new bugbears for moralizing politicians. Like saloons before them, jooks could be attacked for their clientele, namely, black men and women and working-class women. During a court case in 1939, a state prosecutor said, "They are . . . the arch incubators of vice, immorality and low impulses. Nothing in modern economy has so clarified our concept of hell's half acre." Florida's "Dance Hall Act" of 1937 singled out popular jook joints as a social menace, banning all dancing without a special license. New state laws banned slot machines and most gambling on September 30, 1937. Predictably, the moral courage of the legislators did not extend to the deplorable conditions of the agricultural workplace, only the recreational habits of the exploited labor.[15]

Jook joints would have been an obscure footnote in history if not for the fact that young white people began to build and frequent their own. In the 1940s, swing jazz had been co-opted by white musicians and an older white audience. Younger white dancers eschewed Lawrence Welk in favor of more kinetic black jazz that moved the body with more urgency. Of course, the fact that older white people frowned upon or misunderstood the hot jazz and jitterbug dancing only made them more attractive to the younger "hepcat" generation.[16]

For many, jook joints were strictly off limits for moral reasons, especially for women. But even for those uninterested in booze, sex, or gambling, the jook joint represented an alternate world where the usual restrictions on feminine expression did not exist. Ethel Skipper grew up curious about the jook joints she heard so much about, but she remained skeptical: "All I could think about was if the church people would have found out that I was at a jook they would have had me at church. I was never raised to go to a place like that." But after she married, she asked her husband to take her out during one of his Saturday night outings. She sat against the wall wide-eyed, taking it all in, especially the dancing, until a beer bottle exploded nearby. She quickly lost her nerve and asked to be taken home.[17]

In the 1930s, white journalists changed the spelling and meaning of the word. To "jook," a verb, meaning to be unruly and wicked, became a "juke," meaning a dance club or coin-operated phonograph. The real goal was to strip the word of any suggestion of sex or race that would have hurt sales of the coin-fed contraption in white society. The word "saloon" had been similarly banned by the press in deference to the liquor interests, who did not want drinking and bars to be associated with the word and the connotations it still carried after Prohibition.[18]

In 1941, groundbreaking black linguist Dr. Lorenzo Turner confirmed that "jook" was of African origin, where it was a vulgar term meaning to misbehave in a disorderly and wicked fashion. Turner was astonished to learn of the word's "widespread use in Florida and the extension of meaning to something respectable or at least semi-respectable." Turner also chastised *Time* magazine for using the Anglicized spelling "juke" in a recent publication. "It is always jook, rhyming with book," the *Miami Herald* wrote.[19]

Activities such as drinking, gambling, and casual sex that may have been acceptable for white men took on more sinister tones when attributed to black men in the press. Therefore, jook joints earned a bad reputation in a city already rife with organized crime, gambling, and prostitutes. It comes as little surprise that when World War II began and venereal disease once again became a concern to military authorities, jook joints would become public enemy number one.

THE "BLACK SPOT"

As a "wide-open" city in one of the nation's most infected states, Tampa had a long history of sexual disease. The Works Progress Administration reported how Tampa's first cigar-making immigrants quickly became infected after arriving in Tampa: "Youth and ignorance prevented the Spanish immigrants from foreseeing the obvious consequences derived from their continuous visits to houses of prostitution. From the very beginning of the establishment of the Spanish hospitals [in the 1890s] in this community, it might be said that the treatment of venereal diseases has been one of their main practices. The [VD] problem is still faced by these clubs [in the 1930s]."[20]

In the 1940s, Tampa became an important location for the U.S. war effort. MacDill Air Base opened in April 1941, augmented by Drew Field (near the future site of Tampa International Airport) and Henderson

Field (south of the University of South Florida's main campus). At their height, these air bases alone housed more than 43,000 servicemen around the city. Tens of thousands more workers and servicemen came to Tampa for business or pleasure. The port regularly hosted vessels while the shipyards ran night and day to construct minesweepers and concrete liberty ships.[21]

During the war, men and women worked, traveled, and played on a scale the country had never seen. The war also drew millions of women from rural areas to cities such as Tampa. With women entering the workforce on such a large scale, they had unprecedented freedom to recreate outside the home. While workers made sacrifices, they often played as hard as they worked. Round-the-clock shifts at shipyards and factories gave rise to long nights of dining, drinking, and dancing. By dissuading women and families from having children, the war may have incentivized women to date *more* rather than less.[22]

Mary Henry of Tampa presents an excellent example of a woman mobilized for the war industry. Orphaned as a child in Tennessee, she moved to Miami and worked as a secretary there in 1940. Her sister called her in 1941, telling her about the lucrative shipbuilding jobs in Tampa. Miss Henry promptly went to work at Tampa Ship Repair. A union organizer courted her throughout the war years, and she discovered the delights of Tampa's nightlife. Henry especially loved the Columbia and Las Novedades, where the atmosphere was elegant, the food exquisite, and the dance floor jumping.

> When you worked at Tampa ship repair, everybody thought the next day was gonna be it. I mean, we all had a good time. And there were so many nice places to go dancing and everything. Like I said, my husband and I practically lived [on the dance floor] when we were dating. My husband was a galvanizer in a union. He'd pick me up at 12:30 [at night, after my shift]. We'd go right down Twenty-Second Street to the Seabreeze and stay until three in the morning. Oh, and they had the best band and we had the best time and the best food and everything. As I tell my daughter, if I never have another good time, I lived to see it! The Seabreeze was the place!

Oh, I'll tell you, I can't talk fast enough to tell it all! It was a wonderful life outside of being in the war. Those were the days. I don't mind telling you, I just had a ball.[23]

For soldiers stationed in Tampa, entertainment was typically not so wholesome. It is unsurprisingly difficult to persuade young soldiers mobilized for war far from home to avoid the intimate company of women. Tampa's criminal underworld had its hooks deeply set in the city's government and police, and its overlords must have anticipated a bonanza for the prostitution operations in its territory. The Army Air Corps quickly discovered that visiting Tampa was unhealthy for its personnel. Any time servicemen were granted leave in the city, there was a good chance they would return infected with VD.

Military officials immediately recognized the threat of venereal disease as an alarming number of draftees, especially African Americans, were found to be infected. No other factor cost the military as much lost manpower. In World War I, VD caused 357,969 American casualties, 100,000 more than incurred on the battlefield. In 1941–42, 329,000 infected soldiers missed 4,175,000 days of service. A congressional report revealed that out of the first two million men examined by the armed forces, the infection rate in Florida was the worst in the nation. More than 5 percent of white inductees were infected, a rate matched only by Texas and surpassed by New Mexico. At more than 40 percent, the infection rate for Florida's black examinees was the highest in the country. Florida also suffered from the highest rates of deaths from sexually transmitted disease in the nation.[24]

Like mobilization itself, the campaign against VD had been long overdue and had to make up for years of neglect. Before the war, the military had little apparent interest in what public health officials had to say. Early in 1941, a doctor from the Public Health Service (PHS) released a book called *Plain Words About Venereal Disease* in which he lambasted the army for taking so little action to address the issue. Only the outbreak of war prevented the army and PHS from having a potentially unpleasant public debate. With some harmony restored in the federal anti-VD effort, the military recognized the scope of the crisis and actively collaborated with the PHS. Throughout the war, the PHS supported the military's anti-VD efforts through expertise, support of state and local programs, writing or supporting helpful legislation, and a flood of education-propaganda materials.[25]

Since official statements urging servicemen to avoid the company of prostitutes had limited effect, authorities had to forcibly reduce or eliminate the trade. The assistance of local governments and law enforcement was essential to the anti-VD program. The Southern states all suffered from the same misguided racial policies and neglect, but climate determined a heavy military presence in the South. Federal military and health officials found that their initial policies could not compete with years of racism, corruption, and complacency.[26]

Congress gave federal officials more leverage over uncooperative local governments in 1941. The May Act expanded the military's jurisdiction into the civilian areas that surrounded its bases, allowing it to bypass local civilian authorities, assume control of local law enforcement, and restrict soldiers from visiting locales deemed hazardous. Early in the war, the military invoked the May Act twice, once in Tennessee and once in North Carolina. These types of intervention cost the local economy dearly as soldiers confined to base could not spend money in the community. Suddenly local politicians in the South found there were dire consequences for defying the military's requests. Merchants who lost revenue due to government neglect and the May Act would surely make their ire felt at the ballot box. For the rest of the war, the military could get the best results merely by threatening to invoke the May Act, as it did in Tampa and Miami in 1942.[27]

Captain Robert Dyer, head of the venereal disease protective service for the entire Army Air Corps, named Florida's air bases the "black spots" of military VD infection in the summer of 1942.[28] Tampa's air bases lost fifteen thousand man-days to VD that summer, and 17 percent of personnel had syphilis.[29] At that time, Hillsborough County treated almost 2,000 civilians for VD and the army turned away 1,100 prospective servicemen because of infection. It was the draftees' responsibility to get treatment to be eligible or otherwise face arrest. After treatment, some men intentionally contracted syphilis again to delay enlistment.[30]

Just over half of the soldiers managed to stay clean. Thirty percent of soldiers made contact with prostitutes after drinking alcohol or being led

BASES OF THE THIRD AIR FORCE

MAJ. GEN. WALTER H. FRANK
COMMANDING GENERAL

Corruption and permissiveness resulted in a high rate of sexual infection among military personnel during World War II, worse than their counterparts across the South. (Melvin Asp papers, University of South Florida Tampa Special Collections) by a friend, while 15 percent went into town actively looking for prostitutes. The going rate at the time was anywhere between one and five dollars, plus the cost of a hotel room. Of the many ("dozens" at the time) bases under the Third Air Force in the Southeast (from Arkansas and Louisiana in the west to Florida and the Carolinas in the east), Tampa's MacDill and Drew Fields ranked worst in VD infections.[31]

Gilbert Osincup, chairman of the health and housing division of the state defense council, said, "Prostitution and venereal disease are going to be wiped out in Florida, come what may and regardless of what heads may fall." Captain Robert Dyer, head of the Third Air Force's VD protective service, told Tampa's Rotary Club, "If the local authority does nothing to clear up the situation in a very few days, the army will take over the job and then we'll get action." The army urged local authorities to round up prostitutes and prosecute their business allies: operators of jooks, nightclubs, hotels, restaurants, taxi cabs, and rooming houses, who often depended on the indulgence of local enforcement. Major Onis Hazel of the Army Air Force said, "We propose drastic action to protect our men from this evil. The racket of prostitution moves into every army camp before it is even completed."[32]

Camp Followers, Soiled Doves, and Victory Girls

In a letter to the editor, a Tampa resident wrote to the *Tampa Tribune*, "I hear so much about the problem with delinquent girls and women who frequent hotels on week-ends and get drunk and scream all night long in gaiety." Any dedicated newspaper reader would have been alarmed by the ubiquitous stories in the press about out-of-control women.[33]

Florida witnessed a new wave of migration into the state during the war, an estimated one million servicemen and one million civilians, many of them young women in search of work and love. Many saw the war as an opportunity to escape their rural homes for a new life in the big city. Knocked free of their old lives by the shudder of war, these "loose" women were a public menace in the eyes of the FBI. Tampa was inundated with female teens adrift from all over the country. The police arrested six to eight a day simply for being in Tampa.[34] In a statement to the *Tribune*, Police Chief Woodruff said of the girls migrating to Tampa,

"They come to see soldier boy friends, and fail to find them; they come to get married and decide they don't want to get married; they come as brides of soldiers sent to a Tampa base, and drift without compass or rudder after they have gone; they come for adventure and romance."[35]

On another occasion, Woodruff described the problem in more detail.

We arrested two girls the other night. They were sisters, one 16 and the other 18, both from Iowa and were married. They just wanted to come to Florida. There are hundreds of others who come to Florida without the slightest idea of whether they can get a job when they get here. In some instances we have arrested women whose soldier husbands have left the country. They stay here having what they call a good time. We have also picked up wives of men who are working at night on defense jobs. They get liquored up and get into trouble. We have the names of hundreds of women and are checking on them every day.[36]

Reports of court hearings heaped on details about the female offenders. "There was a girl of 15," the *St. Petersburg Times* read, "whose too-wise eyes were out of place in a soft baby face that itself didn't go well with a mature figure. She was dressed in a red dress, bright red ankle sox and oxfords. She flared as Judge Fisher warned she'd probably be sent to the girls' industrial school in Ocala." When brought to court in Clearwater, a seventeen-year-old girl said she didn't understand the charges brought against her. The judge asked if she knew what "immoral" meant. She answered that she did not, then the judge asked if she was a loose woman. "I wasn't loose," she demanded, saying she had gone out with a girlfriend, not a man.[37]

Molly, nineteen, came from a small Florida town to attend business school and live with relatives. She met a shipworker who already had a family here. She found out too late and was eventually detained in a beer parlor. Mary, fifteen, ran away from home after her family moved here. She was arrested in a raid on a cheap hotel. A month later, she was arrested again. Small-town Texan Peggy came to marry her boyfriend, stationed at Drew Field. Their romance fizzled when she met another soldier, "then others," and she ended up single and received VD treatment at the stockade before being shipped home. Irene, sixteen, came to Tampa with her mother and sister from the panhandle. She was arrested when a soldier tried to rent a hotel room with her. Her mother quickly took her back up north. Millie, nineteen, came to Tampa with her sister, got a job, dated a shipyard worker, and "played around and had a good time." She was arrested at a jook. The *Tribune* did not print similar stories about black women.[38]

In July 1942, the FBI sent a team of instructors to brief Tampa's law enforcement officers on methods for suppressing prostitution. The FBI came armed with literature to help local law enforcement in their crackdown. Bureau Chief J. Edgar Hoover saw the spread of VD as a form of sabotage—tens of thousands of potential soldiers and workers were not utilized as a result of infection. The bureau announced, "drastic measures are justified in combating the evil, just as drastic measures are being taken to deal with saboteurs who use explosives to disrupt the war program."[39]

One FBI anti-VD guide named "taverns" and "jukes" as the most troublesome spots. The only place more dangerous to soldiers than a jook was an actual house of prostitution, the manual stated. Prostitutes may have been public enemy number one, but single women, especially young women, were seen as a menace, as well. Authorities named the conditions that they thought made a young girl ripe for prostitution or promiscuity. Among them were the criteria of bad family situations, delinquent parents, or being from a community with no recreational facilities. Other criteria included:

> She is a product of a broken home.
> She is the daughter of an employed mother.
> A girl forced into too early retirement [bedtime].
> She is a child-bride of a man in the service.
> She may have a misguided sense of patriotism and believes she is contributing to the war effort by giving herself to the man in uniform.[40]

Two days after Tampa's law enforcement conference, local officials announced their retaliation against Tampa's jooks and prostitutes. That summer, city aldermen gutted Tampa's alcohol and jook ordinances and replaced them all. The new guidelines banned single women from jooks after 10:00 p.m. and from employment after midnight. The ordinance also restricted female employees from drinking or dancing on the job, preventing the use of flirtatious "B-girls" to sell drinks. A local ordinance stated, "It is unlawful for any woman of ill fame to be on the streets, frequent bars or theaters after 9pm." New guidelines empowered local officials to easily revoke licenses of uncooperative business owners and barred felons from running jooks.[41]

With no state law against prostitution, local police favored vagrancy and loitering charges to detain women. Since vagrancy was the charge most often leveled against suspects, county courts increased bonds for the charge from $25 to $1,000—a hefty fee for even the most upscale professional prostitute. City Council increased bonds for vagrancy from $25 to $200. A state law passed in 1941 gave police authority to quarantine VD carriers, and in 1943 the legislature finally outlawed prostitution outright.[42]

Treatment of syphilis involved a five-to-six-week regimen of painful arsenic injections, making it difficult to persuade carriers to undergo the full course of treatment. Patients could lose all of their symptoms after the first treatment but still carry and spread the disease. Of course, military men had no option, but the state found that the anti-VD campaign required new legal and institutional support. With a strengthened state law, police could detain women for three to five days without habeas corpus and send them to the state hospital at Ocala for "a painful course of arsenic injections" lasting six weeks.[43]

A handful of prewar ordinances proved helpful in screening the population. In the late 1930s, Mayor Robert E. Lee Chancey enacted an ordinance requiring barbers, beauticians, and food handlers to undergo health exams. Ten percent had VD. Another 36 percent of domestic servants tested positive when a similar ordinance regulated them.[44] The police wanted a curfew for all women throughout the entire city—not just the jooks—but one was never passed. Sex and jooks were so closely related in people's eyes that Alderman D'Arpa declared, "If you keep women out after midnight, there won't be an open jook, because women are their principal article of trade." Alderman Frecker admitted that the situation was out of control "because of our failure as city representatives to exercise any control over the jooks. And I think we should be ashamed to take our pay from the city."[45]

The biggest single law enforcement component of the anti-VD campaign was the raiding of jook joints in the black areas of Tampa. These sweeps looked for any suspicious single woman, who the police detained, if only to forcibly test her for VD. The war effort superseded the basic rights citizens enjoyed in peacetime. This policy was a drastic departure from the more permissive times before the war, when Tampa's police readily ignored vice. Roundups started in August 1942 and fell heavily on the black jook joints. Charlie "Moon" Vanderhorse, the popular black owner of the Little Savoy, was arrested for employing a minor. More than half of those arrested in a raid on August 3, 1942, were women—seventy-two in all, most of them black. A few were white married women.[46]

From June 1942 through May 1943, officers made 1,542 arrests with 1,311 convictions. The city stockade and state camps brimmed with syphilis cases. The old stockade was used for female prisoners but was far too small. The jail and stockade were designed for a city of 50,000, Tampa's population in 1920, not Tampa's wartime population of 150,000 or 200,000 compounded by a campaign against wartime sex and disease. In the summer of 1942, it held more than 250 prisoners instead of the designed capacity of 160. Authorities had to refrain from further arrests until more space could be made available, and the city added a 125-bed "sleeping porch" to the stockade. The city built a large clinic in the stockade in September 1942 so patients would not have to be driven to the existing clinic near Central Avenue. The authorities arranged to have treatment continue after the prisoners had completed their sentences.[47] The Hillsborough County Federation of Women's Clubs protested to the city that conditions and food at the stockade were "a disgrace to Tampa womanhood."[48]

In effect, the "crackdown," "clean-up," or "all-out war" on VD was directed against unmarried women. In 1942, the Florida Board of Health received federal funds to create Rapid Treatment Centers where infected women could be quarantined and treated. The state selected four old Civilian Conservation Corps camps deep in the Ocala forest, where an inmate could be expected to spend weeks or months of treatment for VD and training to become more "productive" and "moral" citizens. Although the newspapers claimed the site "resembles [an] ideal tourist camp," stays there probably weren't so pleasant. The average age of the inmates was nineteen years old, and a quarter of them were not Florida residents. The camps opened in August 1942 and could cure up to five

Whether run for white people or black people, jook joints featured music, drinking, and dancing in a setting that encouraged intimacy among patrons. The high-backed booths provided a modicum of privacy, and some offered event rooms by the night or hour. (Florida Archives)

hundred women every month. The war on VD was in full swing and thousands of women were incarcerated, but then why did the problem get worse?[49]

<h2 style="text-align:center">CRACKDOWN</h2>

In autumn 1942, the press optimistically declared that Tampa was "on the road to recovery" from the VD plague. Tampa's vice squad, health department, and jook joint operators cooperated in a sustained crackdown on prostitutes. The stockade overflowed with women, who the VD clinic tested and treated.

In October 1942, M. D. Sinclair, head of Tampa's Vice Squad, claimed an easy victory over prostitution and VD: "From my standpoint I believe this is true because arrests are falling off. I can't give an estimate, not even a rough one, of how many prostitutes and others we picked up at the height of the clean-up, but I do know things have quieted down now."[50]

Military officials were not so optimistic. Rates of VD infection had fallen, but not nearly enough. Police Chief Woodruff answered allegations of foot-dragging by claiming that his best efforts were already underway. In September 1942, the army declared thirty-two Tampa businesses "out of bounds" for military personnel. That same month, military officials asked Tampa police leadership to meet at MacDill Air Base. There, the military asserted that rounding up women was not enough. The pimps and associate purveyors had to feel the pinch, too. The tactic was encouraged by the Public Health Service:[51] "It was early observed that the mere arresting of girls who were fined or even convicted of prostitution was inadequate to eliminate clandestine or commercialized prostitution. It was only when cities and communities emphasized the role of middlemen—facilitators, bellhops, cab drivers, and other individuals who procured customers for prostitutes—that any repression program could succeed."[52]

As head of the Venereal Protective Service for the Army Air Corps, Captain Robert Dyer had the most to gain from decreased prostitution. Dyer knew that to stop prostitutes, one had to go after their procurers: "Prostitutes operate here mainly through jook joints, taxicabs, cheap rooming houses and hotel bellhops, and they employ paid agents who arrange for their contact with soldiers. To make their business profitable, they must have this cooperation, and to a considerable extent, the protection or indulgence of law enforcement officers."[53] The government enlisted private industry in the fight against VD. Jook operators replaced soft, dim lights with bright white illumination and sawed off the high backs of their booths so the police could see every patron from the street. They closed early and deterred prostitutes. With the guidance of the Social Protection Division, the National Hotel Association endorsed wartime standards for hotel operation. The SPD and Office of Defense Transportation mandated that uncooperative cab drivers have their certificates revoked. The National Cab Association and affiliated unions joined the effort. Even the liquor industry was recruited to pressure bars to clean up their act.[54]

Despite all of the pressure brought to bear against prostitution, Tampa's leaders did not take the campaign very seriously. Police Chief Woodruff dismissively claimed, apparently with a straight face, "Tampa never had a great deal of crime." Whatever they said in meetings, Tampa's police showed no interest in pursuing the real sources of prostitution. Instead, they became proficient at rounding up women to demonstrate that progress was being made. But sweeping the streets of women did little to change the ugly reality of VD in Tampa. Instead of declining, by the summer of 1943, VD rates had increased to new crisis levels.[55]

As the situation worsened, a local businessman said, "Tampa is getting closer and closer to becoming off limits. It would be a catastrophe to the city, and would take ten years to overcome it." On June 4, 1943, Major General St. Clair Streett wrote an open letter to Mayor Chancey threatening to invoke the May Act in the army's "self-defense," which would make prostitution a federal offense and place Tampa off-limits to troops:[56] "The venereal disease rate among soldiers stationed in the vicinity has been constantly higher than in any other community. . . . The inescapable fact that the venereal disease rate among military personnel stationed in the Tampa area has risen markedly during the last six months gives serious cause to doubt the efficacy of enforcement measures."[57]

In the summer of 1943, VD infection rates for Tampa's three air bases reached an alarming 45 percent, while the rest of the Third Air Force averaged just 8 percent. The national syphilis infection rate was forty-five per thousand. Florida's was 170 per thousand, almost four times the national average, the worst of any state in the nation.[58]

The headlines shared news of Tampa's "Failure to Suppress Vice Lords." During the crisis of 1943, federal investigators shared evidence that Tampa was part of a circuit of professional prostitutes, "who are brought into Tampa, their fares paid, addresses given, their administration expenses looked after locally." Streett also emphasized that the police needed to concentrate on pimps and purveyors rather than on the routine roundups of women. He claimed that state and local laws were sufficient but that they had not been enforced adequately. While federal investigators hinted at the presence of organized crime, Tampa's newspapers took as little interest in the subject as the police department and mayor's office. The *Tribune* pointed out, "During the three-hour discussion in which the army put its cards in the table, not one public official opened his mouth to make this or a similar statement, 'All right, we're going to go after the owners of places where venereal disease has been contracted.'" George Hall of the Junior Chamber of Commerce took the city's aldermen to task when he said in a hearing, "I've been up here plenty of times when you gentlemen have had requests for revocation of permits before you, and you have not taken action."[59]

Mayor Chancey gave in to federal pressure gradually, which proved much too slow for the military. Chancey did little to prompt local businessmen to curb the conditions that led to the infections, despite new laws and plenty of support from public health and military officials.[60] By 1943, Chancey was up for reelection and became more sensitive to bad publicity. He chose to respond to the public digs of federal officials by appealing directly to Tampa's voters. By means of a white-only primary system and the White Municipal Party, white voters chose the invariably Democratic candidates, making most elections a mere formality.

It was obvious Chancey was not seeking black votes when he insisted that the VD menace was merely a black problem: "As a whole the charge is true, but the Army didn't distinguish between races in summing up the total. I understand the venereal disease rate among white people is lower than in many other cities." In a radio speech to the "Good women of Tampa," Chancey said, "As a citizen I resent petty politicians publicizing to the world that Tampa is a Sodom and Gomorrah. We know it is a slander to the good name of our community."[61]

After months of urging by federal authorities, Chancey appointed a Social Protection Committee, promoting Margaret Ansley from a child welfare worker to the committee's VD specialist. He also appointed M. D. Sinclair chief of a special VD squad that quickly raided black jook joints and pool halls, rounding up over fifty, most of them teenagers. It soon became apparent that the police were hindering local efforts. In a public meeting, Ansley said, "We as a community have a great apathy toward social problems." She accused Chief Woodruff and Sinclair of dismissing her suggestions and giving her the "run around." To Sinclair, she said, "You haven't been discourteous, rather just indifferent, careless. I remember I've apologized because I felt I was appearing dumb for coming back again and again. I was trying to offer the information I had." The city health officer identified "considerable opposition" to Chancey's orders to clean up prostitution in 1942. Mayoral candidates Curtis Hixon and Luther Cobbey assailed Chancey for allowing vice to flourish. After he lost his bid for reelection to Curtis Hixon in 1943, Mayor Chancey spent the remainder of his term shaking up the police department, probably in an attempt to clean up his public image.[62]

A variety of procedures strengthened the campaign. Beginning in November 1942, VD clinics sent letters detailing where every case was contracted. Copies of these letters were then sent to the "place of procurement" itself, the Third Air Force, the sheriff's office, Tampa's police chief, the state hotel commission, the state beverage commission, and any other interested parties. Such a paper trail made it easier for the various authorities to cooperate and identify undesirable business owners. While jooks were the focus of most crackdowns, all kinds of places were under new scrutiny: laundries, tourist cabins, restaurants, public parks, and taxi companies.[63]

Officials placed new emphasis on health cards. Many of the young women in town were "camp followers"—the girlfriends or wives of servicemen stationed in Tampa. Often treated as vagrants, camp followers were legal as long as they had a Tampa health card that certified they were free of communicable disease. Health cards became a way to force women, once again mostly black women, to be tested for VD without being arrested. Law enforcement required food servers and domestic workers, typical jobs for black women at the time, to have health cards to keep their jobs. Heavy penalties and fines awaited employers whose workers did not have health cards.[64]

Another constructive approach to the problem included new black training personnel for all black soldiers. According to public health officials, "Negro . . . personnel can better understand the mores, folkways, and race psychology of the Negro soldier than similar white personnel, and can thus be used more advantageously." Black counselors would appeal to the soldiers' positive virtues, such as "racial pride, competitive spirit, and patriotism," to change the behavior of black soldiers. A local Negro Recreation Committee ensured that black soldiers could enjoy healthy and wholesome activities as alternatives to the jooks, including various clubs, dances, and parties that had long been available to white soldiers.[65]

The State Board of Health created an anti-VD program specifically for black people in Florida. Dr. R. F. Sondag praised the program's progress. "The negroes have accepted the responsibility of controlling the diseases among their own race and have cooperated with the SBH splendidly. Pamphlets have been distributed to almost every negro home in the state to bring attention to the need for controlling venereal infection." Black clubs and churches spread the word. Negro Wartime Health Committees formed in Jacksonville, Miami, Pensacola, and Tampa. In the first six months of 1943, about 18,500 new cases were treated.[66]

Police Chief Newberger began employing undercover informants who testified against defendants in cleared courtrooms to protect their identities. Newberger called meetings with hotel operators and taxi drivers. Taxi cab drivers were warned by their employers that they would be fired, blacklisted, and turned over to the police if they knowingly transported someone to make a rendezvous with a prostitute. Bellhops were similarly warned not to give servicemen advice on where to find dates.[67]

Just as the campaign was intensifying in Tampa, the military had come to a momentous decision. On December 2, 1944, the military would no longer punish soldiers for contracting VD. The surgeon general and Public Health Service had been advocating against punishment, instituted in 1926, because it often led carriers to conceal their condition or seek ineffective home remedies. The armed forces were essentially penalizing themselves by demoting qualified personnel for a problem they had helped create. Public health officials thought the military should bear some responsibility for uprooting men and exposing them to dangerous locales. Just as soldiers were being left off the hook for becoming infected, the anti-VD campaign was as harsh as ever toward female civilians.[68]

JOOK JOINTS/BARS

Year	Tampa	H. County	Total
1941–42	23	51	74
1942–43	14	25	39
1943–44	15	20	35

A SHORT-LIVED VICTORY

By 1944, the *Tribune* cautiously declared victory over the jook joint menace: "The number of unescorted or free lancing females around the jooks isn't what it used to be—all because of that little phrase, 'vagrancy and S.B.H.' [State Board of Health]. But the soiled doves are in the minority, and most of the participants in the nightlife at the jooks are hard-working Tampans on hand for the beer and dancing."[69] Police Chief McClelland told the *Tampa Times*, "We feel that we have the drinking places in Tampa well under control now and intend to keep them that way." The anti-VD campaign had changed the rhythms of the city. Most civilians left Tampa's jooks and bars to the soldiers, migrating to places in the county. With alcohol hard to come by, some jooks opened only on weekends.[70] Liquor licenses declined from 932 in 1941 to 707 in 1944. The war had taken its toll on the area's jooks, with half going out of business.[71]

The Public Health Service wanted local communities to permanently adopt their policies, but they were short-lived in Tampa after the war's end in 1945. After all the work and suffering for the anti-VD campaign, Tampa more or less reverted to its prewar status as the "Sin City of the South." The anti-VD campaign proved to be just as ephemeral as the jitterbug, a dance craze soon forgotten in favor of the next.[72]

While Tampa faced the same problems as it did before the war, Florida was quickly changing. The generation of African Americans who served in the war envisioned another victory after V-J Day: a victory over inequality. The White Democratic Party was part of the larger Democratic Party with one caveat: it excluded black Americans from membership or voting in the party's primary elections. White Democrats dominated the mayor's office, making Tampa a one-party town with a deeply flawed democracy. When the U.S. Supreme Court decided against the white primary in 1944 (*Smith v. Allwright*), Tampa's politicians suddenly had to take its black voters more seriously.[73]

In 1950, the congressional Kefauver Committee visited Tampa to investigate the flourishing organized crime scene in the city. A series of unsolved mob murders in the 1940s and 1950s demonstrated that Tampa was still in the thrall of gangsters.

In many ways, the war had opened Florida to the world like never before. The once obscure somnolent swamp had truly become the Sunshine State in the postwar years. The broken promise of the Florida land boom would be fulfilled over the next generation, bringing millions of new residents from all over the country. More than anything, Florida's status as a tourist destination, coupled with unprecedented migration from the north, changed Florida's politics and demographics. As Florida became a destination for tourists and workers, the Sunshine State's political tone began to slowly change.

A STEAK HOUSE IN THE SKY

Bartke's and the 1950s

If Florida in the 1950s was defined by migration, tourism, development, affluence, and a desire for normalcy, no restaurant represented the state quite like Bartke's Steakhouse, particularly the one located in Tampa International Airport. The eatery represents the heady days of prosperity in the 1950s and the people's boundless faith in the wonders of technology. It also reveals some of the shadows of the 1950s, such as the Cold War, polio, and the limits of technology. Most of all, it is the story of a family, how they came to Florida, what they brought, and what they found. All seemed possible, and nothing was too daring to dream.

With their skills and vision, Frank and Alva Bartke created Bartke's Steakhouse, a restaurant perfectly suited to the desires of Floridians and tourists in the 1950s. Coupled with the novel luxury of air travel, Bartke's airport location provided an elegant atmosphere, modern gadgets, and excellent food. The setting alone provided a great attraction for customers. Bartke's provided the perfect view from the terminal's second floor, where onlookers could watch the airliners take off and land on the airstrips while dining and sipping cocktails. The couple went on to sell their restaurant in New York and run a business empire in the Tampa Bay area.

* * *

Alva Weston never set out to be a restaurateur. Born in 1915, she married and had children (daughters June and Barbara) in her early twenties, but the marriage did not last. In 1941, at thirty-six years old, Alva relocated the family to Leeds, New York, in the Catskill Mountains, where the attractive blond was pursued by several suitors. One of them was Frank Bartke, who had been running bars and nightclubs as a young man. Alva's oldest daughter June, remembers:

> Frank had an old gin mill in those days. My mother met someone else there that she started dating, but she had also met Frank. And Frank was very much smitten with my mother, but she ended up marrying someone else and he went off to World War II. He was a captain in the tank division and he was killed on my birthday in 1945. I think I was ten years old.
>
> After that, we moved back to Albany with my grandmother, and then Frank started coming around. My grandmother was making sure that he did come. [Alva] ultimately married Frank. He basically raised us.[1]

Alva often baked at home to supply Frank's bar with snacks. When his caterers failed to cook for a party at his tavern, Alva, seven months pregnant with Frank's child, cooked for the entire party in their own kitchen. The victuals were then taken to the tavern for serving. Thus began Alva's career as a remarkable restaurateur in her own right. Frank acquired the Embassy Restaurant in Albany and concentrated more of his efforts on providing quality food. The Bartkes took a huge step when they bought Kerslake's, a larger restaurant in nearby Ravena. This became Bartke's, their signature steak house. Cashing in on the postwar American obsession with meat, and above all steak, Frank became an expert in aging and cooking beef. With a new baby, Christine, the Bartkes moved into an apartment over the restaurant. After early success and several expansions, the restaurant boasted nine hundred seats. The sisters found living above the restaurant fascinating after several years in boarding schools.

> June: We had a commissary down underneath the restaurant. It was just like a city down there [where] everything was produced. He aged his own meat with ultraviolet lights and a cooler, and then a butcher

would come in and butcher up the meat: the length of the hair [on the side of beef] would determine when Frank would tell the butcher to cut it, so it was aged, really, truly aged. That was a long time before cryovacking.

It did not take long for the restaurant to gain a following from several nearby towns. Bartke's became a classic destination restaurant for couples and families willing to drive and spend the evening drinking and dining. In fact, Frank seemed to be able to conduct the restaurant like a good band.

> June: He had an organist, and when it got busy, he used to go up and tell her, "Donkey Serenade," because it was [fast and lively] and everybody would move faster when that song came on. The [employees] also remembered that he wanted that played because we were busy and we needed everybody to move quicker. He took care of all the cooking and major stuff and buying the beef and everything. When he was doing all this, we were all together and we learned all this stuff, too. It was a trickle-down effect.

Alva and her daughters became immersed in the family business. While Alva began with baking and cooking, she soon found her calling in the front of house, charming customers and monitoring service. The girls grew up quickly in the big restaurant, where Frank was fond of employing them as diplomats and spies.

> June: I was still in my early teens, and I was not a school person. Eventually I quit school and he let me work in the restaurant. So he would say, "Okay, you have to go over and find out how the food is at all the tables." He wanted us to have peripheral vision. That's what he called it. And you had to go around the table and then come back and tell him what every person was eating.

Frank asked his stepdaughters to innocently play the jukebox while spying on the bartender to be sure he wasn't stealing or giving away drinks. Frank also asked friends dining there to strongly complain when questioned by the sisters to be sure they knew how to cope with angry patrons. Alva was always a customer-oriented charmer with a "treasure chest" of toys and candy.

To Florida

In 1948, when eleven-year-old Barbara had recovered from appendicitis and Alva suffered a minor wound in the kitchen, Alva resolved to take a break with her newly healthy daughter. She chose to go to Florida and visit the beaches of Pinellas County. The sleepy, pristine beaches of Treasure Island swept her away. Barbara remembers, "We went to Sunset Beach and she just loved it. Loved it!"[2]

The owners of the Edward James Hotel ran a department store chain in Washington, D.C., and wanted someone to run their hotel's newly built restaurant. After meeting them on the beach, Alva arranged a lease for the restaurant and bar. When Alva returned to New York, June remembers she announced to Frank, "I don't want to live in the cold anymore. We'll have two restaurants, one in Florida."

In 1950, Frank visited from New York to buy property. When word spread that the steak king from New York might open a local restaurant, the *St. Petersburg Times* wrote a full profile on Frank's kitchen hardware: "The man who sent 100,000 folks from his Catskill Mountain restaurant last year with happy steak-filled stomachs will 'maybe' set up a steak emporium at the Gulf Beaches. Eulogized by Duncan Hines and the Automobile Association of America, this master of turning a slab of beef into a symphony of taste-titillating odoriferousness is Frank Bartke." Frank learned the art of fine dining from his Viennese father, and in America he helped develop "a gadget which has been heralded by steak gourmets as the greatest invention since fillet mignon."[3]

> Bartke took the old-fashioned rotisserie, tipped it over on its side, added a conveyor belt and couple of gimmicks and came up with something that can cook 120 steaks an hour "done to your taste." Enthusiastically explaining his gadget, Bartke mildly derides charcoal broiled steaks. "That wood flavor," he scoffs, "most of the charcoal is bought in briquettes, so where's the wood flavor?"

Using his device, here's Bartke's method of turning out an oozing, crisply singed steak. First, he preheats an aluminum casserole to 550 degrees, then he drops a U.S. Choice Grade steak into it, immediately searing it and sealing in the flavor. His tipped-up rotisserie is heated by forced gas which fires up ceramic tiles to 825 degrees. The casserole is popped onto the endless conveyor belt and [in] 30 seconds, give or take a few, it rolls out the other end [cooked to order].

Frank personally inspected every side of beef he procured and supervised the aging process. His beef would hang in his coolers for the minimum of a month, and he always tried to have an inventory of $15,000 worth of beef ready to butcher as the need arose. Frank also had a secret formula for frying onions and served sides of "super-sized" fried mushrooms with every steak. "We use more mushrooms," Bartke proudly announced, "than any other restaurant in the state of New York."

In terms of atmosphere, Bartke's excelled: "Bartke's has dreamed up and popularized such touches as his 'coffee by candlelight.' Instead of a skimpy cup of java, a Bartke waitress brings a good sized warmer filled with coffee and seated over a burning candle. The candle keeps the brew at just the right temperature and surrounds the diners with light that's a boon to any woman's complexion." They even placed small absorbent pads on the saucer to ensure no coffee would stain white shirts and dresses. A string quartet or organist played dining music, mostly waltzes. Bartke's promotional mailing list included ten thousand loyal fans who received post cards in anticipation of their birthdays and anniversaries and Christmas. "'Most of my customers,' Bartke said, 'take two or three hours to dine. There's none of this hustle-bustle. They take their time and enjoy the meal. Just like in Vienna.'"

As for opening a steak house in Florida, Frank played coy. "Well, maybe I will look over the restaurant field [in Tampa Bay] but I've been in it a long time (20 years) and would like to get away for a while." He was about to celebrate the fourth anniversary of his Ravena restaurant.

For more than a year, Alva ran her fledgling restaurant in Florida while Frank ran the flagship in New York. With Alva often alone in Pinellas, the male-dominated restaurant industry mocked her efforts. The male restaurateurs of Pinellas sniped at her for her entire career.

Barbara: When she opened the Plaid Bar and the restaurant in the Edward James Hotel, she got tremendous flak from the [local] male restaurant owners. It was very sexist then. They were out for blood. And she just charmed them all.

Bad fortune interrupted the tenuous New York-Florida arrangement in 1951. Although Frank had been pleading for a fire hydrant near the Ravena restaurant for years, it would be installed too late. The restaurant burned down with the uninstalled water pipes lying beside the road.

June: The only way they could [explain the fire] was that a busboy dumped the ashtray into a linen and rolled it up and put it into the chute, and so that's where the fire started was in the laundry room. And then, in that area, which was a commissary bottom, was where all the liquor room and everything was. So, once it hit the liquor room, it just blew up. The fire engines came, no water. We just stood there and watched it burn. The heat was so intense. They got the safe out and opened [it]. [The] money that was in there was just ashes.

Frank rebuilt the restaurant but sold it soon after to focus the family's fortunes in Florida. He moved the family to a house on Treasure Island in 1950. During the drive to Florida, Barbara and June encountered segregated facilities for the first time. After their black live-in nanny, Lavina, moved into their home, the family was made aware that mixed racial households were frowned upon in St. Petersburg. Alva was obligated to apply for permission from city officials to have Lavina in their home or she had to leave the beach from 6:00 p.m. until 6:00 a.m. daily. Finally, the city granted permission for the family to convert their garage to an apartment for their help.

The Bartkes ran further afoul of Southern tradition when they became heavily involved in the Republican Party. Alva became active after a friend encouraged her to start a club for Republicans, while Frank assumed posts within the local party organization. The Bartkes supported Congressman William Cramer's successful 1954 campaign, the first Republican to be elected to represent Florida since 1880.

After success and happiness at the Edward James Hotel, the owners saw the great profits the Bartkes made and reconsidered the contract they had signed. In 1952, they broke the lease and asked the Bartkes to leave, who took the case to court. Frank instructed the entire family to dress very plainly in the courtroom, "like we just got off the boat," June remembered. Frank expected their adversaries to show up encrusted in gold and jewels. They did not disappoint. "The owners came in like Astor's pet horse all dressed up with the jewelry." The judge sided in the Bartkes' favor.

In the meantime, Alva never missed a beat on the beach. The restaurant space they left behind at the Edward James Hotel never recovered. The Tropic Terrace Hotel next door was eager to host the Bartkes' excellent restaurant.

Their social and political connections paid quick dividends. Hillsborough County's Aviation Authority came to the beach for a working trip. They were in the midst of planning the conversion of the army's Drew Air Field to Tampa International Airport. The grand new version of the airport needed a touch of glamour and flash. A Madison's Drug Store would provide snacks and sundries, but the airport wanted a fine dining restaurant in the terminal. The Bartkes dazzled the authority with food, drink, and service. Before leaving, authority members urged Frank to bid for the restaurant in the new million-dollar airport terminal. Frank obliged, but Alva was less enthusiastic at the prospect of sinking the family into a large restaurant like the old nine-hundred-seat New York location. Even Frank admitted that he was tired.[4]

Alva ran the Pinellas restaurant and helped set up the airport property with Frank, who operated in Hillsborough County. Frank bought a house and moved the family to Tampa's Beach Park neighborhood. He sold the Sunset Beach home and Alva kept an apartment on Treasure Island. Alva and the children oscillated between Hillsborough and Pinellas counties with the rhythms and demands of business, school, recreation, and family. Every new investment seemed to pay sweet dividends for the Bartkes: apartment buildings, a filling station, hotels, a commissary, dredging operations, real estate, and restaurants in Tampa and St. Petersburg. Sometime after arriving in Florida, Frank went from being a restaurateur to a full-fledged developer.

The Grand Opening

The Tampa International Airport Terminal location would demand all of the Bartkes' knowledge and expertise. It would also become one of Tampa's most iconic restaurants of the 1950s and 1960s. A deluge of articles appeared in local papers about the new airport's restaurant. The first secret to Bartke's success was that if a food critic would not write a review of the business, the Bartkes simply wrote one themselves. They then published them in local newspapers, to be crowned by the small disclaimer "*advertisement*." The restaurant's paid ads and newspapers' genuine reviews are often difficult to tell apart.

A review at the time read, "Frank and Alva Bartke's suave new restaurant and cocktail lounge, occupying the entire top floor and terraces of the terminal building, will also be opened with some pomp and ceremony over the weekend. From its glittering kitchen—a reckless panorama of stainless steel and the latest in cooking mechanics—to table decor, indirect lighting, air-conditioning and soft-color drapes, the latest Bartke's bistro is a monument to the American appetite." In a further aspiration to fashionable modernity, Bartke's featured musicians on the Hammond organ and "architecture from the California school."

The Aviation Authority invited three hundred dignitaries to a grand opening luncheon at Bartke's that preceded the airport's formal opening ceremonies. As a publicity stunt, the Bartkes flew in some menu items, such as rum from Puerto Rico and pineapple from Hawaii. They coordinated the entire dinner for the Aviation Authority's guests, with various flying times (of the propeller-driven Super Constellation airliners of the day) noted on the menu.

If the menu appeared lavish, the guests were not always comfortable that afternoon. The dining room's air conditioner failed, forcing the suited dignitaries to wipe their sweaty brows with cloth napkins. Modern technology was a coy mistress, and the mishaps did not stop there. Rain swept across the tarmac just before the opening ceremony, sending the crowd running to the terminal for cover. When the ceremony began after the shower, the microphone malfunctioned. The grand speeches that followed a quick repair lasted for almost five hours in the steamy August

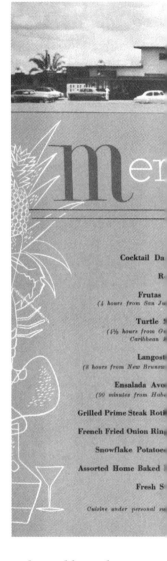

Bartke's menu reflects the optimism of the 1950s and the faith in technology to improve daily life. The opening celebration of Tampa International Airport's terminal featured a lunch with ingredients flown in from all over the hemisphere by airlines that no longer exist. (Florida Menu collection, University of South Florida Tampa Special Collections)

heat. World War I fighter ace and Eastern Air Lines president Eddie Rickenbacker said he felt fortunate to be alive in America at the most exciting time in its history; he also warned that the airport would outgrow its terminal within three years. When it came time to raise the American flag over the airport, the color guard could not be found. The flag was finally raised after a short delay, and an air force band from MacDill played "The Star-Spangled Banner."

The finale of the ceremony occurred when Tony Pizzo, Ybor City's

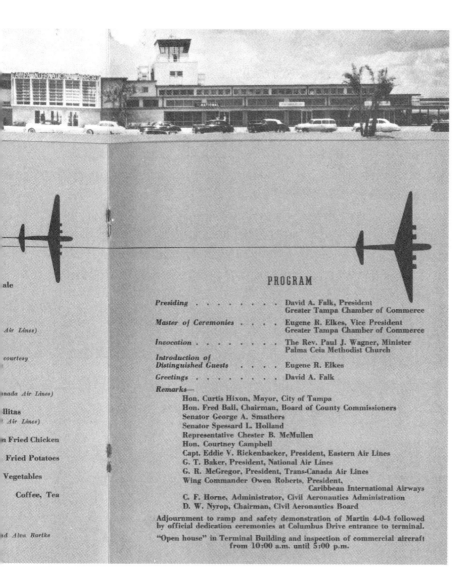

PROGRAM

Presiding	David A. Falk, President Greater Tampa Chamber of Commerce
Master of Ceremonies	Eugene R. Elkes, Vice President Greater Tampa Chamber of Commerce
Invocation	The Rev. Paul J. Wagner, Minister Palma Ceia Methodist Church
Introduction of Distinguished Guests	Eugene R. Elkes
Greetings	David A. Falk

Remarks—
Hon. Curtis Hixon, Mayor, City of Tampa
Hon. Fred Ball, Chairman, Board of County Commissioners
Senator George A. Smathers
Senator Spessard L. Holland
Representative Chester B. McMullen
Hon. Courtney Campbell
Capt. Eddie V. Rickenbacker, President, Eastern Air Lines
G. T. Baker, President, National Air Lines
G. R. McGregor, President, Trans-Canada Air Lines
Wing Commander Owen Roberts, President,
                              Caribbean International Airways
C. F. Horne, Administrator, Civil Aeronautics Administration
D. W. Nyrop, Chairman, Civil Aeronautics Board

Adjournment to ramp and safety demonstration of Martin 4-0-4 followed
by official dedication ceremonies at Columbus Drive entrance to terminal.

"Open house" in Terminal Building and inspection of commercial aircraft
from 10:00 a.m. until 5:00 p.m.

alcalde (mock mayor), staged an invasion of the festivities with his "secretaries of Army and Navy" arriving in three small planes wearing the lavish medaled uniforms of generalissimos. Pizzo's aircraft had a large green hornet (the name of a popular Ybor City gossip column) smoking a cigar painted on the side, and he kissed the ladies' hands in Old World style. Pizzo's cohorts held signs reading "Viva Cuban Coffee!" and gave out a hundred loaves of Cuban bread to the crowd. He apologized for his tardiness but joked that menacing UFOs threw him off course. He then presented Mayor Curtis "Hickson" with the key to Ybor City, and every-one had a good laugh.

Yet there was a certain seriousness in Pizzo's antics. At the steps of an "ultra-modern steakhouse," Ybor City's demonstration reminded all of her distinctive and irreplaceable culture. While the worn Latin favorites such as Las Novedades, Spanish Park, and the Columbia were perfectly suited to quaint, old-fashioned Ybor City, Bartke's tapped into postwar America's latest aspirations. The steak house was the perfect template for consumers to project their dreams onto. A steak dinner strips food of ethnic and regional identities, replacing those old notions with signifiers of luxury and conformity. Affluent people ate steak and drank martinis at places like Bartke's all over the country. After years of rationing in the 1940s, steak became a powerful symbol, and the best steak houses pro-vided atmospheres worthy of the dream. Traveling by air was unattain-able for most Americans. For example, a ticket from New York to Los Angeles would have cost $208, more than $1,500 in 2010 currency. But anyone with money for a steak dinner could fly vicariously at Bartke's.[5]

TAKEOFF

On its menu, Bartke's identified itself as a novel place to be with a logo of a contrived modern jet arcing into the sky. The restaurant was said to be "the most modern on the west coast of Florida if not in the entire state." Although they were still relatively new to Florida, Frank and Alva iden-tified with their new home state and its unbridled business sense. They had reason to be optimistic. They claimed to net about $8,000 in their first month. Less than two years after opening, the monthly volume leapt to over $61,000. The airport restaurant netted more than half a million a year. Just one-quarter of their customers came to the airport to travel; the restaurant's remaining patrons came from the Tampa Bay area seek-ing out the spectacles of the new airport and one of the best steaks in town. Bartke's became a quintessential "destination" restaurant, drawing patrons from a wide area, just as it had in New York.[6]

Frank and Alva marketed the restaurant aggressively. Their self-written "reviews" heaped praise on Florida and their restaurant. One ad boasted,

How far the Tampa Bay area has advanced from the somnolent days of a few years ago is perhaps most perfectly illustrated by the new Tampa International Airport at Drew Field. And nowhere in the port is this development more clearly observed than in Bartke's restaurant and cocktail lounge.

For one thing, the restaurant is far ahead of anything even dreamed of a few short years ago, and for another, diners there can glance out the spacious window at almost any moment of the day or evening to see super air liners landing from or departing to all points of the compass and many parts of the world.

Frank and Alva showed many other restaurateurs the clear trend emerging after World War II: the soaring popularity of steak houses. Many followed in their footsteps, including Steve's Rustic Lodge, and a certain Bern Laxer, who was running a then-humble steak house of his own. June remembers, "We used to go eat there [at Bern's]. And Frank and Bernie had a good rapport, because they were both doing the same thing at different [restaurants]. Bernie used to do all of his own cooking, and he would be in shorts and a t-shirt." Bern did not get into the steak business until 1956, so Frank could have been a key inspiration for Tampa's next great steak house.

Frank discovered the Groetchen Broil-o-Matic steak broiler at a trade show and immediately bought one. Once placed in a wedge-shaped pan, the steak can be inserted into the slot that determines its cooking time. The grill rotates with hot flames over and under the meat. For example, a full rotation over the flames might turn out a well-done steak, while a half turn would produce rare meat. Frank made enough adjustments to his Broil-O-Matic to warrant applying for and receiving a patent.

"He didn't really have to have a cook after that in the kitchen, as far as somebody cooking the steaks," Barbara recalls. Anyone could be trained to rub steaks with Bartke's signature seasoning and put them into the appropriate slots of the broiler. In minutes, the steak would slide out of the contraption perfectly cooked. Slight adjustments could be made to account for steaks of different cuts and thicknesses. "It just went around," Barbara said, "and you'd come around to the other side and it would come down like a runway and it would, plop! There it was. And you knew it was rare, because it came out of the rare hole."

And it made great copy for admen. An "editorial" beamed, "One of the most mysterious facts about the whole deal is that the cooking is done with such perfect timing that the steaks are ready and sizzling hot just in time to meet vegetables and other items as they emerge." The mystery behind Bartke's timing became its central attraction. "Something exclusive is Bartke's steak broiler [called the 'Groetchen Broil-o-matic'], a device considered a genuine achievement in the tasty preparation of food. Almost without exception," the ads enthused, "the visitors insist upon lingering for considerable periods to watch the famous Bartke rotary steak grill in operation." Such an understated tone could not last long. "This machine," another ad claimed, "is a marvel of the culinary art."

Columnist Russel Kay thought so, too. In one of his newspaper articles, he complained about getting poorly cooked steaks at restaurants. When asked for rare, it arrived burnt. When he sent the steak back to the kitchen, another arrived still frozen in the middle. Kay's "column" in the *St. Cloud News* described Bartke's broiler with all the enthusiasm of a snake-oil salesman.

> Thanks to a fellow named Frank Bartke . . . customers are now insured. He has perfected a contraption he calls the Rotary Steak Broiler that automatically cooks a steak to perfection and exactly the same every time. It has compartments designated for each type of steak desired and all the chef has to do is simply put the steak in the proper place on the broiler and he can't go wrong. . . .
>
> I thought I'd seen everything, but this contraption has anything beat I've ever encountered. It is absolutely foolproof and believe-it-or-not will handle 120 steaks an hour, 45 filet mignons at one time and delivers every single one of them exactly as the doctor ordered.[7]

Some could even imagine a day when human chefs would be obsolete. Like many other industries, restaurants increasingly relied upon mechanization for efficiency. Milkshake machines, deep fat fryers, blenders, toasters, and electric stoves had become commonplace by the 1950s. The Broil-o-Matic was just another step in the modern march of progress.

Like the dining room and the airport itself, the shiny metal kitchen was part of the attraction, sleek, modern, and clean. One of their ads described it as "a symphony of gleaming spotlessness." Brownie's Tin Shop—whose motto read, "If it can be made with sheet metal, we can make it"—constructed the dazzling kitchen.

Because the airport location did not have adequate kitchen space, Frank created a commissary on airport property. There, butchers broke down sides of aged beef into cuts, and cooks made sauces, dressings, and soups in bulk for service daily. Bartke's was an early adopter of the keypunch IBM computer to crunch data for payroll, and Barbara remembers that manually keypunching all of the information was "a miserable job." Like hundreds of other restaurants, Frank embraced off-site refrigeration services for meat. He kept up to $20,000 worth of beef on hand in his aging cooler. Frank's chilled arsenal of "prime gold" was nicknamed "Bartke's own private Fort Knox." Bruce Wert ran a wholesale meat firm and "food locker plant" in Pinellas County that stored and aged meat for an extra charge. When a place like Bartke's ran out of steaks, they simply sent for a shipment from their food locker instead of having to order a new inventory. Sometimes a more flashy approach was in order. On one occasion, Frank flew in two hundred pounds of aged beef for a single party.[8]

For all of the novelty Bartke's flaunted, there was little to be found on their plates of food. Instead, Bartke's traded in durable American classics with fine presentation and little pretension. In addition to the touted steaks, their specialties included broiled red snapper, lobster, frog legs, French-fried onions and mushrooms, mashed potatoes, and so on. Over time, the kitchen added other 1950s favorites to the menu, including appetizers such as pigs in a blanket, Swedish meatballs, chicken liver pockets, mini pizzas, and an entire "Chinese" menu. And for dessert, pie and intricately layered parfaits in tall pilsner glasses.

June remembers the buzz created by Bartke's in Tampa:

I was in school then [at the Academy of] Holy Names, and all the kids that were in my class, they were always chattering about, "Oh, Dad's taking us to the airport for dinner tonight." It was the place to go food-wise. And everything was perfect. They had valet parking, they had entertainment, they had the views of the planes coming in and out, and it was just at the right moment to open that in the society we lived in at that time.

The elite came there [to Bartke's] all the time. And then they came back.

Dizzy with Success

The 1950s found Florida dizzy with modern progress in many ways. The Sunshine Skyway Bridge, which linked Pinellas and Sarasota in 1954, cost $22 million and was the biggest open-water crossing of its kind in America. Shopping malls popped up like mushrooms overnight. Florida's population and tourism industry expanded, and metropolitan areas quickly pancaked outward into suburbs. Bartke's new airport location, which sat at the virtual epicenter of the developing "Tampa Bay" market, bore witness to a flurry of development. When Bartke's hosted a banquet for the Drew Park Chamber of Commerce, Mayor Curtis Hixon set lofty goals for Tampa's future. The city's population climbed steadily and, augmented by multiple annexations in 1953, had exceeded a quarter million by 1960. Hixon boasted of City Hall's foresight to acquire cheap and vital property for a large auditorium and several bridges.

Frank himself became a highly successful entrepreneur outside the restaurant business. His partner, Eric Schrommer, provided capital while Frank did the footwork. They created new property by dredging on both sides of the Courtney Campbell Causeway and became one of the leading developers of Rocky Point. They built two Causeway Inns, north and south, on either end of the causeway. Most of Frank's profits went right back into the Bartke's restaurants, and Frank opened yet another location on Rocky Point. Frank invested heavily in Rocky Point because it had all the criteria for a hot tourist spot: waterfront property, a nearby airport, easy access to the expanding interstate road system, and close proximity to the gulf beaches in Pinellas.

Tampans had been complaining about the lack of a city beach for some time. When two boys drowned off the Courtney Campbell Causeway, the demands for a beach grew louder. City leaders considered building a giant 1,200 × 600-foot pool and white sand beach at the causeway's edge at Rocky Point, and Frank was a financial backer. Developers also

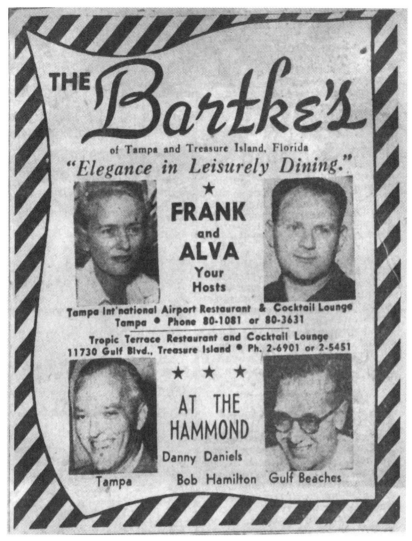

Ads for Bartke's steak houses featured photos of Frank and Alva in addition to the organ players who performed at their restaurants. (Bartke's scrapbook, University of South Florida Tampa Special Collections)

planned an outdoor drama theater and a private beach for the point. The cost for the Rocky Point projects was at least a million dollars. While not all of the plans came to fruition, the city started developing the Rocky Point beach in 1954. Barbara worked the concession stand. The property has since been occupied by luxury hotels.

Bartke's attracted publicity and sponsors with their novel location and good food. The Florida Citrus Commission sponsored "Florida Calling," a radio show that reached a potential audience of twenty million listeners. The musical variety show held a daily contest in which the host called a random telephone number in the United States. The host asked a question over the phone, and if the contestants answered correctly, they won a free ten-day tour of Florida. The first stop: Tampa International Airport to dine at Bartke's and then off on a chauffeured driving tour.

Frank and Alva were selling more than steaks at Bartke's. They sold Florida itself, with the enthusiasm of the recently converted. It wasn't just good for their individual business. The Bartkes were performing their public duty as Floridians. In 1953, an article in the *Gulf Beach Journal* sought to cheer up businessmen with flagging confidence. Despite the prosperity the article described, it said, "Too many of the businessmen are looking at the world through dark blue glasses and missing all the green that surrounds them. People talk themselves into such a state of affairs through a gloomy outlook on life." Only those who marketed their locales as well as their businesses had any chance of success, the article reasoned. The booster, who would inevitably be successful, would be too busy with his growing business and profits to complain. The article offered to point out "a few" examples of model boosters, but gave only one: Bartke's.

> In the restaurant business, a highly competitive field, probably the most outstanding example of a successful enterprise based on promotion, publicity and advertising is the Bartke's at Treasure Island and Tampa. They have shown over a ninety per cent increase over last year, every one of them is crowded, people travel for miles to eat there. Why? They believe in advertising their product. Every newspaper in the area carries their ads, radio, direct mail, every medium is used, based on a percentage of their gross . . . and it pays off. Promotion and follow through, that is the secret.[9]

Bartke's reflected Florida's restless nature in the 1950s. "There is no standing still at the Bartke's restaurants, so far as progress and constant improvement are concerned." Their instant success at the airport called for expansion with a new dining room, augmenting the restaurant's original 250-seat space. An ad trumpeted the expansion:[10] "Late in February [1953], the pressing need for more table space at the Bartke restaurant at Drew Field was met by the addition of the Sky View Terrace Room. The glass wall of the dining room permits diners an unexcelled view of the vast expanse of sky over the airport from which giants of the air lanes soar in for landings, only a few feet from the restaurant balcony."[11] With the new room, Bartke's came into its own, allowing customers an incomparable view of the runway. To further capitalize on the view from the terminal, customers could slide back the glass windows for a better look. Their ads boasted of "Tampa's newest Ultra Modern Horseshoe Bar on the Observation Platform." A new air-conditioning system ensured there would never be sweating patrons after the opening day debacle. Even Bartke's entertainment was "ultra-modern," a Hammond electric organ player. In the hands of a talented player, the Hammond was a modern one-man band popular in churches and jazz halls. Instead of hiring an expensive band, a single organist entertained patrons. The Bartkes sponsored their own thirty-minute radio show on WFLA Monday through Friday featuring Danny Daniels on organ live from the restaurant.

The Bartkes hired Bob Hamilton to play the Hammond at various Bartke's locations. "The artist can literally make his Hammond 'talk,'" wrote a disbelieving journalist. "His novelty tunes include everything from airplanes taking off to barking dogs. His rendition of Hawaiian War Chant includes the beating of the drums and background chants, all played on the organ."[12]

Alva was a natural entertainer herself.

When the Bartke's guests are in a gala mood and the tempo is right, Alva Bartke and Bob Hamilton, the famous organist, are "in the mood," [and] they team up to entertain the diners. A "Snake Number" is played upon insistent requests, the lights are subdued, phosphorescent gloves and other accessories are used, the "black light" is switched on and the fun starts. Alva really only plays a chord and Bob carries the medley of appropriate music and does he turn on the steam!

The customers get quite a charge out of the number—applaud, shout and some merely sit quietly and observe the unbelievable entertainment. In the old slogan of the theater, Alva and Bob have them rolling in the aisles. Food is left untouched, cocktails and highballs are temporarily forgotten and the entire place tries to figure out what is happening. Frank Bartke, Alva's husband, when he pays a visit, just shakes his head in wonderment of what vivacious Alva will dream up next. But Frank beams with pride and the full house of guests proves the popularity of the zany number.[13]

Bartke's became an absolute favorite meeting place for local groups, clubs, and organizations in the Tampa Bay area. Banquets, receptions, conferences, and presentations filled Bartke's schedule. The Disabled American Veterans welcomed a freed POW home from Korea one night. On another, the National Association of Credit Men salivated over their steaks and anticipated profits. College sororities held events beside the Chamber of Commerce. The Business and Professional Women's Club feasted at the same tables as the American Institute of Banking had drunk at the night before. B'nai B'rith and the Union of American Hebrew Congregations sampled kosher delicacies made in the same kitchen where steaks were broiled for the Christ the King Guild. All manner of wedding receptions, baby showers, and marriage anniversaries were celebrated with a trip to Bartke's. One sign that Bartke's had excellent steaks: the cattle consigners from the Florida State Fair dined together there.

In 1953, J. Arthur Turner, the new president of Tampa's Chamber of Commerce, presided over the group's seventieth annual dinner at the brand-new Bartke's on Rocky Point. As the five hundred distinguished guests stepped off their planes and out of their cars, beauty queens handed them flowers, cigars, and Florida oranges. With a slide show illustrating Tampa's many inroads, Turner told those in attendance that he came to Florida as a young man and vowed to stay and be a part of its future. He confided that huge reserves of uranium for nuclear power lay in Tampa's abundant phosphate deposits. He urged the Chamber of Commerce to back a nuclear research facility in the city to extract the resources. If exploited, the uranium could supply power to an entire nation, he enthused. Businessmen dreamed of the day atomic weapons could be deployed against incoming hurricanes.

When Tallahassee's civic leaders contemplated their own airport, they asked the Hillsborough Aviation Authority about Bartke's. Herbert Godfrey of the airport wrote back, "We consider that The Bartke's Restaurant at Tampa International Airport is one of the finer restaurants in the entire Tampa Bay area. The food is superior in quality and the service is outstanding." A meal at Bartke's was so sought-after that one private flyer complained that there was no way for him to go from Peter O. Knight airport to Tampa's airport terminal. With the streetcar system gone in 1946, it was left to Bartke's to offer free transportation to anyone wanting to visit from Peter O. Knight.[14]

The Bartke's empire was at its zenith. Just as Alva feared, they were juggling more than nine hundred seats between their multiple restaurants. But instead of having a flagship that depended upon attracting patrons from a distance, as they did in New York, Bartke's found itself at the center of the action: Tampa International Airport, Rocky Point, and Treasure Island.

SHADOWS OF THE 1950S

Sometimes it seemed too good to be true. Despite the exaltation of the boosters, the 1950s were not a time of unbridled progress and prosperity. There were dark overtones as well, forewarnings of future dangers and reminders of the dark days of the past.

While she attended high school, when Barbara Bartke wasn't working at the commissary in Tampa, she and her friends hung out on the Pinellas beaches. "I'd go to a beach party all night, go home for two hours, get up, take a shower, and go to work. So, I was really worn out." When she graduated high school in 1952, Frank bought her a car as a gift.

A short walk home on the afternoon of September 14, 1954, changed Barbara's life.

> I was a big shot. I was the only one who had a car, and I was going all around with my friends. Something was wrong with the car, and they had a car dealership on Treasure Island at the time, Ford. I had to walk home. Maybe twenty blocks. And I'm walking and I'm walking and I thought, "Jeez, I don't feel good. I'll go home." By the time I got home and got in bed, I couldn't walk.

And then by the time Mom got the doctor there, Dr. Cage . . . said to Mom, "I gotta get her down to Mound Park [today Bayfront Medical Center]. We're not waiting for an ambulance. Come put her in the car." So he drove me down, with Mom in the back seat, and every time we went over a bump, something else died, but I got more paralyzed as we went. They got me in there and they did a spinal tap. And then, by the time they got me in my room, I couldn't move. I was totally paralyzed.

Barbara became Pinellas County's sixty-third polio victim. Although she benefited from good doctors, the methods of therapy were primitive at best. She underwent the standard ineffective treatment for polio then: hot packs of cloth laid on the body and gamma globulin shots to boost the immune system. She was not expected to walk again.[15]

It did not take long for word to spread about Barbara's condition. At the time, polio was poorly understood and many people thought they would become infected if they ate at Bartke's. Polio thrived in the summertime, when infections typically peaked. That fall was a quiet one at the Bartkes' restaurants, and sales dipped for the first time. June Bartke remembers, "When the word got out, she was diagnosed as polio, and she was totally paralyzed. We went from big business to nothing. She was in a hospital, so we suffered financially, emotionally, and everything." In 1955, at a large luncheon at the airport restaurant, county epidemiologist Dr. C. D. Hopkins spoke about the arrival of Salk's vaccine, which, he said, would cure the dreaded polio.

Modern technology enabled more than the defeat of disease. U.S. food production—and consumption—soared to new heights. Eight years after the strict rationing during World War II, Bartke's premiered a lavish Hawaiian luau triple buffet every Sunday evening. It was impressive, the ad-reviews claimed, "not alone in the types and qualities of the food served, but in the infinite variety and the beauty of the flower decked setting." The luau was not just one buffet but three. The first was the cold table. A bowl of solid ice with carnations frozen inside cradled fruit salad. Other items on the cold table included stuffed olives, spiced whole peaches and pears, vegetable and fruit jellies, various meat and vegetable salads, deviled eggs, marinated herring, cottage cheese with chives, corn relish, and cold cuts of ham, turkey, and corned beef.

"Having made your selections," the article continued, "(and almost certainly having taken too much) you repair to a table where a cart with a variety of hot rolls is wheeled up to be eaten with Bartke's famous whipped butter and a pot of fragrant coffee." The volume and variety of the first course must have seemed extravagant to those who had grown up during the Depression and the rationing days of the war. "Having eaten what you can of the oversupply you've taken, you leave your table and go to the steam table section." Diners feasted upon plates piled high with roast prime rib au jus, baked shrimp in a special sauce, au gratin potatoes, and corn soufflé. "Once more you try to eat all of the generous portions but you have the thought of dessert in mind, and probably refuse the new offer of hot rolls."

"Having done the best you can, and having certainly finished the last tender morsel of roast beef at least, you return to the luau once more, this time stopping at the dessert bar." The final feast consisted of fine cheeses (including Blue, Edam, Gruyère, and Liederkranz), a variety of fresh fruit, fruit gelatin, whipped pudding with pineapple and cherries, brownies, and various pies and cakes. During the war, this course alone would have exhausted a restaurant's sugar stamps in one night!

The article concluded with suggestions for some final indulgences,

> When you have gotten through all of this eating (and not until then) and have settled down for a liqueur or perhaps a glass of port, and to light an after-dinner smoke, you will glance at your watch and realize—ten chances to one—that you have consumed at least two hours and in the most pleasant eating experience you probably have had in many a month. They call it a Luau. You can call it a smorgasbord, you can call it a buffet, you can call it what you will, but in the end you will call it a magnificent dinner.

The luau was a savvy marketing tactic to increase traffic on sleepy Sunday nights. Amid all the conspicuous consumption, it may have been easy to forget how many people still went hungry, even in Tampa. International hunger was pervasive, Britain had stopped rationing meat only in 1954, and China starved. In this context, the promotional statement "The Luau is almost unbelievable" could be taken quite literally. As the Cold War unfolded abroad, the Communist menace found willing recruits among the hungry of Europe and Asia. Those unwilling to bend to Soviet domination wanted nothing more than to emigrate to America, land of million-dollar civilian airports, with glitzy Hammond organs and sumptuous Luau buffets.

In Soviet-occupied Austria, Kathe "Tante" Bartke, Frank's aunt, was wanted by the Communists for being subversive. During the war in 1944, several GIs had escaped from a Nazi prison camp near Altenmarkt, and Kathe fed and clothed them and provided a map for their escape. She could have been executed by the Nazis had the GIs been recaptured. Instead of applauding her efforts against the common enemy, the Communists assumed she was a capitalist sympathizer.

One of the soldiers, Joseph M. Suss, remembered the events in an affidavit to the House Judiciary Committee in Congress:

The course of our flight took us through the town of Altenmarkt in Austria. At that time, several of the men in my party were sick, weak from travel and lack of food. In desperation we decided to seek the aid of a house in Altenmarkt. Fortunately, the house we selected was not hostile to us.

Mrs. Bartke made arrangements to provide us with shelter. She procured food for us, supplied us with a map of the surrounding area and gave us general directions on how to avoid the German troops stationed in the immediate vicinity.

I must point out that Mrs. Bartke did all this for us with considerable risk to herself and without thought of any future compensation. It is quite probable that without her timely assistance, the escape of our party would have failed.

Kathe Bartke found herself on the Soviet-backed government's blacklist. She visited the United States briefly in 1949 but could not stay. When the political situation worsened, Kathe fled again in 1950, barely escaping Communist agents to board an airliner bound for America. Once she arrived, the United States denied all extensions of her visa, and Kathe was ordered to be deported in 1951. A desperate appeal to local politicians rallied Congressmen Bill Cramer, George Smathers, and Courtney Campbell to her cause. Joseph M. Suss, who Bartke had helped escape the Nazis, came to her defense, as well. A bill passed in Congress and was signed into law by President Eisenhower in late 1953. Part of the bill granted Kathe Bartke status as a resident alien. The newspaper added Kathe's accent to her last quote in the article, "Now dot iss ofver, I am zo glad." Kathe lived out the rest of her days working happily in Bartke's commissary and giving her co-workers bear hugs.[16]

The smoldering Cold War produced a troubled international situation. In 1955, when Eleanor Roosevelt passed through Tampa to visit her uncle in Sarasota, reporters interviewed her as she dined in Bartke's airport restaurant. She was alarmed by all of Eisenhower's "sabre-rattling" over Formosa (present-day Taiwan). Mrs. Roosevelt recalled the horrible destruction wrought by the atomic bomb in Hiroshima and advocated strengthened defense to keep America's interests secured. She appeared tired from her constant work as chairman of the board of governors of the American Association for the United Nations. Instead of steak, she dined on simple hot tea and a fruit cocktail before moving on to Sarasota.

CONCLUSION

Bartke's soared through the 1950s, netting more than $500,000 annually, but earnings lagged as the 1960s wore on. The airport's terminal was always overcrowded with spectators, which hampered business. Many of the novel and endearing features of the early 1950s did not age well. Young diners wanted a place that spoke to them, not to their parents. The stewardess uniforms, the Broil-o-Matic, the Hammond organ, and indeed the airport itself, had aged out of fashion. As air travel became more affordable, routine, and uncomfortable, the old glamour had worn off. In the decades after Bartke's emerged on Tampa's restaurant scene, a new generation of steak houses sprang up, including Steve's Rustic Lodge, Iavarone's, Malio's, and Bern's.

The year 1966 turned out to be a pivotal one for the relationship between Bartke's and the Aviation Authority. While Bartke's wanted to expand, the authority said it would no longer invest in the old terminal while they planned for a new one. Bartke's then asked permission to open an additional cocktail bar for travelers on the go. The authority would grant the new bar only if they could agree that the restaurant's lease did not cover the new terminal. Their disagreement festered until both sides enlisted lawyers. The airport and authority quietly collected customer complaints and business grievances. Even if Bartke's somehow extended its lease to the new terminal, the agreement would end in 1972, shortly after the terminal was set to open in 1971. It did not make business sense for Bartke's to invest in a space where they would spend so little time. Winning a new lease seemed out of the question.[17]

Although the authority said in correspondence that it wanted to retain local flavor in the airport's dining scene, the new terminal did not demonstrate that desire. Host International, the corporate head of several large dining chains, was awarded the contract for the new terminal. The days of distinctive airport dining had temporarily come to an end, replaced by corporately owned chains.[18]

Frank and Alva divorced late in the 1960s but remained close. Frank changed things up by founding Bartke's Dinner Theatre on Rocky Point, a successful concept that lasted well into the 1980s. He also donated nearby land for a Shriner's temple. When Frank died in 1979, the family discovered that Frank was routinely paying mortgage payments and nursing home fees for several former workers. Alva and her daughters went on to open several notable restaurants in Pinellas County, where in 1962 they pioneered the "early bird special" for senior citizens that would later become synonymous with sleepy St. Petersburg's retired population and their ubiquitous green benches. Together, the Bartke ladies made a lasting impact with the Careless Navigator, and Red Cavalier, and other restaurants. Alva died in 2005. Together, the Bartke family helped change the face of the Tampa Bay area at the dinner table and beyond.

A SEAT AT THE NATION'S TABLE

Lunch Counter Integration

On February 1, 1960, four black college students quietly sat down at a Woolworth's lunch counter in Greensboro, North Carolina. When they were denied service, they refused to leave and returned day after day to demonstrate. While the national media broadcast footage of the protest, the "sit in" inspired young activists across the nation to openly confront Jim Crow. Legal efforts for equality seemed to stall indefinitely in the courts. Tired of pleas for patience from their elders, dissatisfied young people eagerly joined Youth Councils or formed local groups to take action. Each community's activists and officials responded in their own way. Lunch counter sit-ins became the first viral phenomenon of the civil rights movement that harnessed the audacity of youth. The country would never be the same.

Although the initial Greensboro demonstrations appeared to be spontaneous, they were soon shrewdly calculated to make a greater impact. Concentrating demonstrations on national chain stores made strategic sense for several reasons. The variety stores typically welcomed black patrons to all departments of the store except the lunch counter, where they were forced to order take-out or dine standing. Chains could potentially face boycotts and sit-ins all over the nation and had much more business to lose than local entrepreneurs did. If chains gave in to integration, local businesses would be much more likely to follow suit for economic reasons. There was another more practical reason to single out lunch counters. Tampa mayor Julian Lane recalled, "The main thing the blacks were interested in, of course, was the lunch counters. . . . The restaurants . . . were expensive; even in those days, there weren't many blacks that could afford them." So by choice and necessity, lunch counters became the first target for sit-ins.[1]

Like much of the South, Tampa's reckoning with race relations had been thoughtlessly deferred. The city had traditionally done little to provide housing or recreational facilities for the black ghettoes. Although state and local officials resented any interference by Washington, D.C., they had become accustomed to using federal dollars to grudgingly provide amenities, namely, public housing, to the people they had sworn to represent.

The black community ached for progress toward equality. The promise of the Supreme Court's *Brown v. Board of Education* decision of 1954, which mandated the integration of all public facilities, had gone unfulfilled. When black parents sued the Hillsborough County schools to integrate in 1959, Judge George Whitehurst, an avowed segregationist, would not consider it.[2]

Downtown Tampa remained the most visible symbol of the city and its commerce. Large department stores like Maas Brothers and Kress acted as downtown's economic barometers and still drew customers from all walks of life. Postwar prosperity, cheap gasoline, suburban housing, and the interstate drastically changed cities across the nation. Over time, fewer citizens entangled themselves in downtown's traffic and parking because they could shop closer to home in the suburbs. During the 1950s and 1960s, downtown atrophied from Tampa's commercial jewel to a symbol of the city's decline.

If downtown had fallen on hard times, the black business district of Central Avenue was also in steep decline. In 1960, Central Avenue was still the main street of segregated Tampa. Walking down Central, one could see reminders of the vitality of Tampa's black community: the Harlem Public Library, Helping Hand Day Nursery, International Longshoreman's Union 1402, the state offices of the NAACP, Rogers Dining Room, The Little Savoy nightclub, La Paris Beauty Salon, Powell's Barber Shop, Pyramid Hotel, El Chico bar, and the Central Life Insurance

Company. The black business district depended on segregation to some extent. An integrated marketplace would see black entrepreneurs at a distinct disadvantage when seeking loans, property, and partners.[3]

In the 1950s, the city neglected housing concerns in favor of larger projects such as a police station, hotel, library, and auditorium. In 1957, the legislature cleared the City of Tampa to receive federal redevelopment funds, but so-called urban renewal rarely revived the places it visited. Redevelopment projects, which included Maryland Avenue, Ybor City, and the Riverfront, would adversely affect 60 percent of Tampa's black population, but no black Tampans served on the city's Urban Renewal Committee. The local government never consulted the people who would be affected. Officials relocated residents to segregated neighborhoods in the most blighted parts of town. Hundreds of people had simply been forced from one ghetto to another.[4]

When he was elected in 1959, Mayor Julian Lane appointed a Bi-Racial Committee to resolve Tampa's racial disputes. It was the first biracial committee in Florida and the South. Tampa was very image-conscious at the time, and no one wanted to repeat the racial violence of other Southern towns. Mayor Lane "often laughed about it," he said, because "the first year I was in office we had two hurricanes, a flood and integration."[5]

BUILDING A MOVEMENT

No single group did more than the National Association for the Advancement of Colored People (NAACP) to provide a mutually supportive network, a pool of leadership, and financial backing for local civil rights efforts. In 1909, white and black citizens formed the NAACP to advocate for black equality. Its Legal Defense Fund, formed thirty years later, spearheaded a legal campaign against Jim Crow policies. This campaign had already seen stunning victories at the Supreme Court, crowned by *Brown v. Board of Education*, which called for equal access to public education. During the 1950s, an educated, talented, and courageous triumvirate ran the Florida Chapter of the NAACP in Tampa: State Field Secretary Robert W. Saunders, Rev. A. Leon Lowry, and attorney Francisco Rodriguez.

Born in 1921, Robert W. Saunders grew up in Roberts City, south of West Tampa, and began his higher education at Bethune-Cookman College in Daytona Beach. He served as a Tuskegee airman during World War II; after the war, Saunders graduated from the Detroit Institute of Technology. When white terrorists fatally bombed NAACP Florida State Secretary Harry T. Moore and his wife in their Mims home, just north of Titusville on the east coast, on Christmas 1951, Saunders was asked to take the hazardous post. He suspended his study of law at the University of Detroit and moved the NAACP's headquarters to Tampa. His cool demeanor and steely resolve saved the Florida chapter from defeat and built an entirely new movement from scratch with the help of his wife, Helen, and stalwart lieutenants.

The Reverend A. Leon Lowry became the inspirational statesman and spiritual soul of the local movement. Born in Savannah and educated at Morehouse College and Andover Newton Theological School, Lowry pastored at several churches, most notably C. T. Walker Baptist Church in Augusta, Georgia, where he had a nine-year tenure.[6] Lowry arrived in Tampa as Beulah Baptist Church's new pastor in 1956. His placement at Beulah seemed like the perfect fit. Lowry, so learned and steeped in activism, preached in the city's first black Baptist church. Free black Tampans too proud to pray from the hot balcony of the segregated First Baptist Church formed Beulah in 1868. As a source of comfort, community, and mutual aid, the churches played a central role in the lives of African Americans.[7]

Tampa's segregation denied black residents opportunity for all but the worst jobs, mostly relegating them to maids, janitors, and menial labor. Most did not get involved in civil rights activism, lacking the time, money, and resolve to defy the power structure, which often included their employers. "It was a dangerous thing," Lowry admitted. "It marked one and made one very, very visible when one took leadership in that area. Places like Ruskin, Mango, Riverview, Plant City, I recall a time when I dared not show my face in some of those areas."

Lowry drew inspiration from fellow activists such as Fred Shuttlesworth and as a one-time pupil of Martin Luther King Jr. As a regional leader of the NAACP, he ran afoul of Florida's white supremacists immediately. The deeply racist Pork Chop Gang, a group of rural legislators from north Florida, formed the Florida Legislative Investigation Committee, or the Johns Committee, in 1956 to root out subversives, starting with the NAACP. The committee first tried to squelch the Tallahassee Bus Boycott and subpoenaed Lowry in 1958 to demand the records of the NAACP. Lowry demonstrated his resolve when he refused to give up the records and walked out while being questioned by the legislature. Shocked by his quiet defiance, the legislature found him in contempt, but he was not arrested. Some black residents thought Lowry and the NAACP were needlessly causing trouble. Tampa's local office was perennially short of funds and support, often borrowing from the state office to survive.[8]

One indispensable Afro-Cuban lawyer, Francisco Rodriguez Jr., provided the local and state movement's legal muscle. Born to Cuban parents in Ybor City, Rodriguez learned quickly about prejudice. His father held Cuban culture and morals above all others, but Junior developed a fondness for the American schools he attended. Other children treated him differently: "I was not accepted completely by the black kids because I was Latin, and certainly I was not accepted by the white kids. I was always the victim of double-barreled prejudice; one of them was linguistics, and the other one was color." When his black peers laughed at his heavy accent, Rodriguez grew to be defensive and redoubled his efforts to master the English language. "I always carried a notebook around, any word that I didn't know—I always jotted it down and got the definition. I did that until I finished college and graduate school. It became almost an obsessive habit with me."[9]

After graduation from Middleton High School, Rodriguez studied English, Spanish, and French at Florida A&M University. He took a teaching job in Fort Pierce on Florida's east coast, where he found the segregation stricter than Tampa's. An unsettling encounter with a white school administrator prompted Rodriguez to reorient his entire life toward activism and service. With the U.S. entry into World War II, Rodriguez joined the Marine Corps. He did not allow his military service in the Pacific to interrupt his education, reading voraciously and studying Chinese culture while stationed there immediately after the war.

Upon his return home, Rodriguez found himself ill-suited to teaching in Hillsborough County's segregated school system. Instead of studying psychology as planned before the war, Rodriguez studied law at Howard University, concluding with graduate work at the University of Pennsylvania and Temple University. In 1951, Rodriguez became licensed to practice law in Florida, and the NAACP moved its state headquarters to Tampa the following year. From the small offices on Central Avenue, Rodriguez shook the state with a stream of litigation: "During those years, I filed practically every law suit that was filed in the state of Florida. I exposed my life to multiple dangers. I was chairman of the legal redress committee for the entire southeast region."

For a young new member like Clarence Fort, Rodriguez was a galvanizing presence. Fort remembers, "Rodriguez, as far as I'm concerned, does not get the credit he deserved, because he was really another spark plug. And we knew that he had our backs as far as anything that went wrong and if we were arrested. Very inspiring. He took on a lot of [high] profile cases. In fact, he was the attorney that handled all civil rights matters, discrimination matters. He was a person who got it done."[10] Twenty-two-year-old Clarence Fort was one of those intrigued by the news from Greensboro. Born in 1938, Fort was raised on his father's farm outside Alachua County, Florida. He paid his own way through a barber college in Texas, and in 1958, Fort found an apprenticeship with barber Melvin Stone in Tampa. He began dating his future wife, who shared an interest in the budding civil rights movement and the NAACP. Fort recalls,

> One night [late in 1958] my wife and I went to a [NAACP] meeting on Central Avenue at Central Life Insurance Company. I think we were the only two young people there. They talked to us about forming a youth council then, and that's how it all got started. I [recruited] some friends of mine who attended my church [and] started talkin' with them, and we had two or three people together and we started from there.
>
> We didn't actually do that much. We had some interaction with a [white Baptist] group down in Palma Ceia. I think what they were really doing was grooming us to become adult members. There was not [yet] a movement around the country wherein they were having demonstrations and wait-ins and sit-ins. Not until 1960. And that's when

we really became involved. It was only after the demonstrations that things began to change in the city of Tampa.[11]

News of the ongoing Greensboro sit-ins deeply inspired Fort, who had plenty of enthusiasm but no strategy to force a change. Saunders was concerned that rash demonstrations would merely get people jailed and strain the chapter's resources further with no sure benefit. Saunders and Lowry empowered Fort to build a larger Youth Council intent on direct action. It is worth quoting Fort's oral history at length to trace his trajectory from a barber to a civil rights leader.

> It was on the news, television, newspapers—it was something new, very dramatic. That was the spark plug. And it just spread like wildfire all over the South. When those students sat down at the lunch counter there, it started around the South. It really opened our eyes. All the years I went to segregated schools . . . all the years of shopping at a restaurant, five-and-ten-cent store, and having to buy hot dogs and hamburgers and stand up and eat them at the end of the counter. Well, all that began to play in your mind and say, "Wait a minute, something's wrong with this system. Are we citizens? Or are we not?"
>
> I went to the senior branch [of the NAACP]. I went to his [Robert Saunders'] office and told him, "Why don't we do that in Tampa?" And he kind of shied away from it because it was something that they didn't get involved in. They could not promote demonstrations of that sort. So, I sort of took it upon myself at that time. Pretty difficult to pull off, because the senior branch could not get involved.
>
> Bob Saunders was with the movement, but he could only do so much as field secretary. They couldn't come out and say, "We are organizing a sit-in demonstration." They couldn't do that. I could do it because I was a young barber . . . self-employed. Everybody else working on other jobs would lose their jobs [for demonstrating]. So that's why I was very into it.
>
> What I actually did to get it up and rolling, I had to go to the . . . two African American high schools, Middleton High School on the east side of town, and Blake High School on the west side of town. I couldn't let it be known I was on campus. I think the principal at

Middleton knew it, and he just told me, "Young man, I don't know you're here," because he certainly would have lost his job if [he] had permitted that to happen. So what I did, I found . . . their student government president. He allowed me to come back and meet with their student council. Same thing at Howard W. Blake [High School].

[Future Judge] George Edgecomb was student council leader at Middleton [High School and] Shafter Scott of Blake [High School]. We sat down and talked about it and . . . recruited some students. We started out with about forty-five kids. In fact, we started out with Blake and Middleton, then some kids joined us from Booker T. Washington Junior High School. They started coming down. So it really was spontaneous and it just caught on fire.

We tried to select people who was pretty level-headed, we thought, that could go in and represent themselves in an orderly manner. . . . That's how we built up our council—I think it swelled to sixty people—and we mapped all our strategy out what we would do.

Our biggest problem in Tampa was the parents of the students. They were working, they were afraid [if] their bosses saw their kids on television, that they would get fired or in the papers. We actually had a couple of parents pull their kids off the stools because they didn't want to lose their jobs.

I was cutting hair at the time, so the barbershop was a meeting place. People came in to get haircuts and they talked about it: pros and cons, whether it was good idea or a bad idea. A lot of African Americans wasn't for it, wasn't for the movement.

Some of the people that told us, "Just wait." And my thing was, "How long do we wait?" We were already behind the North, so how long do we wait? So, that was the urgency of it. That we shouldn't wait any longer.

After having a series of meetings and I started talkin' so strongly about it, the youth [Council] became so involved in it, so it was almost impossible then to hold it back. After [the senior NAACP staff] saw that we were really gonna do it, then they say, "Well, we'll see what we can do; we'll back you up." Once the civil rights battle really got strong in the Tampa Bay area, we had, if not a weekly meeting, we had at least biweekly meetings. And the two speakers would be Reverend Lowry and Francisco Rodriguez.

We had to constrain the youngsters, because we didn't want any violence. It was pretty difficult. They were ready to go. They wanted to do something different. They got a chance to see the news media, what was happening at that time in other parts of the country. And Tampa certainly was not the second city; there was a lot of cities that started before us. Then they saw what happened in Tallahassee. It was just a whole different scenario in the Tallahassee area.

In Tallahassee the police department took it upon themselves to stop the demonstrators. I think they had dogs, they had water hoses, but they mostly had students from Florida A&M [Agricultural & Mechanical University]. They were not high school students like we had here in Tampa.

We split the groups up. I carried a group. We didn't give any dates because we didn't want the press or the students to go back and tell what was going on.[12]

The Reverend A. Leon Lowry leads black youth in front of Woolworth's, while Tampa police escort the activists and keep angry white onlookers at bay. (Department of Anthropology African Americans in Florida Collection, University of South Florida Tampa Special Collections)

The Youth Council wanted to make an impact without encouraging violence. They kept the date of their sit-ins secret and did not notify police. On February 29, 1960, two small groups of black teens entered two downtown lunch counters: Woolworth's and W. T. Grant's. Fort remembers, "I was a little nervous, I have to admit. I guess every civil rights leader is. You're going into something you don't know what to expect, and after you have gone so far it's too late to turn around. . . . But I took the first seat, and then the others started following in and it was, well, it really wasn't bad."[13] Shortly after the demonstrators entered the W. T. Grant's store, the workers behind the counter put up signs saying the lunch counter was closed. The two groups sat for about fifteen minutes and then left. Soon after the demonstrators left, the lunch counters reopened for business. Anticipating this, Fort and his counterpart led their groups back into the lunch counters fifteen minutes later, whereupon the counters were once again closed.

At the Woolworth's sit-in, the counter manager pushed a "closed" sign in front of the demonstrators. A young lady of the Youth Council promptly brushed the sign away.

The employee barked, "You can't tell me how to run this lunch counter."

Waving cash in her hand, the young demonstrator shot back, "You can't tell us how to spend our money either, because ours is just as good as anybody else's."[14]

Five of the six white patrons at the counter left immediately, while one woman could not resist finishing her slice of pie. Management roped off the stools behind the demonstrators to prevent others, mainly white customers, from joining them. "They roped everything off," Fort remembers, "they didn't make us move—they put the ropes behind us." The Youth Council demonstrators stayed until the counter closed at 6 p.m.[15]

Youth Council members had a follow-up meeting at St. Paul's A.M.E. church that evening, where they met with NAACP leadership. "They [the NAACP] didn't try to stop us," Fort said, "They just said, more or less, to act in an orderly manner, be yourself, and stay out of any verbal contact with the other race. I think I was the only one who was supposed to really speak." After debating their next move, the Youth Council decided to sit in again the next day.[16]

Tampa's police department cooperated fully with the demonstrators at the direction of Mayor Julian Lane. On the second day of the sit-ins, the Tampa Police Department called NAACP headquarters. Fort remembered, "The police department called to find out if we were going [to demonstrate], so they could send police protection. And that's the key difference between the other cities and Tampa, the police protection. They didn't let a soul get near us." Police worked with the demonstrators so closely that they directed traffic and prevented citizens from entering the lunch counters while the sit-ins occurred. This prevented the violence that flared up in other towns like Jacksonville, where racial gangs brawled in the street, and Tallahassee, where the police waged a brutal war on demonstrators with tear gas and batons.[17] Mayor Lane explained, "The mayor in Jacksonville was opposed to integration; here I wasn't opposed to it. It was the Christian thing to do."[18]

On the second day of sit-ins, a young man named Joseph Dasher emerged with his own group of black demonstrators. They were not part of the NAACP or any other civil rights organization, and they did not show the same restraint as the official group. The *Tampa Tribune* characterized the group as a "disorderly, mob-like throng." Fort complained that Dasher's "rebel" group was pushing white people around. To make matters worse, Dasher falsely told reporters that he was vice president of the NAACP Youth Council.

Violence erupted at the Greyhound Bus Terminal that day between one of Dasher's demonstrators and a white patron, both of whom were promptly arrested. In another incident at the White Tower restaurant, one of Dasher's demonstrators broke a glass on the floor. The youth evaded police and later told the press, "the glass just dropped out of my hand."[19]

This was just the kind of negative publicity that the Youth Council wanted to avoid. Even Dasher admitted that his group was out of control. When the crowd surged forward toward Morrison's cafeteria, reporters warned the manager. He stood at the door with trembling hands, fumbling for the proper key to lock the doors. Outside, the crowd swelled to two hundred. Some blamed the reporters for not being served at

Morrison's, shouting, "If it hadn't been for you, a few of us could have got inside!" and "A waiter said we'd be served if we got in!" When a bewildered white driver rear-ended another car at a nearby intersection, the demonstrators laughed and jeered.[20]

At another mass meeting at St. Paul's that evening, the Youth Council decided to wear signs identifying them as legitimate NAACP demonstrators. Predictably, the local press used Dasher and his group to discredit the entire movement. "Lunch Counter Mixing Falters, Move Losing Ground Here," the *Tampa Times* announced with a hopeful tone. The press also made much of the "incorrigible" seventeen-year-old Dasher's criminal record, reciting his offenses, including grand theft auto, and punishments. On the one hand, Dasher's group kept the Youth Council from following up their first protests: the violence was far too embarrassing to risk again. On the other hand, many of Dasher's malcontents joined the NAACP Youth Council to get in on the demonstrations, strengthening the group for future sit-ins. Fort remembers, "If I'm not mistaken their [Dasher's] group fizzled out."[21]

After the violence and demonstrations of that second day, March 1, signs of a white backlash first appeared. A six-foot-tall burning cross in the style of the Ku Klux Klan was found on Holstinger Bridge. It could be seen from Blake High School, where many of the Youth Council attended class.[22] The next night, Dillard Elementary, another black school, was vandalized by gunfire.[23] Days later, a gunman shot two .45 caliber rounds into the Reverend A. Leon Lowry's bedroom from a moving car. The shots missed Lowry and his wife, both asleep, by less than four feet.[24]

The shooting of Lowry's home did nothing to distract the campaign but riveted the press. After the shooting, Lowry told the reporters gathered on his front lawn,

> I am now more determined than ever to fight harder for what I believe to be right. And instead of frightening me, this has just solidified my determination to continue the fight to the very end, come what may. If my life is taken, it will be taken, but I am going to fight on through, until this thing is accomplished.[25]

Years later, Lowry recalled being unmoved by threats of violence.

There are bullet holes in the windows of the house that are still there. I couldn't use my telephone at a certain time of night, and we assumed that somebody was cutting it off downtown or someplace. I got many threatening telephone calls, and many instances when I picked up the telephone, the language that came over it was quite profane. More to worry you and to keep you from sleeping and things of that nature.[26]

I have received many phone calls from white citizens in Miami, New York, and even Georgia since we began our sit-downs here and many have stated they are with us in our drive for first-class citizenship. Since the incident, many have volunteered to guard my house because Negroes are aware that this drive is not merely to get a pop or sandwich but the right to move freely.[27]

Governor LeRoy Collins slammed the "sit-downs" from Tallahassee, saying, "I hate to see demonstrations of this kind. They lead to disorder. Disorder leads to danger to the general welfare and I hope we will not have any more of it." Tampa's white newspapers agreed with Collins. The *Tampa Tribune* thought the lunch counter campaign a folly.

The lunch counter of a private store is a poor rostrum from which to demand equal rights. No tax funds are involved. No public control is involved. In the absence of these elements, the courts have held that a store proprietor can serve or not serve whomever he pleases. . . . The freedom not to buy is as valid as the freedom not to sell. The sit-downs can demonstrate the Negro's dissatisfaction with this form of discrimination but they cannot change it. . . . Tampa must show, in dealing with the sit-downs, that its respect for law will withstand these regrettable abrasions of racial feeling.[28]

The third consecutive day of demonstrations was considerably more peaceful than the last. Although Dasher's "rebel" group materialized again, Youth Council members wore armbands that read, "I am an American, Youth Council, NAACP." The rebels referred to themselves as "We Are Too's," indicating that they were American, as well. About two hundred white people, mostly young men, gathered along the sidewalks, muttering dire threats to Dasher's rebel group, who had little direction

and arrived early. One of the rebels was overheard saying of their counterparts in the NAACP, "When are they going to get here?" When the
Youth Council arrived shortly after, the rebels resorted to following them
from place to place.[29] When they arrived in the basement Kress lunch
counter, they found the area darkened. Instead of waitstaff, "closed" signs
greeted the demonstrators.[30]

Clarence Fort provided a voice for the Youth Council's silent demonstrations. In a prepared statement to the press, Fort urged, "If the different parents would register and vote, we wouldn't have to protest, because they could put someone in office who would do something about
the rights of the Negroes." He concluded, "We also feel that if we spend
money in other parts of the store, we should be able to spend it at the
lunch counters and be able to sit and eat."

There was good reason to take heart: the sit-ins were catching on. Si-
multaneous demonstrations, unaffiliated with the NAACP, took place in
St. Petersburg and Sarasota.[31]

THE TABLE OF FRIENDSHIP

Frustrated by the violence and disorder surrounding the wave of demonstrations across Florida, Governor LeRoy Collins resolved to speak
to Florida's citizens on racial matters. His speech of March 20, 1960, was
extraordinary because it was so unheard of for a Southern governor to
provide any genuine leadership in the face of such problems. Audibly exasperated by the destructive passions on both sides of the Jim Crow line,
Collins delivered a speech laden with fables, folk wisdom, and the Bible.
Above all, Governor Collins called for an unprecedented level of racial
dialogue at the local level to resolve tensions.[32]

To set an example and get the process started, Collins called for the
creation of a Committee on Race Relations, choosing respected Tampa
attorney Cody Fowler as its head. Fowler was known to defend black
clients in the courtroom when few white attorneys would. Fowler and
his mother, Maud, were instrumental in founding the City of Temple
Terrace.

Tampa's Bi-Racial Committee was convened on April 2, 1960, as
a direct result of the lunch counter sit-ins and the encouragement of

Governor Collins. Cody Fowler led this group as well, which incorporated white and black representatives from education, law enforcement, clergy, and business. Buried in Fowler's reports was a mission statement of sorts: "We believe in the democratic control of change. . . . These adjustments may be made on the street-corner under the leadership of extremists with disturbance of the peace, threats of violence, and angry passion as the guiding line, unless there is an institution in the community whose task is to deal with them."[33]

Like Collins's speech on race, Fowler's reports often read like an impatient father trying to scold his children without alienating them. Fowler admired the black leadership in the movement while complaining of a lack of visionary white leaders in Florida: "During the whole critical period since 1954, the South has suffered acutely from lack of leaders. As in the great crisis of 1860, the South's political leadership has been almost entirely composed of nay-sayers." The biracial approach would not have been necessary had there been more dynamic leadership from the white establishment in the first place. Black leadership tended to be strong at the time because it had to be to rise above internal debates and external hostility. White leadership was anemic because it perceived that no political gain could come from leading any kind of social change. If the political futures of Julian Lane and LeRoy Collins are any indication, at that time in the South, it was indeed political suicide to cooperate with the civil rights movement.[34]

A store owner in San Antonio, Texas, voluntarily integrated in March, making it the first success of 1960, but further progress was elusive. According to Fowler, "That other cities have not yet succeeded in resolving the dilemma is not surprising when it is recognized that the initial call for leadership was directed at merchants, a group sensitive to so many pressures as to be peculiarly unprepared for the role of leading social change."[35]

Some Southern newspapers were just as skeptical of white leaders' intentions as Fowler. The *Raleigh News and Observer* editorialized,

This thing cannot be solved by a continuance of mass protests by the Negro students. . . . This thing cannot be solved by more mass arrests, either. . . . The issue will not quiet down without a decision—either to cope with the moral question or to cease all food service. . . . This means, too, that the leadership of North Carolina's assailed cities must assert itself.[36]

The *Richmond News Leader* despaired at the contrast between the black student activists and the white thugs who confronted them.

> Here were the colored students, in coats, white shirts, ties, and one of them reading Goethe and one was taking notes from a biology text. And here, on the sidewalk outside, was a gang of white boys come to heckle, a ragtail rabble, slack-jawed, black-jacketed, grinning fit to kill, and some of them, God save the mark, were waving the proud and honored flag of the Southern states in the last war fought by gentlemen. Eheu! It gives one pause.[37]

For those shocked and dismayed by recent events, Fowler sought to explain the many factors that had changed the dynamics of race relations in the South. Fowler's factors of change can be summarized as follows: the South's transition away from agriculture toward an industrial and service economy; changes in the way the U.S. Supreme Court interpreted the rights of black citizens; the new status of Africa as an ideological battleground in the Cold War; mass communication and consumer culture raising expectations of black people; personal communication and the formation of a civil rights network across the nation; better educated black Americans; more liberal religious leaders and religious interpretation of the racial situation; service by black citizens in the armed forces; more aggressive black leadership; increased black buying power; urbanization; increased political rights for black Americans, especially voting; and a gradual liberalizing of racial attitudes among white Americans. Fowler saw the situation quite clearly and wanted Florida's local leaders to do the same.[38] He argued that much racial tension could be diffused by providing more housing, recreational, and employment opportunities for African American citizens. Instead, most Southern leaders were more interested in cracking the whip of law and order.[39]

Fowler saw the events of 1960 as an opportunity for communities to act and integrate voluntarily and peacefully, preempting any need for the courts to get involved. He saw sit-ins "as an appeal of one segment of the citizenry to another." Should the citizens ignore this appeal, "a struggle between Negro citizens and state power" would result. Fowler stated, "Thus what began as an issue of community relations may well end as a question of legal rights and privileges. This was probably inevitable, given the inability of local leadership" to react in a constructive manner. Indeed, few Florida communities created biracial committees or started meaningful community dialogues.[40]

* * *

Fowler knew he was probably fighting a losing battle when trying to convince many white Southerners to peacefully accept desegregation. But he made convincing arguments that the economic well-being of Florida and its citizens depended on a peaceful solution to the crisis. Fowler wrote prophetically,

> The use of economic pressures, rather than legal attacks, could have immense implications. Techniques similar to the lunch counter "sit-ins" could be developed for many other objectives, including employment.[41] Florida's economy, unlike the deep South states, is very much related to its vast number of tourists and huge number of beautiful recreation areas. While de facto segregation is a national, not Southern reality, open policies of complete segregation are condemned by the overwhelming majority of Americans from which Florida's tourists stem. Florida then has a kind of economic vulnerability to national feeling that is incomprehensible in Mississippi.[42] Florida could lose millions in tourist trade and industrial expansion if a policy of racial repression, adapted for a rural economic society, is allowed to unwittingly build up the potential for racial tension and street corner solutions.[43]

But Fowler left wiggle room for the Pork Chop Gang and other segregationists. "All of this would seem to suggest the wisdom of Florida's acceptance of a racial policy that would encourage and expect great variance from community to community." Translated: Integration may be necessary for the Lamb Choppers of Florida's cities, who depended on tourism, but "the rationale of segregation for many rural communities is much more tenable." Fowler never said segregation was just, only that it would be much easier to maintain ("tenable") in Florida's rural communities.[44]

Just three days of sit-ins and the threat of more convinced much of Tampa's business elite to negotiate. While the NAACP applied pressure behind the scenes, Field Secretary Robert Saunders reminded the press, "Although active sit-ins at lunch counters have been discontinued because of the program of Gov. LeRoy Collins to form biracial committees, there is still active protest against segregation in public businesses. . . . All over the state we are receiving reports of increased support in our fight to end discrimination at lunch counters and in employment."[45]

Reverend Lowry attended the first meeting of the committee, which met in the boardroom of the Exchange National Bank. He recalls, "They asked for a moratorium on demonstrations, to which I agreed, while we worked on this matter around the table, negotiating. The first meeting I recall very distinctly, and I felt very frustrated." Reverend Lowry notes that the agenda was dominated by concerns over the finances of the downtown stores. Lowry rose to walk out of the meeting, but local businessman Robert Thomas persuaded him to stay and attend the next session. Fowler wrote of the meeting, "The Commission met with outstanding leaders of the Negro community. The personal respect of many of these leaders for the Negro members of the Commission was a major reason for the Commission's success in effectively terminating many demonstration potentials." Even if the negotiations began with tension and distrust, a dialogue had commenced.[46]

After discussing the issue with several variety store companies, Fowler wrote, "The consensus reached in these discussions was that change was inevitable; that negotiations were imminently preferable to demonstration; there was need for much responsibility in the Negro Community; and that store policies should and would respond flexibly to responsible local leadership."[47] The committee stressed that it needed time to persuade businesses to integrate. But with an aggressive Youth Council urging further demonstrations, Fort felt he had very little time. He alone was expected to hold the youths back from further actions. "This was hard for me," Fort remembered, "because the youths had gotten stirred up then, and they were ready, man."[48]

I was called everything from a sell-out to Uncle Tom. They [Youth Council members] thought I had sold out to the system. And we realized that—well, I did—we had to have time to let them work it out. So, I would just tell them at the meeting that they had to trust me. If I started it, there was no way I was going to sell out and back down. We had assurance from Reverend Lowry, who was still around, and Bob Saunders telling us that they were trying to work it out. And they began to integrate other cities, and we felt that it was just a matter of time before it would come to Tampa. The kids that I was using didn't have money to buy a hamburger anyway. When we really started to integrate with the kids, we had to give the kids money to buy food.[49]

The delay took place mainly because the city's businessmen wanted to know how integration would proceed in other cities and awaited guidance from their respective corporate headquarters. The question was not if Tampa should integrate—it was when and how. After months of discussions, the committee agreed upon a low-intensity method of integration.

To summarize Fowler's notes:

Small groups of three were to visit designated lunch counters three times a day for three days. This was later pared down to groups of two twice a day.

Activists would avoid sitting near or talking to white patrons.

Lunch counter owners and/or corporate headquarters would brief store managers on the change of policy.

Store managers would brief their staffs of the change of policy.

The committee asked Mayor Lane to post a detective in every participating store for the test period of integration.

The committee asked the press not to publicize the days of test integration.

The committee would convene two weeks after the tests for assessment.[50]

About ten chains agreed to participate on Tampa's first day of integrated dining, with at least two black couples to visit each participating store.

One couple would dine at about ten in the morning, and another would dine at two in the afternoon. In this way, integration could maintain a low profile by avoiding the lunchtime rush. The activist group led by James Hammond, Young Adults for Progressive Action, selected discreet adults to participate rather than the high school students of the Youth Council. The NAACP asked participants to order their food and eat quietly. If they encountered any trouble, they were asked to calmly pay their bill and leave, regardless of whether they had finished their meals.

Tampa's first day of integrated dining took place on September 14, 1960. About 150 black Tampans dined at eighteen lunch counters. C. Blythe Andrews, the editor and publisher of the *Florida Sentinel-Bulletin*, was among them. He accompanied "Mrs. Cook, mother of two, and she was obviously nervous":

> I tried to make conversation with her en route, but as we neared the site of North Gate [shopping center], butterflies began jumping in my own stomach. I realized then that I too was nervous about the thought of trouble. We got out and walked in Madison's. There were stares when we sat down, but we were put at ease when a waitress named Violet asked "May I help you?" Mrs. Cook and I glanced at the menu and ordered eggs, French fried potatoes, toast, coffee and grits.[51]

Clarence Fort participated, as well. He had plans to meet an associate to dine with at the Walgreen's lunch counter. When his companion did not arrive, Fort decided to dine alone.

"I was by myself," Fort remembered:

> Now that was a frightening experience. I was too nervous to even eat. And I sat down and I ordered, I think it was grits and eggs. It was early in the morning, with bacon, coffee, and just as I started to butter my toast, two guys came up. Two white guys came up, and they said, "look what we have here, a nigger at the lunch counter." They stood behind me, right behind me. Other people were there; two or three got up and left. But I'd say at least ten remained. So they said, "[W]e're not going to let him eat here." So at this time I called the waitress and said, "Will you give me my bill and let me pay you?" I never touched the food.[52]

Afraid to leave the store, Fort wandered around until he found the manager he knew from the biracial meetings. Fort explained the situation, and the manager told the men, "Look, we're not going to have any trouble here, we're not going to have any trouble in my store. We're going to let these people eat here." When the men would not leave, the manager called the police. The police arrived shortly, and as they walked in, Fort walked out. One of the white men spit at Fort, who looked back and saw the police detain his pursuers, warning them to leave downtown Tampa.[53]

A handful of reactionaries who gathered downtown, four from Plant City and one from Dover, were all arrested after chasing two young black boys down Franklin Street while armed with axe handles and bats. Reverend Lowry urged all black people to jump on the bandwagon "or stay in the shadows where you can't hurt any of us. The day of the 'hankerchief head' and 'Uncle Tom' is gone."[54]

After a week of testing and probing, Tampa had permanently integrated most of its lunch counters. Eighteen lunch counters participated in the precedent-setting event, but that left a great many still segregated. According to the *Sentinel-Bulletin*, there was a miscue, "which occurred when two teachers showed up at a Martin's Pharmacy store and were told that they [Martin's] 'had not come in yet on the agreement to serve Negroes.'"[55]

By December, eleven cities had integrated their lunch counters while another ten had informally integrated. But no changes had taken place in Georgia, South Carolina, Louisiana, or Mississippi. By February 1961, one year after the first Greensboro sit-in, several of Florida's tourist-oriented cities integrated, including Miami, Orlando, Sarasota, St. Petersburg, Daytona Beach, Pompano Beach, and Ft. Lauderdale. It should be noted that no cities north of Orlando joined the trend. With no money at stake in the tourist industry, Florida's segregationist Pork Chop Gang, which dominated politics from their staunch northern districts, stood firm for the old ways.[56]

Many independent, locally owned eateries would not agree to admit black patrons. Beyond lunch counters, there was a whole community of full-service restaurants who had more to lose. Restaurants did not have a department store to maintain profits, nor did they have a nationwide network of outlets to depend on. For many of Tampa's restaurant owners,

WHAT WILL BE NEXT?

CERTAIN TAMPA MERCHANTS HAVE INTERGRATED THEIR LUNCH COUNTERS — WHY? BECAUSE THE NAACP HAS THREATENED TO BOYCOTT ALL MERCHANTS WHO DO NOT BOW DOWN TO THEM.

LUNCH COUNTERS ARE NOT ALL! IT IS JUST ANOTHER STEPPING STONE TO OUR WHITE SCHOOLS AND PLAYGROUNDS AND A CHANCE TO PUT A NEGRO BESIDE YOUR WHITE DAUGHTER. JUST HOW LONG WILL WHITE MEN TOLERATE THIS BEFORE THEY WILL STAND UP AND BE COUNTED??

YOU CAN HELP NOW BY STOPPING ALL BUSINESS WITH ANY STORE INTERGRATING LUNCH COUNTERS.

PLEASE BOYCOTT THESE STORES:

MAAS BROTHERS DEPT. STORE
BELK LINDSEY STORES
WOOLWORTH   KRESS
MADISON   . WALGREEN
NEWBERRY   • GRANTS

AND THOSE IN SHOPPING CENTERS AT:

BRITTON PLAZA   NORTH GATE
HILLSBOROUGH PLAZA   DALE MABRY

DON'T SPEND YOUR DOLLARS FOR INTERGRATION

White Citizens of Tampa

In this leaflet purporting to speak for "the white citizens of Tampa," segregationists urged consumers to boycott the lunch counters in an effort to stop integration. (Sumter Lowry papers, University of South Florida Tampa Special Collections) integration meant more risk and fewer benefits. To some extent, the Jim Crow line maintained itself: without decent jobs, most black people could not afford to dine in restaurants at all.

An important dialogue had begun, however flawed, and the lunch counters were an important first step in equality. Fowler wrote, "The wholesome race relations enjoyed by the citizens of Tampa are due to the fact that leaders of both races have taken time out to sit around the 'table of friendship' to formulate and implement policies and programs for [their] improvement."[57]

THE UNIVERSITY RESTAURANT

The new University of South Florida (USF), with its campus located just north of Tampa and Temple Terrace, was Florida's first university in a major metropolitan area. While this pleased the state's up-and-coming urban legislators, known as the Lamb Choppers, it threatened the disproportionate power of Florida's rural legislators, known as the Pork Choppers, or Pork Chop Gang. Locating a new idealistic university in one of Florida's fastest-growing urban areas during the civil rights movement went against the grain of the Pork Choppers' ideology of white supremacy and conservative social policies. Led by legislator and one-time governor Charlie Johns, the Pork Choppers formed the Florida Legislative Investigation Committee (FLIC). Better known as the Johns Committee, the group singled out civil rights groups and suspected homosexuals in Florida's universities for scrutiny as Communist agents. They never did find a single Communist, but they were able to shake up civil rights activists and university employees—their chosen ideological enemies—from 1958 until 1964 on the taxpayer's dime. The financially struggling University of Tampa had refused to become a state university because of its desire to remain segregated.

USF admitted its first students in 1960, and its first black student enrolled in 1961. Tampa resident Ernest Boger was attracted to USF for being cheap and close to home. He was not an activist, but he was a keen student seeking the "economic advantage" of a degree. He became USF's student number 2,000. "I got a fair amount of [press] coverage just for doing regular things. I did have some concern prior to coming in." He turned out to be a model student. Once Boger joined the band, where he played tuba and valve trombone, he felt like he was part of a group and became "very comfortable." He joined the Russian language club and demonstrated leadership in the intramural basketball team.[58]

On November 24, 1963, just two days after the assassination of President John F. Kennedy, USF's band played a concert. To celebrate afterward, the entire group planned a dinner at the nearby University Restaurant. Opened just months before USF, the University Restaurant was the only major eatery near the isolated campus. With a hearty menu of Italian and American classics, the restaurant catered to nearby brewery and university workers. Previously, Boger felt comfortable dining only in the Latin restaurants of Ybor City.[59]

Being on scholarships, Boger and some other students had to help break down the equipment and tidy up after the recital. He was on the second busload of students and arrived about thirty minutes later than the first group, who had already been seated and placed their orders. A group of rowdy locals were well into a drinking session at the bar. With the food about to arrive for his peers, Boger entered the restaurant: "As I walked in, I could see the manager getting frantic. When you're a person of color you tend to anticipate some of these things, and a lot of times they don't materialize, but when they do, you know exactly what's happening. So I saw him scurry over to our band director and there's some whispering going on."[60] The manager asked about Boger, and the band director replied, "That's Ernie, our Student Assistant." The manager refused to host an integrated party. Moments later, a student announced that Boger would not be served and the band would no longer dine at the restaurant. The news clearly pleased the young white men leering from over their drinks at the bar.

> Boger: By that time, they called a couple other places. [They] called Frisch's Big Boy to be sure there was no problem. Everybody got up and left. I'm sure that hurt them that evening because all the orders were already in and were about to come out as we [the student assistants] arrived. That sent the message from about a hundred people. Then the next day, the students and faculty began to picket. It was about the time that the public accommodation laws were about to be

passed. I don't know if that particularly helped anything because the tide of change was already in place. But to the credit of USF students and faculty, they recognized a situation and stepped up.[61]

The worst predictions of the Pork Chop legislators had come true: white students from an urban university had acted to promote civil rights for African Americans. Boger was content to let the situation go, as Congress seemed poised to take up the civil rights bill after President Kennedy's assassination. Some of his white peers were far less forgiving. Both candidates for USF's Student Association president wanted to form a civil rights committee if elected.

In the days following the incident, students and administrators met on campus to decide a plan of action. Most administrators and faculty advocated a "behind-the-scenes" approach to persuade management to integrate. The more indignant students and faculty formed the short-lived but loftily named Student Congress on Human Relations. Sociology professors Douglas Greene and Jack Ross served as the founding faculty advisors for the group. A member commented at the time, "This incident occurred shortly after the assassination of President Kennedy, a time when emotions were exposed, raw, ready for focusing." Their founding document envisioned USF students and faculty taking part in Tampa's ongoing racial dialogue.

> The turning away of a [black] student provoked indignation that such a situation should exist so near campus and precipitated picketing. [On] January 28, a group of students and faculty spent almost two hours discussing the situation with the management. Management remains steadfast in its refusal to open its facilities to everyone, regardless of race.
>
> At the same time that this letter is being circulated on campus, a conference-request is being lodged with members of the Mayor's Bi-Racial Commission; a well-used step in the negotiation process in Tampa.
>
> Students and faculty at the University of South Florida who agree with the principle that equality of opportunity is a legitimate concern of all have banded together to form the Student Congress on Human Relations (SCOHR). While not affiliated with any national

organization, the group seeks to explore and to develop projects in those areas shared by persons of good will the nation over: health and welfare; housing; education and youth incentives; and, vocational opportunity. Contact has been made with . . . the AAUP, and with such community groups as the Urban League, the Council on Human Relations, and the National Conference of Christians and Jews, in order that a working relationship may be formed for mutual counsel and coordination.[62]

The more militant students favored direct pressure by continuing the picketing of the restaurant. Shortly after midnight on December 6, a group of local toughs approached some USF students who were still picketing at such a late hour. The locals beat several students while they were trying to leave the site. Advocating a nonviolent approach, the student picketers did not fight back "since this would defeat the purpose of the picketing," a student claimed. A small foreign car with three students inside was almost flipped by the assailants. When the students attempted to drive away, the assailants followed them at high speed in two cars before pinning the student's car against a barricade. The thugs pulled the student driver from his car and beat him, requiring him to seek treatment at a hospital.

The university's *Campus Edition*, run in part by students, published editorials condemning the picketing as unconstructive. One student fired back by writing, "Your position on the University Restaurant shows the hypocrisy of your eulogy to President Kennedy, a friend of human equality, which appeared on the same page. If segregation triumphs in this area, the bigots will have the *Campus Times* to thank for it." Another student observed of the campus paper, "There was this wonderful defense of students' rights to wear Bermudas [shorts]. Now there is an issue [integration] fraught with significance."[63]

Chemistry professor Jack Fernandez was a young member of the faculty and the Association of American University Professors. He described the AAUP membership as "furious" over the policy of the University Restaurant. A delegation of four or five members went to meet with Basil Scaglione to gauge his willingness to integrate. Fernandez recognized a tolerant soul in Scaglione, who claimed to have grown up with black neighbors. Scaglione explained that he would happily integrate when Congress passed the proper legislation, which seemed to be within sight.

Fernandez felt that Scaglione was being held to an unfairly high standard and pointed out that black cafeteria employees were not allowed to eat at USF. "If you want to boycott," Fernandez told his colleagues, "start with USF." Instead, the AAUP publicly boycotted Scaglione's restaurant. Fernandez was so frustrated at this selective activism that he resigned from the AAUP, never to return.[64]

The University Restaurant had an especially vocal defender in Sumter Lowry, an avowed segregationist and anti-Communist. Having run unsuccessfully for governor several years before on the Segregationist Party ticket, Lowry found it easier to wage his political battles while not being burdened with any office. He began a campaign of recorded phone messages that both defended and promoted the University Restaurant's "white only" policy. The messages read,

> Let freedom ring. . . . The people of Tampa do not wish to dine among members of the black race. The University Restaurant on Fowler Avenue, recently refused to serve a Negro student from the University of South Florida. Because of this exercise of freedom, the students and faculty at the University of South Florida are being urged to boycott the University Restaurant. The next time you dine out, if you would like one of the best steaks in town and would like to eat your meal in the presence of members of the white race, try the University Restaurant—you will be glad you did. Let freedom ring.[65]

Owner Basil Scaglione briefly considered building a separate dining room to house integrated parties, such as those from USF. True to his word, Scaglione fully integrated the restaurant after Congress passed the Civil Rights Act on July 2, 1964. "There is no other way," Scaglione said days later, "The bill is now the law of the land."[66]

At USF, student efforts toward social justice fizzled quickly. The beating incident put an end to picketing. The SCOHR group went inactive, and no civil rights committee was ever added to USF's student association, today known as student government. But in the city, dedicated black activists, in conjunction with the Bi-Racial Committee, were just getting started.

Robert Saunders noted with some satisfaction that by late 1963, all outlets of the following chains had integrated: W. T. Grants, Woolworths, S. H. Kress, Walgreens, Eckerd Drugs, and Howard Johnsons. Even Maas Brothers had integrated its downtown restaurant, a favorite of lady shoppers. Still, Maas Brothers refused to serve black shoppers outside of their downtown store, and the Super Test Amusement Center, while integrated, would still not serve food to black customers.[67]

In July 1964, newly elected Mayor Nick Nuccio called for a special meeting to ensure that integration continued smoothly beyond Tampa's lunch counters. The operators of Luigi's, Hawaiian Village, Embers Imperial House, and Bill Lum's Old China House attended, as well as representatives of chains including Morrison's Cafeterias, Martin Pharmacies, and Eckerd Drug Stores. Ybor City's most popular restaurants—the Columbia, Las Novedades, and Spanish Park—also joined the effort.[68]

The *Florida Sentinel-Bulletin* sounded optimistic in 1964, praising the spirit of cooperation in the city. "In integrating the parks, swimming pools, theatres, beach, zoo, and hotels, cafes, motels, and almost everything else, there has been no commotion, no bitterness, no squabbles. The Biracial Committee deserves much of the credit[.] We must keep Tampa quiet and sober-minded. We must not shout about little incidents and forget the major progress that has been made. Above all, we must prove that we are first-class citizens by acting like first-class citizens in our dress, by our speech and by our public conduct."[69]

Some white leaders also ensured the success of the campaign. Cody Fowler certainly helped to prove the worth of the Bi-Racial Committee. Mayor Julian Lane's cooperation with the demonstrators meant that Tampa would not be tarnished by the violence seen in Jacksonville, Tallahassee, and St. Augustine. Integration may have been the right thing to do ethically, but Lane's cooperation was politically suicidal. In his bid for reelection, Lane lost many of the white districts that elected him in 1959. The promising political career of Governor LeRoy Collins also ended prematurely after his stand against hate, and he never held elected office again.[70]

Movie theaters, swimming pools, parks, public schools, and restrooms all integrated as a result of Tampa's first civil rights campaign using non-violent passive resistance. The whirlwind lunch counter campaign had been powered by the dedication and discipline of black leaders such as A. Leon Lowry, Francisco Rodriguez Jr., Robert Saunders Jr., James Hammond, and Clarence Fort. It also fed into other campaigns, such as the search for equity in the workplace and training programs for black workers. For the first time, the business community had been pressured by direct action, and it responded. For the moment, the Bi-Racial Committee provided an ideal forum for discussions. Beginning with its lunch counters, Tampa was on its way into a new era.

MOURNING LAS NOVEDADES

Tales of Urban Renewal

Ybor City's oldest residents gathered around the charred remains of a restaurant to ponder the future and meditate on the past. So much had been lost. One of the finest restaurants in Tampa at the time, Las Novedades (Spanish for "the novelties"), was a landmark for tourists and residents alike, a shrine of Ybor City's history and dignity. When it finally closed in the 1970s, the Latin Quarter reeled from the effects of ill-conceived urban renewal programs, and residents lost a vital symbol. The events just before and after its closing reveal a Tampa in mid-transformation: fast food, urban renewal, labor strikes, bullfights, steak houses, race riots, ghosts, gay bars, and arson all play their part in the death of the icon. Las Novedades, Steak 'n Brew, and the El Goya Lounge had one thing in common: one after another, they all occupied the same Ybor City building in the unlucky age of urban renewal.

Born in Asturias, Spain, Manuel Garcia was a proud and principled businessman. He immigrated to Havana as a boy in the late 1890s and as a teenager worked sweeping the floors of saloons and keeping the coins he found among the debris. He came to Ybor City at the turn of the century and worked odd jobs in the cigar factories.[1]

Between 1900 and 1905, Garcia saved enough money to start a family and buy La Fonda, a restaurant next to a small saloon called the Columbia. Hungry drinkers often wandered from the saloon to La Fonda for meals, and business was good. When Prohibition threatened to ruin the Columbia, Garcia became a partner and they merged into a new, larger restaurant during the 1920s.[2]

After splitting with his partners at the Columbia in the 1930s, Garcia moved on to revive the Spanish restaurant Las Novedades in 1939 with his son, Manuel Jr. The eatery, also on Seventh Avenue, originally opened in 1890 but went out of business in the early 1930s. The Garcias revived the restaurant and relocated to the stately building at the intersection of Seventh Avenue and Fifteenth Street. With its delectable Spanish food and dignified service, the restaurant was among Florida's finest restaurants for decades. Awards poured in from the Florida Restaurant Association and magazines such as *Holiday* and *Esquire*.[3]

As the business expanded, Garcia's former partners in the Columbia became competitors. Each restaurant added more elaborate rooms and entertainment to their already impressive operations. A prolonged and genuine rivalry persisted for decades, with each establishment receiving accolades and awards while Ybor City slowly declined around them.

The downturn in local business prompted the restaurants to increase their emphasis on entertainment to draw tourists. While the Garcias hired strolling guitarists to perform for diners, the Columbia maintained an entire orchestra to back up its owner and violinist, Cesar Gonzmart.[4]

During the late 1960s, Manuel Junior's son, Manuel III (hereafter referred to as Manny), worked at Las Novedades, as well. In 1954, his training began when, at the age of eleven, he asked his father for money to go to a movie. His father suggested he wash dishes in the restaurant to earn his way. Over the years, Manny climbed the ladder from salads and sandwiches to soups and sauces. He worked with some of the best chefs in the state and saw how the restaurant functioned. After working as an apprentice through his high school years, he prepared for the next step—college at Cornell University's prestigious School of Hotel Management.[5]

While Manuel was president of the Florida Restaurant Association, he rubbed shoulders with small-time entrepreneurs and prestigious CEOs. He befriended the founders of Burger King and met an associate named Harland Sanders, who started a small company named Kentucky Fried Chicken. The concept of fast food sparked Manuel's imagination, but because of prior commitments, he declined an invitation by Sanders to join the budding chain. In 1963, the Garcia family proudly watched Manny receive his degree from Cornell. The young graduate wanted to run Las Novedades, but his father had a radical suggestion for their business future.[6]

"Son, let's look into this fast food business."

"Dad, what've you been drinking?" came Manny's reply.[7]

Manuel Jr. may have been a traditional man, but he saw the writing on the wall: there was a future in fast food, while Ybor City seemed to have no future at all. The cigar industry had been declining since the 1930s. Termites had devoured the old company housing. Latin veterans relocated after World War II and Tampa's poorest residents often replaced them.

Federal funds radically changed the city in the 1960s and 1970s with interstate roads and urban renewal. Officials routed Interstate 4 through the residential heart of Ybor City, bisecting the community and claiming dozens of homes for the government by eminent domain. Urban renewal programs began with the "Federal Bulldozer" clearing cities of undesirable structures. In the wake of demolition, the invisible hand of the free market and private business would ostensibly build the community anew.

In 1965, the *Tampa Tribune* announced, "Ybor City's transformation into a gleaming new and modern Latin Quarter was approved by the Federal Urban Renewal Administration." In fact, only demolition began that year, destroying dozens of buildings to make way for new developments. Besides rehabilitating run-down Ybor City, urban renewal promised to "preserve and strengthen the distinctive qualities . . . of Tampa's Latin heritage and present-day Latin community."[8]

High expectations accompanied the announcement—would Ybor City rouse from its siesta? Projected maps, city plans, and architects' sketches splashed across the newspapers, touting an "international attraction." While officials claimed that 93 percent of Ybor's historic structures would face demolition, boosters predicted 2.5 million tourists would visit in 1970 and 3.2 million by 1973.[9]

With Ybor's history reduced to rubble, just what would all those tourists come to see? A group of developers planned a hotel, motel, apartments, restaurants, and beer gardens to lure tourists. Investor Dr. Henry Fernandez announced, "We have plans for a three hundred foot tower with a restaurant on the top." Fernandez even considered saving some of Ybor City's old buildings from demolition, a rarity at the time.[10]

Urban renewal marked 708 buildings to be demolished in the first phase. Of Tampa's three urban renewal programs, the largest took place in Ybor City, comprising nine hundred displaced families. Unlike the other projects that relocated only African American families, almost one-third of those relocated from Ybor City were considered white or Hispanic. Officials spoke of a four-year period to move the displaced residents, but no time table existed for redevelopment.[11]

Despite the rosy predictions, urban renewal failed miserably. It was understandably difficult to get profit-seeking entrepreneurs to invest in one of the poorest, most run-down areas of Tampa. Dozens of Ybor's oldest businesses folded or were demolished. Poverty prevailed with no end in sight. Crime continued to rise. Government regulations bound redevelopment plans in red tape. While businessmen and politicians dreamed of giant entertainment complexes, Ybor City's reality had not changed nor were its problems ever really addressed.[12]

The situation did not improve for the Garcia family either. Manuel Sr., Manny's grandfather, the founder of La Fonda and reviver of Las Novedades, died in 1966 at the age of eighty-two. In March 1967, Local 104 of the Hotel and Restaurant Employees and Bartenders International Union, AFL-CIO, filed a lawsuit claiming Las Novedades refused to bargain with them over changes in policy. Workers staged a walkout on February 28, led by the waiters. Three days later, kitchen workers joined the picket lines outside the restaurant. Truman Mincy, a cook and Restaurant Workers Union member who stayed at his post, found his house firebombed by the union with minor damage. Management aggressively sought out waitresses and dressed them in colorful dress uniforms to replace their unionized waiters.[13] Business suffered during a strike by the powerful waiter's union in 1967. Only by importing scab waiters—thereby angering much of the Latin community—did the Garcias beat the strike. It took two years for business to return to its former levels.[14]

In the midst of these difficulties, Manuel Jr.'s extraordinary wife, Clarita, wrote Tampa's single most important cookbook, *Clarita's Cocina*. A scholar of language at the University of Madrid, Clarita could claim an impressive pedigree in hospitality. Her grandfather had run a Spanish inn and her uncle cooked for King Alfonso XIII. Garcia worked as an interpreter before moving to Tampa. A faithful record of Spanish cuisine leavened with her charming notes, *Clarita's Cocina* is still considered to be an essential resource for anyone interested in Tampa's Spanish food. For years, Clarita appeared on various local television programs, showing audiences how to make Spanish favorites. The book also solidified the reputation of Las Novedades as a source of fine cuisine. Doubleday Press published *Clarita's Cocina* in 1970 amid much uncertainty about the future of Las Novedades and Ybor City.

Manny investigated the fast-food industry as his father suggested. Manuel had gotten to know James W. McLamore, who was a director of the Florida Restaurant Association. He was also one of the first franchisees of Burger King and offered Manny a great opportunity. In 1969, instead of opening an outlet in Gainesville as planned, Manny discovered that an Orlando-based franchise was available. The previous owners had no confidence in the Burger King concept and had changed the name of their two restaurants. Someone had to turn the unprofitable business around fast. The franchise would soon have a new neighbor that was sure to bring in customers—Walt Disney World, set to open in 1971. Manny was thrilled with the opportunity and assembled investors to buy out the franchise. He attained exclusive rights to open Burger King outlets in three counties in central Florida (Orange, Osceola, and Seminole).[15]

At first, Manny thought he could run his Burger King empire *and* inherit Las Novedades. He soon discovered the demands of fast food, especially the expansion of a previously failing franchise. His managers pitched Burger King at churches and PTA meetings, anywhere to get the word out. Manny closely watched the local expansion of McDonald's, because the company selected the best future locations. Whenever he had the chance, the young man would suggest that his father sell Las Novedades to help him with Burger King.[16]

Manny observed that the two restaurants had but one thing in common: "Both of them are businesses. Going from the restaurant business to the fast food business was like going from flying a jet to riding a bike." The differences between Las Novedades and Burger King were extreme indeed. Las Novedades had been a destination in Ybor City for more than eighty years when it closed. Employees at Las Novedades were highly skilled and handsomely paid—many worked there for decades. The kitchen turned out refined top-dollar cuisine, sometimes consumed in feasts that lasted hours. The restaurant's atmosphere and decor projected its dignified Old World image.

Burger King began cooking flame-broiled burgers on a conveyor-belt grill in the 1950s and opened uniform outlets across the country. Employees at Burger King are usually young and unskilled and earn minimum wage—no unions or benefits to worry investors. Understandably, few fast-food workers stay at their jobs for long. The food is factory-processed, uniform, and cheap. Burger King customers eat out of paper bags, use disposable utensils, and sit on molded plastic chairs—or just buzz by the "drive thru" and munch in their cars. For better or worse, fast food had come to define modern food service.

While the Garcias toiled for Burger King, developer Jim Walter approached Manuel with an offer of partnership. Walter had gone from building simple "shell homes" for World War II veterans to being a housing construction tycoon. He invited the Garcias to join a slick urban renewal scheme meant to transform the crumbling heart of Ybor City into a Spanish-themed shopping district, a concept known as the Walled City. The scheme was the brainchild of Jim Walter and Cesar Gonzmart, the owner of the Columbia Restaurant. Gonzmart had emerged as Ybor City's most flamboyant businessman, playing violin with the Columbia's orchestra and kissing ladies and babies tableside. Not surprisingly, Manuel distrusted Gonzmart, his greatest rival.

Gonzmart and Walter dreamed quixotically. A feasibility study of the Walled City plan found that to succeed, the complex would require a strong "focal point" attraction. Walter, Gonzmart, and Henry Fernandez, a Tampa optometrist and partner in the project, decided on Portuguese—or "bloodless"—bullfighting as the primary attraction. Only one problem remained: bullfighting was illegal in Florida, so Gonzmart and a team of lobbyists warmed up to legislators in Tallahassee to have a special bill passed. Former Florida attorney general (and a vice president at Walter's company at the time) Jimmy Kynes lobbied for the bill, which received less than sixty seconds of debate on the floor of the legislature before being passed. Governor Claude Kirk asked the legislature to reconsider the bill and to send it to him after a more healthy debate.

Gonzmart reportedly went about in his full Liberace wardrobe of ruffled cuffs and kissed the hands of every secretary he saw.[17]

Like a tall tale, the price and projected revenue generated by the bullfighting grew with each telling: the cost of $5 million and revenues of $10 million grew exponentially. Excited investors from Wall Street, the Columbia Broadcasting System, and the government of Spain dreamed that the Walled City would rival Busch Gardens for tourist dollars. With the help of Louis de la Parte, a powerful state senator from Tampa, the Florida legislature passed a bill that legalized bloodless bullfighting in 1970.[18]

The reaction among the public ranged from curiosity to revulsion. On the *Tonight Show*, Johnny Carson lampooned the unusual Florida law. The next day, throngs of people crowded around Gonzmart's Columbia Restaurant, some asking where the bullfighting was to occur, others demanding that the plans be scrapped. Protestors outside the restaurant lynched Jim Walter and Cesar Gonzmart in effigy.[19]

In a *Tampa Tribune* editorial, Charlie Robins wrote that Ybor City already had an identity built upon its dining, not around bullfighting.

> Ybor City is bean soup, boliche, and yes, even bolita, but it's not blood and sand. In Ybor City, success is measured by one's ability to get the eye of the waiter, not the ear of the bull and the moment of truth comes when one plunges his dessert spoon into the flan or guava shells. In short, Ybor City may be indigestion after dinner, but never death in the afternoon. The city's Latin Quarter can yet survive the bulldozer of urban renewal, but I doubt that it could survive the brave but unblooded bulls or tourist promotion. . . . In fact planners specifically stated their aim was not to build a tourist attraction, but to preserve one.[20]

For those concerned about the bullfighting, Gonzmart offered comfort.

> The attraction will offer much more than bulls, with much singing and dancing, and will be family oriented. In Spain they have these traveling troupes, like rodeos or circuses. They put on Spanish pageants, with horses, clowns, dancing, and midget bullfighters and midget bulls and no swords, no killing. It's a sort of comedy or farce. They are very, very popular. Well, we thought we'd adapt that to our place in

Ybor City. I'll debate them [bullfighting opponents] anytime on television. We're right. They're wrong. They're looking for something that isn't there . . . they've gotten us national attention already.

The bullfighting ring was set to open in October 1971, to coincide with the grand opening of Disney World.[21]

Developers had envisioned a twenty-five acre shopping district surrounding the bullfight arena. The brick streets would guide tourists to antique shops, galleries, boutiques, nightclubs, and a "magnificent Spanish palace motel." Lavish bachelor apartments would attract a younger crowd.[22]

In the meantime, Manuel considered Walter's offer of partnership. Unsure how to react, he asked his son for advice. "It's bloodless bullfighting," Manny snapped, "forget it." As they thought over the offer, several flaws must have come to mind. Unrealistic projections for the "Walled City" construction and attendance raised false hopes among the public. While optimism can be healthy, no one was sure whether 2,500 tourists would come to Ybor City in 1970, never mind the projected 2.5 million. After a pause, Manny said, "Sell it [Las Novedades] to them, I need you here [in Orlando]."[23]

Tampa's realities supported Manny's argument. Amid soaring prices and a tottering economy, urban renewal and arson motivated by insurance fraud gutted Ybor City. In the wake of demolition, the number of businesses declined by 10 percent, and about one out of five restaurants closed in between 1965 and 1969. In 1970, the long-term outlook for almost any businessman in Ybor City was tenuous at best, and the losses were just beginning. Urban renewal and other programs seemed to do nothing but point out the government's (and private interests') inability, or unwillingness, to help.[24]

In 1970, Manuel Garcia Jr. swallowed his pride and sold the restaurant he had run for more than thirty years for half a million dollars. While the sum seems like a good deal of money for the time, Manuel had debts to pay and received much of his payment in kind with antiques and furniture from the restaurant. He accepted a position in his son's booming Burger King operation but could not bring himself to leave his beloved Tampa until several years later.[25]

Gonzmart promised that Las Novedades would remain open, keep its name, and continue to serve its famous Spanish cuisine. He became president of Las Novedades, while Jim Walter became chairman of the board. Besides the addition of "prime western steak" to the menu, the new owners changed nothing about Las Novedades.[26]

Gonzmart gloated over his victory to newspapers and magazines, analyzing his coup: "I think perhaps my flair for showmanship was one reason we were able to remain in business and they were not. We came in with a very elaborate musical production, of which I was the star. And violins dealt them a mortal blow. It destroyed them. Have you seen me perform? I persuaded my dear friend Jim Walter to save it from becoming a lost landmark."[27] Prospects for the Spanish Walled City dimmed quickly. Like the projected profits, the controversy generated by bloodless bullfighting quickly spun out of control. In February 1971, a group unassociated with Ybor held a bullfighting exhibition in Bradenton. The untrained and untested Ocala bull went berserk, broke out of the ring, and charged into the crowd. Two policemen had shot a dozen bullets into the bull's brain before it finally stopped. Three months later, the Florida legislature rescinded the bullfight law, and the Spanish Walled City lost its precious focal attraction.[28]

With the Walled City project shelved, Las Novedades outlived its usefulness, and Gonzmart closed the restaurant in 1972. Tampa historian Tony Pizzo reacted with a solemn reflection: "The Las Novedades was born with the cigar industry. It was across the street from the old Sanchez y Haya cigar factory, the number one factory in Tampa. . . . I think it is a sad moment in Ybor City history. The Las Novedades was probably the oldest restaurant in all of Florida. It's a sad commentary. I just hope Cesar Gonzmart will re-open it."[29] In the meantime, according to the *Tribune* "[Cesar] Gonzmart talk[ed] endlessly about something he calls 'the Magic' of Ybor City, and mentions it in the same breath as the Magic Kingdom of Disney World." The Columbia appeared to be more magical than ever. Manuel Garcia left a large number of imported, hand-painted Spanish tiles at Las Novedades that inspired the Columbia's newly tiled exterior.[30]

In March 1973, the newspapers confirmed the rumors—Las Novedades would be replaced by a steak house chain. Shortly after the announcement, the *Tribune* reported that Bob and Jessica Stubbs, on an annual visit from Illinois, rushed to the restaurant "to have dinner there right away, as if an old friend were dying." Incredulous, Mrs. Stubbs asked, "How can they do this? We've been coming here for the past ten or fifteen years. Where will we go now? They've got steak houses from Maine to California and they have to do this? It's horrible. It's unspeakable."[31]

Waiter Ovidio Martinez said, "We're all sad it's closing. I've spent a lifetime between the Columbia and here. It's all I know. I've come to love this place; I couldn't work in a steakhouse." At Las Novedades, patrons were "treated like kings and queens," Martinez recalled, and that is the difference between "a real Spanish restaurant" and "something else."[32]

In this case, "something else" was Steak 'n Brew. Gonzmart and Walter leased the property to New York–based corporation Longchamps, Inc. Longchamps assured disappointed Ybor residents that "while the décor will become that of a steak house it will be a Spanish type steak house in keeping with the Ybor City atmosphere." The Ybor outlet opened in March 1973 and was part of a ten-unit expansion plan in Florida.[33]

Besides remodeling the kitchen and replacing old plumbing, Longchamps spent $150,000 remodeling the beautiful restaurant with a crazy-quilt of decors. In the end, it looked more like an amusement park ride than a "Spanish steak house." The self-service buffet, dance floor, and stage were decorated with a variety of "nailed down" nostalgic novelties like "fish netting, rum kegs, pewter tankards and plates, wagon wheels, ship lines and moonshine jugs." The overwrought interior had "décor befitting an English pub, a German pub, a deck of a sailing ship, docks of New England, colonial America, the old west, the south seas, a pirate's cove—you name it."[34]

Cesar Gonzmart hailed the sale as another great victory, especially in terms of finance. "I am not a good businessman?" he chided reporters: "I paid zero for the buildings and the business and I owned 50 percent, which we leased for $1 million. Jim Walter took tax losses on his 50 percent, leaving me with 100 percent of the profit. Then I sold the lease and property for $350,000, including $100,000 in cash. I retained the Las Novedades corporation, which gave me a tax advantage for losses incurred in the past, plus we held the name."[35] Gonzmart quipped that his volume was up 40 percent from last year, but his bravado was probably meant to mask the Columbia's own struggles. Under his leadership, the quality of the food and management had declined steeply. Awards for excellence such as Florida Trend Magazine's Golden Spoon Awards stopped coming in. Ybor City couldn't even support a steady daytime trade, and the Columbia closed for lunch. Gonzmart spoke the truth when he said, "It just wasn't profitable to have two fine Spanish restaurants so close together."[36]

Explaining the sale wasn't as easy for Steak 'n Brew hostess Margaret Duarte, who had the unenviable job of greeting shocked customers who thought they would be eating at Las Novedades. "People walk into the lobby," she said, "see the difference, and exclaim, 'You don't have that good Spanish food anymore.' They're disappointed. Even I was disappointed at first. I used to buy bread in the old Las Novedades."[37]

Strong contrasts set Steak 'n Brew apart from Las Novedades. Where waiters had once deboned fish and carved fowl tableside stood the ubiquitous self-service salad bar and cheap "all you can drink" beer and wine. At Las Novedades, waiters wore fine tuxedos and memorized every order. At Steak 'n Brew, staff in hot pants and sneakers greeted customers with name tags that read, "Hi my name is ____." The restaurant hoped to lure young people and families, potentially supplied by the new Hillsborough Community College campus nearby.[38]

Local businesspeople complained that Ybor City drew fewer tourists without Las Novedades. They also doubted that anyone would come to Ybor City to eat at "a steak place." No wonder the *Tampa Times* wrote, "There is a lingering sadness over the passing of the Las Novedades." Tampa was learning too late that the Latin restaurants were the only marketable remnant of old Ybor City.[39]

Steak 'n Brew lasted just over a year before admitting failure in Ybor City. In the public eye, Ybor City became something of a ghost town, inhabited by criminals and poor, trapped residents. In its weakened state, few people were interested in opening new businesses in the crumbling Latin Quarter. No large restaurant could expect to survive there, especially in the shadow of the Columbia, which became Ybor City's flagship attraction. In 1974, owner H. Herbert Wagner Jr. hoped a new Spanish restaurant would occupy the site. When he announced he was "looking for a reputable, specialty-type restaurant to fit in with the building's décor," few could have predicted who the next tenants would be.[40]

A business with a dedicated clientele occupied the site, but it was not a Spanish restaurant. El Goya Lounge, a gay bar and dance club, replaced Steak 'n Brew in 1976 with even more controversy. Florida's second-largest gay club at the time, El Goya became popular for its drag queen revues and dance floors.

Since the Stonewall Riots of 1969 in New York, when gay patrons resisted a brutal police raid, the movement for gay equality had brought gay clubs out of the shadows and into the open. Tampa's vice squad no longer raided gay bars as a matter of routine. The popularity of disco music and dancing in the 1970s raised the profile of gay dance clubs into the mainstream, and El Goya capitalized on the trend. Tampa's nightlife had reached a nadir in the 1970s. Only the gay bars downtown and in Ybor City attracted large clienteles. Tampa still remained "a closet town," according to local gay men, but the clubs thrived by night.[41]

Ybor City's elders may have disapproved of the perceived desecration of Las Novedades, the site of so many wedding and christening receptions. Lingering spirits in the building seemed to haunt its occupants. For years, employees and patrons reported red-eyed demons, vaporous spirits, and the ghost of a man in a white suit. These strange visions lurked far away from the stage and were not part of the dance revues. But they may have been informed by the then-current horror craze in Hollywood, buoyed by hits such as 1973's *The Exorcist* and 1979's *The Amityville Horror*. The ghost stories caught the attention of local journalists.

Employee Jennifer Gerhardt reported,

Shortly after I started working there in 1976, I noticed a man in a white suit sitting at the bar. He looked like a negative of a photograph at first glance. And when I turned around to look back at him, he was gone. Another time, after I became the bar manager, I was locking up at night. . . . Just as we were walking away from the door, we saw this man in white walk down the hallway and through the Garden Bar. He then opened the [locked] door and walked out. We couldn't believe our eyes.[42]

When employees tried to open the door, it was still locked. "We unlocked the door," said the cashier, "to find the chain on the gate still looped and padlocked."[43]

Waiters and customers sighted the mysterious ghost all over the building, and he was often staring back. Some believed the man in the white suit dated back to Las Novedades in the 1950s. As the story went, a quarrel between a waiter and a chef over an order of Crêpes Suzette turned deadly. The mythical murder took place in the confines of a maze-like corridor leading to the ice room. Most of the site's supernatural phenomena were said to have occurred in that hallway, but no one has ever identified any such crimes in the historic record.[44]

The strange occurrences were not limited to one corridor. A figure was known to look over the shoulders of those who gazed into a certain mirror. Curtains parted and closed spontaneously, lights turned on and off, and chandeliers swayed without the slightest breeze. Others saw swirling white clouds in the air, moving as if alive. One could reportedly hear people walking and talking all over the building when no one was there or hear a piano playing haunting melodies in the distance.[45]

A *Tampa Times* article about the ghost sightings intrigued readers so much that the newspaper held a séance there to satisfy collective curiosity. Several mediums sat around a table with reporters and attempted to confirm if supernatural activity flourished there. After an hour of reflection, the mediums and psychics related several profiles of spirits caught in the old restaurant. A girl who was kept in a cage and tortured; a merry violinist; two murdered men; a middle-aged woman who was robbed of her life savings; a chef who specialized in cooking chickens; and reverberations of illegal activities like gambling, smuggling, and prostitution.[46]

Manny Garcia denied the existence of ghosts in the building, and he should know—he practically grew up there. One has to wonder whether the ghost stories were genuine, a publicity stunt, the product of fancy, or inspired by Hollywood. In any case, the ghost stories are an outgrowth of nostalgia—and a pervading sense of loss.[47]

On November 14, 1977, in the darkest hours of morning, a man used a shaky drain spout to climb three stories up the side of the old building. On the summit of the roof, he emptied a can of gasoline into a ventilation duct. After waiting a few moments for the liquid to drain into the old

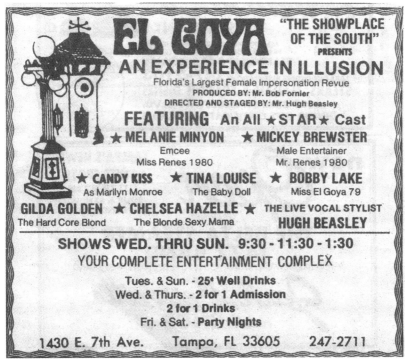

The El Goya Lounge's ads proudly advertised a revue of female impersonators, but the attempted arsons of the building and reported ghosts inside caught far more attention. (*La Gaceta*)

plywood-patched El Goya Lounge, he lit a match and fled. It was some time before anyone noticed the red glow and black smoke emitted by the flames.[48]

In the gathering light of morning, "people saw a landmark die," a *Tribune* article recalled. Five priceless El Goya tile works and a $10,000 grand piano from New York's Metropolitan Opera House were destroyed. A crowd of old Las Novedades customers gathered around the burnt hulk for an impromptu funeral. The *Tampa Tribune* observed, "Most of those who came to see the remains spoke fondly of Las Novedades and memories and festivities that once filled its dining rooms. More than thirty elderly Latins came to pay their respects."[49]

Armando Avales blamed El Goya for the fire: "I came here when it had all the pretty murals and the Goya tile, but it's no more. It's been ruined. You'd eat, drink, and see your people, see your family. It was our life. It's no more at all. It was ruined. Not by the fire, but by people. People who changed its image."[50] Other locals defended the El Goya as the only business putting urban renewal into practice. Armando P. Valdes Jr., a nearby jeweler said, "It was a gay place. These people here, they never bothered nobody. And let me tell you, they had a very profitable business." Another resident said, "It was bringing Ybor City back alive—definitely. Ybor City was a very dead place. Once this place [El Goya] started opening, it brought this place back alive."[51]

No matter how one felt about the El Goya, seeing the shell of the old Las Novedades drove home the hard reality of urban renewal's shortcomings. "It can't be rebuilt," Don Dominick said. "Renovation. Restoration. They can't make it like it was. It's now history, so much like the rest of Ybor City." Mary Fuentes, who was there consoling her seventy-eight-year-old mother, said, "I remember when Las Novedades closed about five years ago. It was a tremendous blow to my parents. If you haven't lived here, or if you didn't live here forty years ago, you can't know what's been taken away from these people. It's hard to live when the history of your people starts to fade away." "Novedades was one of the last authentic traditions around Ybor," resident Arturo Fernandez said. "It was a landmark, it was history. When they closed Novedades, they closed Ybor City too."[52]

Almost six months after the fire, police arrested the suspected arsonist, John Hayward McDaniel, for being a "torch for hire" on behalf of another gay bar called Rene's on Kennedy Boulevard. The two businesses had been fiercely competing for the loyalty of the area's gay population since El Goya opened in 1976, a rivalry that sometimes turned violent.[53]

Police believed that McDaniel, also known as "Champ," received $500 for his services. Because the fire did not completely destroy the building, McDaniel vowed to burn it down again. The arsonist had cooperated with the investigation until the murder of a mobster in the county jail "shut him up tight," said police. The authorities remained silent on who they suspected paid him, but all fingers pointed to Cesar Rodriguez, owner of a dozen bars in Tampa, including Rene's and another gay bar called Kikiki, who had previously been involved in organized crime. His business had suffered badly after El Goya opened.[54]

Constant fires were a reminder that urban renewal had failed in Tampa. As the economy worsened in the early 1970s, incidents of fire insurance fraud spiked, accounting for a third of such claims. In 1978, federal court convicted a ring of sixteen arsonists, real estate agents, insurance brokers, and organized criminals in what was said to have been the largest racketeering trial to date. It did nothing to slow down the arson.[55]

Ybor City's residents continued to witness the painful reverberations of urban renewal. The *Tampa Tribune* wrote of "Broken Promises" and "Broken Hearts," and citizens complained that urban renewal "only succeeded in tearing [buildings] down." City officials and local businessmen still fostered big plans for the area. Cesar Gonzmart, in his usual exuberance, said, "The future is now. I'm not talking long-term plans. I'm saying that soon you'll come back and see a different Ybor City." As if in response to Gonzmart, the *Tampa Tribune* asked, "Has Ybor City's hour arrived? They've heard the grand dreams before."[56]

A dream came true for the owners of the El Goya Lounge. They rebuilt the venue to become an even more popular gay dance club named Tracks. For a time, it was one of the most popular clubs in the city, drawing straight and gay patrons alike. The place was hip, fueled by the emerging rave culture that supplanted disco in the late 1980s. In Tracks, the old dining rooms of Las Novedades served as dance floors, each room with a different visual and musical theme. While most of Ybor City was desolate, Tracks had customers lining up along the sidewalk to get in on the weekends.

Gradually, other entrepreneurs followed the example and opened businesses in the area. A colony of artists gave way to funky new restaurants, bookstores, record shops, and musical venues. These independent businesses lit the way for bigger ventures and more established investors.

Far away, near Mickey Mouse's sprawling empire, Manuel Garcia's Burger King franchise became one of the most successful in the world. His outlets grossed 50 percent more than the chain's average—a difference of a quarter million dollars. With a dozen restaurants by 1980, Manny's annual volume was ten times that of Las Novedades. "Some people tell me we've taken a step backward by going into the hamburger business," Manny Garcia said. "We had some flak from family and friends.

Some laughed when we said we were going to do this. But they don't laugh now." Manny added, "Before we were really running a restaurant. Now, we run a corporation."[57]

The fast-food industry was not without its downside, however. Competition stiffened in the 1980s, resulting in a fast-food marketing war. Television advertising was the key to the corporate struggle. Fast food does not sell well without commercials. Public relations spawned a torrent of multimillion-dollar advertising campaigns such as "Where's the Beef?," "The Whopper Beat the Big Mac!" and "Have You Had Your Break Today?" Garcia and other franchisees fretted over their lack of input into Burger King's bid for global fast-food dominance. The winners were anybody's guess.

In May 1980, a new salvo in the burger wars landed in Ybor City, when McDonald's opened a rare custom-made outlet. Built with Spanish flourishes in design and decor, it still served the same burgers and fries. A path of handlaid brick with old-looking lampposts led to the entrance. Inside, a cement Ponce de Leon statue stood amid ferns and fountains designed to mimic Ybor City. Green lamps, just like those used in cigar factories, illuminated the restaurant's interior. Cigar box art and old photographs of Ybor City adorned the walls, along with a hand-painted mural. The artist painted Las Novedades in the corner of the mural with vibrant colors. Manager Dagmar Gignac said, "You'd be surprised how many people are coming in and reminiscing. We picked decorator pieces from a very traditional part of town." With the remains of Ybor City's failed restaurants, Ronald McDonald festooned his latest addition.

Fast food launched the Garcia family into a whole new strata of wealth and success. They even considered reopening Las Novedades. Looking back on the end of Las Novedades, Clarita Garcia concluded that Tampa had squandered Ybor City's genuine heritage.

We enjoyed good business, and the loyalty of the local Tampans was so rewarding, but it became harder and harder to attract people to the area. It was the late sixties and the beginning of the seventies when unrest, riots, muggings, etc. were rampant in the area. Then progress stepped in to further clinch the ability to operate soundly. Why progress? Interstate 4 with only one exit to Ybor City. Manuel fought long and hard for the City Fathers to preserve Ybor City. The fine Spanish restaurants had put Tampa on the map, and they failed miserably to protect that which was a tourist drawing card . . . the Spanish Restaurants.[58]

Manuel Jr. died in 1988, having gone from a single restaurant to running the DavGar Corporation in Florida. Among his pallbearers was an old employee, Serafin Martinez, father of Governor Bob Martinez, also a former mayor of Tampa. The Garcias' franchise of forty-eight Burger Kings was worth $45 million in 1990.[59]

Manny invested in new concepts during the 1980s, including Miami Subs, started the Pebbles chain, and opened fine dining restaurants in Orlando. In 1997, he sold the family's franchise of fifty-seven locations for $55.6 million to pursue his latest ambition. He set up a central commissary Culinary Concepts/Chefs Creations for his restaurants near Orlando, which is now his most profitable business. The company prepares and vacuum seals high volumes of gourmet soups, sauces, and even smoked duck. Disney is among his biggest clients, and his business will soon outstrip that of his Burger King franchise.[60]

Despite all the talk about redevelopment, Cesar Gonzmart kept doing what he did best—being the spokesman for the Columbia Restaurant. As Ybor City's fortunes rose, so did the Columbia's. The Gonzmarts opened several outlets around the state, packaged frozen food, concocted a powdered Sangria mix, and marketed a popular cookbook. Tracks was among Ybor City's top nightclubs throughout the 1980s into the mid-1990s, when franchised bars and restaurants displaced many of the local establishments. Ybor City once again became a popular destination for dining and nightlife. As more people seek out walkable neighborhoods and affordable housing, Ybor City and nearby Tampa Heights have become fashionable for businesses and residents. The shift among young people toward urban living and entrepreneurship has finally stepped in where the federal bulldozers left off in the 1960s.

CONCLUSION

Rapid changes in modern society have influenced the rise and fall of social institutions such as saloons, jook joints, vaudeville theaters, speakeasies, and steak houses. While the preceding chapters have exposed conflicts, injustices, and the social friction accompanying wrenching change,
they should not obscure the fact that, for many citizens, Tampa was an
ideal place to grow up and raise their families. Even at its most troubled,
old Tampa had its wholesome charms. Likewise, even at its best, Tampa
retained a rusty edge of mystery and danger to knowledgeable outsiders
late into the twentieth century.

There is a wistful nonchalance in the way many locals regard Tampa's
illicit past, as if the entire town was in on the joke, and the crimes had
no victims. The first casualty was democracy itself. Tampa's government,
wide open to vice for a time, suffered from a kind of civic indifference.
For much of its history, Tampa's elites seemed to see the city as a recepta-
cle for attracting outside investment rather than an opportunity to create
a genuine community. While Tampa is not unique in this regard, and the
usual bugbears of greed, race, and class played a role, the city seemed especially unprepared for a future of transparent, civic-minded governance
and public service.

After World War II, Tampa tried to distance itself from its own seedy
reputation in order to cash in on the tourism that inundated Florida.
However, the area's remarkable growth ground to a halt, first during the
Great Depression of the 1930s and then again in the post-urban malaise of

the 1960s and 1970s. Despite its public ambition, Tampa's fortunes sank as suburban sprawl left the city center reeling from neglect and poverty. Various programs such as urban renewal proved ineffective in stopping the decline or burnishing the city's troubled image.

The post war population boom in Florida inundated Tampa with a sprawling populace more interested in business and burgers than bolita or boliche. Observers during the 1980s noted that a changing of the guard seemed to be taking place. The influx of new workers from outside the city changed the feeling for residents. The city had almost tripled in population between 1940 and 1990, while Hillsborough County's more than quadrupled. Don Basler, president of the Health Executive Advisory, said of the newcomers, "They were not and never will be a part of 'Old Tampa.' On the other hand, 'Old Tampa' is not so sure it likes what has developed. Many have not adjusted to the change that has occurred." Much of Tampa's old identity, for better or worse, had been abandoned and/or displaced.[1]

Some instinctively understood that Tampa was in a similar position to the one it had been in a century before. While Tampa had the ambition to be a great city and take its rightful place as the "Queen of the Gulf," it did not have the capital to transform itself. That would require a visionary magnate such as Vicente Martinez Ybor. "Tampa's future lies in king-sized projects," the *Tampa Tribune* editorialized in 1985, "most of which will exceed the limits of local leaders and surpass the dreams of even the most visionary natives among us." This prophecy would be fulfilled more than thirty years later with the large Water Street development downtown led by Jeff Vinik, owner of the Tampa Bay Lightning hockey franchise.[2]

Since the 1980s, it has been difficult to identify the signature industry—aside from nude dancing and attorneys—that sets Tampa apart from the rest of Florida. The hand-rolled cigar industry had gradually given way to mechanized production, which did not require skilled workers nor their hefty salaries. Premium hand-rolled clear Havana cigars, Tampa's signature product, disappeared from its factories. The embargo on Communist Cuba beginning in 1961 emphasized that Tampa's fine cigars were a thing of the past. In place of the cigar industry, Tampa cobbled together several other sources of revenue, including shipping via the port, military spending via MacDill Air Force Base, and the requisite modern Florida mainstays of tourism, attorneys, the service industry, and real estate.

Old Tampa may be long gone, but its sense of history remains, which is increasingly crowded out by the pulpy images of pirates and gangsters. Behind those archetypes, however, it is still possible to glimpse a genuine past far more colorful, disturbing, and inspiring than any pirate tale.

NOTES

Introduction: Boom Town on the Florida Frontier

1. Kelly Reynolds, *Henry Plant: Pioneer Empire Builder* (Cocoa: Florida Historical Society Press, 2003), 141–42.

2. For a concise summary of race relations in Tampa, see Nancy A. Hewitt, *Southern Discomfort: Women's Activism in Tampa, Florida, 1880s–1920s* (Urbana: University of Illinois Press, 2001), 24–32, 132–36.

3. José Rivero Muñiz, Eustasio Fernandez, and Henry Beltran, *The Ybor City Story: (1885–1954). Los Cubanos en Tampa* (Tampa, Fla.: n.p., 1976), 4, 23–24; Reynolds, *Henry Plant*, 141.

4. Of course, the massive Moorish behemoth never made a dime. The hotel limped on after Plant's death, in 1899, but never prospered. The Plant system sold the white elephant in 1904, and after closing in 1930, it became the home of the University of Tampa the following year. Reynolds, *Henry Plant*, 156.

5. Muñiz, Fernandez, and Beltran, *The Ybor City Story*, 7.

6. Muñiz, Fernandez, and Beltran, *The Ybor City Story*, 7–8.

7. *Tobacco Leaf*, July 12, 1895; L. Glenn Westfall, *Don Vicente Martinez Ybor, the Man and His Empire: Development of the Clear Havana Industry in Cuba and Florida in the Nineteenth Century* (Ph.D. dissertation, University of Florida, 1977), 73.

8. Muñiz, Fernandez, and Beltran, *The Ybor City Story*, 11–12.

9. Gary Mormino, "Tampa and the New Urban South: The Weight Strike of 1899," *Florida Historical Quarterly* 60, no. 3 (1982): 337–56; Also see Westfall, *Don Vicente Martinez Ybor*.

10. Muñiz, Fernandez, and Beltran, *The Ybor City Story*, 14–15.

11. *Tobacco Leaf*, February 5, 1987; *U.S. Tobacco Journal*, March 18, 1987; *New York Times*, May 16, 1887.

12. Muñiz, Fernandez, and Beltran, *The Ybor City Story*, 24–26, 40.

13. Works Progress Administration Tampa office records, box 15. University of South Florida Special Collections, Tampa (hereafter cited as WPA Records).

14. Joan Marie Steffy, *The Cuban Immigrants of Tampa, Florida, 1886–1898* (master's thesis, University of South Florida, 1975, 22–23; Gary Mormino, "Tampa and the New Urban South," 337–39.

15. Steffy, *The Cuban Immigrants of Tampa, Florida, 1886–1898*, 17, 18, 35; Karl H.

Grismer, *Tampa: A History of the City of Tampa and the Tampa Bay Region of Florida* (St. Petersburg: St. Petersburg Print, 1950), 215.

16. Gary Ross Mormino and George E. Pozzetta, *The Immigrant World of Ybor City: Italians and Their Latin Neighbors in Tampa, 1885–1985* (Urbana: University of Illinois Press, 1987), 17–38.

17. Reynolds, *Henry Plant*, 150; Steffy, *The Cuban Immigrants of Tampa, Florida*, 55.

Chapter 1. The Sunday Wars: Saloons and Recreation

1. For more about the WCTU's efforts in Tampa and Ybor City, see Hewitt, *Southern Discomfort*, 38–42.

2. F. Valdez, and the Federal Writers' Project of the Work Projects Administration for the State of Florida, *Life Histories: Biographical Interviews of Ybor City Residents* (1936), "John Cacciatore," 2.

3. Grismer, *Tampa*, 212–13; *Tampa Morning Tribune*, June 24, 1887, April 24, 1903. Because of variation in the name over the years, hereafter it will be cited as the *Tampa Tribune*.

4. Westfall, *Don Vicente Martinez Ybor*, 72; *Tampa Tribune*, June, 1887; City of Tampa Archives, "Incorporation History." www.tampagov.net/city-clerk/info/archives/city-of-tampa-incorporation-history.

5. Florida and Allen H. Bush, *A Digest of the Statute Law of Florida of a General and Public Character: In Force up to the First Day of January, 1872* (Tallahassee, Fla.: C. H. Walton, state printer, 1872), 250.

6. The nickname for the laws, also known as Sunday laws, that aimed to control behavior on Sundays, ostensibly to protect the sanctity of the Christian Sabbath.

7. Steffy, *The Cuban Immigrants of Tampa, Florida, 1886–1898*, 19, 28.

8. Tampa City Marshal, *Marshal's Docket*, City of Tampa, 1895–96.

9. Thomas J. Noel, *The City and the Saloon: Denver, 1858–1916* (Lincoln: University of Nebraska Press, 1982), 12. This book successfully contextualizes saloons in the setting of a frontier town in a variety of ways.

10. Frank W. Alduino, *The "Noble Experiment" in Tampa: A Study of Prohibition in Urban America* (Ph.D. dissertation, Florida State University, 1989), 4. Alduino's dissertation traces the development of Prohibition and dry laws in Tampa. His findings helped guide my own research, especially in chapters 1, 3, and 6, which fill out some stories and details not included in his work.

11. Hillsborough County Sheriff's ledger, 1890s. Housed at the Hillsborough County Sheriff's Museum in Ybor City; Alduino, *The "Noble Experiment" in Tampa*, 4; *Tampa Tribune*, June 24, 1897, and January 29, 1891.

12. *New York Times*, January 18, 1903.

13. For a full discussion of Tampa's aversion to taxes and police, see Kim Jules Frosell, *Booster Altruism: Motivations and Restraints on Progressive Reforms in Tampa, Florida, 1900–1921* (master's thesis, University of South Florida, 1994); *Tampa Tribune*, June 18, 1907.

14. Lori Rotskoff, *Love on the Rocks: Men, Women, and Alcohol in Post–World War II America* (Chapel Hill: University of North Carolina Press, 2002), 23.

15. John Kobler, *Ardent Spirits: The Rise and Fall of Prohibition* (New York: Putnam, 1973), 178–79.

16. Alduino, *The "Noble Experiment" in Tampa*, 82.

17. See also Clifford C. Sharpe, "Florida's First Brewery," *Sunland Tribune* 17 (November 1992): 59–66; *Tampa Tribune*, February 13, 15, and 16, 1897.

18. Alduino, *The "Noble Experiment" in Tampa*, 74, 78, 82–83; *Tampa Tribune*, December 13, 1953.

19. *Tampa Tribune*, October 22, 1896; Alduino, *The "Noble Experiment" in Tampa*, 82–83.

20. *Tampa Tribune*, September 20, 1897, October 5, 1897.

21. Federal Writers' Project of the Work Projects Administration for the State of Florida. *Social-Ethnic Study of Ybor City, Tampa, Florida* (1935), 56–57; *Tampa Tribune*, September 30, 1897, October 5, 1897.

22. *Tampa Tribune*, October 1, 1896; August B. Mugge, *My Memoirs* (unpublished manuscript, 1990), 5–6.

23. Mugge, *My Memoirs*, 6; *Tampa Tribune*, July 8, 1897, August 10, 1895, April 23, 1896, and May 29, 1897.

24. Mugge, *My Memoirs*, 7, 69.

25. *Tampa Tribune*, May 29, 1897.

26. *Tampa Tribune*, August 10, 1895.

27. *Tampa Tribune*, August 8, 1895.

28. Resolutions of Tampa City Council, 1889–1901, City of Tampa Archives, 31; *Tampa Tribune*, August 12, 1895.

29. *Tampa Tribune*, February 16, 1896.

30. *Tampa Tribune*, June 9, 1896.

31. Tampa City Council minutes, June 1896, and August 16, 1896.

32. *Tampa Tribune*, October 12, 1896, October 1, 1896, June 14, 1895, July 7, 1896, and September 9, 1896.

33. *Tampa Tribune*, December 13, 1896, January 26, 1897, July 2, 1896, and April 28, 1897.

34. *Tampa Tribune*, October 1, 1896.

35. *Tampa Tribune*, June 24, 1897.

36. *Tampa Tribune*, June 30, 1896.

37. *Tampa Tribune*, June 5, 1897, and June 24, 1897.

38. *Tampa Tribune*, July 3, 1896.

39. *Tampa Tribune*, April 21, 1899, October 13, 1897, July 2, 1896, and June 24, 1897.

40. City Council Minutes, *Tampa Tribune*, June 24, 1897, and October 13, 97.

41. *Tampa Tribune*, June 5, 1897.

42. *Tampa Tribune*, June 5, 1897, and June 26, 1897.

43. *Tampa Tribune*, July 9, 1897.

44. *Tampa Tribune*, June 24, 1897, and October 13, 1897.

45. *Tampa Tribune*, May 1, 1896; Mugge, *My Memoirs*, 7, 69.

46. *Tampa Tribune*, June 28, 1900.

47. *Tampa Tribune*, May 1, 1896, July 7, 1896, September 9, 1896, and October 13, 1897.

48. *Tampa Tribune*, July 9, 1897.

49. Alduino, *The "Noble Experiment" in Tampa*, 8–11; *Tampa Tribune*, May 6, 1902, May 10, 1902, September 19, 1902, and November 23, 02.

50. *Tampa Tribune*, May 6, 1902.

51. *Tampa Tribune*, May 25, 1902.

52. *Tampa Tribune*, May 25, 1902.

53. *Tampa Tribune*, May 27, 1902, and June 1, 1902.

54. *Tampa Tribune*, May 27, 1902, and June 1, 1902.

55. Alduino, *The "Noble Experiment" in Tampa*, 12–13; *Tampa Tribune*, June 27, 1902, and October 24, 1902.

56. Frosell, *Booster Altruism*, 52; *Tampa Tribune*, February 4, 1900, and February 26, 1901.

Chapter 2. "Some of the Soldiers Did All Their Fighting in Tampa": The Spanish-American War

1. Steffy, *The Cuban Immigrants of Tampa, Florida, 1886–1898*, 82; Muñiz, Fernandez, and Beltran, *The Ybor City Story*, 34.

2. *Tampa Tribune*, August 2, 1892

3. *Tampa Tribune*, August 14, 1893.

4. *Tampa Tribune*, August 14, 1893. Apparently, no one was hurt by the shots.

5. *Tampa Tribune*, August 16, 1892, and September 8, 1892.

6. *Tampa Tribune*, September 13, 92. El Piral does not appear in the oldest available City Directory, Shole's from 1899.

7. Alfred J. López, *José Martí: A Revolutionary Life* (Austin: University of Texas, 2014), 266; *Tampa Tribune*, November 24, 91.

8. Muñiz, Fernandez, and Beltran, *The Ybor City Story*, 64–65.

9. Muñiz, Fernandez, and Beltran, *The Ybor City Story*, 91–92.

10. Muñiz, Fernandez, and Beltran, *The Ybor City Story*, 93.

11. Steffy, *The Cuban Immigrants of Tampa, Florida, 1886–1898*, 98.

12. *Evening Independent*, February 13, 1967; Steffy, *The Cuban Immigrants of Tampa, Florida, 1886–1898*, 98; Grismer, *Tampa*, 206.

13. This theory was pioneered by U.S. Admiral Hyman G. Rickover's own investigation into the issue in 1974; he published his findings in 1976. Dana Wegner later confirmed Rickover's findings. Both concluded that spontaneous combustion of airborne coal dust likely set off the explosion. Since the coal and gunpowder bunkers were placed too close together in the *Maine's* design, the ignition of the coal bunker led to a chain reaction in the gunpowder bunker, setting off the catastrophic explosion that doomed the ship and most of its crew. For Wegner's findings, see Edward J. Marolda, *Theodore Roosevelt, the U.S. Navy, and the Spanish-American War* (New York: Palgrave, 2001), 7–17.

14. *Tampa Tribune*, February 24, 1895; William J. Schellings, *The Role of Florida in*

the Spanish American War, 1898 (Ph.D. dissertation, University of Florida, 1958), 20; City Council Minutes, April 2, 1898.

15. *U.S. Tobacco Journal*, April 30, 1898; *Evening Independent*, February 13, 1967.

16. Steffy, *The Cuban Immigrants of Tampa, Florida, 1886–1898*, 113, 124–25; *Tampa Tribune*, January 22, 1898, January 26, 1898, February 16, 1898, February 17, 1898, and March 8, 1898.

17. Donald H. Dyal, Brian B. Carpenter, and Mark A. Thomas, *Historical Dictionary of the Spanish American War* (Westport, Conn.: Greenwood, 1996), 259.

18. Dyal, Carpenter, and Thomas, *Historical Dictionary of the Spanish American War*, 259.

19. Steffy, *The Cuban Immigrants of Tampa, Florida, 1886–1898*, 112.

20. Charles Johnson Post, *The Little War of Private Post: The Spanish-American War Seen Up Close* (Boston: Little Brown, 1960), 37–45, 58–59.

21. *Tampa Tribune*, August 12, 1951.

22. *New York Times*, May 15, 1898.

23. Alduino, *The "Noble Experiment" in Tampa*, 42; *Tampa Tribune*, February 24, 95; Mormino, "Tampa's Splendid Little War," 37–42.

24. George Kennan, *Campaigning in Cuba* (New York: Kennikat, 1971), 3–4.

25. Kennan, *Campaigning in Cuba*, 3–4.

26. *Tampa Tribune*, July 10, 1898, and February 24, 1995; Steffy, *The Cuban Immigrants of Tampa, Florida, 1886–1898*, 120, 127; Mugge, *My Memoirs*, 8; See also William J. Schellings, *Tampa, Florida: Its Role in the Spanish American War, 1898* (master's thesis, University of Miami, 1954).

27. Grismer, *Tampa*, 208–9.

28. *New York Times*, May 22, 1898.

29. *Tampa Tribune*, May 12, 1898.

30. Geoffrey Mohlman, Susan Greenbaum, Karen Mayo, and Brent Richards Weisman, *Soldiers and Patriots: Buffalo Soldiers and Afro-Cubans in Tampa, 1898* (Tampa: University of South Florida, 1999), 55.

31. *Tampa Tribune*, March 16, 1952.

32. Mohlman, Greenbaum, Mayo, and Weisman, *Soldiers and Patriots*, 25, 55; Poulney Bigelow, "In Camp at Tampa," *Harper's Weekly* (June 4, 1898), 550; *Tampa Tribune*, March 16, 1952.

33. Mohlman, Greenbaum, Mayo, and Weisman, *Soldiers and Patriots*, 25; Bigelow, "In Camp at Tampa," 550.

34. *Tampa Tribune*, March 16, 1952.

35. *Tampa Tribune*, April 16, 1947.

36. Anna Northend Benjamin, "Christian Work in Our Camps," *Outlook* 59 (July 2, 1898): 566–69; Alduino, *The "Noble Experiment" in Tampa*, 44–45.

37. Steffy, *The Cuban Immigrants of Tampa, Florida, 1886–1898*, 113; *Tampa Tribune*, February 24, 1995; Mormino, "Tampa's Splendid Little War," 39–40.

38. Post, *The Little War of Private Post*, 71–72.

39. Post, *The Little War of Private Post*, 72.

40. *New York Times*, May 15, 1898.

41. Vincent J. Cirillo, *Bullets and Bacilli: The Spanish-American War and Military Medicine* (New Brunswick, N.J.: Rutgers University Press, 2003), 57.

42. United States, Walter Reed, Victor C. Vaughan, and Edward O. Shakespeare, *Report on the Origin and Spread of Typhoid Fever in U.S. Military Camps during the Spanish War of 1898* (Washington, D.C.: U.S. Government Printing Office, 1904), 484, 500 (hereafter cited as U.S. Typhoid report); Sun Tzu and Tom Butler-Bowdon, *The Art of War: The Ancient Classic* (Chichester, U.K.: John Wiley & Sons, 2002), 60; Cirillo, *Bullets and Bacilli*, 69; *Tampa Tribune*, May 18, 1998.

43. Cirillo, *Bullets and Bacilli*, 76; U.S. Typhoid report, 486, 491, 496.

44. U.S. Typhoid report, 501; Cirillo, *Bullets and Bacilli*, 72, 91; Dyal, *Historical Dictionary of the Spanish American War*, 284.

45. U.S. Typhoid report, 485.

46. Edward F. Keuchel, "Chemicals and Meat: The Embalmed Beef Scandal of the Spanish-American War," *Bulletin of the History of Medicine* 48, no. 2 (Summer 1974), 253–55.

47. Keuchel, "Chemicals and Meat," 253–55; *Atchison Daily Champion* (Kansas), January 24, 1899.

48. Post, *The Little War of Private Post*, 56–57.

49. Cirillo, *Bullets and Bacilli*, 243; Keuchel, "Chemicals and Meat," 249, 257, 261.

50. Keuchel, "Chemicals and Meat," 250.

51. Cirillo, *Bullets and Bacilli*, 108.

52. *Tampa Tribune*, April 16, 1947.

53. Since the Rough Riders was the best-known unit in town owing to Roosevelt's penchant for publicity, many soldiers falsely claimed to be in its ranks. Alduino, *The "Noble Experiment" in Tampa*, 44–45.

54. *Tampa Tribune*, October 11, 1949.

55. *Tampa Tribune*, October 11, 1949.

56. Mohlman, Greenbaum, Mayo, and Weisman, *Soldiers and Patriots*, 45, 47, 54.

57. Willard B. Gatewood Jr., "Negro Troops in Florida, 1898," *Florida Historical Quarterly* 49, no. 1 (July 1970): 1–15.

58. *New York Times*, May 14, 1898.

59. *Tampa Tribune*, May 12, 1898.

60. *Tampa Tribune*, June 19, 1898, and May 12, 1898.

61. *Cleveland Gazette*, July 2, 1898; *Tampa Tribune*, June 8, 1898.

62. *Tampa Tribune*, October 11, 1949.

63. *Tampa Tribune*, June 8, 1898.

64. Gatewood, "Negro Troops in Florida, 1898," 9; Alduino, *The "Noble Experiment" in Tampa*, 45–47; The Second Georgia Regiment was called in to restore order after riots, particularly among the unruly black soldiers; *Tampa Tribune*, June 8, 1898; *Augusta Chronicle*, June 11, 1898; *Atlanta Constitution*, June 11, 1898; *The (Cleveland) Gazette*, June 25, 1898, and June 27, 1898.

65. *Tampa Daily Times*, June 7, 1918.

66. James W. Covington, "The Rough Riders in Tampa," *Sunland Tribune* 3, no. 1 (1977): 8.

67. Post, *The Little War of Private Post*, 87.

68. Tampa Bay Hotel Menu, July 4, 1898, Henry B. Plant Museum, Tampa, Fla.

69. "History of Hillsborough County: Tampa's Part in the Spanish American War," Works Progress Administration Records, USF Tampa Library Special Collections.

70. Alduino, *The "Noble Experiment" in Tampa*, 81.

Chapter 3. Theater of Shadows: Vice, Corruption, and Indecency

1. *Tampa Tribune*, May 19, 1897, December 29, 1898, and July 2, 1901.

2. City Council Minutes, August 17, 1900, February 26, 1901, June 27, 1903, August 17, 1900, October 26, 1900, and February 25, 1901; *Tampa Tribune*, July 13, 1901, and November 23, 1901

3. For a concise discussion of bolita and organized crime, see Mormino and Pozzetta, *The Immigrant World of Ybor City*, 280–86.

4. Ann L. Henderson and Gary Ross Mormino, *Spanish Pathways in Florida, 1492–1992* (Sarasota, Fla.: Pineapple, 1991), 19; *Tampa Tribune*, September 16, 1903.

5. Mormino and Pozzetta, *The Immigrant World of Ybor City*, 282.

6. Mark H. Haller, "Policy Gambling, Entertainment, and the Emergence of Black Politics: Chicago from 1900 to 1940," *Journal of Social History* 24, no. 4 (Summer 1991): 719–20; *Tampa Tribune*, February 21, 1896, and January 24, 1895. See also this author's book for an inside view of the money laundering operation, Crichton McKay, Alice McKay, and Andrew T. Huse, *Crichton and Alice McKay* (Tampa: University of South Florida Tampa Library, 2000).

7. *Tampa Tribune*, February 4, 1902.

8. Haller, "Policy Gambling, Entertainment, and the Emergence of Black Politics," 720, 722, 724, 728, 733–34.

9. Haller, "Policy Gambling, Entertainment, and the Emergence of Black Politics," 734.

10. *Tampa Tribune*, December 11, 1903, December 20, 1903, October 9, 1904, February 14, 1905, and March 7, 1905.

11. *Tampa Tribune*, June 17, 1904.

12. *Tampa Tribune*, April 25, 1905, and May 2, 1905.

13. *Tampa Daily Times*, February 20, 1973; *Tampa Tribune*, April 30, 1904.

14. *Tampa Tribune*, January 16, 1906, February 19, 1908, and June 28, 1909.

15. *Tampa Tribune*, June 29, 1909.

16. *Tampa Tribune*, September 9, 1908.

17. T*ampa Tribune*, August 8, 1912, and February 13, 1911.

18. Polk County voted itself dry in 1896, and blind tigers soon sprung up around all the phosphate mines and worksites. There is no shortage of articles covering the tragedies arising from such lawless places; see, for example, *Tampa Tribune*, May 20, 1903.

19. *Tampa Tribune*, October 22, 1905.

20. *Tampa Tribune*, October 22, 1905.

21. *Tampa Tribune*, August 23, 1905, August 25, 1905, October 10, 1905, October 19, 1905, October 20, 1905, and October 21, 1905.

22. *Tampa Tribune*, October 25, 1905.

23. *Tampa Tribune*, October 25, 1905, August 14, 1907, August 16, 1907, May 20, 1908, and January 5, 1909.

24. *Tampa Tribune*, July 8, 1896, January 18, 1903, and January 31, 1903.

25. *Tampa Tribune*, December 1, 1900, December 2, 1900, March 30, 1901, and March 31, 1901.

26. *Tampa Tribune*, December 1, 1900, December 2, 1900, March 30, 1901, and March 31, 1901.

27. *Tampa Tribune*, August 25, 1903, and September 4, 1903.

28. *Tampa Tribune*, August 25, 1903, and September 4, 1903.

29. *Tampa Tribune*, September 20, 1903, November 26, 1903, and April 6, 1905.

30. *Tampa Tribune*, September 2, 1906, September 6, 1906, and October 12, 1906.

31. *Tampa Tribune*, January 18, 1908, and January 23, 1909.

32. *Tampa Tribune*, February 7, 1904, March 9, 1905, December 13, 1903, May 12, 1905, November 24, 1903, August 10, 1907, and October 12, 1905.

33. *Tampa Tribune*, March 30, 1912, and April 2, 1916.

34. *Tampa Tribune*, August 21, 1914, and August 22, 1914.

35. *Tampa Tribune*, April 21, 1955; *Tampa Times*, June 6, 1916; Alduino, *The "Noble Experiment" in Tampa*, 119; A study of civic corruption in Pennsylvania during the 1960s revealed many commonalities between Wincanton, Pa., in the 1960s and Tampa in the early twentieth century: a politically weak system incapable of reform, an elite obsessed with controlling money in the community, minimal caretaker policies by the local government, a numbers racket at the core of the corruption, control of the police by criminals, fake arrests, and widespread bribery. John A. Gardiner, *The Politics of Corruption: Organized Crime in an American City* (New York: Russel Sage Foundation, 1970), 18–25.

36. *Tampa Tribune*, January 14, 1902.

37. *Tampa Tribune*, April 13, 1902, and February 8, 1999.

38. *Variety* 25, no. 13 (March 1, 1912): 15. Douglas Gilbert, *American Vaudeville: Its Life and Times* (New York: Dover, 1963), 35–37.

39. *Tampa Tribune*, April 20, 1902, and October 27, 1901.

40. *Tampa Tribune*, July 4, 1902.

41. *Tampa Tribune*, June 2, 1901, June 21, 1901, June 23, 1901, and June 21, 1902.

42. *Tampa Tribune*, January 8, 1903.

43. *Tampa Tribune*, March 29, 1900.

44. *Tampa Tribune*, March 20, 1903.

45. *Tampa Tribune*, April 5, 1903, April 11, 1903, July 3, 1903, and August 5, 1905.

46. *Tampa Tribune*, May 28, 1907, September 17, 1908, and June 20, 1909.

47. *Tampa Tribune*, September 21, 1911.

48. *Tampa Tribune*, December 28, 1909.

49. *Tampa Tribune*, January 19, 1910.

50. City Council Minutes, April 19, 1910, and April 20, 1910.

51. *Tampa Tribune*, January 26, 1910.

52. *Tampa Tribune*, June 16, 1909, June 17, 1909, June 23, 1909, January 10, 1910, January 11, 1910, June 22, 1909, and January 30, 1910.

53. *Tampa Tribune*, September 21, 1911.

54. *Tampa Tribune*, March 22, 1912.

55. *Variety* 25, no. 13 (March 1, 1912): 15. This article is used throughout.

56. *Tampa Tribune*, February 21, 1912.

57. Jessica R. Pliley, *Policing Sexuality: The Mann Act and the Making of the FBI* (Cambridge/London: Harvard University Press, 2014), 77–81.

58. *Tampa Tribune*, September 19, 1911.

59. City Council Minutes, September 17, 1911, September 19, 1911. Ordinance 566 passed unanimously, a rare feat in council.

60. City Council Minutes, September 17, 1911, September 19, 1911; Athanasaw and Sampson v. United States, 227 U.S. 326 (1913): 327–33.

61. *Tampa Tribune*, March 4, 1912.

62. *Tampa Tribune*, March 4, 1912; Athanasaw and Sampson v. United States, 227 U.S. 326 (1913): 327–33.

63. Athanasaw and Sampson v. United States, 227 U.S. 326, 327 (1913).

64. *Tampa Tribune*, June 27, 1912, March 6, 1913, and March 22, 1912.

65. *Tampa Tribune*, April 12, 1913.

66. *Tampa Tribune*, May 14, 1915, June 24, 1917, February 9, 1929, February 10, 1929, and January 15, 1931. *Tampa Times*, February 8, 1929, and January 14, 1931. See also L.J. Bailey, "US vs. L. Athanasaw, Violation of White Slavery Act," BOI microfilm records, case 2807, roll 136 (Oct 26, 1911): 4.

67. *Tampa Tribune*, September 27, 1915.

68. Alduino, *The "Noble Experiment" in Tampa*, 97–99; Deets Pickett, Clarence True Wilson, and Ernest Dailey Smith, *The cyclopedia of Temperance, Prohibition and Public Morals* (New York: Methodist Book Concern, 1922), 3.

69. *Tampa Daily Times*, October 1, 1915, and October 2, 1915.

70. Pam Iorio, "Political Excess Shaped by a Game of Chance: Tampa, Bolita, and the First Half of the Twentieth Century," *Sunland Tribune* 26 (2000): 27–36.

71. Hal Morgan and Andreas Brown, *Prairie Fires and Paper Moons: The American Photographic Postcard, 1900–1920* (Boston: D. R. Godine, 1981), 123; *Tampa Tribune*, February 11, 1916.

72. *Tampa Tribune*, February 11, 1916, and April 28, 1916.

73. *Tampa Tribune*, March 17, 1916.

74. *Tampa Tribune*, March 19, 1916, October 31, 1915, November 4, 1915, and April 15, 1916.

75. *Tampa Tribune*, April 14, 1916.

76. *Tampa Tribune*, April 6, 1916.

77. *Tampa Tribune*, April 13, 1916, and April 10, 1916.

78. *Tampa Tribune*, April 17, 1916.

79. *Tampa Tribune*, April 27, 1916.

80. *Tampa Tribune*, April 24, 1916; *The "Noble Experiment" in Tampa*, 22–23.

81. *Tampa Tribune*, April 24, 1916, and April 29, 1916.

Chapter 4. Collective Action: Soup Houses, Boycotts, and Cooperatives

1. For an excellent history of the labor culture in Cuba and Tampa, see Louis A. Pérez, Jr., "Cubans in Tampa: From Exiles to Immigrants, 1892–1901," *Florida Historical Quarterly* 57, no. 2 (1978): 129–40. Gerald E. Poyo, "The Impact of Cuban and Spanish Workers on Labor Organizing in Florida, 1870–1900," *Journal of American Ethnic History* 5, no. 2 (1986): 48.

2. Poyo, "The Impact of Cuban and Spanish Workers on Labor Organizing in Florida, 1870–1900," 48, 51–52, 54, 56, 57, 59.

3. Louis A. Pérez, Jr., "Reminiscences of a Lector: Cuban Cigar Workers in Tampa," *Florida Historical Quarterly* 53, no. 4 (April 1975): 443–49. See also George E. Pozzetta and Gary R. Mormino. "The Reader and the Worker: 'Los Lectores' and the Culture of Cigarmaking in Cuba and Florida," *International Labor and Working-Class History*, no. 54 (1998): 1–18. For a comprehensive history of the lector, see Araceli Tinajero, *El Lector: A History of the Cigar Factory Reader* (Austin: University of Texas Press, 2010), 9–44.

4. Robert P. Ingalls, *Urban Vigilantes in the New South: Tampa, 1882–1936* (Knoxville: University of Tennessee Press, 1988), 38–42.

5. This type of relationship between figures of authority over subjects was basically an extension of patriarchy (father-son) applied to the village or workplace. This type of relationship may have been sturdy in Spanish society but was not nearly as durable in the United States. For more on this subject, see Clark S. Knowlton, "Patron-Peon Pattern among the Spanish Americans of New Mexico," *Social Forces* 41, no. 1 (1962): 12–17.

6. Grismer, *Tampa*, 183.

7. Muñiz, Fernandez, and Beltran, *The Ybor City Story*, 19; Steffy, *The Cuban Immigrants of Tampa, Florida, 1886–1898*, 24; Joe Scaglione, "City in Turmoil: Tampa and the Strike of 1910," *Sunland Tribune* 18 (November 1992): 29–36.

8. *Tampa Tribune*, August 4, 1901.

9. *Tampa Daily Times*, August 24, 1893

10. *Tampa Daily Times*, August 24, 1893, August 26, 1893, and August 31, 1923.

11. The factory was located at Howard Avenue and present-day Oak Street, where the West Tampa Library now stands. *Tampa Tribune*, December 27, 1953.

12. Pérez, "Cubans in Tampa," 129–40.

13. Durward Long, "Labor Relations in the Tampa Cigar Industry, 1885–1911," *Labor History* 12, no. 4 (Fall 1971): 552.

14. *Tampa Tribune*, July 9, 1899; *U.S. Tobacco Journal*, August 12, 1899

15. See also Mormino, "Tampa and the New Urban South," 337–56.

16. *Tampa Tribune*, July 13, 1899, and July 20, 1899.

17. *Tampa Tribune*, July 13, 1899.

18. *Tampa Tribune*, July 13, 1899, and July 20, 1899; *U.S. Tobacco Journal*, August 9, 1899.

19. *Tampa Tribune*, August 12, 1899.

20. *U.S. Tobacco Journal*, September 5, 1899.

21. *La Gaceta*, November 9, 1984; Muñiz, Fernandez, and Beltran, *The Ybor City Story*, 22–23; see also Durward Long, "La Resistencia: Tampa's Immigrant Labor Union," *Labor History* 6, no. 3 (1965).

22. Steffy, *The Cuban Immigrants of Tampa, Florida, 1886–1898*, 26–27; Long, "La Resistencia," 193–96; *U.S. Tobacco Journal*, May 25, 1901.

23. *La Gaceta*, November 9, 1984; Muñiz, Fernandez, and Beltran, *The Ybor City Story*, 22–23; *U.S. Tobacco Journal*, August 31, 1901.

24. Long, "La Resistencia," 203.

25. *New York Times*, April 9, 1901; *U.S. Tobacco Journal*, July 29, 1901.

26. *La Gaceta*, August 31, 1984.

27. *Tampa Tribune*, July 27, 1901.

28. *Tampa Tribune*, August 1, 1901.

29. *Tampa Tribune*, August 3, 1901.

30. *Tampa Tribune*, August 3, 1901, and November 2, 1901; Long, "La Resistencia," 207.

31. *Tampa Tribune*, August 6, 1901.

32. *Tampa Tribune*, August 10, 1901.

33. *New York Times*, August 7, 1901.

34. Long, "La Resistencia," 207.

35. *Tampa Tribune*, August 10, 1901, August 20, 1901, August 21, 1901, and August 30, 1901; *New York Times*, August 7, 1901.

36. *Tampa Tribune*, August 13, 1901, and August 15, 1901.

37. *Tampa Tribune*, August 16, 1901; *U.S. Tobacco Journal*, August 17, 1901.

38. *Tampa Tribune*, August 21, 1901.

39. *U.S. Tobacco Journal*, September 14, 1901.

40. *Tampa Tribune*, August 31, 1901, and August 21, 1901.

41. *U.S. Tobacco Journal*, September 16, 1901, September 21, 1901, and August 24, 1901.

42. *Tampa Tribune*, August 29, 1901.

43. George Pozzetta, "Immigrants and Radicals in Tampa, Florida," *Florida Historical Quarterly* 57, no. 3 (January 1979): 348; *L'Alba Sociale*, August 15, 1901

44. *Tampa Tribune*, September 19, 1901

45. *New York Times*, September 21, 1901; Ingalls, *Urban Vigilantes in the New South*, 79, 81; See also *Tobacco Leaf*, September 25, 1901; *Tampa Tribune*, September 19, 01; Long, "La Resistencia," 210.

46. *Tampa Tribune*, September 24, 1901.

47. Ingalls, *Urban Vigilantes in the New South*, 81; *U.S. Tobacco Journal*, October 21, 1901; Long, "La Resistencia," 210.

48. Long, "La Resistencia," 213.

49. *Tampa Tribune*, August 9, 1908; Long, "Labor Relations in the Tampa Cigar Industry, 1885–1911," 553.

50. Long, "Labor Relations in the Tampa Cigar Industry, 1885–1911," 554.

51. Long, "Labor Relations in the Tampa Cigar Industry, 1885–1911," 553.

52. *Tampa Tribune,* June 16, 1904.

53. Scaglione, "City in Turmoil," 5.

54. Long, "Labor Relations in the Tampa Cigar Industry, 1885–1911," 553; Scaglione, "City in Turmoil," 5.

55. The *Tobacco Journal* told his story in a sympathetic light. *U.S. Tobacco Journal,* September 3, 1910.

56. Gene Burnett, "Death and Terror Scar Tampa's Past," *Florida Trend* (December 1975): 78; Scaglione, "City in Turmoil," 6.

57. *Tobacco World,* September 19, 1910; Scaglione, "City in Turmoil," 7.

58. Burnett, "Death and Terror Scar Tampa's Past," 77.

59. Burnett, "Death and Terror Scar Tampa's Past," 77.

60. Or possibly Castencio.

61. Today John F. Kennedy Blvd.

62. Scaglione, "City in Turmoil," 4, 7.

63. Burnett, "Death and Terror Scar Tampa's Past," 78.

64. Long, "Labor Relations in the Tampa Cigar Industry, 1885–1911," 554–55; Scaglione, "City in Turmoil," 3.

65. *Tampa Tribune,* October 11, 1910.

66. Stefano Luconi, "Tampa's 1910 Lynching: The Italian-American Perspective and Its Implications," *Florida Historical Quarterly* 88, no. 1 (Summer 2009): 38–39; Scaglione, "City in Turmoil," 1; *Tobacco Leaf,* October 20, 1910.

67. Burnett, "Death and Terror Scar Tampa's Past," 80.

68. Long, "Labor Relations in the Tampa Cigar Industry, 1885–1911," 555.

69. *Tampa Tribune,* August 8, 1908.

70. *Tampa Tribune,* February 15, 1919, and June 15, 1918.

71. *Tampa Tribune,* March 10, 1919, and March 12, 1919.

72. *La Gaceta,* May 5, 1989.

73. *Tampa Tribune,* December 24, 1916.

74. *U.S. Tobacco Journal,* March 23, 1918.

75. *Tampa Tribune,* March 6, 1917.

76. *Tampa Tribune,* March 6, 1917.

77. *Tampa Tribune,* February 15, 1919, and June 15, 1918.

78. *Tampa Tribune,* March 11, 1919.

79. *Tampa Tribune,* March 11, 1919.

80. *Tampa Tribune,* April 3, 1919.

81. *Tampa Tribune,* August 23, 1919, and September 30, 1919.

82. *Tampa Tribune,* October 27, 1919; *Tampa Daily Times,* April 29, 1918.

83. *Tampa Tribune,* October 28, 1919.

84. *Tampa Tribune,* November 4, 1919.

85. *Tampa Tribune,* November 5, 1919.

86. *Tampa Tribune,* November 8, 1919.

87. Grismer, *Tampa,* 247; *Tampa Tribune,* April 19, 1918; *El International,* July 2, 1920.

88. *La Gaceta*, November 18, 1984; *Tampa Tribune*, November 29, 1920; *Tampa Citizen*, November 12, 1920.

89. *El International*, July 2, 1920.

90. Valdez, *Life Histories*, 3.

91. *Tampa Citizen*, November 25, 1921.

92. *Tampa Tribune*, November 30, 1920.

93. *Tampa Daily Times*, December 12, 1920.

94. The CMIU paid out $1 million in 1920. Durward Long, "The Open-Closed Shop Battle in Tampa's Cigar Industry, 1919–1921," *Florida Historical Quarterly* 47, no. 2 (1968): 120; *Tampa Citizen*, February 4, 1921; *Tampa Daily Times*, February 5, 1921.

95. *Tobacco Leaf*, December 18, 1920.

96. *Tampa Tribune*, July 10, 1929.

97. *Tampa Tribune*, June 16, 2004.

Chapter 5. War, Fear, and Bread during World War I

1. *Tampa Tribune*, February 6, 1917.

2. *Tampa Tribune*, January 30, 1917.

3. The *Tribune* was echoing similar remarks given by former President Teddy Roosevelt condemning "hyphenated Americans" as would-be enemies. *Tampa Tribune*, March 3, 1917, February 5, 1918, August 23, 1917, and April 1, 1917.

4. A good example of ineffectual wartime vigilance can be found in the American Protective League, an organization of civilian volunteers who never found a single spy.

5. *Tampa Tribune*, February 28, 1907.

6. *Tampa Tribune*, January 23, 1918.

7. U.S. Bureau of the Census, *Historical Statistics of the United States, Colonial Times to 1970, Bicentennial Edition, Part 2.*, Bureau of Labor Statistics, 2011. For an excellent discussion of the state of bread and bakeries in the United States at the time, see Aaron Bobrow-Strain, *White Bread: A Social History of the Store-Bought Loaf* (Boston: Beacon, 2012), 20–37.

8. David I. McLeod, "Food Prices, Politics, and Policy in the Progressive Era," *Journal of the Gilded Age and Progressive Era* 8, no. 3 (July 2009): 365–67.

9. Mrs. Julian Heath, "Work of the Housewives League," *Annals of the American Academy of Political and Social Science* 48 (July 1913): 124; McLeod, "Food Prices, Politics, and Policy in the Progressive Era," 365–66.

10. *Tampa Tribune*, December 16, 1916.

11. In public, Sauls went by J. L. Sauls, using the initials of her husband, James. *Tampa Tribune*, December 16, 1916.

12. State and county food boards helped represent the interests of the U.S. Food Administration under Herbert Hoover; *Tampa Tribune*, December 16, 1916, and September 13, 1918.

13. *Tampa Tribune*, December 15, 1916.

14. *Tampa Tribune*, May 4, 1917.

15. *Tampa Tribune,* January 21, 1917.

16. *Tampa Tribune,* May 15, 1917, February 23, 1917, and January 17, 1917.

17. *Tampa Tribune,* April 11, 1917, and April 14, 1917.

18. The *Plant City Courier* was quoted in *Tampa Tribune,* May 27, 1917. *The Nation* 107, no. 2766 (July 6, 1918): 3.

19. *Tampa Tribune,* May 24, 1917, and May 27, 1917.

20. *Tampa Tribune,* June 9, 1917.

21. Officer McCants would soon have more legal basis for his broad interpretation of sedition. The Espionage Act of 1917, passed on June 15, just days after the musical incident at the German Club, was meant to safeguard mobilization and the U.S. military. The Sedition Act of 1918 amended the Espionage Act by aiming at anti-American speech. For many, German music with or without vocals gave comfort to the enemy and detracted from the war effort. *Tampa Tribune,* June 9, 1917. See also Stephen M. Kohn, *American Political Prisoners: Prosecutions under the Espionage and Sedition Acts* (Westport, Conn.: Praeger, 1994).

22. *Tampa Tribune,* June 9, 1917.

23. *Tampa Tribune,* June 10, 1917.

24. *Tampa Tribune,* June 12, 1917.

25. *Tampa Tribune,* November 20, 1917.

26. *Tampa Tribune,* November 20, 1917.

27. *Tampa Tribune,* February 15, 1917.

28. Donald Brenham McKay, *Pioneer Florida* (Tampa, Fla.: Southern, 1959), 380–81.

29. *Tampa Tribune,* April 16, 1917.

30. *Tampa Daily Times,* June 19, 1917. Initial reports about the liberty bond drive were drawn from this issue.

31. *Tampa Daily Times,* June 19, 1917.

32. Despite its voluntary nature, the purchase of Liberty Bonds was often seen as a gauge of one's patriotism. Those who refused to purchase bonds often met public violence and intimidation.

33. *Tampa Daily Times,* June 19, 1917.

34. *Tampa Daily Times,* June 15, 1917.

35. *Tampa Daily Times,* June 19, 1917, and June 20, 1917

36. Formed in 1916, the U.S. Shipping Board was responsible for the development of a Merchant Marine and naval reserve. When the United States entered the war, the board supervised the Emergency Fleet Corporation, a government-owned company that executed the will of the USSB. The EFC immediately commandeered every contract for the construction of ships weighing more than 2,500 tons. For more on the USSB, see Edward Nash Hurley, *The Bridge to France* (Philadelphia: Lippincott, 1927). *Tampa Daily Times,* July 16, 1917, and June 30, 1917; *Tampa Tribune,* September 11, 1917.

37. *Tampa Tribune,* January 17, 1918, and January 18, 1918. The initial accounts of the drownings are drawn from these issues.

38. Because of the chronic labor shortage, local African American workers were often able to obtain better jobs than in peacetime.

39. When a foreign-born resident attains citizenship, he or she is known as a naturalized citizen. Foreign residents who do not become citizens are known as un-naturalized citizens. *Tampa Tribune*, February 14, 1918.

40. *Tampa Tribune*, February 14, 1918.

41. *Tampa Tribune*, February 26, 1918.

42. *Tampa Tribune*, February 26, 1918. The account of the courthouse meeting was taken from this issue. For insight into Tampa's citizen committees and vigilantes, see Robert P. Ingalls, *Urban Vigilantes in the New South: Tampa, 1882–1936* (Knoxville: University of Tennessee Press, 1988).

43. *Tampa Tribune*, February 26, 1918.

44. *Tampa Tribune*, February 26, 1918.

45. *Tampa Tribune*, February 26, 1918.

46. *Tampa Tribune*, February 27, 1918.

47. For a concise example of this scholarship of the home front, see "Policing the Home Front: From Vigilance to Vigilantism," in *Uncle Sam Wants You: World War I and the Making of the Modern American Citizen*, ed. Christopher Capozzola and Joseph Nicodemus (Oxford: Oxford University Press, 2008). *Tampa Tribune*, February 27, 1918.

48. *Tampa Tribune*, February 21, 1918.

49. In this case, "mother's bread" refers to typical white bread.

50. *Tampa Tribune*, February 21, 1918.

51. *Tampa Tribune*, August 31, 1917, and January 23, 1918.

52. *Tampa Tribune*, January 23, 1918.

53. *Tampa Tribune*, April 11, 1918.

54. In Tampa, deviled or devil crabs referred to a popular street food: fried blue crab croquettes seasoned with a light tomato base and spices, coated with Cuban bread crumbs, and fried.

55. *Tampa Tribune*, April 8, 1918, and April 9, 1918.

56. "Our First Year in the War," *Literary Digest*, April 6, 1918, 25.

57. "Our First Year in the War," *Literary Digest*, April 6, 1918, 25. Harold Dwight Lasswell, *Psychopathology and Politics* (New York: Viking, 1960), 120. *Tampa Tribune*, April 8, 1918.

58. *New York Times*, April 8, 1918, 10.

59. *Tampa Tribune*, April 10, 1918.

60. *Tampa Tribune*, April 9, 1918, and April 10, 1918.

61. *Tampa Tribune*, April 9, 1918.

62. *Tampa Tribune*, April 11, 1918.

63. *Tampa Tribune*, February 15, 1903, February 18, 1908, September 22, 1916, and November 19, 1896.

64. *Tampa Tribune*, April 9, 1918, and April 10, 1918.

65. *Tampa Tribune*, April 21, 1918, May 10, 1918, February 2, 1919, April 13, 1918, April 11, 1918, April 14, 1918, and May 7, 1918.

66. Florida Quarterly Bulletin of the Department of Agriculture 28, 108–10. August Schinderhans, *The Truth in the World War: An Expose for Better Americanism* (Dallas: 1921), 18.

67. George Nox McCain, *War Rations for Pennsylvanians; the Story of the Operations of the Federal Food Administration in Pennsylvania, including Personal and Biographical Sketches of its Officers and Members, with Dramatic, Humorous and Unusual Episodes in the Experience of County Administrators during the World War* (Philadelphia: John C. Winston, 1920), 238. William Manchester, *Controversy and Other Essays in Journalism, 1950–1975* (Boston: Little, Brown, 1976), 238.

68. "Annual Report of the Commissioners of the District of Columbia Year Ended June 30, 1919." Report of the Health Officer. District of Columbia Health Dept. 3, 1919, 24.

69. Quarterly bulletin (New York: New York Department of Health, 1918), 221.

70. *Tampa Tribune*, April 16, 1918.

71. U.S. Department of Justice, *Annual Report of the Attorney General of the United States* (Washington, D.C., 1918), 23. Army War College Library, *Monthly List of Military Information Carded from Books*, issues 28–45. List for April 21–May 20, 1918, 12.

72. *Tampa Tribune*, September 13, 1918, October 31, 1918, and June 6, 1918.

73. *Tampa Tribune*, July 5, 1918.

74. *Tampa Tribune*, July 5, 1918.

75. *Tampa Tribune*, August 6, 1917.

76. *Tampa Tribune*, August 1, 1918, and March 29, 1918. Erik Kirschbaum and Herbert W. Stupp, *Burning Beethoven: The Eradication of German Culture in the United States during World War I* (New York: Berlinica, 2015), 37.

77. Leland Hawes, "Club Felt the Wrath of Wartime," *Tampa Tribune*, December 13, 1998.

78. *Tampa Tribune*, September 23, 1918.

79. *Tampa Tribune*, December 13, 1998.

80. *Tampa Tribune*, October 9, 1918.

81. *Tampa Tribune*, October 14, 1918.

82. *Tampa Tribune*, November 2, 1918.

83. *Tampa Tribune*, December 15, 1918.

84. *Tampa Daily Times*, December 12, 1918.

85. *Tampa Tribune*, December 18, 1918.

86. *Tampa Tribune*, October 20, 1990.

Chapter 6. The Noble Disaster: Prohibition and Speakeasies

1. Catts would have undoubtedly opposed the Sturkie Resolution, passed by the Florida Democratic Party, that condemned religious prejudice and secret societies such as the Ku Klux Klan. Alduino, *The "Noble Experiment" in Tampa*, 101–2; David Chalmers, "The KKK in the Sunshine State: The 1920's," *Florida Historical Quarterly* 42, no. 3 (1964): 211.

2. Herbert Asbury, *The Great Illusion: An Informal History of Prohibition* (New York: Greenwood, 1968), 145.

3. *Tampa Tribune*, April 6, 1919.

4. *Tampa Daily Times*, January 1, 1919.

5. Valdez, *Life Histories* (B. M. Balbontin), 2.

6. Edward Behr, *Prohibition: Thirteen Years That Changed America* (New York: Arcade, 1996), 13.

7. Behr, *Prohibition*, 116.

8. *All-Florida Magazine*, November 7, 1965.

9. Theyre Hamilton Weigall, *Boom in Paradise* (New York: A. H. King, 1932), 176–77.

10. Alduino, *The "Noble Experiment" in Tampa*, 63–64.

11. George Chauncey, *Gay New York: Gender, Urban Culture, and the Makings of the Gay/Male World, 1890–1940* (New York: Basic, 1994): 306–8.

12. *Tampa Daily Times*, January 1, 1919; Leo Stalnaker Scrapbook, Stalnaker Papers, University of South Florida Tampa Special Collections, 5.

13. *Tampa Bay Life*, June 1992, 23; Alduino, *The "Noble Experiment" in Tampa*, 115.

14. Alduino, *The "Noble Experiment" in Tampa*, 115–16; *Tampa Tribune*, November 25, 1990.

15. *Tampa Tribune*, August 7, 1919.

16. Alduino, *The "Noble Experiment" in Tampa*, 136; *Tampa Tribune*, February 12, 1921.

17. All statistics from Polk's City Directories, 1919–1937.

18. *Tampa Daily Times*, January 1, 1919.

19. *Tampa Tribune*, May 7, 1978.

20. Pamela Gibson, "Sin City, Moonshine, Whiskey and Divorce," *Sunland Tribune* 21 (November 1995). The region had long been known for especially strong spirits. A scholar has noted that years before Prohibition, "Recurrent testimony strongly suggests that the strength of the whiskey circulating in Southwest Florida not only served to make the partakers drunk, it began addiction from the first drink." Abuse of such moonshine lead to damage of the body and brain.

21. See Richard Cofer, "Bootleggers in the Backwoods: Prohibition and the Depression in Hernando County," *Tampa Bay History* (Spring/Summer 1979); Alduino, *The "Noble Experiment" in Tampa*, 121.

22. *Tampa Daily Times*, February 11, 1974.

23. Daniel Okrent, *Last Call: The Rise and Fall of Prohibition* (New York: Scribner, 2010), 166; Alduino, *The "Noble Experiment" in Tampa*, 125; *Tampa Tribune*, November 25, 1990.

24. *All-Florida Magazine*, November 7, 1965.

25. Alduino, *The "Noble Experiment" in Tampa*, 124; Kobler, *Ardent Spirits*, 256–58.

26. *Tampa Life*, June 15, 1929.

27. *Tampa Tribune*, November 12, 1930.

28. Alduino, *The "Noble Experiment" in Tampa*, 147; Stalnaker Scrapbook, 23–24.

29. The history of Tampa's gangsters has since become a cottage industry of sorts and need not be covered here. Alduino, *The "Noble Experiment" in Tampa*, 146–47, 150, 151–54.

30. *Tampa Tribune*, December 8, 1932.

31. *Tampa Tribune*, November 11, 1920, February 10, 1921, February 6, 1921, and March 1, 1921.

32. *Tampa Tribune*, June 25, 1921.

33. Alduino, *The "Noble Experiment" in Tampa*, 128–29.

34. *Tampa Tribune*, October 13, 1923.

35. *Tampa Tribune*, December 5, 1921

36. *Tampa Tribune*, March 26, 1922, March 28, 1922, and January 16, 1924; *Tampa Daily Times*, December 11, 1923, and April 6, 1922.

37. *Tampa Tribune*, April 17, 1922, April 18, 1922, and June 22, 1922.

38. *Tampa Tribune*, January 12, 1923.

39. *Tampa Tribune*, March 13, 1923.

40. *Tampa Tribune*, October 13, 1923.

41. *Tampa Tribune*, October 18, 1923

42. *Tampa Tribune*, October 24, 1923

43. *Tampa Times*, October 29, 1923.

44. Chalmers, "The KKK in the Sunshine State," 210–211.

45. *Tampa Tribune*, March 7, 1924; Alduino, *The "Noble Experiment" in Tampa*, 173–75.

46. *Tampa Times*, November 1, 1923.

47. *Tampa Tribune*, November 8, 1923, and November 6, 1923.

48. *Tampa Tribune*, November 3, 1923, and November 4, 1923; Alduino, *The "Noble Experiment" in Tampa*, 180, 186–87; *Tampa Times*, January 23, 1924.

49. *Tampa Tribune*, December 12, 1923.

50. *Tampa Tribune*, January 16, 1924, April 9, 1923, and January 22, 1924.

51. Alduino, *The "Noble Experiment" in Tampa*, 35, 125.

52. *Tampa Tribune*, April 18, 1924, and May 15, 1924.

53. *Tampa Tribune*, January 22, 1924, July 16, 1924, August 5, 1924, April 24, 1924, July 16, 1924, and August 5, 1924; *Tampa Times*, April 23, 1924.

54. *Tampa Tribune*, August 15, 1924.

55. *Tampa Tribune*, August 31, 1924, August 15, 1924, and October 26, 1924.

56. *Tampa Tribune*, November 25, 1990; For more on the election of 1923, see Robert J. Kerstein, *Politics and Growth in Twentieth-Century Tampa* (Gainesville: University Press of Florida, 2001), 66.

57. *Tampa Tribune*, December 15, 1926; Alduino, *The "Noble Experiment" in Tampa*, 129; Kyle S. VanLandingham, *In Pursuit of Justice: Law & Lawyers in Hillsborough County, 1846–1996* ([Tampa, Fla.]: Hillsborough County Bar Association, 1996), 48. Stalnaker listed his four legislative priorities as follows: first, to ban the teaching of evolution; second, to close all dance halls on Sundays; third, to require all motorists to stop before crossing railroad tracks; and fourth, to require the flying of the American flag on all schools (public and private) while classes were in session. His appointment was among the last made by Tampa's council-style government. Permissive Mayor John Perry Wall did not approve. An admiring clerk at the sheriff's office compiled a scrapbook documenting Stalnaker's tumultuous tenure on the

bench. "Prepared for Judge Leo Stalnaker, Municipal Judge, 1927," the inscription reads, "in recognition of his great services to Tampa. By Jessie Wauchofe, Clerk, County Sheriff's Office."), hereafter referred to as Stalnaker Scrapbook, p. 36. For a full biography, see Morison Buck, "Leo Stalnaker (1897–1986)" (Digital Collection, Florida Studies Center Publications, 2000), Paper 2500.

58. Stalnaker Scrapbook, 4.

59. *Tampa Tribune*, June 16, 1927.

60. *Tampa Tribune*, June 16, 1927; Stalnaker Scrapbook, title page, 1, 2.

61. Stalnaker Scrapbook, 5.

62. Stalnaker Scrapbook, 14.

63. Stalnaker Scrapbook, 45.

64. Stalnaker Scrapbook, 2; *Tampa Tribune*, June 24, 1927.

65. Stalnaker Scrapbook, title page, 7.

66. Stalnaker Scrapbook, 7.

67. Stalnaker Scrapbook, 4, 7, 19.

68. Stalnaker Scrapbook, 5

69. Stalnaker Scrapbook, 4, 12.

70. Stalnaker Scrapbook, 2.

71. Stalnaker Scrapbook, 24.

72. Stalnaker Scrapbook, 2.

73. Stalnaker Scrapbook, 6, 7.

74. See the Buck biography of Stalnaker.

75. *Tampa Tribune*, June 8, 1917.

76. *Tampa Tribune*, June 8, 1917, November 15, 1905, September 2, 1902, May 26, 1904, and July 30, 1901.

77. Stalnaker Scrapbook, 17.

78. *St. Petersburg Times*, August 26, 1927; Stalnaker Scrapbook, 17.

79. *Tampa Tribune*, August 30, 1927, and November 25, 1990; *Evening Independent*, July 30, 1927; Stalnaker Scrapbook, 20.

80. *Tampa Tribune*, August 30, 1927; *St. Petersburg Times*, August 26, 1927.

81. Stalnaker Scrapbook, 15, 23; *Evening Independent*, August 3, 1927.

82. *Tampa Tribune*, August 30, 1927; Stalnaker Scrapbook, 31.

83. *Lincoln Star* (Nebraska), August 28, 1927.

84. *Tampa Tribune*, August 5, 1927.

85. Stalnaker Scrapbook, 24, 25, 33.

86. Stalnaker Scrapbook, 16.

87. Stalnaker Scrapbook, 18.

88. Stalnaker Scrapbook, 36, 39.

89. Stalnaker Scrapbook, 12, 44.

90. Stalnaker Scrapbook, 11, 42.

91. Stalnaker Scrapbook, 24, 31, 33, 45.

92. Stalnaker Scrapbook, 40.

93. Stalnaker Scrapbook, 45.

94. Stalnaker Scrapbook, 44, 50.

95. *The Municipal Judge*, rear of Stalnaker Scrapbook.

96. Stalnaker Scrapbook, 47; *Tampa Tribune*, October 5, 1927.

97. VanLandingham, *In Pursuit of Justice*, 48.

98. *Tampa Life*, June 27, 1929.

99. *Tampa Life*, August 17, 1929, June 27, 1929, and July 13, 1929.

100. *The Spade* (Tampa), April 20, 29.

101. *Tampa Life*, June 22, 1929, August 31, 1929, and June 27, 1929.

102. *Tampa Life*, June 27, 1929, July 13, 1929, and June 15, 1929.

103. *Tampa Life*, June 8, 1929.

104. *The Spade*, April 20, 1929, 1.

105. *Tampa Life*, August 3, 1929, and June 8, 1929.

106. It seems the sermon referred to specific girls, perhaps a club or cheerleading squad.

107. *Tampa Tribune*, August 15, 1930; *Evening Independent*, December 3, 1930.

108. *Tampa Tribune*, May 17, 1930, July 31, 1931, November 25, 1990, and January 18, 1930. See Buck biography.

109. IN RE PETITION OF LEO STALNAKER FOR REINSTATEMENT AS ATTORNEY AT LAW. [NO DOCKET NUMBER] SUPREME COURT OF FLORIDA. 150 Fla. 853; 9 So. 2d 100; 1942 Fla. LEXIS 1095, June 30, 1942.

110. *Tampa Tribune*, November 12, 1930, and October 23, 1929.

111. Alduino, *The "Noble Experiment" in Tampa*, 19.

112. Alduino, *The "Noble Experiment" in Tampa*, 220–22; *Tampa Tribune*, May 7, 1933, and May 10, 1933; *Tampa Daily Times*, December 4, 1933.

Chapter 7. Jook Joints, World War II, and "Venereal Disease"

1. Stetson Kennedy, *Pedro and Estrella*, WPA Life Histories Project, Library of Congress, 1939.

2. *Tampa Tribune*, December 31, 1941.

3. *Miami Herald*, October 5, 1941, and November 30, 1941; Theodore Pratt, "The Land of Jooks," *Saturday Evening Post* (April 26, 1941): 20.

4. Pratt, "The Land of Jooks," 20–21, 40–43.

5. It would take another twenty years before the television documentary "Harvest of Shame" made the plight of migrant workers known to mainstream America. Pratt, "The Land of Jooks," 20–21.

6. Pratt, "The Land of Jooks," 21, 40, 41.

7. Pratt, "The Land of Jooks," 40, 20–21.

8. For a good source on the background of jook joints in Florida, see Madeleine Hirsiger Carr, *Denying Hegemony: The Function and Place of Florida's Jook Joints during the Twentieth Century's First Fifty Years* (Ph.D. dissertation, Florida State University, 2002); The Florida Supreme Court decided the proper spelling is "jook" in Arnold v. State, 1939. See also, H. L. Mencken, *The American Language: An Inquiry into the Development of English in the United States* (New York: Knopf, 1945), 710.

9. Madeleine Hirsiger Carr, *Jookin': Working Class and Culture in the Making of a Florida Jook Joint* (unpublished manuscript), 7.

10. Carr, *Jookin,'* 8; Carr, *Denying Hegemony,* 81; Pratt, "The Land of Jooks," 21.

11. Pratt, "The Land of Jooks," 43; Carr, *Jookin,'* 8; Stetson Kennedy, Herbert Halpert, and Zora Neale Hurston, *Let the Deal Go Down* (Jacksonville, Florida, 1939), audio. Retrieved from the Library of Congress, accessed December 12, 2017: https://www.loc.gov/item/flwpa000011/.

12. Zora Neale Hurston, *Their Eyes Were Watching God: A Novel* (New York: Perennial, 1990), 125.

13. Carr, *Denying Hegemony,* 23.

14. Carr, *Denying Hegemony,* 72–73.

15. Carr, *Denying Hegemony,* 113, 116.

16. James Marcus, "The First Hip White Person," *Atlantic Monthly* (February 2001): 119–23.

17. Carr, *Jookin,'* 11.

18. Carr, *Denying Hegemony,* 75.

19. *Miami Herald,* October 5, 1941.

20. See Works Progress Administration Records, Box 15, "Medical History," USF Special Collections.

21. For an overview of Tampa's industrial contributions to the war effort, see Gary R. Mormino, *Hillsborough County Goes to War: The Home Front, 1940–1950* (Tampa, Fla.: Tampa Bay History Center, 2001).

22. See Marilyn E. Hegarty, *Victory Girls, Khaki-wackies, and Patriotutes: The Regulation of Female Sexuality during World War II* (New York: New York University Press, 2008).

23. Interview with Mary Henry at her home in Tampa, March 30, 2000.

24. United States, *Techniques of Law Enforcement against Prostitution* (Washington: U.S. Government Printing Office, 1943), 8; M. Hibben, "Venereal Disease in the Armed Forces," *Editorial research reports 1943,* vol. 1 (Washington, D.C.: Congressional Quarterly Press, 1943). Retrieved from http://library.cqpress.com/cqresearcher/cqresrre1943010900. Claire Strom, "Controlling Venereal Disease in Orlando during WWII," *Florida Historical Quarterly* 91, no. 1 (Summer 2012): 110.

25. John Boyd Coates and Ebbe Curtis Hoff, *Preventive Medicine in World War II* (Washington, D.C.: Office of the Surgeon General, Dept. of the Army, 1955), 158. Chapter 10, on venereal disease, from volume 5 on communicable diseases, was particularly helpful. All citations of this source come from that chapter.

26. *Preventive Medicine in World War II,* 139–42.

27. *Preventive Medicine in World War II,* 142, 158, 161.

28. *Tampa Tribune,* August 26, 1942.

29. *Tampa Tribune,* August 26, 1942.

30. *Tampa Tribune,* July 29, 1942.

31. *Tampa Daily Times,* August 13, 1943; *Tampa Tribune,* July 24, 1942.

32. *Tampa Daily Times,* August 26, 1942; *Tampa Tribune,* July 24, 1942.

33. Strom, "Controlling Venereal Disease in Orlando during WWII," 95, 110; *Tampa Tribune,* January 6, 1943.

34. *Tampa Tribune,* September 6, 1942.

35. *Tampa Tribune*, May 2, 1943.

36. *Tampa Tribune*, September 6, 1942.

37. *St. Petersburg Times*, August 11, 1942.

38. *Tampa Tribune*, May 2, 1943.

39. *Tampa Tribune*, July 20, 1942.

40. *Techniques of Law Enforcement against Prostitution*, 55.

41. *Tampa Tribune*, May 27, 1942; *Tampa Daily Times*, October 26, 1942; *Tampa Tribune*, July 24, 1942.

42. *Tampa Tribune*, July 29, 1942.

43. Strom, "Controlling Venereal Disease in Orlando during WWII," 86.

44. *Tampa Tribune*, August 20, 1943.

45. *Tampa Tribune*, August 1, 1942.

46. *Tampa Tribune*, August 3, 1942.

47. *Tampa Tribune*, September 3, 1942.

48. *Tampa Tribune*, August 20, 1943; *Tampa Tribune*, June 30, 1942; *Tampa Daily Times*, August 5, 1942.

49. *Tampa Tribune*, July 29, 1942; *Tampa Daily Times*, January 16, 1944; Strom, "Controlling Venereal Disease in Orlando during WWII," 86, 102, 109.

50. *Tampa Daily Times*, October 26, 1942.

51. *Tampa Tribune*, September 12, 1942.

52. *Preventive Medicine in World War II*, 174.

53. *Tampa Tribune*, August 26, 1942.

54. *Preventive Medicine in World War II*, 165.

55. *Tampa Tribune*, May 2, 1943.

56. *Tampa Tribune*, August 20, 1943.

57. *Tampa Daily Times*, June 7, 1943.

58. *Tampa Tribune*, July 29, 1943; *Tampa Tribune*, June 7, 1943.

59. *Tampa Tribune*, August 13, 1943, and August 20, 1943.

60. *Tampa Daily Times*, June 10, 1943.

61. *Tampa Tribune*, June 7, 1943; *Tampa Daily Times*, September 1, 1943.

62. *Tampa Tribune*, June 5, 1943; *Tampa Daily Times*, June 10, 1943; *Tampa Tribune*, August 20, 1943; *Tampa Daily Times*, November 17, 1943.

63. *Tampa Tribune*, August 20, 1943.

64. *Tampa Daily Times*, November 25, 1943.

65. *Preventive Medicine in World War II*, 89–91; *Tampa Daily Times*, February 8, 1944.

66. *Miami Herald*, July 11, 1944.

67. *Tampa Daily Times*, September 1, 1943.

68. *Preventive Medicine in World War II*, 142–146.

69. *Tampa Tribune*, June 25, 1944.

70. *Tampa Tribune*, June 25, 1944.

71. *Tampa Tribune*, June 25, 1944.

72. *Preventive Medicine in World War II*, 175; *Tampa Tribune*, June 25, 1944.

73. *Tampa Daily Times*, February 10, 1944.

Chapter 8. A Steak House in the Sky: Bartke's and the 1950s

1. June and Barbara Bartke and Andrew T. Huse, *June Bartke and Barbara Bartke oral history interview* (Tampa: University of South Florida Tampa Library, 2008), http://digital.lib.usf.edu/?t30.17. All quotations of June and Barbara Bartke are derived from this recording. The other vital source for this narrative is the Bartke's Restaurant Scrapbook at the University of South Florida's Special Collections Department. Unless otherwise indicated at a paragraph's end, the narrative is based on the interview and the stories and ads preserved in the scrapbook. When possible, I have cited the clippings from the scrapbook, but in many cases no identifying information was preserved.

2. The Bartke family participated in Florida's new "land boom" of the postwar years, which is covered in Gary Mormino, *Land of Sunshine, State of Dreams: A Social History of Modern Florida* (Gainesville: University Press of Florida, 2008), 44–75, and postwar tourism in Florida, 76–112.

3. *St. Petersburg Times*, November 5, 1950. The profile of and quotes from Frank are derived from this colorful article.

4. St. Petersburg Times, November 5, 1950.

5. *Wall Street Journal*, July 22, 2010.

6. Financial information drawn from Hillsborough County Aviation Authority Central Records.

7. *St. Cloud News*, June 1, 1953.

8. *Gulf Beach Journal*, March 6, 1953; *St. Petersburg Independent*, July 1, 1953.

9. *Gulf Beach Journal*, August 14, 1953.

10. *St. Petersburg Independent*, February 25, 1953.

11. *St. Petersburg Independent*, May 13, 1953.

12. *Gulf Beach Journal*, November 7, 1952.

13. *St. Petersburg Independent*, January 21, 1953.

14. Hillsborough County Aviation Authority Central Records.

15. For a discussion of polio cases at that time, see David M. Oshinsky, *Polio: An American Story* (Oxford: Oxford University Press, 2005), 161–69.

16. *Clearwater Sun*, August 20, 1953.

17. Hillsborough County Aviation Authority Central Records.

18. For a history of airports at the time, see Alastair Gordon, *Naked Airport: A Cultural History of the World's Most Revolutionary Structure* (New York: H. Holt, 2004), 123–71.

Chapter 9. A Seat at the Nation's Table: Lunch Counter Integration

1. "Civil Rights Protests in Tampa: Oral Memoirs of Conflict and Accommodation," *Tampa Bay History* 1, no. 1, University of South Florida, Tampa (1979): 54.

2. *Chicago Defender*, August 10, 1959.

3. *The Florida Sentinel-Bulletin*, August 27, 1960.

4. Robert W. Saunders, *Bridging the Gap: Continuing the Florida NAACP Legacy of Harry T. Moore, 1952–1966* (Tampa, Fla.: University of Tampa Press, 2000).

5. "Civil Rights Protests in Tampa," 49, 51. Although the press referred to the

group as the Bi-Racial Committee, the group referred to itself as the Bi-Racial Commission, and the two titles were used interchangeably.

6. A. Leon Lowry and Otis R. Anthony, *A. Leon Lowry* (Tampa: University of South Florida Tampa Library, 1978) http://purl.fcla.edu/usf/dc/a31.82.

7. Lowry and Anthony, *A. Leon Lowry.*

8. Lowry and Anthony, *A. Leon Lowry.*

9. Francisco A. Rodriguez and Otis R. Anthony, *Francisco Rodriguez, Junior* (Tampa: University of South Florida Tampa Library, 1978).

10. Clarence Fort and Andrew T. Huse, *Clarence Fort Oral History Interview* (Tampa: University of South Florida Tampa Library, 2006). http://purl.fcla.edu/usf/dc/f55.3.

11. Fort oral history.

12. Fort oral history.

13. "Civil Rights Protests in Tampa," 42.

14. *Florida Sentinel-Bulletin*, March 1, 1960.

15. "Civil Rights Protests in Tampa," 43.

16. "Civil Rights Protests in Tampa," 43.

17. "Civil Rights Protests in Tampa," 44.

18. "Civil Rights Protests in Tampa," 49, 51.

19. *Tampa Tribune*, March 2, 1960.

20. *Tampa Tribune*, March 2, 1960.

21. *Tampa Daily Times*, March 1, 1960; "Civil Rights Protests in Tampa," 44; *Tampa Daily Times*, March 2, 1960.

22. *Tampa Daily Times*, March 2, 1960.

23. *Tampa Daily Times*, March 3, 1960.

24. *Florida Sentinel-Bulletin*, March 15, 1960.

25. Lowry and Anthony, *A. Leon Lowry.*

26. Lowry and Anthony, *A. Leon Lowry.*

27. *Florida Sentinel-Bulletin*, March 15, 1960.

28. *Tampa Tribune*, March 1, 1960, and March 4, 1960.

29. *Tampa Tribune*, March 3, 1960.

30. *Tampa Tribune*, March 3, 1960.

31. *Tampa Tribune*, March 3, 1960.

32. An audio recording of the speech can be found in the LeRoy Collins Papers, University of South Florida Tampa Special Collections. Reading the speech does not convey the frustrations of the governor. Digitizing the speech off of a reel-to-reel tape recording provided me with a whole new perspective on the governor's profound frustration.

33. Steve Lawson and Cody Fowler Papers, University of South Florida Tampa Library. Fowler's reports on desegregation efforts can be found in box 4.

34. "The Student Protest Movement, Winter 1960," Special Report, Southern Regional Council. April 1, 1960, page 1, Lawson/Fowler Papers, box 4.

35. "The Student Protest Movement, Winter 1960," 2.

36. *Raleigh News and Observer*, February 16, 1960.

37. *Richmond News*, February 22, 1960.

38. Fowler Commission on Race Relations, "To Florida Leaders in Civic, Religious, and Business Affairs," (Tallahassee, October 17, 1960): 1–3; Fowler Commission on Race Relations, "Report of the Fowler Commission on Race Relations," (Tallahassee, December 2, 1960): 18. Lawson/Fowler Papers, University of South Florida Tampa Library, box 4.

39. "To Florida Leaders in Civic, Religious, and Business Affairs," 5.

40. "The Student Protest Movement, Winter 1960," 1–2.

41. "The Student Protest Movement, Winter 1960," x.

42. "Report of the Fowler Commission on Race Relations," 19.

43. "To Florida Leaders in Civic, Religious, and Business Affairs," 6.

44. "Report of the Fowler Commission," 19.

45. *Chicago Defender*, May 7, 1960.

46. "Report of the Fowler Commission on Race Relations," 13; Lowry oral history.

47. "Report of the Fowler Commission on Race Relations," 8.

48. "Civil Rights Protests in Tampa," 45.

49. Fort and Huse, *Clarence Fort Oral History Interview*.

50. "Proposed Method of Desegregation of Down Town Lunch Counters, also Ybor City and Sears, August 1960." Lawson/Fowler Papers.

51. *Florida Sentinel-Bulletin*, September 17, 1960.

52. "Civil Rights Protests in Tampa," 48.

53. "Civil Rights Protests in Tampa," 48.

54. *Florida Sentinel-Bulletin*, September 20, 1960.

55. *Florida Sentinel-Bulletin*, September 17, 1960.

56. *Chicago Defender*, February 20, 1961.

57. "Proposed Method of Desegregation of Down Town Lunch Counters, also Ybor City and Sears, August 1960."

58. Ernest P. Boger and Andrew T. Huse, *Ernest Boger* (Tampa: University of South Florida Tampa Library, 2003). http://purl.fcla.edu/usf/dc/u23.16. USF would not have an intercollegiate basketball team until 1970.

59. Mary Lou Harkness and Carl Dulac, *M. L. Harkness* (Tampa: University of South Florida Tampa Library, 1977); Boger and Huse, *Ernest Boger*.

60. Boger and Huse, *Ernest Boger*.

61. Boger and Huse, *Ernest Boger*.

62. University of South Florida Archives, Papers of John Allen, University of South Florida Tampa Special Collections. Box 10, folder 3.

63. *Campus Edition*, December 16, 1963.

64. Dr. Jack Fernandez interview with author, August 14, 2014.

65. Audio telephone message dated January 3, 1964. Sumter Lowry Papers, University of South Florida Tampa Special Collections. Box 1, folder 47.

66. *Campus Edition* (University of South Florida), January 20, 1964, and July 16, 1964.

67. Saunders memo November 22, 1963, Robert Saunders Papers, University of South Florida Tampa Special Collections. Box 6, folder 5.

68. Fowler Commission memo, July 15, 1964, Lawson/Fowler collection, box 1.

69. *Florida Sentinel-Bulletin*, August 22, 1964.

70. "Civil Rights Protests, in Tampa," 51–52; *Florida Sentinel-Bulletin*, September 3, 1960.

Chapter 10. Mourning Las Novedades: Tales of Urban Renewal

1. Manuel Garcia III interview with author, July 31, 2001.

2. Garcia interview. The Columbia claims in its cookbook that they took over a failing business. In fact, no business in Ybor City felt safe, and the Columbia closed for lunch in the early 1970s.

3. Garcia interview.

4. *St. Petersburg Times*, June 23, 1974.

5. Garcia interview.

6. Garcia interview.

7. Garcia interview.

8. *Tampa Tribune*, May 13, 1979.

9. *Tampa Tribune*, May 13, 1979, and June 30, 1965.

10. *Tampa Tribune*, May 13, 1979, and June 30, 1965.

11. *St. Petersburg Times*, September 12, 1966.

12. The failure of urban renewal was clearly apparent in the mid-1960s. For a critical analysis of the program written at the time, see Martin Anderson, *The Federal Bulldozer: A Critical Analysis of Urban Renewal, 1949–1962* (Cambridge, Mass.: MIT Press, 1964).

13. *Tampa Daily Times*, March 15, 1967, and April 13, 1967.

14. Garcia interview.

15. *Tampa Tribune*, December 19, 1976. Walt Disney World changed Orlando and Central Florida in profound ways. See Richard E. Foglesong, *Married to the Mouse: Walt Disney World and Orlando* (New Haven: Yale University Press, 2001).

16. Garcia interview.

17. *Tampa Tribune*, May 13, 1979; "Bull Fight Correspondence," Louis De la Parte Papers, box 2, folder 6, University of South Florida Tampa Special Collections.

18. *Tampa Tribune*, May 13, 1979.

19. *Tampa Tribune*, May 13, 1979.

20. *Tampa Tribune*, June 21, 1970.

21. Author unknown, *Call: Man and the Telephone* (Fall 1970): 19; *Tampa Tribune*, May 29, 1970.

22. Author unknown, *Call*, 19.

23. Garcia interview.

24. Tampa's Model Cities Program, *Second Year Action Plan: Part One; Problem Analysis* (City Demonstration Agency, City of Tampa, Florida, May 15, 1970), B1a.1.

25. Garcia interview.

26. *Tampa Tribune*, May 5, 1970.

27. *Tampa Tribune*, May 29, 1970.

28. *Tampa Tribune-Times*, May 13, 1979.

29. *Orlando Sentinel*, November 26, 1972.

30. *Orlando Sentinel*, November 26, 1972; Garcia interview.

31. *Tampa Tribune*, May 13, 1973.

32. *Tampa Tribune*, May 13, 1973.

33. *Tampa Tribune*, November 7, 1972; *Tampa Times*, June 7, 1974; *Tampa Times*, June 23, 1973.

34. *Tampa Tribune*, November 7, 1972; *Tampa Tribune*, May 13, 1973; *Tampa Times*, June 7, 1974; *Tampa Times*, June 23, 1973.

35. *Tampa Tribune*, May 29, 1970.

36. *St. Petersburg Times*, November 19, 72.

37. *Tampa Tribune*, November 7, 1972; *Tampa Tribune*, May 13, 1973; *Tampa Times*, June 7, 1974; *Tampa Times*, June 23, 1973.

38. *Tampa Times*, March 24, 1973.

39. *Tampa Times*, March 24, 1973.

40. *Tampa Times*, March 24, 1973.

41. *Tampa Times*, June 7, 1974, September 7, 1974, and July 14, 1975. For an article about Tampa's gay population in 1973, see *Tampa Times*, February 6, 1973, and *Tampa Tribune*, April 4, 1976. While the city's nightlife was in decline, a different kind of community was on the rise in Ybor City. Taking advantage of cheap rents, a community of artists and artistic-minded people collected in Ybor City. While the Chamber of Commerce tried to court financiers, the artist colony imbued Ybor City with a do-it-yourself funky artistic aesthetic that persisted long after the colony had disappeared. The colony held an annual Artist and Writer's Ball that became the inspiration for Ybor's Guavaween festivities held around Halloween. For more, see Paul Wilborn, *Cigar City: Tales from a 1980s Creative Ghetto* (St. Petersburg, Fla.: St. Petersburg, 2019).

42. *Tampa Times*, August 29, 1981.

43. *Tampa Times*, August 29, 1981.

44. *Tampa Times*, August 29, 1981.

45. *Tampa Times*, August 29, 1981.

46. *Tampa Times*, October 31, 1981.

47. Garcia interview.

48. *Tampa Times*, May 23, 1978.

49. *Tampa Tribune*, November 14, 1977; *St. Petersburg Times*, November 14, 1977.

50. *Tampa Tribune*, November 14, 1977.

51. *St. Petersburg Times*, November 14, 1977.

52. *Tampa Tribune*, November 14, 1977.

53. *Tampa Tribune*, November 14, 1977.

54. *Tampa Tribune*, November 14, 1977; *Tampa Times*, May 4, 1978. For more about Rodriguez, see the profile printed in the *Tampa Tribune*, November 1975.

55. Tampa was home to 82 arson fires in 1978, with that number rising to 146 in

1979. Even more buildings burned in 1980. *Tampa Daily Times*, March 11, 1975, and October 5, 1980.

56. *Tampa Tribune-Times*, May 13, 1979.

57. *Tampa Tribune*, December 19, 1976.

58. Letter from Clarita Garcia to Roland Mantiega, February 12, 1990. Tony Pizzo papers, Special Collections, University of South Florida.

59. Garcia interview; Letter from Clarita Garcia to Roland Manteiga; *Orlando Sentinel*, July 29, 2002.

60. Garcia interview; Letter from Clarita Garcia to Roland Manteiga; *Orlando Sentinel*, July 29, 2002. For more about Manny Garcia III's impressive career, see "Many Happy Returns," Robert W. Tolf *Florida Trend* (Posted February 1, 2003, and updated in 2008).

Conclusion

1. *Tampa Tribune*, February 1, 1984.

2. *Tampa Tribune*, June 30, 1985.

BIBLIOGRAPHY

Primary Sources

Athanasaw v. United States, 227 U.S. 326–27. United States Supreme Court, 1913.

Bartke's Restaurant Scrapbook, University of South Florida Tampa Special Collections.

Benjamin, Anna Northend. "Christian Work in Our Camps." *Outlook* 59 (July 2, 1898): 566–69.

Boger, Ernest P., and Andrew T. Huse. *Ernest Boger*. Tampa: University of South Florida Tampa Library, 2003. http://purl.fcla.edu/usf/dc/u23.16.

Governor LeRoy Collins Papers, University of South Florida Tampa Special Collections.

Coates, John Boyd, and Ebbe Curtis Hoff. *Preventive Medicine in World War II*. Washington, D.C.: Office of the Surgeon General, Dept. of the Army, 1955.

District of Columbia Health Department. "Annual Report of the Commissioners of the District of Columbia Year Ended June 30, 1919." Report of the Health Officer. District of Columbia Health Dept. Vol III, 1919.

Federal Writers' Project of the Work Projects Administration for the State of Florida. *The Negro in Florida Cities: Tampa*, 1930.

Federal Writers' Project of the Work Projects Administration for the State of Florida. *Social-ethnic study of Ybor City, Tampa, Florida*, 1935.

Florida Department of Agriculture. *Florida Quarterly Bulletin of the Department of Agriculture*, vol. 28.

Fort, Clarence, and Andrew T. Huse. *Clarence Fort Oral History Interview*. Tampa: University of South Florida Tampa Library, 2006. http://purl.fcla.edu/usf/dc/f55.3.

Fernandez, Jack. Unpublished interview with author, 2014.

Florida and Allen H. Bush. *A Digest of the Statute Law of Florida of a General and Public Character: In Force up to the First Day of January, 1872*. Tallahassee, Fla.: C. H. Walton, State printer, 1872.

Garcia, Manuel, III. Unpublished interview with author, 2001.

Harkness, Mary Lou, and Carl Dulac. *M. L. Harkness*. Tampa: University of South Florida Tampa Library, 1977.

Heath, Mrs. Julian. "Work of the Housewives League." *Annals of the American Academy of Political and Social Science* 48 (July 1913): 121–126.

Henry, Mary. Unpublished interview with author, 2000.

Hibben, M. "Venereal Disease in the Armed Forces." *Editorial research reports 1943* (Vol. I). Washington, D.C.: Congressional Quarterly Press, 1943.

Hillsborough County Aviation Authority Central Records.

Hillsborough County Sheriff's ledger. Housed at the Hillsborough County Sheriff's Museum in Ybor City, 1890s.

Kennedy, Stetson. *Pedro and Estrella*. WPA Life Histories Project, Library of Congress, 1939.

Kennedy, Stetson, Herbert Halpert, and Zora Neale Hurston. *Let the Deal Go Down*. Jacksonville, Florida, 1939, audio. Retrieved from the Library of Congress, accessed December 12, 2017: https://www.loc.gov/item/flwpa000011/.

The Steve Lawson and Cody Fowler Papers, University of South Florida Tampa Special Collections.

Library of Congress Digital Collections.

Lowry, A. Leon, and Otis R. Anthony. *A. Leon Lowry*. Tampa: University of South Florida Tampa Library, 1978.

Sumter Lowry Papers, University of South Florida Tampa Special Collections.

McKay, Crichton, Alice McKay, and Andrew T. Huse. *Crichton and Alice McKay*. Tampa: University of South Florida Tampa Library, 2000.

Milo Smith & Associates. *A Plan for Preserving Tampa's Latin Heritage*. Tampa, Fla.: Milo Smith + Associates, 1970.

Mugge, August B. *My Memoirs*. Unpublished manuscript, 1990.

New York Department of Health. Quarterly bulletin. New York: New York Department of Health, 1918.

The Henry B. Plant Museum. Tampa, Fla.

Post, Charles Johnson. *The Little War of Private Post: The Spanish-American War Seen Up Close*. Boston: Little Brown, 1960.

Rodriguez, Francisco A., and Otis R. Anthony. *Francisco Rodriguez, Junior*. Tampa: University of South Florida Tampa Library, 1978.

Saunders, Robert W. *Bridging the Gap: Continuing the Florida NAACP Legacy of Harry T. Moore, 1952–1966*. Tampa, Fla.: University of Tampa Press, 2000.

Saunders, Robert W., and Canter Brown. *Dr. Robert W. Saunders, Sr.* Tampa, Fla.: University of South Florida Tampa Library, 2002.

Robert Saunders Papers, University of South Florida Tampa Special Collections.

Leo Stalnaker Papers, University of South Florida Tampa Special Collections.

Supreme Court of Florida. "Re: Petition of Leo Stalnaker for reinstatement as attorney at law." [No docket Number]. 150 Fla. 853; 9 So. 2d 100; 1942 Fla., June 30, 1942.

Tampa Board of Trade Minutes, City of Tampa Archives

Tampa City Council's minutes, resolutions, and ordinances. City of Tampa Archives.

Tampa's Model Cities Program. *Second Year Action Plan: Part One; Problem Analysis*. City Demonstration Agency, City of Tampa, Florida, May 15, 1970.

United States. *Techniques of Law Enforcement against Prostitution*. Washington, D.C.: U.S. Government Printing Office, 1943.

United States, Walter Reed, Victor C. Vaughan, and Edward O. Shakespeare. *Report on the Origin and Spread of Typhoid Fever in U.S. Military Camps during the Spanish War of 1898*. Washington, D.C.: U.S. Government Printing Office, 1943.

U.S. Bureau of the Census, *Historical Statistics of the United States, Colonial Times to 1970, Bicentennial Edition, Part 2*. Bureau of Labor Statistics, 2011.

United States Department of Justice. *Annual Report of the Attorney General of the United States*. Washington, D.C., 1918.

University Archive, University of South Florida Tampa Special Collections.

The USF Department of Anthropology African Americans in Florida Collection, University of South Florida Tampa Special Collections.

Valdez, F. *Life Histories: Biographical Interviews of Ybor City Residents*. Federal Writers Program, 1936.

Variety 25, no. 13 (March 1, 1912).

Weigall, Theyre Hamilton. *Boom in Paradise*. New York: A. H. King, 1932.

Works Progress Administration Tampa Office Records, University of South Florida Tampa Special Collections.

Writers' Program (U.S.). *Tampa Guide*. Tallahassee, Fla.: Florida State Planning Board, 1941.

Secondary Sources

Alduino, Frank W. *The "Noble Experiment" in Tampa: A Study of Prohibition in Urban America*. Ph.D. dissertation, Florida State University, 1989.

Alger, R. A. "The Food of the Army During the Spanish War." *North American Review* (January 1, 1901): 171–72.

Anderson, Martin. *The Federal Bulldozer: A Critical Analysis of Urban Renewal, 1949–1962*. Cambridge, Mass.: MIT Press, 1964.

Asbury, Herbert. *The Great Illusion: An Informal History of Prohibition*. New York: Greenwood, 1968.

Bailey, L. J. "US vs. L. Athanasaw, Violation of White Slavery Act," October 26, 1911, 2807–6, page 4, case 2807, roll 136. Bureau of Investigation Microfilm Records, 1911.

Behr, Edward. *Prohibition: Thirteen Years That Changed America*. New York: Arcade, 1996.

Bobrow-Strain, Aaron. *White Bread: A Social History of the Store-Bought Loaf*. Boston: Beacon, 2012.

Burnett, Gene. "Death and Terror Scar Tampa's Past." *Florida Trend* (December 1975): 77–80.

Buck, Morison, "Leo Stalnaker (1897–1986)." Digital Collection, Florida Studies Center Publications, 2000.

Burnett, Gene. "How Tampa Survived a 'Splendid Little War.'" *Florida Trend* (December 1981): 102–3.

Campbell, A. Stuart, and William Porter McLendon. *The Cigar Industry of Tampa, Florida*. Gainesville: University Press of Florida, 1939.

Carr, Madeleine Hirsiger. *Denying Hegemony: The Function and Place of Florida's Jook*

Joints during the Twentieth Century's First Fifty Years. Ph.D. dissertation, Florida State University, 2002.

Chalmers, David. "The Ku Klux Klan in the Sunshine State: The 1920's." *Florida Historical Quarterly* 42, no. 3 (1964): 209–15. http://www.jstor.org.ezproxy.lib.usf.edu/stable/30140018.

Chauncey, George. *Gay New York: Gender, Urban Culture, and the Makings of the Gay/Male World, 1890–1940*. New York: Basic, 1994.

Cirillo, Vincent J. *Bullets and Bacilli: The Spanish-American War and Military Medicine*. New Brunswick, N.J.: Rutgers University Press, 2004.

"Civil Rights Protests in Tampa: Oral Memoirs of Conflict and Accommodation." *Tampa Bay History* 1, no. 1. University of South Florida, Tampa (1979).

Cofer, Richard. "Bootleggers in the Backwoods: Prohibition and the Depression in Hernando County." *Tampa Bay History* (Spring/Summer 1979): 17–23.

Coffey, Thomas M. *The Long Thirst: Prohibition in America, 1920–1933*. New York: Norton, 1975.

Cooper, Patricia A. *Once a Cigar Maker: Men, Women, and Work Culture in American Cigar Factories, 1900–1919*. Urbana: University of Illinois Press, 1987.

Capozzola, Christopher, and Joseph Nicodemus, eds. *Uncle Sam Wants You: World War I and the Making of the Modern American Citizen*. Oxford: Oxford University Press, 2008.

Covington, James W. "The Rough Riders in Tampa." *Sunland Tribune* 3, no. 1 (1977): 1–9.

Dyal, Donald H., Brian B. Carpenter, and Mark A. Thomas. *Historical Dictionary of the Spanish American War*. Westport, Conn.: Greenwood, 1996.

Foglesong, Richard E. *Married to the Mouse: Walt Disney World and Orlando*. New Haven, Conn.: Yale University Press, 2001.

Frosell, Kim Jules. *Booster Altruism: Motivations and Restraints on Progressive Reforms in Tampa, Florida, 1900–1921*. Master's thesis, University of South Florida, 1994.

Gardiner, John A. *The Politics of Corruption: Organized Crime in an American City*. New York: Russel Sage, 1970.

Gatewood, Willard B., Jr. "Negro Troops in Florida, 1898." *Florida Historical Quarterly* 49, no. 1 (1970): 1–15. http://www.jstor.org.ezproxy.lib.usf.edu/stable/30145817.

Gibson, Pamela. "Sin City, Moonshine, Whiskey and Divorce." *Sunland Tribune* 21 (1995): article 4. Available at: https://scholarcommons.usf.edu/sunlandtribune/vol21/iss1/4.

Gilbert, Douglas. *American Vaudeville: Its Life and Times*. New York: Dover, 1963.

Gordon, Alastair. *Naked Airport: A Cultural History of the World's Most Revolutionary Structure*. New York: H. Holt, 2004.

Grismer, Karl H. *Tampa: A History of the City of Tampa and the Tampa Bay Region of Florida*. St. Petersburg: St. Petersburg Print, 1950.

Haller, Mark H. "Policy Gambling, Entertainment, and the Emergence of Black Politics: Chicago from 1900 to 1940." *Journal of Social History* 24, no. 4 (Summer 1991): 719–39. http://www.jstor.org.ezproxy.lib.usf.edu/stable/3788854.

Hegarty, Marilyn Elizabeth. *Victory Girls, Khaki-wackies, Patriotutes: The Regulation of Female Sexuality in the United States during World War II.* New York: New York University Press, 2008.

Henderson, Ann L., and Gary Ross Mormino. *Spanish Pathways in Florida, 1492–1992.* Sarasota, Fla.: Pineapple, 1991.

Hewitt, Nancy A. *Southern Discomfort: Women's Activism in Tampa, Florida, 1880s–1920s.* Urbana: University of Illinois Press, 2001.

Hurley, Edward Nash. *The Bridge to France.* Philadelphia: Lippincott, 1927.

Hurston, Zora Neale. *Their Eyes Were Watching God: A Novel.* New York: Perennial, 1990.

Ingalls, Robert P. *Urban Vigilantes in the New South: Tampa, 1882–1936.* Knoxville: University of Tennessee Press, 1988.

Iorio, Pam. "Colorless Primaries: Tampa's White Municipal Party." *Florida Historical Quarterly* 79, no. 3 (2001): 297–318. http://www.jstor.org.ezproxy.lib.usf.edu/stable/30150855.

———. "Political Excess Shaped by a Game of Chance: Tampa, Bolita, and the First Half of the Twentieth Century." *Sunland Tribune* 26 (2000): 27–36.

Kennan, George. *Campaigning in Cuba.* New York: Kennikat, 1971.

Kerstein, Robert J. *Politics and Growth in Twentieth-Century Tampa.* Gainesville: University Press of Florida, 2001.

Keuchel, Edward F. "Chemicals and Meat: The Embalmed Beef Scandal of the Spanish-American War." *Bulletin of the History of Medicine* 48, no. 2 (Summer 1974); 253–55.

Kirschbaum, Erik, and Herbert W. Stupp. *Burning Beethoven: The Eradication of German Culture in the United States during World War I.* New York: Berlinica, 2015.

Knowlton, Clark S. "Patron-Peon Pattern among the Spanish Americans of New Mexico." *Social Forces* 41, no. 1 (1962): 12–17.

Kobler, John. *Ardent Spirits: The Rise and Fall of Prohibition.* New York: Putnam, 1973.

Kohn, Stephen M. *American Political Prisoners: Prosecutions under the Espionage and Sedition Acts.* Westport, Conn.: Praeger, 1994.

Lastra, Frank Trebín, and Richard Mathews. *Ybor City: The Making of a Landmark Town.* Tampa, Fla.: University of Tampa Press, 2006.

Lasswell, Harold Dwight. *Psychopathology and Politics.* New York: Viking, 1960.

Long, Durward. "The Historical Beginnings of Ybor City and Modern Tampa." *Florida Historical Quarterly* 45, no. 1 (1966): 31–44. http://www.jstor.org.ezproxy.lib.usf.edu/stable/30145699.

———. "An Immigrant Co-operative Medicine Program in the South, 1887–1963." *Journal of Southern History* 31, no. 4 (1965): 417–34. doi:10.2307/2205341.

———. "Labor Relations in the Tampa Cigar Industry, 1885–1911." *Labor History* 12, no. 4 (Fall 1971): 551–59.

———. "La Resistencia: Tampa's Immigrant Labor Union." *Labor History* 6, no. 3 (1965): 193–213.

———. "The Making of Modern Tampa: A City of the New South, 1885–1911." *Florida Historical Quarterly* 49, no. 4 (1971): 333–45. http://www.jstor.org.ezproxy.lib.usf.edu/stable/30140624.

———. "The Open-Closed Shop Battle in Tampa's Cigar Industry, 1919–1921." *Florida Historical Quarterly* 47, no. 2 (1968): 101–21. http://www.jstor.org.ezproxy.lib.usf.edu/stable/30140294.

Lopez, Alfred J. *José Martí: A Revolutionary Life.* Austin: University of Texas Press, 2014.

Luconi, Stefano. "Tampa's 1910 Lynching: The Italian-American Perspective and Its Implications." *Florida Historical Quarterly* 88, no. 1 (Summer 2009): 38–39.

Luebke, Frederick C. *Bonds of loyalty: German-Americans and World War I.* Dekalb: Northern Illinois University Press, 1974.

Marcus, James. "The First Hip White Person." *Atlantic Monthly* (February 2001): 119–23.

Marolda, Edward J. *Theodore Roosevelt, the U.S. Navy, and the Spanish-American War.* New York: Palgrave, 2001.

McCain, George Nox. *War Rations for Pennsylvanians; the Story of the Operations of the Federal Food Administration in Pennsylvania, including Personal and Biographical Sketches of its Officers and Members, with Dramatic, Humorous and Unusual Episodes in the Experience of County Administrators during the World War.* John C. Winston Co., Philadelphia, 1920.

McKay, Donald Brenham. *Pioneer Florida.* Tampa, Fla.: Southern, 1959.

McLeod, David I. "Food Prices, Politics, and Policy in the Progressive Era." *Journal of the Gilded Age and Progressive Era* 8, no. 3 (July 2009): 365–67.

Mencken, H. L. *The American Language: An Inquiry into the Development of English in the United States.* New York: Knopf, 1945.

Mohlman, Geoffrey, Susan Greenbaum, Karen Mayo, and Brent Richards Weisman. *Soldiers and Patriots: Buffalo Soldiers and Afro-Cubans in Tampa, 1898.* Tampa: University of South Florida, 1999.

Morgan, Hal, and Andreas Brown. *Prairie Fires and Paper Moons: The American Photographic Postcard, 1900–1920.* Boston: D. R. Godine, 1981.

Mormino, Gary Ross. "GI Joe Meets Jim Crow: Racial Violence and Reform in World War II Florida." *Florida Historical Quarterly* 73, no. 1 (1994): 23–42. http://www.jstor.org.ezproxy.lib.usf.edu/stable/30148725.

———. *Hillsborough County Goes to War: The Home Front, 1940–1950.* Tampa, Fla.: Tampa Bay History Center, 2001.

———. *Land of Sunshine, State of Dreams: A Social History of Modern Florida.* Gainesville: University Press of Florida, 2008.

———. "Tampa and the New Urban South: The Weight Strike of 1899." *Florida Historical Quarterly* 60, no. 3 (1982): 337–56. http://www.jstor.org.ezproxy.lib.usf.edu/stable/30146795.

———. "Tampa's Splendid Little War: Local History and the Cuban War of Independence." *OAH Magazine of History* 12, no. 3 (Spring 1998): 37–42.

Mormino, Gary Ross, and George Pozzetta. *The Immigrant World of Ybor City: Italians and Their Latin Neighbors in Tampa, 1885–1985.* Urbana: University of Illinois Press, 1987. http://www.jstor.org.ezproxy.lib.usf.edu/stable/25163218.

Muñiz, José Rivero, Eustasio Fernandez, and Henry Beltran. *The Ybor City Story:*

(1885–1954). *Los Cubanos en Tampa.* [Tampa, Fla.]: [publisher not identified], 1976.

Noel, Thomas J. *The City and the Saloon: Denver, 1858–1916.* Lincoln: University of Nebraska Press, 1982.

Okrent, Daniel. *Last Call: The Rise and Fall of Prohibition.* New York: Scribner, 2010.

Oshinsky, David M. *Polio: An American Story.* Oxford: Oxford University Press, 2005.

Pérez, Louis A., Jr. "Cubans in Tampa: From Exiles to Immigrants, 1892–1901." *Florida Historical Quarterly* 57, no. 2 (1978): 129–40. http://www.jstor.org.ezproxy.lib.usf.edu/stable/30140461.

———. "Reminiscences of a Lector: Cuban Cigar Workers in Tampa." *Florida Historical Quarterly* 53, no. 4 (April 1975): 443–49. http://www.jstor.org.ezproxy.lib.usf.edu/stable/30150299.

Pickett, Deets, Clarence True Wilson, and Ernest Dailey Smith. *The Cyclopedia of Temperance, Prohibition, and Public Morals.* New York: Methodist Book Concern, 1922.

Pliley, Jessica R. *Policing Sexuality: The Mann Act and the Making of the FBI.* Cambridge, Mass.: Harvard University Press, 2014.

Poyo, Gerald E. "The Cuban Experience in the United States, 1865–1940: Migration, Community, and Identity." *Cuban Studies* 21 (1991): 19–36. http://www.jstor.org.ezproxy.lib.usf.edu/stable/24485700.

———. "The Impact of Cuban and Spanish Workers on Labor Organizing in Florida, 1870–1900." *Journal of American Ethnic History* 5, no. 2 (1986): 46–63. http://www.jstor.org.ezproxy.lib.usf.edu/stable/27500452.

Pozzetta, George E. "Immigrants and Radicals in Tampa, Florida." *Florida Historical Quarterly* 57, no. 3 (January 1979): 337–48. http://www.jstor.org.ezproxy.lib.usf.edu/stable/30148528.

Pozzetta, George E., and Gary R. Mormino. "The Reader and the Worker: 'Los Lectores' and the Culture of Cigarmaking in Cuba and Florida." *International Labor and Working-Class History*, no. 54 (1998): 1–18.

Reynolds, Kelly. *Henry Plant: Pioneer Empire Builder.* Cocoa: Florida Historical Society Press, 2003.

Rotskoff, Lori. *Love on the Rocks: Men, Women, and Alcohol in Post–World War II America.* Chapel Hill: University of North Carolina Press, 2002.

Scaglione, Joe. "City in Turmoil: Tampa and the Strike of 1910." *Sunland Tribune* 18 (November 1992): 29–36.

Schellings, William J. *Tampa, Florida: Its Role in the Spanish American War, 1898.* Master's thesis, University of Miami, 1954.

———. *The Role of Florida in the Spanish American War, 1898.* Ph.D. dissertation, University of Florida, 1958.

Sharpe, Clifford C. "Florida's First Brewery." *Sunland Tribune* 17 (November 1992): 59–66.

Schinderhans, August. *The Truth in the World War: An Expose for Better Americanism.* Dallas: 1921.

Steffy, Joan Marie. *The Cuban Immigrants of Tampa, Florida, 1886–1898*. Master's thesis, University of South Florida, 1975.

Strom, Claire. "Controlling Venereal Disease in Orlando during World War II." *Florida Historical Quarterly* 91, no. 1 (Summer 2012): 86–117. http://www.jstor.org.ezproxy.lib.usf.edu/stable/23264824.

Thompson, Troy. "'A Black Spot': Florida's Crusade against Veneral Disease, Prostitution, and Female Sexuality During World War II." *Florida Public Health Review*, no. 2 (2005): 115–20.

Tinajero, Araceli. *El Lector: A History of the Cigar Factory Reader*. Austin: University of Texas Press, 2010.

Tzu, Sun, and Tom Butler-Bowdon. *The Art of War the Ancient Classic*. Chichester, U.K.: John Wiley & Sons, 2010. http://public.eblib.com/choice/publicfullrecord.aspx?p=644957.

VanLandingham, Kyle S. *In Pursuit of Justice: Law & Lawyers in Hillsborough County, 1846–1996*. Tampa, Fla.: Hillsborough County Bar Association, 1996.

Westfall, L. Glenn. *Don Vicente Martínez Ybor, the Man and His Empire: Development of the Clear Havana Industry in Cuba and Florida in the Nineteenth Century*. Ph.D. dissertation, University of Florida, 1977.

Wilborn, Paul. *Cigar City: Tales from a 1980s Creative Ghetto*. St. Petersburg, Fla.: St. Petersburg, 2019.

INDEX

Polk County, 61, 287n18, 287n18
Port Tampa, 7, 44, 49, 92
Post, Charles, 36, 42, 47, 54
Powell, Alexander B., 46–47
Pratt, Theodore, 182–84
Prohibition, x, 15, 19, 24, 76, 79, 80, 115, 138, 142, 143–79, 149, 153, 167, 188, 261
Prostitution, 42, 49, 81–83, 185, 188, 190–91, 193, 195, 196, 199–203, 272
Public health, 190, 201, 203–4
Public Health Service (PHS), 190, 199, 203–4

Racial segregation, xi, 2, 6, 53, 108, 211, 231–59, 281n2
Railroads, xiv, 2, 7, 17, 35, 54, 70, 74, 179, 298n57
Reconstruction, 2, 13, 127
Reed, Walter, 48
Republican Party, 211
Resistencia, La (aka La Sociedad de Torcedores, labor union), 91–97
Reynolds, Fred, 132, 134
Rinfore, Reedy, 155
Rodriguez, Alejandro, 94–95
Rodriguez, Cesar, 274
Rodriguez, Francisco, Jr., 233, 235–36, 239, 259
Roosevelt, Theodore, 45, 139, 286n53, 293n3
Rough Riders, 46, 49, 55, 286n53

Saloons, x, xi, 7, 8, 9–29, 24, 31, 36, 38, 41–42, 49–55, 58–66, 62, 70, 72, 74, 76, 79–81, 88, 101, 143–44, 146–48, 168, 176, 184, 186–88, 260, 282n9
    Unlicensed saloons ("Blind tigers"), 12, 14, 24, 59, 61, 146, 287n18
Sanchez y Haya (Cigar manufacturer), 4, 268
Sauls, Jennie, 117, 118
Scaglione, Basil, 256–57
Schleman, Arthur, 64–65, 75
Sexually transmitted disease, x, 6, 180, 182, 188, 190–205, 279
    Syphilis, 191, 196–997–201
Smuggling, 150–52, 173, 272, 279
Soda fountains, 27, 28, 41, 42, 148
Soup houses, ix, x, xi, 6, 35, 87–88, 90–97, 99, 100, 103, 109
Spade, The (newspaper), 175–76
Spain, ix, 1, 3, 5, 12, 15, 24, 30, 34–35, 46, 57, 59, 86, 88, 138, 260, 264 266

Spanish Americans, 4, 5, 6, 25, 31–43, 59, 60–61, 105, 147, 149, 165, 188
Spanish Civil War, 181
Spanish-American War, x, 24, 35, 43–44, 46, 54–55, 88, 123, 127
Spanish Club. See Centro Español
Spanish Park (restaurant), 216, 258
Speakeasies, x, xi, 146–50, 152–61, 165, 167–70
Stalnaker, Leo, xi, 162–78
Steak 'n Brew, 260, 269, 270–71
Steamships, 2, 5, 54, 73, 119, 123
    Mascotte, 2
    Olivette, 2, 34
Stecher, George, 120, 138
Stephens, Jack (J.J.), 48, 50, 62, 63, 64–65
Stough, Henry, 80–84
Stovall, Wallace, 103, 124, 166
St. Petersburg, 80, 211, 212, 230, 244, 251
Suarez, Manuel "El Gallego," 58, 62
Sunday Laws, ix, x, 6, 7, 10–14, 16–17, 19–29, 60–62, 70, 72, 74, 82, 282n6

Tampa, City of
    Board of Trade, 3, 10, 86–87, 91, 92, 99, 106
    City Council, 17, 19–20, 22, 28, 56, 73, 76, 105, 115, 118, 121, 136, 163–64, 175, 196
    City Hall, 17, 97, 133, 154, 220
    Corruption, 29, 56–68, 72, 74, 76, 77, 80, 82, 146, 157, 162–63, 166, 175–76, 178, 191, 192, 288n35
    Formation, 1–11
    Police Department, 10, 11, 13–14, 17, 20–22, 25–27, 29, 32, 43, 48–49, 51–52, 55, 56–58, 60–69, 71–73, 75–76, 79, 82–83, 86, 89, 93, 95, 97, 101–3, 110, 112–13, 120, 132, 135, 139, 145, 146, 148, 153–63, 166, 167, 168–72, 175–78, 181, 190, 193, 196, 197, 199–204, 233, 239, 240–41, 251, 268, 271, 274, 179, 282n13, 288n35
    Relations with military, 188–205
Tampa Bay Hotel, 3, 14, 35, 37, 38, 41, 44, 46, 55, 64, 281n4
Tampa Daily Times, 23, 82–83, 88, 102, 124, 127, 162, 170, 204, 209, 242, 270, 272
Tampa International Airport, 188, 206, 212, 213–17, 214, 222, 225, 227
Tampa Life (newspaper), 175–77

ANDREW T. HUSE works as a librarian at the University of South Florida in Special Collections. He writes and speaks about Florida history and foodways.